Notes / Ex

The great Christian historian, Eugen Rosenstock-Huessy argued that the age of the university, which he saw as starting roughly 500 years ago, was about to come to an end. The university system shifted from the stone foundation of God to the shifting sands of post-Christian ideologies. Therefore, it is collapsing, spiritually, intellectually and financially. But, right on time, Providence brings forth this volume from a group of Christian scholars presenting a new model. It is sustainable spiritually and economically. May God breathe life into this plan.

Jerry Bowyer
Financial economist, theologian, speaker and author of The Maker Versus the Takers:
What Jesus Really Said About Social Justice and Economics

A clear track to the needed Education Revolution from the chaos and corruption of secularism that is stealing the soul of our youth and robbing them from their God purposed potential. An essential read!

Greg Denham
Pastor of Rise Church San Marcos, CA and Founder of The Context Movement.

A fierce battle is on for America's soul. It will be won by whoever wins education. This book lays out a fresh strategy for infusing truth, purpose and virtue into the next generation. Bolstered by a rich understanding of history, philosophy, sociology and theology, the book asserts that America's freedom and worldview foundations can be preserved and revitalized by a new reformation. The book demonstrates that God has raised up a team of thought leaders to light the torch of truth to illuminate the path to a brighter future for our nation and our world.

Dr. Ché Ahn
Founder and President, Harvest International Ministry , Founding and Senior Pastor,
Harvest Rock Church, International Chancellor, Wagner University
Founder, Ché Ahn Ministries

Secularism is failing the nations. The Church needs to step forward to complete Christ's commission to disciple the nations. This timely book shows how to do it.

Kevin Swanson
Author, Radio Host, Pastor, Director,
Generations and Christian Home Educators of Colorado

The Third Education Revolution can serve as a timely blueprint for the 21st Century Church to escape the education wilderness of secularism and pragmatism. This seminal work considers theological and historical aspects of the problem and provides a methodology and a new and workable Christian pedagogy. Noted scholars contributed to this profound and culture-shaping book which exhibits "Christ in whom are hidden all the treasures of wisdom and knowledge" (Col. 2:3).

E. Ray Moore, Th.M., Chaplain (Lt. Colonel) USAR Ret.
Chairman of Christian Education Initiative and Director of Exodus Mandate

The Third Education Revolution is a clear and striking call to re-center education on Truth. The crisis of contemporary educational models worldwide lies in the inability of a post-modern, post-Christian naturalism to provide cogent arguments for the validity of reason and self-consciousness, and, hence, for the validity of any notion, in any context, of objective truth. If there is no truth, then education is reduced to an exercise of power and manipulation. Education then becomes indoctrination, rather than an exchange of thinking, creativity and imagination that offers freedom from the bondage to ideologically driven power. *The Third Education Revolution* is a collection of essays that opens the reader to a global, cross-cultural, and cogent call for a student-centered educational process that has truth as its end, goodness as its character, and beauty as its creative expression. I strongly encourage the careful examination of this text as a springboard to the recovery of the learning necessary for flourishing communities.

Scott B. Key, PhD
Vice-President for Academic Initiatives C. S. Lewis Study Center Professor Emeritus, Philosophy, California Baptist University

Our modern crisis of worldviews has positioned the global church for a radical educational partnership that has been missing in its Sunday School culture. Now seasoned Kingdom thought leaders are joining with dedicated pastor/educators to equip the church to new levels of leadership influence. It is time to fan into flames the fires that burned hot in the spread of the early church impact on pagan culture. This can become the church's finest hour.

Dr. Joseph Umidi
Executive Vice President, Regent University

We live in a time of great upheavals. The church must not walk away from her responsibility to make nations Christ's disciples by teaching them to obey the ways of God's kingdom. We compartmentalize some things as sacred and others as secular. The Bible requires us to do God's will in every area of life. In this book, Vishal Mangalwadi and his team of experts from around the world in many fields give us much more than lessons from history, philosophy, theology and pedagogy. They give us a war strategy to take education back for the glory of God and the advancement of His kingdom on the earth.

David Balestri
National Convener, Australian Coalition of Apostolic Leaders

Most African countries have an interesting devotion to pre-scripted education imported from the West. Nations have practiced this education with minimal changes in the philosophy but with massive additions that lead to overcrowded curricula and teacher-centered methodologies. We have very many 'undocumented' graduates and those who have few sellable skills. Our economies will remain 'left behind' unless our education philosophy and pedagogy become transformed. This book offers historical evidence that humanism is not the only way. In this book, humanism is dethroned and Biblical truth is enthroned. Educating our youth in truth will bring back sanity, stability and progress to our politics, culture, economics and the church.

Gillian Kabatereine Kasirye (PhD)
Curriculum Expert – Makerere University and
National Fellowship for Born Again Pentecostal Churches – Uganda.

The amoral power of indoctrination must end. *The Third Education Revolution,* God willing will spark a reformation to recover sanity from decades of darkness. As the mortal enemies of objectivity collapse, resurgence of ideological freedom and imagination will commence. This collection of essays will refresh the global conscience with truth, beauty, goodness, and wisdom. Biblically inspired and Gospel motivated, this brilliant collection of essays endeavors to salvage the faculties of the soul, benefit the poor and privileged, and revitalize the world's economy. Pastors, professors, and parents who long to reverse the deadly chaos of secularism, now is the time to 'create a truth-based educational ecosystem' whereby cultural confusion may heal and redeemed humanity may thrive. May the King advance His Great Commission and excite Great Awakening by the strategic influence of this work. Soli Deo Gloria!

Dr. Samuel Musgrave
Pastor, Trinity Community Church, Clovis, CA

The Bible transformed societies because it was the foundation of Europe's medieval and modern education. Universities studied everything because the Bible taught that all things were created by God's living Word and for His glory. That included my fields of mathematics, physics, chemistry and biology. This book explains how God's Spirit of truth can use the power of the human brain, soul and spirit to understand and teach the truth revealed in God's works and words. The proposed education revolution will make the church (in Paul's words) "the pillar and foundation of the truth," bringing wisdom to academia.

Frank Karlsen, PhD Dr.Philos

Professor in Micro and Nanosystem technology, Molecular Biology and Microbiology Department of Microsystems. Faculty of Technology, Natural Science and Maritime The University of South-Eastern Norway.

Jesus commanded His followers to "disciple ALL nations" (Matthew 28:19). If we do not have a revolution in our education we will lose many generations. Education and Family are two of the most powerful ways for discipling nations. I know Vishal Mangalwadi well. His books have been revolutionary. I encourage you to read this book *The Third Education Revolution* to obey Jesus' command.

Loren Cunningham

Founder Youth With A Mission University of the Nations

Our universities actively promote a rigid, anti-liberal left-wing curriculum that is certain to despoil our civilizations. Meanwhile, too many of our churches have long since forgotten their responsibility to make known God's greater wisdom to rulers and authorities (Ephesians 3:10). This book offers an answer to both problems, by challenging churches to re-discover their age-old mandate to be "pillars of the truth" as they become centers for higher education that is truly liberal and renews our civilizations. The third educational revolution that Vishal Mangalwadi champions can come none too soon!

Robert Osburn, PhD

Senior Fellow, Wilberforce International Institute

The Third Education Revolution is a profound collection of wisdom and strategy. It has the potential to create a loving ekklesia of competent lawyers and reformers with Christlike character who, like modern Esthers, Deborahs, Josephs, and Daniels, establish and administer justice, mercy, and grace in the earth.

Justice and Righteousness are the foundation of God's throne. It follows from that to identify, prepare and educate redeemers of law, government, and business, is an integral part of discipling cities and nations. This has been my mission for seventeen years. I have collaborated with Christian legal professionals across the globe in integrating their faith and calling to fight for the sanctity of life, promote religious freedom, secure justice for the poor, advance peace and reconciliation, and foster integrity under the rule of law. The strategy proposed in this book will extend that mission to all areas of life.

Mark Mudri,
Facilitator Advocates Oceania, Co-founder of Lighthouse Prayer Tower &
Executive member Global Council Advocates International

Shall we subject our children to further indoctrination of the atheistic worldview that is pervasive in today's educational institutions? If we desire to equip our next generation with discerning minds for God's truth, beauty and goodness, then it's time to break the status quo. Parents, students - let this book encourage you and expand your vision with a doable long-term plan. Consider your strategic part in this revolution. Hear the cry, heed the lessons and hone our resources to begin affecting the change!

Karen Chen
Educator, homemaker, homeschooling mom

Each day we ship our children off for seven hours to be profoundly influenced, taught and raised by strangers. Should we be surprised, then, if our children act, think and behave contrary to how we 'raised' them to walk with God? A war is on for the souls of our children and the classroom is the primary battleground. If you want your children to mature in knowledge of truth and their relationship with the LORD, you have to take responsibility for what, when, where, how and why they learn. This book shows the way for a better future for your children and nation.

Dr. Albert Mu, D.O.
Family Physician, Part-time Homeschool Dad

The Third Education Revolution is an inspiring vision. It invites us to be a part of what God is doing in history. The German word for education *"Bildung"* ("making into an image") requires us to bring universities back under "the Spirit that gives life" (2 Corinthians 3:6 and John 6:63). Vishal Mangalwadi's vision of transformation through education stands in this context. God's living spirit transforms humans through inward encounter with the word and the truth. And here lies the key and the power of transforming lives, cultures and our world. Get inspired to become part of a new revolution

Harald Jung, PhD,
Prof. and Dean at Liebenzell International Univ. (IHL)
President of Heidelberg-Institute of international Studies + Leadership, Germany

Must Christian families give their children — God's image — to Caesar to be deceived? This book presents a challenge that the Church needs to hear. It outlines a concrete idea on how to realign the Church to God's exciting calling to bring truth into the marketplace of ideas and thereby disciple nations. To disciple is to educate. We become what we learn (Luke 6:40).

Man's Utopian dreams have always led to destruction. Unchecked power in human hands destroys. Truth, not the state's coercive power, is the time-tested road to liberty and peace.

Mark Shepard, B.S., M.Eng., Electrical Engineering
Former State Senator, State of Vermont, USA
Founding member Christian Education Initiative (https://christedu.org)
Businessman (Industrial automation sector)

Education is an implicit component of the Great Commission, and all education is religious in nature. Vishal Mangalwadi and other scholars have shown in earlier books, and also here, that the Bible is the source of much that we enjoy today in the modern world, including science and technology, the arts, democratic governance, etc. Today, the humanist narrative has become the highway of societal decay under oppressive technocracies. The Church must accept that to be salt and light in this world it has to reform the educational system. That is the way to disciple nations and human flourishing. Tracing the history of Christendom's previous education revolutions, this volume presents a plan for a third revolution, leading the world to the way, the truth and the life.

Philip Panicker, PhD
Senior Lecturer of Engineering (Mechanical, Aerospace and Electrical Engineering)

The Third Education Revolution boldly seeks to restore the soul of education in which learning is the pursuit of truth and virtue. The book reveals why educators no longer see teaching as a sacred calling and why education has ceased being a civilizing process to nurture 'habits of the heart' that discerns what is true, good and beautiful. This visionary book explores how to restore schools as vital faith-based enterprises to equip students with expertise in research, critical thinking and communications. Students should be cultivated as thought leaders by providing an enriching and blended curriculum of classic books and ideas that have impacted our world for better or worse. Education should be independent of governments in order to shun politicization and indoctrination and do far more than merely prepare students for jobs. It will foster education for the flourishing of the transcendent mind.

David J. Theroux
Founder and President, Independent Institute
Founder and President, C. S. Lewis Society of California

God is on a serious reclamation project to get His church from making believers to discipling nations. As God takes us through this next kingdom reformation, a key to its success and sustainability will be a revolution in education. The critical thinking and prophetic insight throughout "The Third Education Revolution" should be considered necessary reading for every Christian in this crucial time in history. I couldn't be more enthusiastic about this book and this movement.

Brian D. Beattie PhD
Pastor - Freedom House CEO / National Director - Transform Our World - Canada
Partner - Global Transformation Collective

THE THIRD EDUCATION REVOLUTION

Reintegrate Veritas and Virtue into Education
By Returning it to the Church

EDITORS
VISHAL MANGALWADI
DAVID MARSHALL

FRESNO, STUTTGART, CHENNAI

Published in Fresno, CA by Sought After Media for Kingdom Education Hub. For more information please contact:
Manager@SoughtAfterMedia.com
1077 N. Willow Ave
Ste 105 PMB 1010
Clovis, CA 93611-4411
USA

ISBN: 979-8-9887831-6-9

Contents

FOREWORD

The desire for truth-based education is growing in Africa, Asia, and Latin America. I have seen evidence of that hunger as Chancellor of Kumi University in Uganda (Africa) and as Chairman of the Dream School in Korea. *The Third Education Revolution*, written by visionaries from around the world, responds to this global need for a new paradigm for teaching young people. It calls for fundamental reforms that restore education to the Church as part of her ministry.

Most of the contributors were inspired by Vishal Mangalwadi, the leader of this ambitious project. I've known Vishal for more than 30 years. I first met him while studying Christian worldview in L'Abri Fellowship. I later had the privilege of translating and publishing his book about William Carey (1761-1834) into Korean.

Carey, the pioneer of modern missions, was a cobbler-turned-linguist and educationist who led the Serampore Mission and College which became Asia's first vernacular university. Carey's team began creating an educational eco-system that transformed South Asia. Vishal's insight into how 'the Light of the World' dispelled India's darkness greatly challenged me. It helped me see how the Gospel had also transformed South Korea — my nation.

As an Asian, Vishal possess rare insight into western civilization from a solid biblical foundation. His grasp of biblical truth gives him a unique framework from which to analyze the world. The essays in this book show how those insights, drawn from the Bible and a broad survey of history are now inspiring a global movement to reshape our future.

I applaud Vishal's insights into Europe's first and second education revolutions. These laid the foundations of the modern world. My experience of managing biblical curriculum and in the core educational elements of training, learning and inspiring convinces me that the innovative suggestions outlined in this book may yield remarkable results.

A yawning gap between opposing worldviews now forms the front- line of spiritual warfare. This battle has to be fought in the sphere of education where truth has been discarded. Secularized education has produced apocalyptic consequences. Postmodern education allows the worst of human nature to influence every domain of life. The Third Educational Revolution arrives at the best possible moment. Covid-19 created a new "post-contact" world.

Digital education has become the new normal around the globe. In the same week as the Pandemic hit my nation, I had the honor of hosting some of these visionaries in South Korea, in February 2020. The ideas behind this book were set on the table just at the moment when history was about to prove their value. The need for education reform could not be clearer, in a world plunged into such chaos.

Running a boarding school was part of my own engagement in education. For over 20-years I have observed how the bible-based learning transforms students' character. I have come to appreciate how beautiful, innovative and creative such education can be when students and teachers live together in a well-designed learning community. My dream is to use a wholesome curriculum that educates children from infants all the way to an alternative university.

For a long time I have observed that many young Africans crave college education but cannot afford it. This is why I appreciate how insightful, innovative, and realistic Vishal's proposals are. I pray that the vision set forth in this book will soon become a reality.

Dr. James Hwang, M.D, Ph. D
Chairman, Erom Group
President of Loving Care Hospital
Chancellor of Kumi University

I

The Third Education Revolution

Chapter 1

Towards A Third Education Revolution

Vishal Mangalwadi[1]

The Third Education Revolution

For a thousand years the church has sent students to the universities. It is time for universities to send students to the local church.

Imagine that students enroll in accredited universities and schools but attend classes in the local church. Professors come to church online. The poorest students get to learn from the world's best teachers. Academic Pastors (AP) mentor students individually and in small groups. Students save up to 75% on tuition and contribute to their family's economy. Students who cannot live with their parents, room and board with elders and deacons trained to teach them the necessary life-skills.

An Academic Pastor (AP) revives the lost idea that teachers are God's gift to build-up saintly character. He/she is a homeschooling parent trained to serve as a church-college parent. In other words, an AP is a Youth Pastor version 2.0. He oversees studies and arranges face-to-face seminars and webinars for students to interact with experts. He also teaches students to love their neighbors by devoting six hours a week to serve the needy in the local community. Students go physically to universities, science labs and institutions to learn what cannot be taught online.

This kingdom education revolution will organize a global network of scholars and professionals to create a truth-based educational ecosystem. Ideologies will be examined without corrupting truth and morality. Education will cease being indoctrination. It will open minds to discern what is true, beautiful, good and wise.

---

1 Prof. Vishal Mangalwadi, M.A. LLD is the visionary behind *The Third Education Revolution.*

Subject Matter Experts (SME's) will create, edit, adapt and translate online curricula from kindergarten to university. Professionals who know online learning, test formation, lecture scripting, videography and worldview will assist SME's to create online curricula.Internships in the community will help students develop vocational and leadership skills.

Educational micro-financing will develop the capacity of resource-deprived churches to become centers of education. AP's will recommend needy students for micro-financing to benefit from "Imaginal Education" (see Chapter 6 by Tom Rudmik) on their way to becoming future-ready graduates. Scholarship funds and grants will supplement educational banking.

A new dark age has descended upon the world. Secularization has robbed teachers of the respect that the Church had bestowed upon them. Teaching is no longer a sacred calling. A teacher has become a vendor in an educational shopping mall (university) where he sells his department's wares. In the absence of divine revelation, universities no longer know what is logic or language, the difference between right or wrong, male or female, marriage or family, nation or justice, self and God: an intellectual revolution is required to restore the soul of education. Learning must earn public respect as a pursuit of truth and virtue. If students go to college mainly seeking pleasure, power, prestige or a license to get a job then the college cannot expect any more respect than a club or a workshop.

Students should go to church-college to gather the best available information. They must be helped to develop expertise in the art of research, critical thinking and effective communication. They should learn languages and master classics. They should learn to value physical fitness, a sportsman's spirit and personal discipline. Students should form teams that turn needs in their community into opportunities for service. They should be helped to travel across continents in order to learn as well as serve in different cultures. This education will also train thought leaders by offering courses in classic books, ideas and biographies that have impacted history for better and for worse.

Amoral universities have become swamps breeding corrupt politicians, civil servants, businessmen, journalists and judges. They can teach students how to make a great robot, but not how to be a good spouse, parent, neighbor or citizen. This revolution will make education a training in servant-leadership. It will do more than prepare students for job markets. It will guide them to find the meaning and purpose of life as they discern their personal calling and prepare to fulfill their vocation. Once again, education will become a civilizing process. It will nurture the "habits of the heart" to better love God, serve neighbors and steward creation.

The Second Education Revolution

Europe's second education revolution began five hundred years ago, in 1520, when Martin Luther published *an Open Letter to the Christian Nobility of the German Nation Concerning the Reform of the Christian Estate.*

Three years earlier, Luther had sounded the trumpet for reforming the church when, on October 31, 1517, he nailed the 95 Theses to the door of the University Church in Wittenberg. Quickly he realized that Europe could not be delivered from institutional corruption without also reforming the university. Wisdom requires humble reason to learn from divine revelation and live in its light.

Luther was not alone. After two centuries of an elitist Renaissance, a number of learned and devout contemporaries had arrived at similar convictions. These included Desiderius Erasmus and reformers such as Ulrich Zwingli, William Tyndale, Philip Melanchthon, John Calvin, Theodore Beza, John Knox and Andrew Melville. Their educational efforts inspired the Council of Trent (1545–63) to transform a section of the Roman Catholic Church into a global force for education.

Some chapters in this volume explain how the 'obedience that comes from faith' (Romans 1:5; 16:26) turned scholars into reformers. They risked their careers and their lives to champion truths that eventually became the faith-foundations of the modern world.

An obvious example is the "truth" of human equality. In Luther's *Open Letter* this truth became the divinely revealed foundation of education-for-all. The belief that all men are "created equal" had never been "self-evident" in any culture.

No study of hierarchical European society, divided between nobility, clergy and serfs, could have taught a social scientist that all human beings were equal. Martin Luther learned that truth from the Bible's doctrine of the priesthood and kingship of *all believers*. His *"Letter"* articulated the radical idea that all men were created in God's image, and all were sinners. The Lamb of God was sacrificed because God loved the whole world. The Gospel is that any sinner could become a child of God through repentance and faith. Every child of God ought to serve his Father as a priest and govern the earth to ensure that God's will is done in his earth.

This theological seed of human equality sprouted and blossomed into a principled not pragmatic - policy of universal education. In the USA, George Whitefield (1714-1770), the great revivalist of the First Great Awakening, taught the truth of human equality most emphatically. His Bible teaching made this peculiar and revealed truth appear "self-evident" to America's founders.

Roman Catholic monasteries, nunneries, cathedral schools and universities had been educating priests since Europe's first education revolution. They, however, did not educate everyone. Luther's argument was that, since every child of God must serve the Father as his holy priest, every child needs to be educated. It took awhile for the biblical idea of the kingship of all believers to transform feudal Europe. God's just, righteous and compassionate will cannot be done on earth unless everyone knows God, discerns and does his will.

Why did Luther seek the nobility's help for his novel proposal of universal education? In 1520, he was still a Roman Catholic priest. He knew that most of his fellow priests would not share their power with everyone. They were no different than today's high priests of secular education. After all, who wants to give away his source of power and livelihood? Owners of the education industry will likely find umpteen reasons to resist *The Third Education Revolution* which we propose, because every revolution disrupts the *status quo*.

The idea of human equality was God's word, a divine "seed." Luther's *Letter* planted it in Europe's soul. The Lord Jesus himself had taught that the 'kingdom of heaven' is sown as a seed. God's kingdom comes as an idea that is communicated in words (Matthew 13: 1-32). This seed-word is the sword of the Spirit. (Ephesians 6:17; Revelation 19:13-15)

Luther's *Letter* on education asked Christian nobility to obey God's word and support education for every child of God. The reformers' obedience made the revealed "truth" of human equality a pillar and foundation of modern liberties—social, political and economic (1 Timothy 3:15). For five centuries now this sword of the Spirit has been conquering oppressive cultures built on hierarchical philosophies and customs. If God is "Our Father" (Matthew 6:9) then we are all brothers and sisters. Luther was the prototype "Protestant." The doctrine of "the priesthood of *all* believers" that he articulated was a protest against his own church and the culture of serfdom. However, protests do not liberate, truth does.

Obedience to the truth of human equality motivated Luther to transform German dialects into a literary language by translating the Bible. The move from Latin to German made it possible to educate everyone in their heart language.

If every child is to know truth, then a child's mother tongue should be the language of primary education. Classical languages such as Latin, Sanskrit, Literati Chinese and Arabic became barriers to widespread intellectual development. They were the primary means of discrimination. They kept the masses away from the centers of power.

Making the language of the people the language of learning is the matrix of modern democracy. You cannot have a "government of the people, by the people, for the people" unless it functions in the language of the people. That phrase was popularized by Abraham Lincoln's Gettysburg Address on November 19, 1863, and the basic idea was borrowed by Sun Yat-Sen in China. Few know that the phrase came from the prologue of the 1384 edition of Wycliffe's translation of the Bible into medieval English.

It is important to understand why the revealed, non-self-evident truth of the gospel became the source of modern ideas of human equality and political liberties. In 1520, Martin Luther published three books. The first, *Open Letter to the Christian Nobility of the German Nation Concerning the Reform of the Christian Estate*, applied the truth of human equality to education. The second, *On the Babylonian Captivity of the Church*, examined how religion had become Europe's source of slavery. His third book was *A Treatise on Christian Liberty*. This book, dedicated to the Pope, was published 12 years prior to Machiavelli's political treatise, *The Prince*.

Machiavelli, an Italian diplomat, saw politics as a pursuit of power. Luther, a student of divine revelation, considered it a pursuit of liberty. He wrote at a time when most Christians were bonded serfs in Germany. Luther's Bible study on *Liberty* began the West's long quest for freedom because the Bible began to be written when God liberated the Hebrews from slavery in Egypt. Luther's Bible study on *Liberty* culminated in the American *Declaration of Independence* (1776). It acknowledged the theological truth that the Creator - not the state, and not evolution had granted an "inalienable right" to liberty for every human being.

As a professor, the very first course that Luther taught was on the philosophy of Aristotle. Then he was ordered to teach the Bible. He submitted a written request to be excused because, he said, he was not qualified to teach the Bible. He was overruled and told to study the Bible in order to teach it. The first book of the Bible that he taught was Psalms. Then he taught Paul's epistle to the Romans. That started Europe's Reformation. By 1520 Luther was teaching Paul's epistle to the Galatians. Paul wrote: "It is for freedom that Christ has set us free. Stand firm, then, and do not let yourselves be burdened again by a yoke of slavery" (Galatians 5:1). This began Europe's quest for political freedom.

How did the Messiah liberate slaves?

The Apostle John answers that question in Revelation 5:9-10. The gospel, i.e., the good news, is that Jesus Christ was crucified as God's sacrificial lamb. He shed his blood to purchase Satan's slaves in order to make them sons of God. Where slaves serve their master, Satan; Sons govern their Father's kingdom. The reformers' growing understanding of this truth of the kingship of *all* believers (Revelation 1:5-6; 2: 26-27; 3:20-21) transformed the hierarchical governance of the Scottish church. After that, these biblical principles of liberty were applied also to political governance. Republican ideas of freedom developed over time in Geneva and France. They were first applied at a national level in Scotland. Then those ideas spread to other nations such as Holland and Switzerland in 1648 and in England substantially after 1688. British colonies in North America experimented with them and finally in 1787 those biblical ideas of liberty shaped the Constitution of the USA.

The Presbyterian system of the Scottish Kirk replaced the Roman Catholic hierarchy with a bottom-up social structure. Churches began to govern themselves by electing their own elders for human beings had been created to rule (Genesis 1: 26-30). Human sin had turned rulers into slaves of Satan (John 8:34) and the Savior came to restore sonship-kingship to all God's children.

Reformers such as John Knox and Andrew Melville fought to apply these theological/egalitarian truths to the way their church and government should be structured. They described their reforms as building the "New Jerusalem" and the "Kingdom of Heaven" on earth. George Buchanan, their older contemporary, called this biblical reorganization of society, "Popular Sovereignty."

The reformers' efforts did not create utopia, but they changed history. A century later the imperfections of their innovations were apparent. While it was easy to appreciate their success, it was difficult to call it the "New Jerusalem." Therefore, the Scottish Enlightenment proposed a compromise: use a Greek term for these Bible-driven experiments; call the new system of governance "Democracy."

No Scottish scholar suggested that their egalitarian system of governance had come from Greece. Everyone knew that the reformers built it upon their understanding of the Bible. They accepted the term "democracy" partly because that made it easier to impute the imperfections of their governance upon man, rather than on God.

Europeans knew that the only political system that Greece ever exported was brutal imperialism. The modern myth that western democracy came from Greek city-states was invented in the USA, at Columbia University (New York) in the early twentieth century. It was popularized by a lapsed Roman Catholic, Will Durant.

The sixteenth century protestors reformed nations because they knew that the only way to make the "voice of the people" (*vox populi*) the "voice of God" (*vox Dei*) was to educate citizens. Every student's mind needed to be renewed by revealed truths which are, at first, counter-intuitive. Take for example the Bible's revolutionary dictum, "The meek shall inherit the earth" (Psalm 37:11; Matthew 5:5). It poses an ethical challenge to the postmodern belief that education has only one purpose: "pursuit of power."

Without an education that writes God's word upon human hearts, the voice of the brainwashed mob becomes the voice of the Devil. That's why in his classic, *The Republic* (375 BC), Plato categorized Greek democracy as the worst of all political systems. He hated Athenian democracy because it killed his mentor Socrates. Plato advocated authoritarian rule by "philosopher kings" as the ideal way to govern cities, if not to build utopia.

Plato's disciple, Aristotle, mentored the Macedonian prince, Alexander, to become a ruthless philosopher-tyrant. A thousand years after *The Republic* was written, English philosopher Alcuin, who played a crucial role in Europe's first education revolution, agreed that the voice of ignorant, manipulated masses could not be trusted to govern nations. In opposition to classical thought, Protestant nations became free nations because they educated every child in God's wisdom. That made it possible for the U.S. Constitution to begin with the phrase "We, the people." The pagan West would have said, "We, the victorious army that defeated the British Empire."

The Constitution began by affirming *popular sovereignty* because it was a political vision built upon the theological truth of the "kingship of *all* believers." The revealed truth that all God's children, not just a victorious militia or a philosopher-despot, should govern God's creation, is the root that has nurtured and sustained the American experiment.

The Constitution of my motherland, India, followed the American Constitution. It also started with the phrase "We, the people" because the founders of modern India were products of Christian education. They did not study in Hindu ashrams or Muslim madrassas. By the end of the nineteenth century, when many of them went to universities, the "Enlightenment" had begun to darken "Christian" education. Thankfully, however, India's Constituent Assembly knew that our hierarchical society, based on caste and gender discriminations, needed to be rebuilt on the revealed truth that all men and women are created equal. Education had to deliver India from the Hindu myth that the god Brahma created castes inherently unequal; the Brahmins from his mouth and the Shudras from his feet. "We, the people" can be sovereign only if every child is given equal opportunity to develop his/her potential and become a servant-leader. Once postmodernism makes education nothing but pursuit of power, prestige, wealth and status, then it becomes a problem in a society already divided as a religious hierarchy. If theology is nothing but mythology, then there is no reason for India to choose the Christian "mythology" of human equality.

The West Without Its Soul

The contemporary term "postmodernism" implies that the modern era's intellectual foundations are now in ruins. Thomas Paine's *Age of Reason* (published in three parts in 1794, 1795, and 1807) has ended as an 'Age of Nonsense' championed by the West's elite universities. The "Enlightenment" became intellectual and moral "endarkenment" as a result of divorcing human reason from divine revelation. Western philosophers now know that the human mind cannot know the truth if it is nothing more than an evolved monkey mind. It is no longer "self-evident" to an average American student that all men are *created*; let alone "created equal." It is hard to get people to believe a myth that zillions of accidents evolved everyone equal.

Inequality is a self-evident, observable fact. President Obama is honest in admitting in a 2017 documentary, The *Final Year*, that human equality is a *story*. In his worldview it is a (pragmatically) useful myth that should be believed. For without this Christian myth, a black man could not have become the president of the USA.

The problem is: what if a goddess-worshipping feminist prefers to believe the myth that females are more evolved than males? Or, what if Nazis and Brahmins prefer the *story* that Aryans are the most evolved race? Then why shouldn't people think that the only "true story" is that white races are supreme? Should education teach stories or should it be a pursuit of veritas — the truth?

President Obama did not transform America's foundational "self-evident" *truth* of human equality into a "useful *story*." This feat was achieved by occult alchemists who championed a philosophy called Pragmatism.

The pioneer of the pragmatic theory of truth was philosopher, logician and scientist Charles Sanders Peirce (1839–1914). Psychologist-philosopher William James (1842–1910) popularized this "humanist" theory. John Dewey (1859–1952), made *Pragmatism* the philosophical foundation of secular, state-controlled education. Dewey wrote volumes on more topics than most people can think about. However, he omitted discussing the question of truth as it is a matter of the spirit. An animal or a bio-machine cannot know what is true or good.

Reviving the Soul

Can I "know" the dream you had last night? Neither my senses nor my logic can figure out what you dreamt. Meditation, mystic experience, parapsychology, astrology, telepathy, hypnosis and spirit-channeling are also powerless. The only way for me to know your dream is for you or God to reveal it to me in words.

You can reveal your private truth because language is revelatory.

The Apostle Paul turned Europe's pagan, story-based slave-culture into a truth-based culture of liberty because he understood the "spiritual" nature of his role as a teacher-revealer. Paul wrote to the church in Corinth,

> "These are the things God has revealed to us by his Spirit. The Spirit searches all things, even the deep things of God. For who knows a person's thoughts except their own spirit within them? In the same way no one knows the thoughts of God except the Spirit of God. What we have received is not the spirit of the world, but the Spirit who is from God, so that we may understand what God has freely given us. This is what we speak, not in words taught us by human wisdom but in words taught by the Spirit, explaining spiritual realities with Spirit-taught words. The person without the Spirit does not accept the things that come from the Spirit of God but considers them foolishness, and cannot understand them because they are discerned only through the Spirit. (1 Corinthians 2:10-14)"

Truth (*veritas* in Latin) was the soul of the Western university. Secularization forced the university to give up the hope of finding truth because it precluded the supernatural, spiritual dimension of reality. Language and logic, imagination and intuition are matters of the spirit.

Since Immanuel Kant's (1724-1804) critique of reason, philosophers have known that, without revelation, the human mind cannot know true truth. Cambridge philosopher Ludwig Wittgenstein (1889–1951) spent his university years trying to figure out language. He came to the same pessimistic conclusion as the Indian sage, the Buddha, that once we exclude St. Paul's worldview of the spirit, human words become incapable of knowing and communicating truth. The best your words may do is to express your feelings — real or fake.

Philosophers of pragmatism may throw you out of their universities if you claim to know and teach truth. Why are they so intolerant? Because they know that the "Enlightenment's" confidence in human reason has failed. Now the best you can do is "hope" that your rigorous scientific method allows you to confidently "assert" a proposition. You are not allowed to call your convictions "true." Pragmatism has enslaved universities to agnosticism. You are required to affirm that your beliefs are only relatively true; your ethics are adjustable; no one should trust you; your media spins stories 24/7 to manipulate your audience. This intellectual culture has made America's political-bureaucratic elite a manipulative "swamp."

President Obama's belief that human equality is not a self-evident *truth* but a useful *story* comes from Dewey's contemporaries, Carl Jung (1875-1961) and Joseph Campbell (1904-1987). Once these astute thinkers realized that the "Enlightenment's" reason cannot know the truth, they turned to myths in search of meaning. For the scientific truth about man was terrible. It was asserted by Burrhus Frederic Skinner (1904 – 1990). His worldview implied that the American Declaration of Independence was deluded; freedom and dignity were theological illusions.

Skinner was a celebrated psychologist, behaviorist, author, inventor and social philosopher. He taught psychology at Harvard University from 1958 to 1974. His 1971 book *"Beyond Freedom and Dignity"* was on the New York Times' bestseller list for eighteen weeks. For him the self-evident, scientific truth ("assertion") was that spirit, God, soul or self do not exist. The Buddha, Nietzsche, Freud and William James were right: The term "God is dead" means that man (self) is also dead. Truth is dead.

"I" does not exist. No "I AM" has ever existed — whether human, diabolical or divine. Therefore the idea of liberty was an illusion spread by the Bible's worldview. Skinner insisted that "I did not direct my life. I didn't design it. I never made decisions. Things always came up and made them for me. That's what life is."[2] Skinner's conclusion is postmodern deconstruction of "self" as discussed in my book, *"This Book Changed Everything: The Bible's Amazing Impact On Our World."*

----

2 Quoted in "Unpacking the Skinner Box : Revisiting B. F. Skinner through a Postformal Lens" by Dana Salter in *The Praeger Handbook of Education and Psychology Vol. 4* (2008) edited by Joe L. Kincheloe and Raymond A. Horn, Ch. 99, p. 872.

Skinner's "determinism" was not hyper Calvinism. It was logical scientism. He was revolting against the fact that the Bible had embedded the myth of "human dignity" into American culture. Freedom had been enshrined in the Declaration of Independence as America's foundational belief because of a Calvinist, Jonathan Edwards (1703 – 1758). He was America's first philosopher and revivalist. He taught this revealed "truth" in his 1754 book *"The Freedom of the Will."*

Theological notions of 'freedom' and 'dignity' that built America did not fit into Skinner's anti-spiritual, materialistic worldview. As a secular scientist /atheist he had to dismiss the American idea of freedom as a "myth." His reason for promoting atheism was pragmatic. Believing the "Christian myth" of an inalienable right to liberty makes it difficult for scientists to modify and control human behavior and to organize society for a happier life.

America's anti-spiritual education system is correct: "truth" and "freedom" are matters of "spirit," not of chemistry. Therefore education controlled by secular state has to destroy the worldview foundation of freedom. It is only a matter of time before graduates, brainwashed and indoctrinated by state-education, destroy freedoms built upon revealed truths. Philosopher kings already control American universities and mass media. Their protégés are eager to control citizens. Brainwashed citizens have no philosophical basis for resisting authoritarian rulers. Under threat, many will surrender their liberties.

Myths enslave because "stories" cannot be questioned. The truth liberates because it has to be examined and debated. Truth demands evidence and reason. That's why truth-(veritas)-based education opens the mind. In *The Book That Made Your World: How the Bible Created the Soul of Western Civilization* I explained how the Bible made the West a uniquely thinking civilization.

The greatest danger to *The Third Education Revolution* will come from pastors and elders who might see a church college as their opportunity to brainwash students.

A wise pastor, however, will grow by humbling himself and allowing students to question his assumptions. He will study and rethink what his seminary had taught him. Fundamentalism is indoctrination. Theology means using reason to make sense of revelation. Building a questioning and investigating culture within a church college will make Christianity America's most robust worldview.

Having lost truth, the West has little option but to reject the *exceptionalism* of its unique liberty. Therefore, please allow me to give one more example of why divorcing divine revelation from human reason must destroy American prosperity.

The July 4, 1776 Declaration of Independence said that governments are instituted to protect "inalienable rights" that the Creator (not the state) has bestowed upon every human being. This includes one's right to pursue happiness. As president, George Washington repeatedly reminded the nation that the right to pursue happiness implies the right to private property. In his formal presidential addresses, writings and prayers, at least 48 times Washington referred to every citizen's right to "sit under his own vine and fig tree with no one making him insecure and afraid."[3]

That imagery, affirming the right to private property, comes from 1 King 4:25; 2 Kings 18: 31; Micah 4:4; and Zechariah 3:10. One could say that that seed from God's word produced America's economic success. The belief that every person has a right to the wealth that he or she creates or inherits comes from the fact that God himself commanded, "Thou shalt not steal" (Exodus 20:15 KJV).

The God who requires the wealthy to love their poor neighbors sincerely and sacrificially, commanded both the rich and the poor "Thou shalt not covet" what belongs to your neighbor (Exodus 20:17 KJV). A nation prospers when the poor do not covet but create wealth for themselves. Education must restore in citizens the Creator's lost image. God did not loot. He "worked" to fill this beautiful earth with abundance.

To teach that "struggle for existence" and "survival of the fittest" help us evolve is to encourage loot. Evolution never commanded anyone "You shall not covet or steal" but to be creative like your Father. Postmodern universities have already destroyed America's founding faith that the Creator endowed each person with inalienable rights. They give to socialists the right to covet and loot what belongs to others.

3 Peter A Lilback, *George Washington's Sacred Fire* (Providence Forum Press, 2006) pp 317-318

They indoctrinate students to believe that anyone who inherits wealth is unjustly "privileged," and theorize that "the capitalists" who create wealth necessarily loot others — especially poor workers. This economic ethic of loot has promoted the immoral attitude that the poor have an inalienable right to covet and loot the property that belongs to capitalists. They believe that wealth belongs to the poor anyway.

At the moment of this writing, in the summer of 2020, some "wise" so-cialists have been advising poor voters in America, "please don't take the trouble to loot shops because that is dangerous for you." The wealthy "fund the police." Therefore they own the law enforcement system. Vote for socialism. That will give us the power to loot the capitalists on your behalf. We'll call it "tax." A tax is whatever the Government chooses to call tax. If you give us the power to loot, we'll give you a monthly check. That will free you to sit in front of a TV, enjoy drugs, play games and gamble. The wealth created by the hardworking tax-payers will more than take care of all your medical and educational expenses, even if you came into America illegally. If you vote for socialism, we'll get the power to punish the capitalists who make America wealthy." This ideology taught in universities is guaranteed to make everyone equal — equally poor.

By rejecting divine revelation, the West has become a beautiful castle which has at its foundation nothing but sinking sand. The biblical root that nourished the West's magnificent tree has been eaten up by worms. The trunk of the tree — education — is infected with debilitating intellectual viruses. A *Third Education Revolution* is needed to revive foundational truths of the modern world.

The Church has become intellectually weaker than the University because it abandoned its own universities. It decided to train its leaders in semi-naries and Bible schools that were intellectually inferior to the universities. The Church appears too weak to take education back from deceiving spirits. Yet, all authority over visible and invisible realms has been given to the Church's head. The resurrected "Ruler of the kings of the earth" (Revelation 1:5) gives to his body the command to shepherd his little lambs. Along with that responsibility comes the authority to teach all nations. That is a mandate to bring all nations under his discipline (Matthew 28:18-20).

Europe's First Education Revolution

Sixteenth century reformers who educated Western Europe and its colonies, including the USA, were products of Europe's first education revolution. It began with the Frankish king Charlemagne (748-814 A.D.) who was made the Roman emperor in 800 A.D.

Charlemagne began his rule with an assumption that to convert someone to Christianity meant to baptize that person. Therefore he ordered pagans to be baptized ("converted") forcefully on "pain of death." That policy of forced conversions was abandoned because the English philosopher Alcuin (735 – 804) persuaded Charlemagne:

> "Faith is a free act of the will, not a forced act. We must appeal to the conscience, not compel it by violence. You can force people to be baptized, but you cannot force them to believe."[4]

Alcuin explained to Charlemagne what St. Boniface (675 – 754), the apostle to German Barbarians, had emphasized a century earlier. That is, *to convert means to educate.* Conversion is the spiritual process of God's Spirit of Truth writing His law in the heart and mind of a repentant sinner. This process makes a rebel a "new creation" (2 Corinthian 5:17) who lives in "the obedience of faith" (Romans 1:5).

Twentieth Century missions failed to disciple nations because many "evangelicals" made the mistake of thinking that to convert means to lead people to pray "The sinner's prayer." They failed to see that the obligation to disciple nations meant to fill the earth with the knowledge of God as the waters cover the seas (Isaiah 11: 1-9).

Charlemagne's intellectual transformation resulted in what is called the *Carolingian Renaissance.* It produced a flowering of scholarship, literature, art and architecture. Charlemagne learned to read. He became such a lover of books that priests had to read to him while he ate. His favorite author was St. Augustine of Hippo (354-430). That made Augustine's educational curriculum Europe's standard for almost a thousand years. All the pioneers of the Second Education Revolution studied it. Charlemagne's court produced books that taught elementary Latin. It financed a royal library that contained in-depth works on language and Christian faith.

---

4 N. R. Needham, *2,000 Years of Christ's Power.* Part Two: The Middle Ages. Grace Publications Trust, (2000) p. 52

While scholars wrote in Latin, Charlemagne also supported translation of Christian creeds and prayers into vernaculars along with teaching grammar and music. He encouraged monasteries to establish Scriptoriums. Fasting, praying and performing religious rituals continued, but monks also dedicated their lives to copy every available manuscript. They wrote books on history, poetry, art, music, architecture, technology and law along with Bible exegesis, commentaries and theology.

Alcuin was Charlemagne's "minister." As such he taught the emperor rhetoric, dialectic (logic) and astronomy. Einhard (775 – 840) tutored the Emperor in arithmetic. He had been educated at Fulda monastery where St. Bonafice was buried. The education revolution that began with an Emperor-Priest team peaked in the founding of the university of Bologna in Italy (1088). There priests studied Justinian Law. Other universities followed teaching medicine and philosophy, along with scriptures and theology. Reflection on divine revelation (Theology) was the queen of all sciences. It justified the use of reason, God's image in man. It gave meaning to every intellectual discipline and to life itself. For the Bible commanded believers to "think about" what it says instead of believing blindly (Philippians 4: 8).

Popes licensed universities because the Bible exhorted Christians to "think." That deep respect for the life of the mind made university the educational arm of the Church, for the Church and by the Church. Church owned universities trained God's ministers to serve the Church and the king. That is why Prime Ministers still serve the Crown. The University of Harvard spelled out its motto as "*Veritas Christo et Ecclesiae.*" Translated from Latin it means that the university was created to help students seek "Truth for Christ and the Church."

Following Charlemagne's example, most kings employed educated "ministers" of the church as their court "ministers" (chaplains and advisors). That's why the officer who advises the British monarch is still called the "Prime Minister." Other "ministers" support his sacred responsibility to govern the nation with God's justice, righteousness, wisdom and compassion.

The University of Bologna, run by monks, taught Law because the Church had already built Europe's best, most trusted and powerful justice delivery system. Church-owned universities trained monks, priests, chancellors and bishops in God's Law which had been codified in civil and canon laws of the Justinian Code. Law education trained ministers of God's justice to serve the Church as judges, chancellors and advocates.

Jewish Roots of European Education

Any genius can invent a script which only he can decipher. A written language creates and enriches a culture only if others are taught to read it. The earliest known writing-systems were developed in Iraq and Egypt more than 1,000 years before Abraham and 3,000 years before Christ.

Abraham grew up in Iraq and spent a brief time in Egypt. His grandson Jacob took his extended family into Egypt where they lived for four hundred years, first as honored guests and then as slaves. These slaves were freed without an armed revolution. They returned to Canaan, to the land God had promised them. God's promise was that He would make them a "great nation."

Most slaves would have been illiterate. Moses, their leader, would have learned to read and write, for he grew up in the palace, adopted by an Egyptian princess.

Today's "experts" would have required Moses to tell stories to illiterate oral learners. But his God was politically incorrect. He gave to illiterate shepherds a text, the Ten Commandments. God wrote it on two tablets of stones. Moses put a copy of that sacred text in a wooden chest (Ark) and covered it with gold. A copy of God's word was sacred. The oral learners were not allowed to worship idols or invent myths about their deities. Not an imaginary god, but the sacred, written text of the Covenant between God and Israel was put in the heart of the camp, in the holiest of holy places.

What would make Israel a "great nation?" They would need to reject made up gods and stories about them. They would need to know the true God and His word that is truth. God made things more difficult: He required them to learn to write and make copies of His law. His word must be written, carved or stitched everywhere, so that ultimately it gets written upon their hearts. The Savior God required slaves to become thinkers. They needed to meditate upon God's written word day and night. Shepherds and brick-makers would become a great nation by becoming teachers of God's word.

God required free-slaves to make sure that every child knows and reveres God's word (Deuteronomy 6:7).

When rescued slaves were wandering in the wilderness, Moses taught them that military conquests will not make them a great nation. Slaves will be transformed by meditating upon God's written word and obeying it. That internalization of God's word will create the socio-cultural capital necessary to transform them into a great and wise nation:

> See, I have taught you decrees and laws as the Lord my God commanded me, so that you may follow them in the land you are entering to take possession of it. Observe them carefully, for this will show your wisdom and understanding to the nations, who will hear about all these decrees and say, "Surely this great nation is a wise and understanding people." What other nation is so great as to have their gods near them the way the Lord our God is near us whenever we pray to him? And what other nation is so great as to have such righteous decrees and laws as this body of laws I am setting before you today? (Deuteronomy 4: 5-8).

Beyond Law

The holiest of holies housed more than God's moral law. Just before writing the Ten Commandments (Exodus 20), God asked Moses to write the history of the Amalekites' attack on vulnerable wanderers. Thus the very first section of the sacred texts that Moses wrote and put next to the Covenant was the history of this specific battle. "The Lord said to Moses, [you] 'Write this [history] on a scroll as something to be remembered and make sure that Joshua hears it'" (Exodus 17:14).

Why did God ask Moses to write history?

Moses, the old man, had climbed up a hill to pray and watch the battle as his young assistant, Joshua, led untrained troops to victory. If one of Joshua's contemporaries was to write the "story" of that battle, the narrator might have described victorious Joshua's leadership, battle strategy, courage and prowess. But Hur and Aaron witnessed the conflict as well as the fact that the battle's outcome was determined by Moses' prayer. The two witnesses grasped the truth.

A flattering story would have hurt Joshua and Israel. It would have made Joshua put his trust in his sword. But his sword was completely useless before Jericho's impregnable walls. Joshua needed to be reminded that the living God had brought the Hebrews out of slavery. Reliance upon Him had made them victorious over the Amalekites. Only a humble and exclusive reliance upon the living God would enable them to win the promised land occupied by nations stronger than former slaves who had nothing.

God was active in human history then and He is active now. Secularizing providential history corrupts truth. Chapters by Gottfried Sommer and Stephen McDowell in this volume remind us of the truth about how Europe and America were civilized and educated.

Pagan shrines did not have sacred texts. They installed idols of man-made gods. Why would anyone worship gods of stone, wood or metals? Pagans worshipped imaginary gods who did not intervene in history. That's why they had no option except inventing stories to teach people why imaginary gods should be worshipped.

God prohibited Jews and Christians from inventing gods and myths. In place of stories, Moses was commanded to put historical truth in the holiest of holy. This is what made the Jews "the people of the book" which was, in fact, a library of books. They revered sacred scrolls, not idols. God's Spirit commanded, inspired and enabled men to write His truth. Words written by Moses and other prophets were the word of God.

Truth must be written down. Enough people must learn to read and orally communicate truth to others. For truth, not myth, must be the intellectual foundation of a free people.

The Temple and the Cathedral

Where would the son of a carpenter or fisherman go to learn to read and write? He went to the local synagogue. During the week the local priest served as the teacher.

What if the local priest failed to answer a student's penetrating questions? In that case a 12-year-old carpenter's son took his questions to the Temple in Jerusalem. For the Temple was the intellectual capital of Israel. It was much more than the place for worship and rituals. The Temple was the sun that radiated God's light to the nation. It was Israel's *de facto* university. Jewish scholars congregated in the Temple. That included experts in public health and scribes who studied, copied and exegeted the Scriptures in order to shed light on topics of vital interests. The Rabbis came to the temple to teach wisdom to priests as well as to the people. Priests and Levites then took God's wisdom to the remotest parts of the nation. Law experts applied God's absolute and man's relative laws to the complexities of new and specific cases.

Jesus of Nazareth went to the Temple to learn from the best-available experts. At the end of the day, however, he was a self-taught teacher — a *Rabbi*. That made Jesus a model of a learner-centered education discussed by Dr. Amanda Forbes in a later chapter.

Jesus studied, fasted and prayed. He was baptized with God's Spirit of wisdom, knowledge and understanding. (Isaiah 9:2). God's Holy Spirit made his words "life and Spirit" that came from the Father (John 6:63). His words were the seed that brought Heaven's kingdom into the soil of the human soul.

The Lord Jesus sent his apostles not as a militia but as sowers of the seed of God's word. He did not ask them to subjugate unbelievers with swords. He sent them to spread God's word which is the sword of the Spirit. Their mandate was to implant God's word in the human heart. God's truth-word was the sword that would conquer Satan's kingdom of deception:

> "For the word of God is alive and active. Sharper than any double-edged sword, it penetrates even to dividing soul and spirit, joints and marrow; it judges the thoughts and attitudes of the heart" (Hebrews 4:12).

Paul was Christ's Apostle who brought God's word to Europe. He didn't attack the Roman Empire with a metal sword. This man who started winning pagan Europe was a man of "letters." He branded himself as a "preacher and a teacher of the truth to Gentiles." (1 Timothy 2:7, Titus 1:1, etc). Paul's vision of an Academic Pastor is described by Dr. David Glesne. Pastor Joe Suozzo explains in his chapter that Paul established local churches that were "the pillar and the foundation of the truth." (1 Timothy 3:15)

Paul believed in "truth" because he believed in the spirit. He was the Jewish Rabbi who sowed the seeds of Europe's first education revolution. Irish monks were among those who watered those literary seeds of western civilization. The Carolingian Renaissance nurtured the saplings the monks and nuns had planted.

This vision of ancient Israel and God's kingdom transformed medieval cathedrals into centers of education. Some of these Cathedral schools grew into universities that continue until this day. Notre Dame in Paris is a classic example. Other famous European universities grew out of monasteries. That is why a chapel is always the most important building in every traditional college in Oxford and Cambridge. Both of them were Augustinian monasteries. Our book cover captures that theological and historical matrix of medieval and modern education.

From the First to the Second Education Revolution

The Second Education Revolution became necessary in the 16th century because pagan weeds suppressed the wheat that Paul had planted and faithful monks and nuns had nurtured.

"Christian" professors and priests suppressed the revealed truth by relying upon pagan rationalism and myths. That forced the reformers to confront Scholasticism. Dr. Gottfried Sommer's chapter explains how the second education revolution reformed European universities by subjecting Aristotelian logic to the searchlight of divine revelation.

One of the tragic confrontations climaxed in Oxford on October 16, 1555. University professors, students and citizens gathered around bishop Stephen Gardiner and several priests in the public square on the Broad Street to watch reformers Bishop Latimer and Bishop Ridley be burnt at the stake. Bags of gunpowder were hung around their necks to make their murders a spectacle!

The two martyrs knelt down near the cross and prayed. The older saint, Bishop Hugh Latimer, encouraged his fellow martyr: 'Be of good comfort, Master Ridley, and play the man; we shall this day light such a candle by God's grace in England as shall never be put out.' (Foxe's book of Martyrs 1583 edition.)

Sure enough, within years Oxford University began to be reformed. It rejected the intellectual darkness into which Scholasticism had fallen and embraced Psalm 27:1, *Dominus illuminatio mea* ("The Lord is my light") as its motto.

Oxford was able to burn reformers alive because by the sixteenth century Christian universities had become the source of Europe's darkness. They had allowed Scholasticism to mix God's revealed truth with Aristotelian Rationalism as interpreted by Muslims such as Avicenna and Averroes. Adding Platonic philosophy to that intellectual cocktail had made intellectuals stagger with dizziness. The Psalmist knew, "The unfolding of your words gives light; it gives understanding to the simple." (Psalm 119:130).

There are universities today that love darkness more than the light. The revolutionaries who choose to confront darkness will need to deny themselves and take up their cross. They should believe the promise that the darkness shall not overcome the light. (John 1:5)

Chapter 2

Three Teachers Who Made Our World

David Marshall[1]

Three of the most influential men who ever lived were teachers: only one died a natural death. All three recognized the importance of tying education to ultimate truth. Upon their words and actions, great civilizations arose. Education not only in the West, but around the world, was founded largely upon the bedrock of the third teacher's lessons. But now the world is scandalized by his words, as were those who first heard them, and has brought in bulldozers to shove the House of Teaching onto a foundation of shifting sand.

Socrates and Greco-Roman Civilization

In his account of the last days of his teacher, Plato made it plain that the Education Wars of Ancient Athens were theological at heart.

Socrates was tried for "corrupting the youth." To be specific, Plato said, Socrates challenged what he saw as unworthy portraits of the divine: Kronos swallowing his sons, Zeus killing his father, the gods squabbling over Troy. "This is the reason why I am a defendant in the case," Socrates explained, "Because I find it hard to accept things like that being said about the gods" (*Euthyphro, echoed in The Republic*). Socrates preferred death to being banished from his hometown because he agreed with his critics that educators held the future of Athens in their hands:

> "It is right to care first that the young should be as good as possible, just as a good farmer is likely to take care of the young plants first."

Socrates was thus made to drink hemlock at age 70 for challenging the teaching of harmful ideologies to children.

---

1 Author and speaker Dr. David Marshall is an educator who has taught in America, China, Japan and Taiwan.

Plato's own student, Aristotle, wrote about every subject imaginable, helping develop such fields as Ethics, Logic, Literary Criticism, Political Science, and Biology. All three Athenian teachers caught a glimpse of the Creator which thinkers in the Stoic school would expand (the Stoics adored Socrates), and to which St. Paul would appeal on Mars Hill. But tares were mixed with wheat in the teachings of the Greek sages. Aristotle's student, Alexander the Great, conquered much of the world for fun and glory. The empire he created split in three, then was conquered by the Romans, who invented concrete and forms of public murder that made drinking hemlock seem merciful. (Mercy being one aspect of divine truth which the Greco-Romans sorely neglected.)

Confucius and Chinese Civilization

Like ancient Greece, late Zhou-era China was fractured politically, but joined by language and national myth, when its greatest pedagogue stepped on stage. Confucius, whom Chinese still call "First Teacher," and whom even communist textbooks identify with the "mainstream" of Chinese tradition[2], was like Socrates, an itinerant lecturer who dreamed of bringing greater justice to the fractured states of his world through education.

While Socrates was dissatisfied by the absurdity and potential harm folded into ancient Greek myths, Confucius seemed to catch a clearer monotheistic vision. Traditional Chinese texts which Confucius quoted and supposedly edited (*Book of Poetry and Book of History*) spoke of *Shang Di*, the word for "God" which Chinese Christians use to this day: Confucius used the later and largely synonymous term *Tian*, or "Heaven."[3] Confucius said that his satisfaction in life came not from any fame he might gain, but because "My mind soars aloft, and does not Heaven know me?" (14: 27) Thus Confucius did not fear death:

> "If a man hears the Truth (Tao) in the morning, and dies in the evening, that is enough."

---

2 David Marshall, "Chinese History Lessons," First Things, February 2017

3 The debate over Chinese names for God is centuries old. I explained in a book entitled Fulfillment: A Christian Model of Religions, why I believe Tian is both a synonym for Shang Di and given New Testament precedent, a serviceable name for God in the mouth of Confucius and some early Chinese. (Though Shang Di is better now, because of how the word Tian evolved after Confucius.) For a popular-level explanation, see my True Son of Heaven: How Jesus Fulfills the Chinese Culture.

And so, caught in a city under siege, he told his students calmly that since Heaven had called him (as teacher) to the mission of preserving civilization, "What can the men of Kuang do to me?"

Yet Confucius was a humble man. His humility consisted of self-awareness, but also of forgetting himself in pursuit of learning and the call of Heaven. He also spoke of a "Holy Person" or "Sage" greater than himself, whom he could not hope to meet, but who would bring some great benefit to humanity.

Confucius' educational reforms did not ruffle as many feathers as those which Socrates unleashed, and he lived out his days in peace, dying about 479 B. C. Curiously, the greatest student in his school, the philosopher Mencius, suggested that a true Sage should be looked for every 500 years. Counting from Confucius' death, that would bring us to the first decades of the Common Era, and the rule of one Pontius Pilate in a sub-imperial state entity far to the west.

The Third Teacher

The third great teacher, who began ministry five centuries after Confucius walked calmly off stage, changed life on this planet the most fundamentally of all. Numerous writers tell how that teacher transformed not only the western world and its colonies, but even states which managed mostly to remain independent, such as Ethiopia, China, and Japan. Chapters in this book reflect the on-going impact of his life, actions, teachings, and death upon Europe, North and South America, Africa, Australia, India, and Indonesia. But it was not just the death of this teacher, it was also what J. R. R. Tolkien would call the "eucatastrophe" following his death – the "good disaster," a sudden dramatic twist in the story that surprised everyone but somehow made greater sense of life itself, even that season of life from death that we call "spring" – that blew the fog from history, and let in a dose of sunlight that still makes the world blink. (And often, close its eyes.)

The Third Teacher's influence on the Far East began about 630 AD, when Alopen, an ethnically Persian monk from eastern Iran, arrived at the court of the Tai Zong emperor, one of the greatest rulers in all China's long history. The emperor set up this foreign monk in the state library to translate the books he had brought. Tai Zong seemed impressed by what he understood, writing a "blurb" that was recorded on a stone stele in

781 which would be erected nearby: "Having examined the principles of this religion, we find them to be purely excellent and natural." (You can see that stone in the Confucian temple in downtown Xian in the "Forest of Steles," first monument on your left as you go through the door.) The emperor recommended that the doctrine about origins brought by the "Religion of Light" from the West be "published throughout the Empire."

Later, students of this greatest of all teachers did indeed set up schools around China, Japan, Korea, and Vietnam, some of which grew into major universities which thrive to this day, along with educational institutions around the world described by other contributors to this volume. This was part of what Vishal Mangalwadi, in the last chapter, called the First and Second Education Revolutions.

Teachers and Civilization

The most influential man who ever lived was a teacher, not an emperor, president, tech tycoon, or sports star. While he lectured brilliantly to large outdoor audiences at times (his "Sermon on the Mount" transfixed Tolstoy and transformed India and America), his "home room" held but a dozen men plus some women. (Even the great Chinese scholar Hu Shi, a fan of John Dewey's pragmatic thinking, credited this man's students with "teaching us that women are human beings).￼" The great teacher had no written credentials, nor did he own so much as a one-room school house on the prairie with a chalk board and some chunks of slate, let alone computers linked to academic databases. His textbook was an anthology of ancient poetry, biographies, laws, and sermons. When his host asked a girl who had snuck into class to help her fix dinner for the men, he replied, "Let her be. This young lady has chosen the better part." When he dropped by a local drive-in for a drink, he promised "living water" to the minority woman at the counter, who felt as if he could see into her broken heart, and the sin, pain, and frustrated hopes that lay there. He commissioned her as a teacher to her home village.

Start with a teacher who models truth by how he lives as well as what he says, and on his shoulders, you might build a great civilization, and bless the world. But get those central teachings wrong, and – well, parts of my hometown of Seattle burnt in the 2020 summer, thanks to the heresies taught in our public schools and universities, which I will describe in a later chapter. A heresy is not a complete lie, it is a partial truth. For the danger in the notions our children are taught today — and the public schools in many lands seem united in denying, covering up, or perverting the central truths that the world's greatest teacher taught— is not that they are simple falsehoods. The problem is that they are broken, partial, often angry truths, as the sand upon which a house bound to fall is made of crushed bits of rock.

Grassroots Education

These three founders of civilization were hardly teachers in the modern sense. In some ways, they were more like parents. They taught for love, not money. They took students on educational field trips up Mount Tai or on the Sea of Galilee. Rather than give pre-packaged lectures on a strictly defined "subject," they let young people ask any question, or allowed circumstances, dinner party debates, and chance encounters to guide inquiry. This may be why, as a student of the Third Teacher and admirer of the other two, and founding Academic Principal of an international school in China, I pulled students out of class on the slightest pretext. They picked tea leaves, waded in the surf, climbed Mount Lao, interviewed fishermen and Buddhist monks, walked through lotus fields and dragged a pine tree back to school to dress up for Christmas. Education does not always happen in nice, neat rows with noses pointed forwards.

Mind you, there is a place for lectures, and the Third Teacher modeled that as well. Mere phrases from his sermons inspired great novelists and overthrew tyrants. So, too, the public lectures of prophets like Elijah, John Wesley, and Martin Luther King, changed the world. My own classroom teachers — Mrs. Morton telling stories of Berlin when the Russians arrived at the end of World War II, Jerome Silbergeld magisterially laying out the history of Chinese thought in art, the great historian Donald Treadgold offering his last day "sermon" in Russian History — inspired me for life.

But I am convinced, as an educator, that the three sages who founded civilizations still have much to teach us about the style of education as well as its content.

The richest learning is student-initiated. It is not confined within walls. Students are best corrected in love, often by adults who know them well and have their best interests at heart. It might be nice if parents don't have to go too deeply in debt to finance their children's learning. In short, the best education reflects the way a father and mother train their children, complemented by the accumulated knowledge of a community that also cares for the next generation.

Great teachers, like good parents, also understand that education is a serious thing, and should be connected to the deepest aspects of life.

Our carefully-designed curriculum in China proved insufficient when life taught students hard lessons: when a young math teacher died suddenly, a student with a beautiful singing voice suffered a breakdown, or students fought in the hall.

Such moments are the final test of education, when one asks ultimate questions about truth, right living, and the meaning of existence. The answers that teachers like Socrates and Confucius offer, center on profound, even if incomplete, moral visions. Tests might not be handed out midway through the semester. Your teacher may ask you, "What is justice?" "Whose coin is this?" "Should this woman not have been healed on the Sabbath?" Or "Who do you say that I am?" Or for an "open book" test, perhaps he will send you through local villages to preach and heal. For as Andreas Wieland will show in the next chapter, the best teachers understand that the final test of good teaching comes in the living.

Which is why a teacher is a dangerous thing. And a teacher called by God to change the world is even more dangerous.

The Third Teacher warned that it would be better to have a millstone tied around one's neck and be thrown into the sea, than to cause "one of these little ones" to stumble (Mark 9:42). Even more than Socrates, He recognized that the teaching of the educational "authorities" of his time had been theologically compromised, and the love of the true God had grown cold.

Setting a Schoolhouse on Sand

One day, while teaching at Siebold University, an exclusive state school near Nagasaki, Japan, I met one of my students in the library with a sheath of papers in her hand. The papers appeared to constitute an essay.

"What are you writing about?" I asked.

"Women and Religion," she answered.

> "Are you writing about the Taliban?" (An easy guess: this was right after American forces had invaded Afghanistan, and the cruelty of the Taliban was much on people's minds. And "religion" was a suspect concept in Japan anyway.)
> "Yes!"
> "Do you know when Japanese women were first publicly educated?"
> The student pondered a moment. "After World War II?"
> "Hah! Don't you know your own history, and who brought the changes to Japanese society that allow you to study in this very school?"

No, I didn't ask this latter question. I knew my student couldn't know the answer, and saw no cause to be mean.

In fact, Methodist missionaries Elizabeth Russell and Jennie Gheer, followers of the Third Teacher, founded what is now "Living Water College" (Kwassui) on the hill across from Glover Garden in 1879, against opposition by those in government circles who thought girls should stay home. But Japanese are not taught the role Christians played in bringing education to their country (although Japan media seems less prejudiced against Christianity than, say, those in China or the United States.)

These days education around the world is built upon a wide variety of fundamental dogmas – Secular Humanism, Critical Race Theory, different forms of Islam, Hindu Fundamentalism, a mix of socialist, humanist and Confucian thinking in China – like factions in the crowd who squabbled among themselves but joined to condemn Jesus. Likewise our public schools seem now to agree only to purge the truths from our children's minds that gave their world life. In the public school texts I have seen you will be hard-pressed to find an honest description of the role the Third Teacher played in history, reform, the development of science, or even in great art. Instead, in a later chapter, I will describe the falsehoods I have found in some of those texts.

Teaching in an increasingly repressive communist country, sometimes I pushed the envelope a little. My students read passages from the Bible in World Literature and World History, since no one can understand either field without coming to grips with the words of Jesus. Whether in American, Japanese, or Chinese schools, I seldom felt free to tell students all I knew about the impact of His life. But as a historian, I tried to correct some of the lies they had been taught. And I knew that, as my Chinese students spread out to leading universities in the West, they would be told more untruths.

The world needs a *Third Education Revolution* first of all because truth matters. It matters for its own sake and, as great teachers recognize, it matters to the character of society.

In formerly Protestant countries, we now hear increasingly shrill and unified voices raised on behalf of what is called "Cancel Culture." Dissidents from the narrow half-truths of neo-Marxist "Critical Studies" are being purged from the quiet green alcoves of university campuses. A shocking percentage of protestors and rioters on behalf of half-truths and quarter-truths turn out to be public school educators.[4] The younger generation is not only being told lies; worse, it is being shielded from important truths.

Socrates complained that in Greek myth, Zeus killed his father. Likewise, the academic establishments of the world murder the truth that sets humanity free - the truth that had built many of those universities, stone upon stone.
Those stones are now falling apart because the university has lost its universality: the cohesion of mere facts in Truth which the first two teachers sought, and the Third Teacher embodied.

Hedgehogs, Foxes, and the Unity of Truth

The 2nd Century Christian thinker, Clement of Alexandria, said that "Truth is one," but noted that it had been torn to pieces by the ideologies of his day. "The dawn of light," which he identified with the Third Teacher, brought fragments of truth back together again into a whole. Even some atheists in Academia sense that truth is unraveling under their noses.

Dr. Stevan Harrell, a kind and amusing anthropologist who ran the interdisciplinary Honors Program at the University of Washington and guided my research on the True Buddha school of esoteric Buddhism, spoke with frustration in his retirement speech of the political war that "tears us apart." Anthropology was left with "no common purpose." For many scholars, he found, "Scholarship is politics."

4 Ruth Milkman, Stephanie Luce, and Penny Lewis,
Changing the Subject: A Bottoms-Up Account of Occupy Wall Street in New York City

Even as a leftist himself (Harrell couldn't conceive of an ethnologist voting Republican), he perceived that political fanaticism was tearing his field to bits: "The leftist-to-liberal majority in cultural anthropology won't tolerate people with any other politics."(Meaning not conservatives, but those who tried to ignore politics and do ethnographic study in peace.)

Harrell distinguished between "hedgehogs" (scholars who burrowed deeply into their ever-narrowing fields as anthropology sub-divided and most professors came to care about more and more confined areas of specialization) and "foxes," who like to scurry between different disciplines in order to hunt for chunks of truth wherever they may find it.

The truth is that not even "foxes" in the modern Academy dare range far, for fear of the Hound of Heaven. For while faith in God, however vague, has lent unity and purpose to many of history's greatest teachers, and inspired the first universities as Vishal said, religious enthusiasm is frowned on in the Academy even more severely than unorthodox politics, especially if it is allowed to sully one's research.

Consider how a simple question can lead a student with a fox-like disposition out of the burrow of a narrowly-defined discipline, to varied truths and then, if educators give her proper encouragement, lead her to God's Truth.

Helping run that school by the sea in China, I guided a bright young student in a personal research project. Since his parents were marine biologists (his Mom gave me shells from a trip to Antarctica), we decided to study a practical maritime problem, "Will our School be Flooded by Global Warming in the next 50 years?" A simple question, one would think.

We borrowed a tape measure from the office and measured the elevation difference between high tide in the Niwa River flowing by the school, and the front steps of the school. So our study began with basic math.

But then, like an impertinent river at flood, this "simple" question began pouring into neighboring fields. My student was writing in English, and doing research in Chinese and English: *languages*. He had to gauge both flooding from our little river and storm surge from a shallow bay out front: *meteorology* and *hydraulics*. We scanned a map of the bed of that bay: cartography. He checked newspaper records of past typhoons, to see how much storm surge was possible: *history*. But had some disasters been misreported? *Political science* and *psychology*.

To do a thorough job of answering related questions such as "How much will the sea rise?" Or "Should the school sell this land to some gullible chump, and move to higher ground?", Other fields would come quickly into play: *geography, oceanography, the physics of air pressure, planetology* (comparing the effects of Carbon Dioxide on other planets) *glaciology* (which influences the rate of sea level rise), *dendrology* (study tree rings, to determine past warming), the *biology* of the algae blooms that filled the bay in summer (other students later took this one on), and then *real estate, economics,* and *ethics . . .*

In the end, the answer we found was simple. "Probably not. In a worst-case scenario, a heavy storm surge during a typhoon might flood the basement. We may need a few sandbags in 20 years or so, if there's a big storm circling in from the north at high tide."

But that is where a real-world "story problem" is bound to take you. Like the path in front of Bilbo Baggins' front door, every trail leads to the end of the world. All history comes from one beginning, and leads to many forks in the dark, mysterious woods of the future.

The great teachers understood that important questions bring all of life to bear. So the history of the universe can be told with a cup of water in hand. And a simple inquiry may lead to further questions that scare modern educators.

If we all just randomly evolved by ruthless struggle in a purposeless universe, why should we tell investors or buyers if our school proves to be built on shaky ground? What obligation do we have to future generations? Ask that question in a university, but however "foxy" the professor may be, don't expect him to bring up abortion or the National Debt, still less God telling Moses on Mount Sinai, "Thou shalt not kill," or the words of the Third Teacher: "Love God with all your heart, soul, mind and strength, and love your neighbor as yourself."

Suppose one does drown in that hypothetical future storm surge? What then?

Former Oxford Professor of the Public Understanding of Science, Richard Dawkins, warned us against asking the "why" question. But why shouldn't students ask about the ultimate purpose and meaning of the objects that we study?

Why do the rising oceans (or the water in my cup) consist of hydrogen and oxygen? Why does a fortuitous resonance involving the "triple alpha process" allow carbon to form in large stars, which is then beefed up to oxygen, in a process that astrophysicist Fred Hoyle first deduced? What ultimate reality explains the dozens of "anthropic coincidences" that allow oceans, and a planet like ours that can host life? Why does Earth lie in a "just right" habitable zone from a sun of certain life-giving properties? Why is the moon, which causes tides that strengthen or weaken storm surges, of a certain size, formed astronomers now suppose by collision with a primordial planet at just the right angle to throw off our present monstrous satellite, which haunts trick-or-treaters, sets tides flowing, and stabilizes Earth's orbit?

Why did God say "Let there be light?"

I often told my World Lit and American Lit students: "Literature is about everything." Great literature, indeed, encourages students to explore questions that raise the human spirit right out of the classroom. Captain Ahab was not looking for a white whale to halt its carbon emissions, but as a picture of his struggle with Nature or God.

Job, too, asked a simple, if not purely academic question: "Why am I suffering?" Instead of giving a direct answer, God sprung a science quiz on him. What elements lie at the core of Earth? What tectonic actions set the boundaries of the sea? Who has explored the Marianas Trench, where (if the movie *Pacific Rim* is right) Godzilla is hanging out? Where does light come from? From what womb (stars) are rain, dew, and frost born? Lead the stars off in a chain, I dare you! How do they influence Earth? Who gives understanding to the human heart? Describe the folk ways of wild goat, horses, donkeys, hawks, eagles, and hippos! How can the ostrich survive with such a bird brain? Would you like to go for a crocodile ride?

Who knows, perhaps Job laughed at this last question despite his suffering, even face-to-face with God. Maybe that was the point.

Maybe God points us to the wonders of Creation, to raise our hedgehog or fox-like consciousness off of our miserable sorrows, to Higher Truth.

"What can I say? I place my hand on my mouth," Job replied.
As he precociously explored the frontiers of 20th and 21st Century science, Job forgot his sorrows for a few moments, lost in wonder.

Richard Dawkins says we should not ask such "Why" questions. That is *why* the modern academy has become too small a classroom for our kids.

Education that loses wonder, and the search for a unifying principle behind the wonders of science through encounter with God, does not "take care of the young plants first," and can even be said to "corrupt the youth."

Churches sometimes give answers that are too pat. We forget the mystery that Job faced, and the questions he could not answer. Confucius said, "To know what you know, and know what you don't know – this is knowledge (wisdom)." Socrates recognized that the wisdom ascribed to him could only reflect his rare recognition of his own oft-admitted ignorance.

Yet I fear even more that most educators no longer dare ask ultimate questions and honestly consider possible answers. I and other writers will show in later chapters how some of our teachers falsify history and hide great literature and philosophy from our children.

The Third Education Revolution follows the lead of the Third Teacher. We seek to recapture the curiosity and boldness of the ancient sages. We seek to allow students to return to a child-like state of wonder, and ask questions without borders.

I sometimes compare the "Grassroots Education" model of the ancient sages to homeschooling, with its spontaneous, love-based, no-holds-barred, student-initiated, out-of-doors character.
It is not that the secular Academy is too big and scary for our quaking Christian souls that need to fly to a safe space. It is that the secular Academy has become too tired, frightened, and timid to produce the free men and women who can create a civilization worthy of the name.

When we say there is something rotten in the state of education, and praise sages of the past – or the Medieval Church or Protestant Reformation – it is not because we wish merely to return to some imagined Golden Age. Christianity helped create modern science, and we intend to make wise use of the instruments it molded for learning.

"What is truth?" A Roman official once asked the Third Teacher, and our modern Academy echoes that question. But Pilate did not wait for an answer, though he asked the right person. Many of our teachers are even more anxious to burrow into their holes and avoid a vision of the heavens that leads to such ultimate questions.

The Third Education Revolution begins with the insight that "The fear of God is the beginning of wisdom," and with humanity's third great Teacher: Wisdom made flesh, who dwelt among us, full of Grace and Truth.

Chapter 3

Loss and Recovery of Virtue in Education

Andreas Wieland[1]

Is corruption the new normal?

From a global and historical perspective, education has never produced
so many students with so many credentials and the technical skills. In
2020 more children than ever receive at least some education and many
of them seem academically qualified for positions of leadership. This is
encouraging because it shows that one of the Sustainable Development
Goals (SDG's) of the United Nations is being reached. One should not
scoff at such real progress.

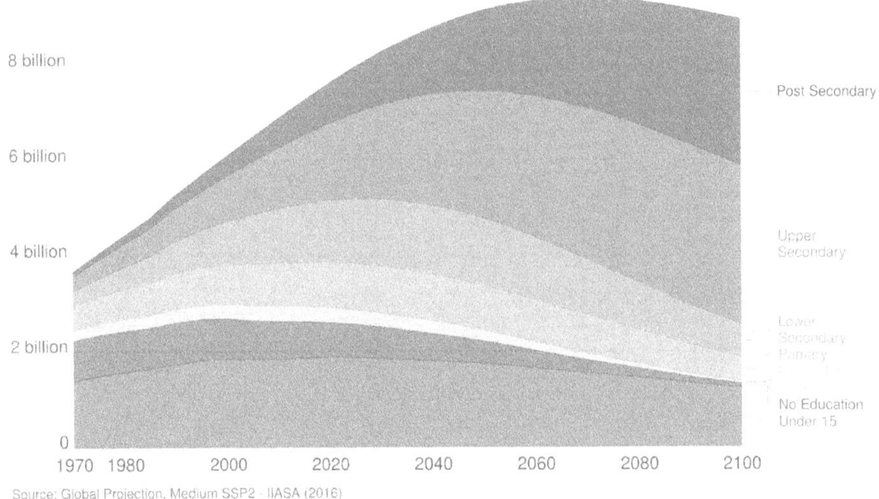

1 Andreas Wieland, a Theologian-Psychologist is the Founder-Director of Truth
and Transformation e.V. in Germany. He serves as the Director of Administration
for the Education Revolution proposed in this book.

I have taught Business Ethics at two German universities over the past five years. I usually begin my first lecture by having students scan a business newsletter. They are asked to look for articles that touch on ethics. After a little hesitation and thought they usually start speaking up, having realized that almost every piece in the newsletter has something to do with ethics: stories about corruption, abuse of managerial power, legal issues, global trading, human rights and sustainability.

The fact that top managers and leaders who attended prestigious ivy-league Universities still entangle themselves in such a mass of ego-centrism, corruption, and manipulative behavior is troubling, to say the least. Business expands around the world, yet moral corruption seems to keep pace.

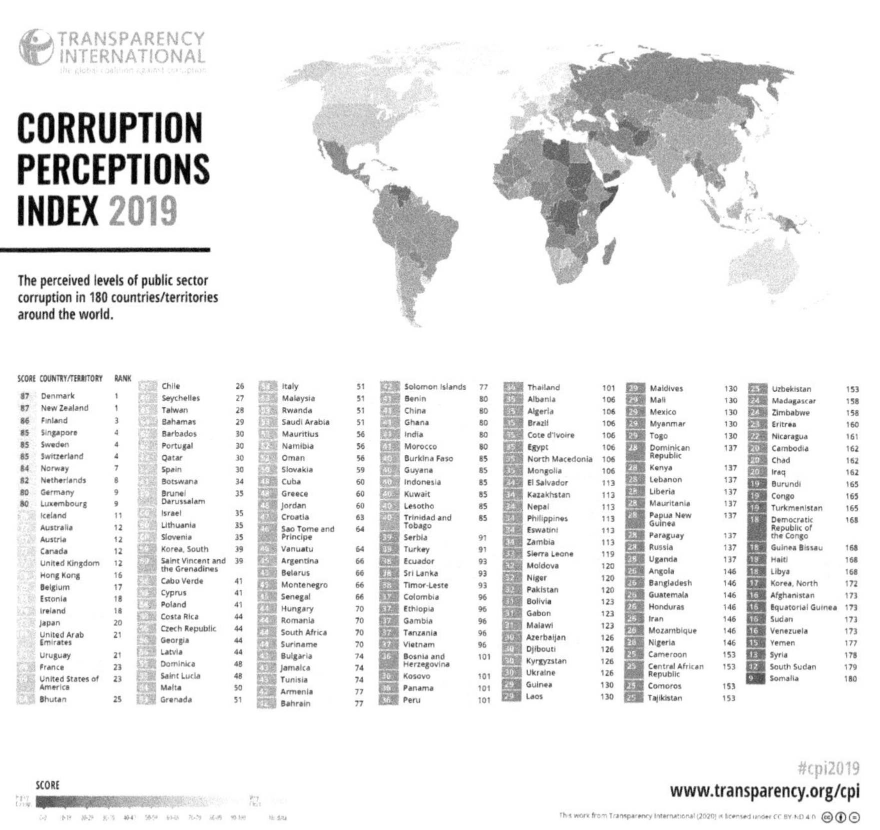

SCORE	COUNTRY/TERRITORY	RANK
87	Denmark	1
87	New Zealand	1
86	Finland	3
85	Singapore	4
85	Sweden	4
85	Switzerland	4
84	Norway	7
82	Netherlands	8
80	Germany	9
80	Luxembourg	9
[illegible]	Iceland	11
[illegible]	Australia	12
[illegible]	Austria	12
[illegible]	Canada	12
[illegible]	United Kingdom	12
[illegible]	Hong Kong	16
[illegible]	Belgium	17
[illegible]	Estonia	18
[illegible]	Ireland	18
[illegible]	Japan	20
[illegible]	United Arab Emirates	21
[illegible]	Uruguay	21
[illegible]	France	23
[illegible]	United States of America	23
[illegible]	Bhutan	25
[illegible]	Chile	26
[illegible]	Seychelles	27
[illegible]	Taiwan	28
[illegible]	Bahamas	29
[illegible]	Barbados	30
[illegible]	Portugal	30
[illegible]	Qatar	30
[illegible]	Spain	30
[illegible]	Botswana	34
[illegible]	Brunei Darussalam	35
[illegible]	Israel	35
[illegible]	Lithuania	35
[illegible]	Slovenia	35
[illegible]	Korea, South	39
[illegible]	Saint Vincent and the Grenadines	39
[illegible]	Cabo Verde	41
[illegible]	Cyprus	41
[illegible]	Poland	41
[illegible]	Costa Rica	44
[illegible]	Czech Republic	44
[illegible]	Georgia	44
[illegible]	Latvia	44
[illegible]	Dominica	48
[illegible]	Saint Lucia	48
[illegible]	Malta	50
[illegible]	Grenada	51
[illegible]	Italy	51
[illegible]	Malaysia	51
[illegible]	Rwanda	51
[illegible]	Saudi Arabia	51
[illegible]	Mauritius	56
[illegible]	Namibia	56
[illegible]	Oman	56
[illegible]	Slovakia	59
[illegible]	Cuba	60
[illegible]	Greece	60
[illegible]	Jordan	60
[illegible]	Croatia	63
[illegible]	Sao Tome and Principe	64
[illegible]	Vanuatu	64
[illegible]	Argentina	66
[illegible]	Belarus	66
[illegible]	Montenegro	66
[illegible]	Senegal	66
[illegible]	Hungary	70
[illegible]	Romania	70
[illegible]	South Africa	70
[illegible]	Suriname	70
[illegible]	Bulgaria	74
[illegible]	Jamaica	74
[illegible]	Tunisia	74
[illegible]	Armenia	77
[illegible]	Bahrain	77
[illegible]	Solomon Islands	77
[illegible]	Benin	80
[illegible]	China	80
[illegible]	Ghana	80
[illegible]	India	80
[illegible]	Morocco	80
[illegible]	Burkina Faso	85
[illegible]	Guyana	85
[illegible]	Indonesia	85
[illegible]	Kuwait	85
[illegible]	Lesotho	85
[illegible]	Trinidad and Tobago	85
[illegible]	Serbia	91
[illegible]	Turkey	91
[illegible]	Ecuador	93
[illegible]	Sri Lanka	93
[illegible]	Timor-Leste	93
[illegible]	Colombia	96
[illegible]	Ethiopia	96
[illegible]	Gambia	96
[illegible]	Tanzania	96
[illegible]	Vietnam	96
[illegible]	Bosnia and Herzegovina	101
[illegible]	Kosovo	101
[illegible]	Panama	101
[illegible]	Peru	101
[illegible]	Thailand	101
[illegible]	Albania	106
[illegible]	Algeria	106
[illegible]	Brazil	106
[illegible]	Cote d'Ivoire	106
[illegible]	Egypt	106
[illegible]	North Macedonia	106
[illegible]	Mongolia	106
[illegible]	El Salvador	113
[illegible]	Kazakhstan	113
[illegible]	Nepal	113
[illegible]	Philippines	113
[illegible]	Eswatini	113
[illegible]	Zambia	113
[illegible]	Sierra Leone	119
[illegible]	Moldova	120
[illegible]	Niger	120
[illegible]	Pakistan	120
[illegible]	Bolivia	123
[illegible]	Gabon	123
[illegible]	Malawi	123
[illegible]	Azerbaijan	126
[illegible]	Djibouti	126
[illegible]	Kyrgyzstan	126
[illegible]	Ukraine	126
[illegible]	Guinea	130
[illegible]	Laos	130
29	Maldives	130
29	Mali	130
29	Mexico	130
29	Myanmar	130
29	Togo	130
28	Dominican Republic	137
28	Kenya	137
28	Lebanon	137
28	Liberia	137
28	Mauritania	137
28	Papua New Guinea	137
28	Paraguay	137
28	Russia	137
28	Uganda	137
26	Angola	146
26	Bangladesh	146
26	Guatemala	146
26	Honduras	146
26	Iran	146
26	Mozambique	146
26	Nigeria	146
25	Cameroon	153
25	Central African Republic	153
25	Comoros	153
25	Tajikistan	153
25	Uzbekistan	153
24	Madagascar	158
24	Zimbabwe	158
23	Eritrea	160
22	Nicaragua	161
20	Cambodia	162
20	Chad	162
20	Iraq	162
19	Burundi	165
19	Congo	165
19	Turkmenistan	165
18	Democratic Republic of the Congo	168
18	Guinea Bissau	168
18	Haiti	168
18	Libya	168
17	Korea, North	172
16	Afghanistan	173
16	Equatorial Guinea	173
16	Sudan	173
16	Venezuela	173
15	Yemen	177
13	Syria	178
12	South Sudan	179
9	Somalia	180

Transparency International (TI) produces a global ranking of how much corruption can be found in a given country every year. It is called Corruption Perceptions Index (CPI, www.transparency.org). The latest report shows that more than two thirds of countries score below 50 out of 100 possible points (where 100 means no corruption and 0 means highly corrupt). The section "Countries to watch" focuses on outstanding developments. The trend is that western countries get lower scorings as time goes by. To give an example, in the 2019 analysis TI wrote: "With a score of 77, Canada dropped four points since last year and, more significantly, seven points since 2012". In its CPI 2018 press release Transparency International said: "The 2018 Corruption Perceptions Index (CPI) released today reveals that the continued failure of most countries to significantly control corruption is contributing to a crisis of democracy around the world." Corruption is not only problematic for individuals and businesses but also for whole nations and democracies, according to TI.

Leaders who studied at "Christian" Higher Educational Institutions have stumbled and fallen, too. Lawsuits against Christian pastors and CEO's of Christian Organizations because of stealing, sexual harassment or abuse, fraud and deception fill blogs and headlines of Christian and secular media.

The best-seller rack also shows troubling trends. In 1998 Robert Greene wrote his classic "*The 48 Laws of Power.*" It is still the no. 1 bestseller in the field of Political Philosophy, no. 3 in Social Philosophy on Amazon. com. The book posits that power is "a-moral," in other words, merely a technical or a pragmatic and personal matter. You should train yourself to apply the 48 laws, which Greene compares to rules in a game, the game of life, if you want to be successful. His book can be used as a training manual on how to use power for one's own benefit.

Almost all of the people responsible for such problems have studied at some university. Can all these phenomena be attributed solely to personal ethical weaknesses, independent of their educational careers? Might these problems not suggest that our present system of higher education does a poor job at character formation?

Many authors discuss integrity, character, and virtue in business: some from a secular perspective, some from a generally Christian or a strictly biblical point of view.

John C. Maxwell is one who writes from a Christian perspective, thrusting his finger into the bleeding wound of corruption in the business world and calling leaders to changed behavior. Maxwell emphasizes character and integrity, arguing that the virtues of honesty, self-sacrifice, generosity and active listening are indispensable qualities of a leader. Ken Blanchard, Leighton Ford, Bill Hybels, Oswald Sanders and many others offer similar arguments.

The character of a leader is formed, according to Robert J. Clinton in *"The Making of a Leader,"* through a series of tests, by which God challenges him and teaches him the skills he needs to master. Clinton makes his case by meticulous analysis of both positive and negative case studies from the biographies of biblical and historical leaders. How do universities deal with character formation and the development of virtues?

In *"Character and Virtue in Theological Education"* (Langham, 2019), Marvin Oxenham points out that virtue formation has been widely discussed in higher education since the early 1980's: programs, degrees, papers and publications have appeared in many forums. Even UNESCO has gotten into the act. But this seemingly encouraging trend is not as promising as it may sound. Oxenham writes:

> "Overall, the place of character and virtue education in the university is hazy at best, and the process of bringing character education to a level of appropriate engagement is laborious. Virtue is not a priority, and in some universities character education is considered anti-liberal, sectarian and anti-intellectual. In others, it is applauded in theory but is nowhere seen in practice. In a few universities, character education is affirmed but generally relegated to the extra-curricular realm." (2019, 42)

So higher education in general seems to flourish as never before, but with little effective emphasis on the character of the student. (See Chapter 16 by Karla Perry.) But there seems to be little focus on education as character building. And this in turn leads to problems in our families, cities, companies and nations.

What is Virtue?

What exactly do we mean by virtue? And what qualities constitute a good character?

Oxenham (2019, 24) quotes Arthur (2017, 28): "Virtues constitute stable dispositional clusters concerned with praiseworthy functioning in a number of significant and distinctive spheres of human life." The eminent philosopher Alvin Plantinga quotes from Calvin College's Statement of Purpose for the Core Curriculum:

> "Virtues are settled dispositions to feel and act in certain ways. A compassionate person is inclined, as if by nature, to be moved by human suffering. A person in possession of the virtue of honesty has the disposition to tell the truth. Vices are also dispositions. A callous person, bearing within his breast a heart of stone, disregards the needs of others as a matter of habit. A person saddled with the vice of deceitfulness has the disposition to lie whenever lying seems convenient. A particular array of virtues and vices, taken together, makes up a person's character." (2002, 130)

The fact that individuals who are not Christians also develop virtues is due to two reasons: a) God's common grace which gives wisdom and knowledge to all humanity, and b) biblical values remain in post-Christian cultures, although people often do not know where they came from and why they make sense. Vishal Mangalwadi is among the authors who have described how the gospel has lent many cultures such a heritage, both in the West and elsewhere.

A Biblical Approach to Building Character Through Education

For Christians, the most important source for reflection on character building is the Bible, God's inspired Word. Here we find tremendous amounts of information about character building. To simplify matters, one can say that in the Bible one finds three facets of answers to this question. Character is counter-intuitive, counter-cultural and opposed to hypocrisy. Biblical morality is both obvious and subtle, telling us truths which seem counter-intuitive, but prove true on deeper reflection if applied practically. Therefore the Bible stands against superficial pretenses as concerns morality.

If one wants to identify concrete examples and texts to prove this, one should follow a double approach, because the Bible teaches character in two ways: by the examples of heroes and villains (and villainous heroes), and by direct precept, command and instruction.

Besides these two ways there is one more perspective we need to look at when identifying concrete biblical data: does the Bible teach principles or give examples of the development of character and training in virtues?

Old Testament Virtues and Character Building

Noah demonstrated a stubborn trust in something that seemed foolish to most of those around him, namely God's order to build a huge ship in the middle of dry land. From the outside Noah's actions made no sense. Noah defied both his cultural narrative and what looked like common sense. Yet his actions reflect humility and love for God.

Abraham likewise left his homeland and headed into a strange desert, displaying counter-intuitive virtue. "He trusted God, and God counted it as righteousness." Faith and obedience are inseparable. But like Noah, Abraham also revealed truth by doing wrong. His cowardice in trying to hide the fact that Sarah was his wife when they first entered Egypt shows two things: a concrete example of a vice and that the Bible is no naïve propaganda or tract for easy success. The Bible shows the weakness of its heroes without restraint and it privileges flawed sincerity over polish, glamour and pretense.

This can also be clearly seen in the life of Moses, who saved the Jews from Egypt, and in the life of David, Israel's greatest king. Both characters are described as close to God and even as his "friend," but the biblical accounts do not spare us their misconduct. Both are revered throughout the Old and New Testaments. But we are forthrightly told how David committed adultery with Bathsheba, murdered her husband and covered up his sins. Moses' failings are treated with the same merciless honesty. Israel's great liberator was ultimately not allowed to enter the Promised Land he had dreamt of all his life.

What can we conclude from these observations? Even virtuous biblical characters wander. We should look up to, but not idolize them. The fact that they fall, points us to the perfect picture of human virtue, Jesus Christ.

Other texts describe virtue explicitly. Proverbs emphasizes the virtues of humility, faithfulness, truthfulness, hard work and honesty—ways which lead to a life that prospers and is blessed by God. Ecclesiastes reminds us that only limited joy is to be found under the sun, indirectly pointing us to a higher realm. Yet other verses encourage us to enjoy life and the blessings God has given. Here the virtue of celebrating comes to the fore, combined with an Old Testament fear of God that roots worldly joys in a transcendent perspective.

The prophetic writings are among the great moral tracts of world literature. But a few texts stand out even in this glorious environment, like Micah 6:8:

> "He has told you, O man, what is good; and what does the Lord require of you but to do justice, and to love kindness, and to walk humbly with your God?"

This text may be viewed as a summary of all that the Old Testament says about character formation. It is set in a courtroom where God is the judge, Micah is His authorized representative, the mountains are witnesses and Israel is the accused. God does not ask much of his people Israel but simply: do justice, love kindness and walk humbly in His sight. These are simple virtues, but not easy to live out in the long run. And they challenge our cultures, self-will, and superficial understanding of what is right. We tend to seek our own advantage at all costs, love power not kindness and are rebellious not humble.

So far we have witnessed a somewhat static depiction of virtue and vice in the lives of Old Testament heroes, and a direct description of the value of such core virtues as honesty, humility, love and justice. But how does character develop to bring out such virtues? This is the key question for those who seek to reform education.

Old Testament stories illustrate the development of character. Moses was expelled from Egypt as a murderer, then lived in Midian as a shepherd for 40 years before he was ready to lead the people of Israel out of Egypt. The story of Jacob also shows how circumstances can form character. Jacob won by deceit, creating turmoil and ended up being deceived himself by his father-in-law. After wrestling with God before meeting the brother he had deceived many years before, it appears that he finally understands that only God's blessing counts. It is at this point of spiritual growth that he is given a new name that is still on the lips of generals and diplomats, "Israel." From that day on Jacob limps but has found reconciliation with God and his brother. Again and again, growth comes through trials.

Moses affirms the importance of early character training, not only for the Jewish nation but as a testimony to neighboring lands:

> "See, I have taught you decrees and laws as the Lord my God commanded me, so that you may follow them in the land you are entering to take possession of it. Observe them carefully, *for this will show your wisdom and understanding to the nations*, who will hear about

all these decrees and say, 'Surely this great nation is a wise and understanding people' . . . Only be careful and watch yourselves closely so that you do not forget the things your eyes have seen or let them fade from your heart as long as you live. *Teach them to your children and to their children after them.* (Deuteronomy 4: 5-9)

"Fix these words of mine in your hearts and minds; tie them as symbols on your hands and bind them on your foreheads. *Teach them to your children, talking about them when you sit at home and when you walk along the road, when you lie down and when you get up.* Write them on the doorframes of your houses and on your gates, so that your days and the days of your children may be many in the land the Lord swore to give your ancestors, as many as the days that the heavens are above the earth." (Deut. 11: 18-21)

Solomon, child of a redeemed relationship between David and Bathsheba, also affirmed the importance of childhood training focused on virtues. There are numerous passages in the book of Proverbs like the following:
> *Discipline your children, for in that there is hope*; do not be a willing party to their death (Proverbs 19:18).

The New Testament repeats this command to focus on character development at a young age:
> "Fathers, don't make *your children* angry. Instead, train them and teach them the ways of the Lord as you raise them" (Ephesians 6:4, NIRV)

So character should be developed at a young age, and parents are responsible for helping instill virtues in children. But character further develops through God's providence in later life.

New Testament Virtue and Character Development

Christians recognize Jesus Christ as the embodiment of righteous character. But one should consider his example with caution.

The heart of the New Testament is that no man can be justified by his own good works: righteousness before God can only come through faith in Christ's death on the cross and resurrection. We should not fall into the common trap of looking at Jesus merely as the perfect human being to be emulated. We should not think that asking people to live like Jesus will heal this broken world. The New Testament contradicts such simplistic views.

For one thing, New Testament heroes like Peter and Paul are almost as broken and flawed as Old Testament ones. They are portrayed as virtuous and worthy of imitation, but we are not spared full portraits of their failures as well. So the New Testament does not promise that if we implement a set of virtues then we and the world will be transformed. On the contrary, the whole Bible demonstrates that people who are flawed can be used by God to change the world. It seems even to be part of Jesus' "educational program." He brings his disciples to a point where they surrender with a feeling of complete unworthiness; then he calls them to service. It is when Peter gives up after fishing all night that his nets almost tear from a huge catch. Before we can be used, we must surrender our self-oriented lives to Christ, and be ready to obey him.

But did Jesus directly initiate character training? If he did, that would confirm the necessity of this aspect of education and give us a blueprint for how it should be conducted.

In the gospels we encounter a teacher of shocking humility. He washes the feet of his students and dies on a cross after enduring an unjust trial at which he offered no sharp rebuke. He speaks of the strength that lies in weakness, telling his followers to take up their crosses, and explaining to them that they will be "blessed" when they turn the other cheek or are meek, poor in spirit, or persecuted. Especially in ancient Europe, which worshipped cruel and assertive conquerors like Alexander and Caesar, Jesus' behavior is counter-intuitive. He does not defend himself, argue, or seek control, but declares himself the servant of all, who has come to die for those who will kill him.

The gospel is also counter-cultural in that Jesus does not conform to man-made laws and rules. He welcomes sinners, lepers and social outcasts, but reveals the hypocrisy and deceit of some religious authorities. His sincerity is demonstrated in his repeated calls to look on the inner man, not on appearances: a widow with a few coins - not a publicly lauded philanthropist - is the greatest benefactor. A tax collector becomes a saint. A loose-living Samaritan woman who thirsts for living water will be her town's evangelist.

In the Great Commission (Matthew 28), Jesus commissioned his apostles to disciple nations by teaching them to *obey* all he had com-manded. We can teach or inform children what Jesus taught but fail to ask them to obey those teachings. These two teaching tasks, being informed and obedient, are quite different. One imparts information; the other forms character. Facts can be imparted by someone who walks into a classroom, tosses out data, then goes home to live a life no one in the class is supposed to ask about. An instructor may even teach good and virtuous truths about Jesus Christ, then leave the building and completely contradict in his actions what he had been teaching just minutes earlier. This is the scandal and challenge we face in schools, universities and churches.

Another aspect of Jesus' teaching style might be called "exalting through humility." In John 21 Jesus confronts Peter with his prior threefold denial of him. Jesus asks Peter three times whether he loved him more than these (other disciples). Peter's reply is a clear and affirmative "yes." Each time Jesus asks, Peter is humbled and saddened more because he thinks Jesus is doubting the truthfulness of his answer. Every time this happens, Jesus follows with a commissioning call: "Feed my sheep;" "Take care of my sheep." Jesus thus burns into Peter's soul three facts: a) Jesus knows what I have done (repeating the number of times Peter denied Jesus), b) Jesus primarily wants my love and unambiguous commitment and, c) Jesus commissions me even though he knows how flawed I am. This, combined with the reception of the Holy Spirit, enables Peter at Pentecost to boldly stand in front of the people of Jerusalem and proclaim the Gospel of a Savior who restores what is broken, heals the sick and calls for unswerving surrender.

Before his death Jesus promised the Holy Spirit (John 13-17). Jesus explained that the Spirit would teach his disciples, reinforcing what he had said and done. So character is built as the Holy Spirit works in a believer, reminding him of God's Word and generating trust, obedience, wisdom and courage focused on Jesus Christ.

Paul writes to his younger colleague, Timothy: "The goal of this command is love, which comes from a pure heart and a good conscience and a sincere faith" (I Timothy 1: 5). Here Paul repeats in a specific context that the goal of the "command" / teaching (Greek: παραγγελίας) is love, echoing Jesus' famous "Golden Rule" and his summary of "all the Law and Prophets." Taken together with other texts in the Pauline corpus it is clear that the training of character is the primary goal of teaching, not just raw knowledge:

> "Knowledge puffs up while love builds up. Those who think they know something do not yet know as they ought to know" (1Corinthians 8, 1-2).

> "If I have the gift of prophecy and can fathom all mysteries and all knowledge, and if I have a faith that can move mountains, but do not have love, I am nothing" (I Cor. 13:2).

Clearly the goal of spiritual development is love, not mere theoretical Bible expertise. Our fatal error lies in failing to cultivate virtue through education.

Finally, the Epistle of James also shows what it means to be a "wise" and "understanding" follower of Christ:

> "Who is wise and understanding among you? Let them show it by their good life, by deeds done in the humility that comes from wisdom." (James 3:13)

So wisdom and understanding, the true goal of education, form a good life full of humble good deeds.

Summary of Biblical Teachings on Character Formation

In short, the Bible teaches the following nine truths about Christian training in virtue:

1) Character building is counter-intuitive and counter-cultural. It does not happen "by chance" or "organically" but *it needs to be intentionally fostered.*

2) Character building is *modeled by an exemplary life of love.* It does not develop through mere abstract and impersonal teachings.

3) Character building *should never be seen as a way to be saved.* Rather, character most fully develops in those followers of Jesus Christ, who have fully grasped the Gospel of salvation by grace alone.

4) Character building should begin with parents and teachers of young children. At an early age, children are more moldable and able to build character than later in life (Proverbs 22:6).

5) Character building *orients itself to God's word and the person of Jesus Christ.* Virtues can be seen in Jesus clearer than anywhere else (1 Pet 1:15-16).

6) Core virtues begin with *love, humility, honesty, justice, and obedience.*

7) The *Holy Spirit plays a central role in character formation* as he puts God's word on our minds, reminds us of Jesus Christ (John 14:26), and enables us to stay humble as we see Jesus loving imperfect human beings based solely on his love and grace.

8) Character building occurs most powerfully in difficult times, as the Holy Spirit reveals sin, and confirms God's love and His calling on us.

9) Character building happens in tension between the call to virtue and the recognition that we lack that virtue. In the process of growth, we are called back to God in need, again and again.

Conclusion:

Let us look again at the present state of society and recognize the urgent necessity of a deep-rooted change in the philosophy of our educational system. *The Third Education Revolution* we envision focuses (among other things) on the building of character because contemporary problems are so evident and ugly. Every nation needs good chemists and economists and these subjects must be taught by experts. However, a professor immersed in keeping up with the latest research in chemistry cannot be expected to also take responsibility for his students' characters. For learning healthy life-skills every student needs to relate to a life-coach — an Academic Pastor (see Chapter 7 by David Glesne). Character training must not be viewed as an extracurricular hobby, for a nation's future depends on the goodness of its citizens. No one should accept simplistic and short-term suggestions of what temporal band-aid ought to be applied to our gaping spiritual wounds. We desperately need a long-term solution for reforming our national character. We need changed people in key positions bringing truthfulness, humility, and justice back into society.

If we wish to see our nations change, we need to foster strong character building in our organs of instruction, beginning in the home, and ending at the university and church. Virtues must be discussed and thought through in these realms of life. Mothers and fathers, teachers and professors, statesmen and civil servants, pastors and theologians need to grasp their responsibility as role models for young people.

Bibliography:

- Arthur, J. et al. (2017). *Teaching Character and Virtue in Schools*. London: Routledge.

- Clinton, R. J. (2012). *The Making of a Leader*. Colorado Springs: NavPress.

- Greene, R. (2000). *The 48 Laws of Power*. New York: Penguin.

- Maxwell, J. C. (2007). *The 21 Irrefutable Laws of Leadership*. Nashville: Thomas Nelson.

- Oxenham, M. (2019). *Character and Virtue in TheologicalEducation:* An Academic Epistolary Novel. Carlisle, UK: Langham.

- Plantinga, C. (2002). *Engaging God's World: a Christian Vision of Faith, Learning and Living*. Grand Rapids: Eerdmans

Chapter 4

From Home-School to Church-College

Joe Suozzo[1]

America's Humble Beginnings and Education

About one mile from the church where I pastor is a small historical land-mark that reminds our community of America's simple beginning. The Georgia Road School House is described by the township's website as having been built in 1735 and had been in continuous use until 1956. When I drive by this little school, I often think about what life and education would have been like for the country more than 250 years ago.

We know from history that more than 85% of the families during that time either owned or worked on small farms. Until the middle of the 20th century, children would have been required to attend school only six months of the year. The other six months would have involved working with their families' businesses and farms; planting, harvesting and other hands-on chores that made children a vital part of the family economy.

But perhaps what is even more intriguing than the humble size of the school and its academic calendar was its curriculum, taught for more than eight generations of America's history. Three text books were widely used during that time: the New England Primer, the Hymnal and the Bible. From the Pilgrims' landing in 1620 through the 1840's, primary education in America was largely training in the Word of God.

The New England Primer was first compiled in 1688 by a British journalist, Benjamin Harris and was used for more than 150 years in America. The way the alphabet was taught gives us a hint of its content.
> *"A: in Adam's fall we sinned all;*
> *B: The life to mend, this book (the Bible) to attend;*
> *C: Christ crucify'd, for sinners dy'd."*

---

1 Joe Suozzo has been serving in pastoral ministry and missions for the past 30 years. He has a burning passion to see young people discipled and educated through the church so that the nations may be transformed for God's glory.

Though the primer went through many revisions, it generally included the Lord's Prayer, the Apostle's Creed, Westminster's Short Catechism, and the Ten Commandments.

Various editions included an account of John Roger's martyrdom with a picture of him burning at the stake while his own children watched. Questions like 'What is the chief end of man, what is the first commandment of the book and what is faith in Jesus Christ?' were also included.

To give an even greater glimpse of America's spiritual fervor during those years: after the First Great Awakening with Johnathan Edwards in 1720, alongside the New England Primer, was published John Cotton's "Milk for Babes", which included 64 questions and answers concerning church and doctrine.

We also see the primacy of God's revelation in the founding of America's colleges. Harvard, Yale and Princeton were all founded on a charter to equip pastors, missionaries and business people with applied theology as the apex of learning. Harvard's first seal after its founding in 1638 was *In Christi Gloriam* ("For the Glory to Christ").

Yale's initial charter in 1701 was that *"Youth may be instructed in the Arts and Sciences through the blessing of Almighty God."* When Princeton was founded in 1746, its first elected president was the famous preacher and philosopher Jonathan Edwards himself, with a mandate to *"train ministers."*

In short, the curriculum that was taught to the first children and young people in America was theological in nature and was designed to bring young people into a saving faith in Christ. The first settlers had a vision for their nation and that vision included a knowledge of Scripture. One could argue that primary education in early America was teaching children and youth to interact with their world biblically. As believers in Christ we know that, if America is unique and great, it is because of that vision and foundation that these early founders laid in their children's hearts.

America's Twilight

Looking at America today you would be hard pressed to find many overt signs of this heritage. The idea of applied theology in primary or secondary schools, or in the university setting now seems fantastic. Aside from the

Christian College and Private Christian School movements, over these last 130 years, education in America has become a thoroughly secular endeavor. Not only is God put on the periphery of student life, but any parent or teacher or even student who dares to introduce Him, could be sued, expelled or severely warned. All of this is under the banner of *"separation of church and state,"* a phrase that is often pulled out of context from one of Thomas Jefferson's letters.

The overall driving philosophy of education today is what is called "essentialism", which simply means that curricula are designed to teach the essentials, including math, English, history and science. While all of those "essentials" have a rich theological basis within Western Civilization, they have now been severed from their inspired beginnings and fail to acknowledge how the Reformation and Scripture inspired many of the West's mathematicians, scientists and literary giants.

You would be hard pressed today to hear about how Isaac Newton was a lover of God and how he authored several commentaries and theological treatises on the Bible. The influence of the church and faith are almost never discussed when looking at the works of Shakespeare. When it comes to science, the Church is portrayed as the villain and the role of God relegated to hostile territory - ignoring the fact that the biblical faith birthed modern science. In books like *The Bible, Protestantism and the Rise of Natural Science, The Book That Made Your World* and *For the Glory of God,* scholars such as Peter Harrison, Vishal Mangalwadi and Rodney Stark have presented the evidence needed to understand why modern science was born in Western Europe and not in China, India or Egypt and why in the sixteenth-seventeenth centuries and not in the fifteenth century.

God's Divine Revelation or Man's Wisdom

How did America stray from a country that saw its primary obligation to instruct their children in the Lord to where we are today? We could point to several factors, ranging from Descartes' Rationalism to the teaching of Darwinism (scientific materialism) to Dewey's vision for modern education that included a militant form of humanism. But the short answer is that the role of the Bible as God's guiding book of revelation was diminished and was ultimately disregarded.

When the Pilgrims and Puritans arrived during the 17th century, they found truths like human equality and divine creation in the Word of God. As education became the secular state's prerogative, human wisdom (and folly) eclipsed the Bible as a source for authoritative guidance. Rather than as revealed by God, truth was soon deemed "self evident."

Compare the Puritan vision for education in the 17th century with that of Americans in the 19th century. In 1647, the General Court of Massachusetts Bay Colony decreed that every town of fifty families should have an elementary school. Their stated goal was to ensure that their children would learn to read the Bible and receive basic teaching rooted in the little Westminster catechism and other Calvinistic doctrine.

However, by 1837 another vision emerged: Horace Mann, known as one of the fathers of secular American education, instituted the first state board of education in Massachusetts. Mann, who had been raised in a Christian home, was bitterly opposed to Calvinistic doctrine and ultimately embraced universalism. He therefore lobbied for "nonsectarian religious education." While Mann believed children in public schools should be taught the ethical principles of Christianity, he denied that they should be given the doctrines commonly taught in the New England Primary and other theologically based curricula.

From 1837 to the present, America has continued to see a slow bleed of its biblical foundations in education. Perhaps the final straw came in 1962, when the Supreme Court decided in a landmark case that prayer to begin the school day was unconstitutional. It shouldn't be a surprise that the last vestige of God in school, the Pledge of Allegiance, is now also under attack, with more and more schools choosing to either eliminate God from the pledge altogether or not recite it at all.

Without a Vision the People Perish

As we look at America today, I think we can all see the effects of eliminating God's Word over time from our children's hearts. As King Solomon penned many centuries ago, indeed, *"without revelation a people perish."* (Proverbs 28:19) As we look at the lives and hearts of our children due to what they are being taught today, we, as believers, feel the weight of this perishing in a number of areas.

The first and most obvious sign of decline is church attendance and faith in God. From 2009-2018 those claiming Christian faith declined from 77% to 65% and those claiming to be either atheist or agnostic increased from 17% to 26%. 100 years ago more than 70% of Americans attended church regularly, today it is 37%. And the greatest bleed in terms of church attendance and faith is among the youngest Americans, the Millennials (Americans born between 1981 and 1996, now young adults), with only 28% attending church regularly and more than 50% claiming either atheism or agnosticism.

It should be no surprise that, as the influence of faith in God and His Word declines in American life, there would also be a moral decline. No area reflects this more than the state of the family and sexuality. Besides the fact that more than 40% of marriages end in divorce, the Millennials are marrying less, living more together and reluctant to have families. Along with this dismal state of affairs we also see how the definition of family, marriage and gender radically changed as we moved further and further away from the Bible's definition of marriage and sexuality.

As America strays further from its biblical and Puritan roots, the more materialistic science and moral relativism have become central to the way many see life. The pursuit of happiness has little to do with pursuing God and His glory, but with living a life of self-gratification, material prosperity, ease and pleasure. These world views have deeply penetrated our culture and education system. Evolutionary theory and secularism are now established tenets for teaching humanities and sciences.

As believers we know that, as America strays further from revelation, disorder, disunity and disillusionment will follow. Inner-city streets are now characterized by regular violent protests. The Media has abandoned any pretense at objective journalism and a robust discussion of objective truth, and has become a party in the cultural wars. In the suburbs we see an epidemic in opioid addiction and a rise in teenage suicide. Such ills are a natural consequence of young people being taught a worldview that cannot possibly make sense of the meaning and purpose of life, family, nation and creation. We understand that, unless God revives this nation to turn back to Him, America will continue its decline.

A Vision for Tomorrow: Homeschool to Church Campus

How shall we recapture America's heart for God? While prayer is certainly primary to revival, perhaps the second greatest way to influence the nation is through the education of young people. The early Puritans understood this and guided the first schools with the basics of Scripture and applied theology. During that unique time in America's history the children were given the New England Primer in which theology, prayer, Scripture and creeds gave the ultimate meaning to life, making sense of the rest of knowledge. They understood that, if America were to be blessed, such blessings must come by turning hearts to the Creator — the very center of life and the cosmos.

What will it take to create an education revolution that can reach the hearts of the next generation for the Lord? Perhaps the greatest means of achieving this goal is for the Church to take back education. When we develop a curriculum that is based on a Christian worldview, young people can be discipled and mentored while working towards their BA degrees.

In 2020 the world of education was rocked by COVID-19. The partial or complete shut-down of almost the entire empire of education opened the door for fundamental innovation. The world has now tasted the benefits of online education, and there has never been a greater openness to radical innovation. What should we do?

The first step should be to recruit students into church campuses from the Christian Homeschool community. Even beforeCovid, over 1.6 million children were being educated at home in America. After the crisis, that number may double or triple, now that parents recognize the ease of online learning and the joy of spending more time together as families.

The Christian homeschool community is an army already on the field, ready to be mobilized for the Lord, and can contribute in a unique way to launching an education revolution through the church.

How to Attract Homeschool Students to Church Campus

There will be two aspects to recruiting young people into college campuses. The first will be to offer AA and BA programs of which the goal would be to instill the truths of God's Word into a young person's mind and heart. The development of courses like Sociology 101, Psychology 101 and World Civilization would not only introduce these disciplines from the point of view of Scripture, but include the rich background of church history in those given areas. These courses would be developed with guidelines that would be accredited and recognized by a range of both Christian and secular universities.

One example would be the development of a two year AA program. The average AA degree requires 60 credits. Over a 2-year period or less, 36 of those credits could be taught by an academic pastor with the help of a professionally-developed curriculum (see Chapter 7 by David Glesne for an explanation of this concept), while the other 24 credits could be acquired through the online vehicle. This will create flexibility in the student's schedule and open the door for mentoring, discipling and practical ministry within the local church. Again: the goal during those first two years would be to give the student a deep abiding faith in Christ, and a liberal arts education that would be taught from a Christian worldview.

Church Colleges will recruit homeschoolers and others while they are still in high school. A number of local Christian colleges and Community Colleges already offer what is called dual enrollment. At a significantly discounted rate, young people will earn up to 30 credit hours even before they graduate from high school which, in most American-based university settings, represents an entire year of college. If young people begin participating in the Church College as high school students to receive these credits, they will naturally matriculate into the Church-College and related universities as students.

Besides the great benefit to the student of mentoring and discipling and being equipped to go into the world as an ambassador for Christ, another benefit of the Church College would be the savings. The average cost of a 4 year college is $25,000-$35,000 per year.

The average debt per student at the end of that time is about $35,000, a great sum for a young person starting out in life. We estimate that earning college credits in local churches with 20 students will bring that cost well under $10,000 per student, allowing them to graduate debt free.

A final benefit of the Church College will be the transformation of America itself. Young people who graduate from church campuses are more likely to begin families and careers as strong witnesses for Christ. This will have a salting influence within the nation and the world. The Puritans began with such a vision of educating young people with a strong faith. It was the faith of America's citizens through the 20th century that built the country into a source of good for the world, notwithstanding its many sins and failures. That goodness can be restored through education that is Bible-based.

As "church-college" turns into a global movement, many young people will be attracted by the prospect of a low cost degree within a faith community. As millions of young people go into the world with such an education, many could begin serving in civic government, medicine, research, business, the corporate world and other industries, carrying with them the light of the gospel to the glory of God. These young people can become a spiritual army of tomorrow, battling immorality and toxic worldviews now promoted in modern universities.

A Life that Still Speaks After 300 Years

Jonathan Edwards (1703-1758) was initially educated at home and went to Yale at the age of 13, receiving his MA by the time he was 17. Many recognize his impact on America: his preaching was partly responsible for our nation's First Great Awakening. You may also know him as the first president of Princeton Seminary. The legacy of his sermons and his guidance of Princeton is still felt today.

Perhaps a less known feature of Edward's life was a biography he wrote on David Brainerd (1718-1747), who was one of the first missionaries to the Native Americans. Brainerd gave his life in service to those Indians. That biography was read by a simple shoe cobbler in England, William Carey. Deeply moved, Carey committed his life to India and became known as the Father of Modern Missions. Carey's example sparked a missionary movement that is still felt around the world today. That movement has been responsible for millions coming to know Christ as Savior.

Edwards' life is an example of what a Bible-based education can accomplish: how one life can bring glory to God around the world, as Samson Selladurai and Stephen McDowell point out, down through the centuries. May God give us grace to see many young Jonathan Edwards, see America revived, its foundations restored and its children receiving the precious Word of God.

"God is able to do more than we possibly can ask or imagine, through His power within us. To Him be glory in the church and in Christ Jesus throughout all generations. Amen!" (Ephesians 3:20-21).

Chapter 5

Blended Learning: A Student-Centered Education

Amanda Forbes[1]

Education has changed dramatically as a result of the COVID-19 pandemic. Only time will tell how those shifts will affect learners long- term, but one fact is already clear: the time has come for what is called "blended learning." National-board-certified veteran 4th-8th grade teacher Alfonso Gonzalez wrote that Blended Learning is becoming the new normal as schools around the world recreate themselves in response to the crisis.[2]

Blended learning can be defined as a style of education in which three elements are present: 1) Some learning takes place online, giving students a degree of control over the time, pace, location, order and style of studying; 2) At least part of the learning takes place away from the home in a supervised location; and 3) The modes of learning within a course are connected to provide a coherent experience.[3] Simply put, blended learning combines online and in-person learning in order to offer students a multi-dimensional yet cohesive education experience.

More than a method for delivering education, blended learning is a shift in educational philosophy that places learners at the center. This matters greatly because for too long and in too many contexts, students have had little autonomy and too little was expected of them. In fact, many

---

1 Dr. Amanda Forbes is Executive Director of Trinity Education, an international education nonprofit committed to providing accessible, discipleship-driven higher education to the poor around the world.

2 "Blended Learning in the Age of COVID-19" by Larry Ferlazo. August 19, 2020. *EdWeek*: https://www.edweek.org/teaching-learning/opinion-blended-learning-in-the-age-of-covid-19/2020/08

3 Christensen Institute: https://www.christenseninstitute.org/resources/topic/education/blended-learning/

students have been crippled by styles of teaching that have left them as passive recipients of knowledge and ideas. Blended learning can help us to reorient our approach to education, rendering students more hands-on and cultivating the skills they will need for success in other areas of life. Most importantly, it can help students accept their rightful role as the type of learners God has created us to be — alive, engaged, stewards over our own minds that were made to glorify Him.

Why Student-Centered Blended Learning Matters for the Church

Much has been written about blended learning and more will emerge as this model explodes in popularity. Michael Horn's and Heather Staker's book *Blended: Using Disruptive Innovation to Improve Schools* (2014) is a helpful introduction, along with the website Blended Learning Universe (BlendedLearning.com). In this chapter, however, I want to focus not on definitions or various methods to implement blended learning, but on how the Church can use this approach to improve the lives of families, communities and nations.

My first serious introduction to this method came in 2014 when the non-profit organization that I co-founded launched a program using blended learning in a slum of Nairobi, Kenya. The program focused on post-secondary students and was implemented at a Kenyan church that operated a school and community center in the heart of some of the deepest poverty I have ever seen. We prepared a robust online program for the students under the guidance of trained in-person facilitators from the local ministry. Over the years, we launched other blended learning programs in Kenya, Tanzania, Mozambique, South Africa, Haiti, Rwanda, and Uganda, providing accessible online training opportunities for students and in-person guidance from local facilitators. Practical online training in marketable subject areas like web design and office management has been valuable for students, but the aspect of our non-profit's work that proved to have the biggest impact has been the blended learning and Christian worldview training integrated into our programs.

Our first programs in Nairobi hold a special place in my heart, as it was there that some of the deepest seeds of discipleship took root and grew into strong young leaders. One of the top students we worked with was able to land a technical role with a company outside the slum, with the result that the entire course of his life was altered. A few other Kenyan students were accepted into a U.S.-accredited online university and were enabled to pursue higher education credentials to improve their futures. Most importantly, though, worldviews shifted. Regnius, one of our former Kenyan students, attested that before joining our non-profit's program, even though he was a "Christian," he did not believe that he was made in God's image and vested with the authority to create. He also used to think that poverty was a curse over his generation, inherited from his grandparents and passed along to his children and generations to come. The worldview course gave him the morale to work diligently in order to make a difference in society, fulfilling his purpose in life to glorify God.

From the beginning a critical part of our vision was to engage the Church in providing blended learning programs to the youth in their communities. The rallying cry behind this vision was Ephesians 3:14, as we believed God's intent is to make known His wisdom through the Church. Surely revealing truth through education, using Christ-centered facilitators and modern educational technology, is one way to achieve that goal. Some churches caught this vision quickly but, by and large, it has been disciple-ship-minded individuals, especially school administrators and nonprofit leaders, who have taken on the mantle of leadership. I personally believe that the Church is missing a massive opportunity to disciple and educate our generation of young people, especially in parts of the world where few viable alternatives for studying beyond high school are available.

George Marsden, an emeritus professor at the University of Notre Dame, has expressed puzzlement as to why Protestant leaders have taken so little interest in Christian higher education. In the U.S., for example, he points out how universities were primarily the domain of the church well into the nineteenth century, as they had been throughout Western Civilization. The roles of professors and clergymen were not clearly distinguished, as most educators were members of the clergy. This is a far cry from today, where Christianity is often viewed as completely foreign to the enterprise of education.[14] Marsden does not propose returning to "a lost golden age," but among his suggestions is that "serious Christians should concentrate on building distinctly Christian institutions that will provide alternatives to secular colleges and universities."[4]

---

4 George Marsden. (January 1991). *The Soul of the American University.* https://www. first- things.com/article/1991/01/the-soul-of-the-american-university.
Ibid.

Nowadays, building a distinctly Christian institution may be less arduous than ever, as one no longer needs first to secure piles of capital and large swaths of land, construct elaborate and costly buildings, and then import faculty from around the world. Instead, leading universities and professors on every continent are making curricula available for free to anyone with an internet connection. Experienced teachers and mentors can connect digitally with students wherever they live. A well-designed online environment can replace multi-million-dollar campuses.

And most importantly, research suggests that this model of education may actually be superior to traditional methods. The U.S. Department of Education shared a meta-analysis that reviewed empirical studies from 1996 to 2008 focusing on online education in K-12 and higher education. The findings? On average, online students performed modestly better than students in traditional classroom settings. And students using blended learning did better than those who studied solely online (Means, Toyoma, Murphy, Bakia, and Jones, 2010, cited in Smith and Brame, nd).[5] Blended learning shouldn't be viewed as an inferior learning option, because it isn't!

Perhaps one of the most promising aspects of blended learning is how it allows educators to focus on the needs of individual students. In fact, "the concept and definition of blended learning is more focused on transformation of instructional models toward student-centered learning…. Simply, blended learning is a delivery mechanism for personalized learning."[6] Research has shown that individualized learning is far more effective for students than traditional classroom settings. Renowned education scholar Benjamin Bloom wrote in 1984 about what he called the "Two Sigma Problem," which referred to the fact that the average tutored student scored above 98% of students in a conventional classroom setting.

Astutely, Bloom did not advocate that all students be educated through one-on-one tutoring, although he did see the remarkable effects of tutoring as evidence that most students can learn far more than they do in

---

5 "Blended and Online Learning" by Blaine Smith and Cynthia Brame. N.d. *Vanderbilt University Center for Teaching*. https://cft.vanderbilt.edu/guides-sub-pages/blended-and-online-learning/

6 Susan Patrick, Kathryn Kennedy, and Allison Powell. (October, 2013). *Mean What You Say: Defining and Integrating Personalized Blended and Competency Education*. iNACOL. https:// files.eric.ed.gov/fulltext/ED561301.pdf.

conventional settings. Instead, he believed that research and instruction should seek alternatives to one-on-one tutoring (which he thought was too expensive for most societies) to achieve the same effect.[7]

According to Seattle Pacific University professors David Denton, David Wicks, and Vicki Eveland, Blended Learning may help solve the Two Sigma Problem. Instructors can replicate certain elements of one-on-one tutoring through blended learning, including improving instructional materials, enhancing interactions among peers, considering differences among students and engaging higher-level thinking[8] More-over, blended learning can offer a more enriching learning environment. In his study of this model in two Michigan high schools, Vandermolen (2010) found that most students agreed that online activities provided education opportunities different from those found in traditional classrooms, and strongly disagreed with the idea that online time would be better spent in the classroom.[9]

What this means is that we have an unprecedented opportunity to make high-quality education available anywhere churches can be found. Blended learning can make this possible, giving churches an opportunity to provide curriculum and mentoring that focuses on the needs of students in local communities.

While this model may sound like "new wine for new wineskins," is there a biblical basis for any of these shifts? Does Scripture say anything about how we educate? Might it even encourage this shift from a teacher-centered, school-based model to a learner-centered, online and church-based model?

---

7 Bloom, Benjamin S. (1984). The 2 Sigma Problem: The Search for Methods of Group Instruction as Effective as One-to-One Tutoring. *Educational Researcher*, vol. 13 (no. 6), pp. 4-16.

8 Denton, David, Wicks, David, and Eveland, Vicki. (2013) Closing the 2 Sigma Gap: Eight Strategies to Replicate One-to-One Tutoring in Blended Learning. Sloan Consortium Blended Learning Conference.

9 Vandermolen, Richard Mark, *The examination of the implementation of blended learning instruction on the teaching and learning environment in two west Michigan school districts* (2010). Master's Theses and Doctoral Dissertations. 296. http://commons.emich.edu/theses/296

A Biblical Rationale for Student-Centered Learning

Christians should care deeply about personalizing learning because, as David Marshall hinted in Chapter Two, it is the model Jesus showed as he led his twelve disciples and interacted with the many individuals he encountered. It is also the model we see throughout the Bible as God individually discipled men and women to follow him. Martin Luther lectured in the university classroom and, along with his wife Catherine, also discipled dozens of students in his home in Wittenberg. Francis Schaeffer followed that model in the L'Abri Fellowship. Yet, it remains true that the contemporary Church isn't known for using strong personalized learning methodologies. Most churches prefer mass instruction and uniform strategies that can be replicated across churches and mission agencies. In the Bible, however, we find immense value placed on the uniqueness of each individual and their particular formative journey. Moses and Joshua; Elijah and Elisha; Jesus and the twelve disciples; and Paul and Timothy are prominent examples. This of course doesn't exclude mass instruction, which God used throughout Scripture to teach and guide people (e.g. Moses instructing the children of Israel, Jesus teaching the crowds, Paul addressing mass audiences), but it shows the need to take a balanced view of the importance of one-on-one and large-group instruction.

In the early chapters of Genesis, we catch a glimpse of the first time God Himself interacted with man: creating Adam and Eve in God's image and then giving them instructions for life in the Garden. Here is no picture of pedantic hand-holding or crippling reliance on the instructor, but an empowering command to exercise dominion and stewardship in "on-the-job" training. God sets boundaries (e.g., telling Adam and Eve what they may consume for food, creating male and female for one another), but He also gives immense creative license. Surely human teachers can learn from the "hands-off" approach of our Creator?

Genesis three introduces a new dilemma, as we are no longer dealing with sinless pupils but with fallen creatures who have fumbled their assigned roles and defied instructions. God steps in, not with heavy-handed punishment at first, but with dialogue and questioning. He initially calls to Adam and asks, "Where are you?" and even allows Adam's deflection to "the woman" to go unanswered. He then follows up with Eve directly, who finally comes out and explains: "The serpent deceived me, and I ate."

For anyone who has ever served as a parent or teacher, the wisdom of God's approach is evident. Two-way dialogue leads the interaction, not one-way accusations, allowing the man and woman to process what they had done and gain the opportunity to own their guilt and responsibility. Genesis 4 follows a similar dialogic process between God and man, this time with Cain at the center of the narrative. Most university professors do not have the luxury of playing such a role in mentoring individual students. That is why *The Third Education Revolution* proposes a unique mentoring role for Academic Pastors (see Chapter 7 by David Glesne).

As the human story unfolds in Genesis, God reveals his specific will to individuals, telling them his purposes and inviting men and women to step out in obedience. The accounts of Noah, Abraham and Jacob all reflect this pedagogy. The Exodus narrative develops divine education as it tells us of the first "tablet-based" education provided through the Ten Commandments when God commands Moses: "Come up to me on the mountain and wait there, that I may give you the tablets of stone, with the Law and the Commandment, which I have written for their instruction" (Exodus 24:12). The principle works for modern tablets, too: clear instruction is provided by the teacher, but the responsibility for obedience and application remains with the student. As we know from Scripture and from life, some take that responsibility more seriously than others. The responsibility of students to initiate and act on learning is elucidated time and time again throughout the Old Testament:

> "Receive instruction from his mouth, and lay up his words in your heart." - Job 22:22

> "Hear, O sons, a father's instruction, and be attentive, that you may gain insight." - Proverbs 4:1

> "Keep hold of instruction; do not let go; guard her, for she is your life." - Proverbs 4:13

> "Hear instruction and be wise, and do not neglect it." - Proverbs 8:33
> "Whoever heeds instructions is on the path to life, but he who rejects reproof leads others astray." - Proverbs 10:17

> "Whoever ignores instruction despises himself, but he who listens to reproof gains intelligence." - Proverbs 15:32

"They have turned to me their back and not their face. And though I have taught them persistently, they have not listened to receive instruction." - Jeremiah 32:33

In the New Testament, Jesus carries forward this model of learner-centered instruction as He pours himself into a small circle of men and women, often engaging with them personally or in small groups. Jesus demonstrated immense care for the needs of the individual (as he also did for the needs of the massive groups that gathered around him). Much could be said about Jesus' teaching style, and a few of my co-authors have said more, but it is sufficient for my purposes to say Jesus was intensely personal in his pedagogical orientation (among many examples, one could point to Jesus's interactions with the woman at the well, Zacchaeus, Peter on the beach after the resurrection, and the leper who came back to thank Jesus).

As the gospel spread throughout the ancient world, God raised up many teachers, but also firmly planted the responsibility for learning and application with learners, not with teachers. The Apostle Paul has much to say about this responsibility, including in the following three deeply revealing verses:

> "But thanks be to God, that you who were once slaves of sin *have become obedient from the heart to the standard of teaching to which you were committed*" (Romans 6:17).

Paul taught Christians to be committed to a high standard of teaching, but could not force them to obey. They had to submit to truth with willing hearts.

> "That is why I sent you Timothy, my beloved and faithful child in the Lord, *to remind you of my ways in Christ, as I teach them everywhere in every church*" (1 Corinthians 4:17).

Clearly Paul did not rely solely on large-group instruction, but sent Timothy to personally reinforce what the Corinthians had been taught.

> "Study to show yourself approved unto God, a workman that needs not to be ashamed, rightly dividing the word of truth" (2 Timothy 2:15).

As Vishal Mangalwadi has pointed out about this verse, it "implies that ultimately Timothy (the learner) not his teacher, Paul, is responsible for what Timothy learns."[10]

---

10 Email communication, August 25, 2020.

Moving toward Student-Centered Blended Learning

Maybe such research and exegesis is nothing new to you and you've been utilizing learner-centered methods and blended learning for many years. Or perhaps this is a new paradigm that you hadn't considered before. Wherever you might be on this spectrum, I'd like to propose a few steps that I believe we can all apply in whatever educational settings we serve, whether in designing a curriculum, teaching at a church, homeschool, or classroom, or helping create the pedagogical model for *The Third Education Revolution*.

Action Item #1 — Consider how you can replace teacher-centered methods (e.g., lectures, large-group instruction) with learner-centered methods (e.g., activities that engage the learners, personalized learning, small-group instruction). It is remarkable to me how we teachers (who should know better) so easily fall back on teacher-centered methods. I'm not saying that all teacher-centered methods are bad, as we still obtain much of our knowledge by listening collectively and Scripture often displays large-group instruction as a worthy example. However, I challenge teachers to think about how to meaningfully, personally engage each student, as often this is far harder to do than delivering a lecture to a classroom. As I have worked with students in many parts of the world, it has been one of the most rewarding experiences of my work to see how quickly students embrace learner-centered methods, especially in regions where the education system hasn't encouraged this form of learning.

Action Item #2 — Evaluate what is best done in-person and what can be accomplished more effectively online or by means of technology. As part of our non-profit's work, we have moved many traditional classroom activities online, choosing well-designed teaching materials that can be delivered via video, online tutorial, purposeful readings, and quizzes. At the same time, we've taught local facilitators how to engage students in dialogue and discussion, hold students accountable, and support their growth in knowledge and application. This has been an effective strategy, as it has provided access to high-quality content that may not have been available locally and freed up facilitators to engage in the more meaningful aspects of learning with their students.

Action Item #3 — Examine how your students feel about owning their learning and consider ways to build their sense of responsibility. As I've helped introduce student-centered blended learning programs in different countries, I can attest that it is not always a smooth transition for students. However, students do remarkable things to rise to the challenge once they know what's expected of them.

At the Christian university we've worked with in Haiti, we have asked much of students in terms of independence and self-guided learning. We've done things to help with the transition, such as providing an online orientation to acquaint students with their learner responsibilities and preparing facilitators who deeply understand the curriculum. But it's the greatest delight when students go beyond us by coming up with ways to support their fellow Haitian classmates or applying what they've learned in the real world, such as some of the students did in collaboratively starting a tech business in Haiti. Ultimately, this is what we should desire for all of our students: that they would go beyond their teacher and study to show themselves approved before God.

Bible Study for Further Reflection

Read Genesis 1 and 2

- What stands out to you about God's interactions with man in these chapters?
- How does God place the responsibility in man's hands for learning about their new world and gaining experience in it?
- Is there anything you see from these chapters that you could apply as an educator?

Read Genesis 3 and 4

- Why do you think God asked Adam and Eve questions rather than directly pointing out their sin?
- Why might it feel easier to lead with accusations rather than dialogue when interacting with students (e.g., "You didn't turn in your homework," or "You got a bad test grade" etc.)?
- Is there anything you see from this chapter that you could apply as an educator?

Read Exodus 24

- What commitment did the people make after hearing God's words and rules (Exodus 24:3-8)?
- What did Moses do as a teacher to instruct, guide, and shepherd the people for God's glory?
- What forms of instruction (e.g., verbal, written, etc.) do you recognize in this passage?
- What valid hesitations do we feel about conveying content in different formats (e.g., video, live teaching, one-on-one coaching, audio lectures, online games, etc.)?

Read Job 22:22; Proverbs 4:1, 4:13, 8:33, 10:17, 15:32, and Jeremiah 32:33

- After reading the above verses, how would you describe the learner's responsibility in the instructional process?
- Do these verses reveal learning to be more active or passive?
- How can we help learners understand their responsibility in learning?

Read Romans 6:17, 1 Corinthians 4:17, and 2 Timothy 2:15

- Can teachers make students "obedient from the heart?" Why or why not?
- What role does "reminding" (reinforcing, modeling, and personally interacting) play in helping students learn? How is this a more learner-centered approach to education than lectures?
- In the environments where you teach (e.g., homeschooling, Sunday school, parenting, public school, etc.), what challenges have you encountered in seeing students take the responsibility to "study to show themselves approved unto God"?

Chapter 6

From Rote Learning to Imaginal Education

Tom Rudmik[1]

Canada's largest think tank, the Fraser Institute, rates Master's Academy, which I was honored to found in 1997, as the best school of more than 800 in Alberta, Canada. Working with corporate partners, we have developed a complete ecosystem of solutions for unleashing innovation in any organization, using what we call "Imaginal Thinking" processes. Our experience will enable the champions of *The Third Education Revolution* graduate students who are equipped to imagine a greater future for their nations.

This chapter describes the breakthroughs we have achieved. Then it relates our innovations to the Bible's vision of Christ making all things new. Third, it explains our approach to leadership and thinking, which we call "imaginal." Fourth, it shows how our students have adopted these concepts to become leaders. Finally, it describes my vision for the coming revolution by paraphrasing Dr. Martin Luther King's inspirational "I have a Dream" speech.

Part I : Developing Breakthroughs in Learning

My Story

My parents exemplified what it means to live by faith and to believe God for big things. With just a high school education, my father was used by God to touch the nation of Estonia for over 35 years, preaching the gospel during the darkest days of Soviet rule. For thirty-five years Estonians tuned in to his short-wave radio broadcasts twice a week to listen to a message of faith and hope. Thousands of people have testified to the

---

1 Tom Rudmik, educator and entrepreneur, is the founder of Master's Academy and College and Imaginal Education and Imaginal Transformation Inc. Tom is passionate about implementing REAL change and is committed to researching and developing breakthroughs in learning and sharing them with the world

life-giving power that those broadcasts brought. At his funeral my father was given the Medal of Honor from Estonia's president in recognition of the impact he had made on his country.

My father taught us children to 'dream big dreams; nothing is impossible with God.'

I began my teaching career in the late 1970s at the ripe old age of twenty-three — a young, energetic idealist. It did not take me long to see that the system of education was broken. After eight years of teaching in public schools I decided to try private Christian education, supposing that the grass would be greener on the other side of the fence. Private Christian education has many advantages; however, I concluded that that system was broken as well. While Christian education was in some ways superior, it too was run rather like a factory for children. I realized that something new needed to be created, but had no idea of what. But I felt a deep desire for something better.

Then I experienced a "burning bush" moment that changed my life forever. My dream was born: to build a prototypical school for learning in the 21st Century that would impact schools around the world. I had to ask, though, "Who am I to achieve such an ambitious goal?" Then I seemed to hear my father's voice again: "Son, dream big dreams, nothing is impossible to those who believe."

In 1995 our family moved to Calgary, Alberta, and two years later we launched Master's Academy and College: a K-12 Research and Development Christian school. Master's was founded with a vision to create a breakthrough 21st-century learner-centric model for elevating achievement for all students to a degree previously unattainable, a model whose signature goes beyond memorizing existing knowledge to innovation and creativity.

Since then, Master's has repeatedly been ranked by the Fraser Institute, Canada's largest independent think tank, as the top-performing school in all the province. We developed what we call the Profound Learning Model according to our understanding of how God has created us to learn, based on research in neuro, cognitive, and behavioral sciences. Our core premise, as I will explain, is that if there is no physical change in the learners' brains, there is no learning. We therefore strive to create educational conditions which allow children to go beyond cramming information, to understanding and learning in an optimal manner.

Profound Learning Model

The Profound Learning Model emerged as a result of ten years of research and development at Master's Academy and College. It is not a program, technology platform or a "learning adventure." It emerges from intentional beliefs, structures, practices and tools applied in tandem, ideally when several conditions are met:
- When brain-compatible experiences empower student learning.
- When there is a culture of trust, restitution, growth and collaboration.
- When optimal conditions for learning are intentionally crafted.
- When new structures are built to transform the behavior of both teachers and students.
- When 'mastery-for-all' is the goal and closing gaps in learning is the focus.

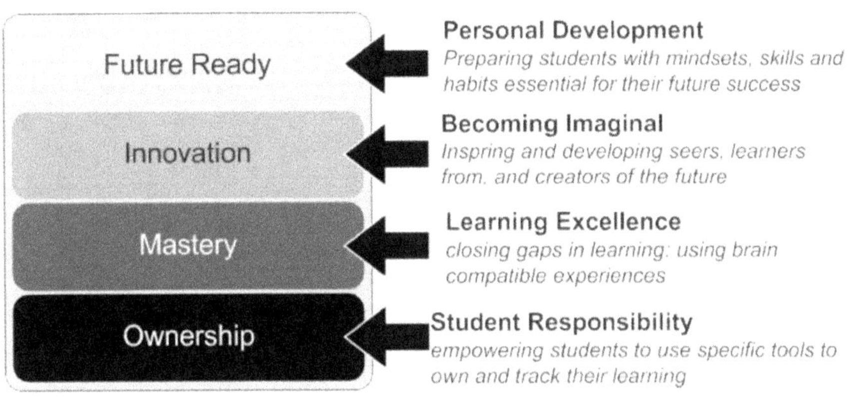

Profound Learning Model — A Tapestry

Profound Learning is marked by nine elements woven into a single tapestry. At any given time, any element may be taking place in any of the layers we call Ownership, Mastery, Innovation and Future Readiness. These elements can emerge under the guidance of any teacher, regardless of technology or location. The following table defines each element and shows how it is put into practice.

Nine Elements of Profound Learning:

1. Culture of Trust
- trust (reducing fear)
- restitution (relationship)
- collaboration vs competition growth mindset

2. Shifting Roles
- role of the teacher (context, conditions, connections)
- role of the student (ownership, empowerment & mastery of learning)

3. Brain-Based
- creating meaning, relevancy, novelty, movement, choice & emotion

4. Quality
- student self-assessment
- tracking Essential Learning Outcomes
- expectations & benchmarks
- doing it right the first time

5. Formative Assessment
- frequent 'check-ups 'before a summative assessment
- identifying gaps in learning
- teacher & peer feedback

6. Personalized Learning
- pacing of learning
- learning preferences
- offering choice (environment, delivery of learning, final product)

7. Closing Gaps
- setting goals to close gaps differentiation in amount & type of instruction
- clustering for mastery
- flexible learning time

8. Collaboration
- positive interdependence
- teaching and learning from one another
- individual success linked to group success

9. Future Ready
- innovation and creativity
- Seven Habits of the Master Learner
- 21st-century skills
- Imaginal Leader competencies
- graduate profile

In 2016 two non-profit organizations, Imaginal Education Canada and the USA, were launched to facilitate development of our digital learning platform and the dissemination of Profound Learning globally.

Why Do Many Attempts Fail?

Numerous reforms have been proposed to the education industry in recent decades. Most of the proposed reforms have addressed mainly the symptoms rather than core problems of the complexities of Education. Failures of those reforms have led to much disillusionment among educators. Problems of education and the failures of proposed reforms are so well documented that there is enough room for finger-pointing and blame to last a lifetime.

For example: why did *No Child Left Behind* fall short? Its focus on teacher performance and raising test scores sounded good on the surface, but failed to address the essential weakness of modern education. The current system does exactly what it was designed to do: produce workers for the industrial age who meet the standards of that Age. Suppose a school succeeds in elevating test scores of all students, would that prepare students for *tomorrow's* world? Or would it graduate students for *yesterday's* era? How can improving an obsolete system bring about the changes desperately needed for our world? Such well-intentioned efforts invariably end up in a blame game, with fingers pointed at teachers, unions, students, parents or politicians. What is required is a bold vision for a *completely new* system of education.

Neuroscience of Learning

Ancient learning theory falsely assumed that students learned most readily by instruction. It thought of the brain as a clean slate on which a teacher writes or an empty vessel waiting for new information to pour in. The brain's biology is not configured to learn best as a result of instruction alone. Of the 10-20% of information that may be retained from that style of teaching, most will be forgotten within a short period. The brain is like a leaky bucket. Recall (if you can!) all the amazing sermons you have heard only to forget them minutes later.

Modern neuroscience shows that students learn by *selection*. The brain chooses new information that is meaningful and connects to prior knowledge to which it can be anchored. The brain wants to learn, figure things out, put the pieces together, and succeed. Therefore, the teacher who teaches best creates conditions in which the student's brain 'chooses' or 'selects' to learn. Under such conditions students learn naturally.

I demonstrate this point in my workshops by speaking to the participants in the Estonian language. Then I ask how many understood what I was saying. Nobody raises their hand unless they happen to know Estonian. If no one in my audience has a concept network for deciphering the Estonian language, no one is able to input any of the information I am conveying. The brain receives information for which it already has a concept network. We grow this knowledge network by anchoring new information. That causes new dendrites to grow in our brain. From an educational perspective, all learning involves neurological growth and biological change.

The brain processes data from all five senses but it also creates outputs or responses to data received. Neural outputs are also patterns embedded into neural networks. When you combine input and output patterns, you begin to understand the notion of habituation and biases. When these patterns form into beliefs, they become powerful mental models or structures that begin to dictate how we view the world and ultimately live in it. In some contexts, this can involve 'confirmation bias,' hearing what you want or expect to hear.

Not only do our brains interpret the world through patterns or mindsets, they also seek data that fit patterns which already exist. In other words, the brain biases information from its environment by accepting input that fits pre-existing networks or patterns. St. Paul recognized this truth when he wrote:

> *"Do not conform to the pattern of this world, but be transformed by the renewing of your mind."*

It is possible to change your mind's "programming" to create new patterns of thinking based on the Word of God. Thus truth sets one free from following embedded patterns of thinking that conform to the world. You can change your brain's programming based on God's revealed truth. The Holy Spirit's role in renewing the mind appears mysterious because this process is spiritual

Part II : It's All God's Idea

Human Nature

I think of humans as consisting of body, soul and spirit. The body is our physical structure and sensing mechanism that connects us to the Universe of Measurement. Our soul is comprised of mind, emotions and will. Our spirit is a place of intuition, conscience and imagination, which can be seen as our eye into the Universe of Unlimited Possibilities, or the spirit realm. The spirit of 'born again' believers has been made new; that is a mystery that Jesus explains to Nicodemus in John 3: 5-15. The moment one receives Christ, one is translated from the Kingdom of Darkness into the Kingdom of Light (Colossians. 1:13), as "new creatures in Christ."

Transformation, however, takes time as our minds are renewed; we replace worldly thinking patterns with scriptural patterns from the Kingdom of God, hence becoming able to discern God's will and plan for our lives. When God speaks to us, it is a Spirit-to-spirit interaction. But ideas and beliefs are interpreted through mental patterns, which need to be aligned to biblical truth. Our patterns of thinking dictate how we live, as Proverbs 23:7 says: "For as he thinks in his heart, so is he." Many books have been written on how to hear God's voice and discern his will.

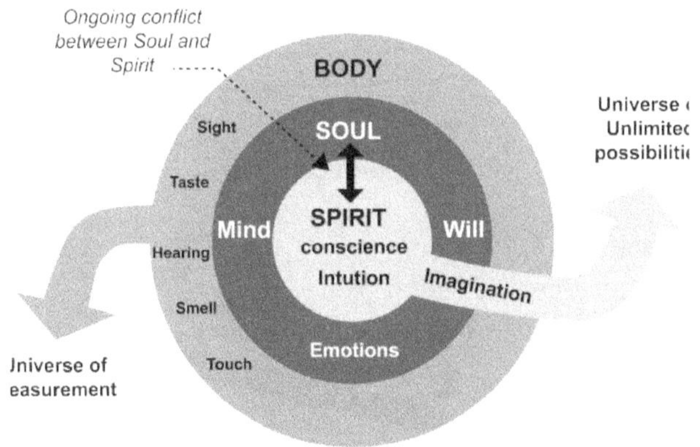

Tripartite Nature of Humans

The Spiritual Foundations of Imaginal Thinking

Imagination is a unique endowment that enables us to see and create the future. Imagination is the eye of the spirit; it is the capacity to engage in the universe of unlimited possibilities in which we invent. All creation starts in the mind of the creator, where one forms images of future creation in a process called "imagination."

Receiving and memorizing information already perceived, created, ordered and codified by our forefathers is necessary. However, as Albert Einstein noted, "Imagination is more important than knowledge. For, while knowledge defines all we currently know and understand, imagination points to all we might yet discover and create."

Once you see the future by imagining, hope affirms that what you are seeing is possible. That generates faith to act. Transforming nations requires Imaginal Leaders because they have not just ideas but inspiring hope for the future. They transform the world by believing that more is possible.

Whether you are an artist, builder or parent, the creator's love sustains the process of creation. Hence, the drivers for Imaginal Thinking are hope, faith and love. *Faith is the substance of things hoped for the evidence of things unseen* (imagination) says Hebrews 11:1

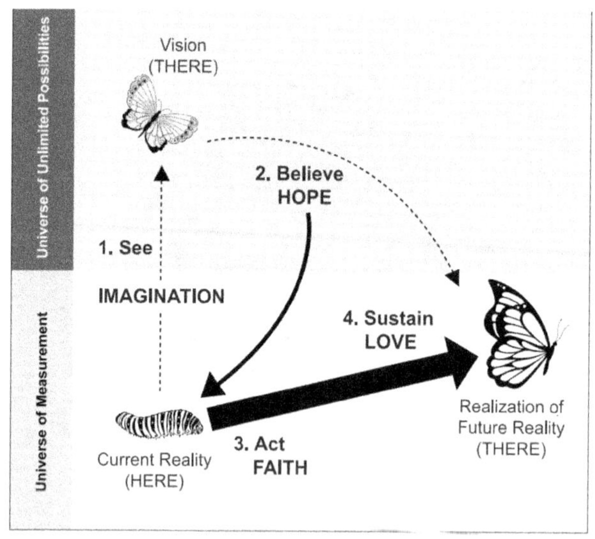

IMAGINATION + HOPE = FAITH

Spiritual Foundation of Imaginal Thinking

Part III: Imaginal Leadership and Thinking Becoming an Imaginal Leader

In May 2012, I was in Nigeria sharing my experience as an educator with hundreds of Christian leaders. I said to them, "Nigeria needs educators to become Imaginal leaders so they can transfer this ability to their students. You can't give what you don't have." At that very moment God spoke to my spirit that now was the time to write a book to help educators, parents and other leaders.

That book, *"Becoming Imaginal: Seeing and Creating the Future of Education" (2013)* was inspired by one of the wonders of nature: how a caterpillar transforms into a butterfly through metamorphosis. The miracle of metamorphosis is presaged within cells embedded in the caterpillar. These cells (figuratively) see and then practically create the butterfly.

Those "Imaginal" cells have both the vision to picture what it will take to become a butterfly and the ability to execute this amazing transformation. Analogously, Imaginal leaders have the capacity to see the future and pull it into the now; they can see beyond what most people envision and have the courage, commitment and know-how to lead the transformation process.

Our ability to be Imaginal is based on the simple truth that we are made in the Creator's image. All creators can see the future and create what they see; Imaginal Leaders do so in ways that transform our world. Imaginal Leader's ability to see and create the future is a latent capacity God has given us. It has been shut down by the educational system of the industrial age, which demanded conformity and compliance.

The world needs more Imaginal Leaders and Organizations that envision a better future and have the courage and know-how to create it. This is why I sought to share universal secrets or keys for unlocking the Imaginal way of living and leading.

I have had the opportunity to lead transformation in education. This industry is highly resistant to any change, let alone disruptive, transformational change. In my experience speaking on this subject and interacting with others, most people agree that traditional education is a broken and obsolete system.

By broken, I mean a system that is under-performing; and by obsolete I mean that, even if the system were performing optimally, it would still fall short of meeting the needs of today's rapidly changing world.

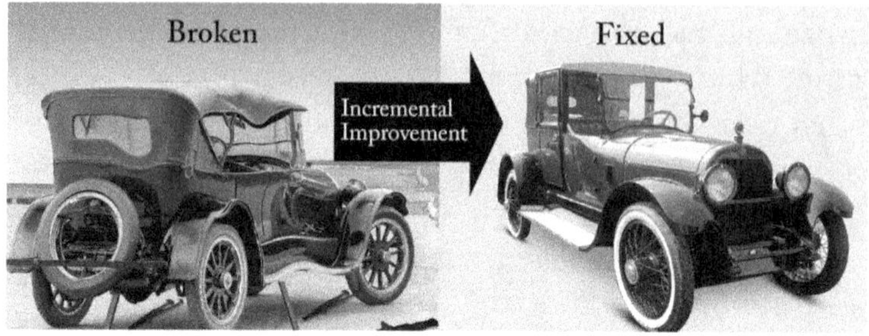

Fixing a System that is Broken

Incremental transformation is significantly different from incremental improvement. The latter focuses on improving processes within an existing system. It assumes that the overall system is fine.

Incremental transformation on the other hand sees an entirely new system. It perceives what is THERE in imagination and strives to pull the future model's new structures into the present, the HERE. Over time, a new system emerges which represents a significant leap into the FUTURE. An Imaginal Leader soon learns that the process to transform an established system is tough. It resists and pushes back change. The change agent has to create conditions for transformation that stakeholders embrace. In short, the Imaginal Leader has to find ways to implement disruptive change while causing the least amount of disruption.

Transforming an Obsolete System

My book argues that it is possible to transform education from a voracious "caterpillar" into an elegant "butterfly." That imagery of an intellectual new-birth symbolizes students being enabled to pursue their destinies beyond limitation.

An Imaginal Leader is one who has the passion, courage and vision to engage in the process of seeing the invisible and creating what others may consider the "impossible." Steve Jobs was such an Imaginal Leader; he was able to live in the tension of his "reality distortion field" to create one of the greatest technology companies, against seemingly insurmountable odds.

Transformation Defined

Webster's dictionary defines transformation as a 'major change in form, nature and function,' analogous to a caterpillar becoming a butterfly. I can change my hair color, but that would not be deemed transformational since the essence of who I am has not changed.

In today's world, many people use the term transformation loosely to mean "change." You will find the term "transformation" plastered all over websites providing consulting services. One website claimed to transform education by bringing teachers' professional practices in alignment with the latest US government's reform attempt, Race to the Top. There was nothing transformational about their services; they were using "best practices" from the past to elevate school performance. Instead of propagating the best practices of the past, we need to develop new practices for the education of the future. And so we are constantly looking for ways to improve our practices.

Transforming education is an immensely challenging task; the system is complex and resistant to change. The mental models that support the current system are strongly entrenched and have been accepted for long. That makes it difficult for most educators to envision a different future. That is why a new way of educating a nation will appear revolutionary to many.

Real revolutions make existing systems obsolete. Automobile ends the age of ox or horse carts; computers end the era of typewriters; video streaming ends cassette or CD industries. Hebrews 8: 13 says that the New Covenant makes the Old obsolete. However, calling something obsolete does not make it so. Imaginal Leaders have to go out and create new models. That is what God enabled us to do in Master's Academy and College.

It prepares students for tomorrow's world while learning from the past.

In 1894, Karl Benz invented an automobile called the Velo. It was an interesting contraption, and I am sure was the topic of many jokes. Such a prototype required tremendous Imaginal abilities, but the Velo was not practical enough to make existing modes of transportation obsolete. That happened only when another Imaginal Leader, Henry Ford, mass-produced the automobile at an affordable price was the horse and buggy rendered obsolete.

That principle applies to education. God has helped us create a prototype school of the future. We are grateful. However the outdated will become obsolete only when the prototype is scaled to the masses. The working prototype of Profound Learning needs a global ecosystem. Then it can be adopted anywhere in the world. We have reached the point at which this vision is possible. By becoming Imaginal, educators can become transformation agents within their school systems. They can also invent radically new systems that are as miraculous as a caterpillar becoming a butterfly.

Need a System for Transformation

Having worked with educators around the world, I have found that most have a difficult time envisioning the future of education. Educators are so firmly entrenched into supporting the existing system that it is challenging to imagine anything different. Sure, we can upgrade technology and pour in resources. We can even modernize the look of a school and call it The Future School. But the fundamental nature of education hasn't changed in a hundred years. There are exceptions, but they are few and far between.

If an educator did come up with a workable vision for the future, it would be difficult to put that vision into practice. This is because most educators are not Imaginal. They are not trained to design complex systems. Michael Fullan, a Canadian leader in education reform, maintains that we have been fighting a fruitless uphill battle. The solution is not how to climb the hill of bringing more innovations or reforms into the system. We need to climb a different hill, so to speak.

> "To break through this impasse, educators must see themselves and be recognized as experts in the dynamics of change by becoming skilled change agents."

development, testing etc. It is
…ases of the innovation project.

…l Leaders

…knowledge that is already known,
…m is to help students learn from
…Bible God gives us both history

…can. Think of the tremendous ad-
…ate from high school. They receive
…or university while developing the
…In school they experience creating
…ined to become futurists. Master's
…ts to be Future Ready, and by this
…tors of the future.

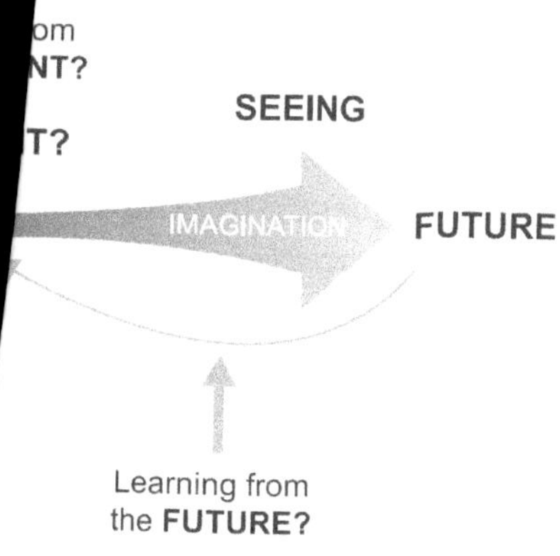

…rning from the Future

…odd since it has not yet occurred. Such
…he future with our imagination. All cre-
…isualizes the object of his creation. The
…o bring what he sees into reality, by means

Imaginal Thinking: A System for Transformation

All knowledge is about the past, while all decisions are about the future. The Imaginal Thinking process is our school's methodology for transformation. It is best experienced in a collaborative workshop setting, and is about imagining the future and learning from the vision we thus gain so that we can create the future we desire or need. Our Knowledge Creation Engine powers the Seven-Step Imaginal Thinking process.

Imaginal Thinking utilizes numerous tools, processes and systems that enable organizations to create robust views of the future, based on strong as well as weak signals from the future. This research is a prerequisite for creating new knowledge that enables scenarios of the future to be created.

Imaginal Thinking Process

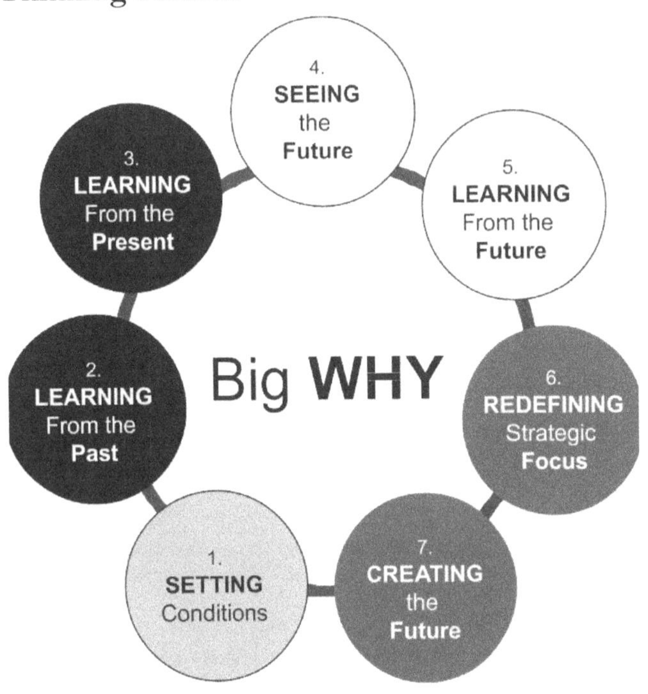

1. Setting Conditions

Are we ready to face the future? Do we have intent? Do we have adequate research to begin the process?

2. Learning from the Past

How did we get here? Who are some of the winners and losers from the past, why? What were the stabilities and drivers for change?

3. Learning from the Present

What emerging trends are shaping our organization's future? What are some weak signals of today that could disrupt the future?

4. Seeing the Futures

What are our possible, probable, plausible, preferred, and preposterous futures?

5. Learning from the Futures

How would we survive or thrive in the futures?

6. Redefining Strategic Focus:

To revisit what we should focus on?

7. Creating the Future:

Where are the opportunities between the THERE and the HERE? How can we translate those opportunities into Innovation projects?

Imaginal Thinking Tools and Processes:

1. Setting Conditions

• Environment: Specialized environment for collaboration and release of the
Imaginal spirit
• Culture: Imaginal Organization culture embraces the contradictory nature of the innovation and business performance 'engines'.

2. Learning from the Past

• Drivers: looking at historical drivers that led to profound changes in our world
• Stabilities: what forces historically were keeping change from happening

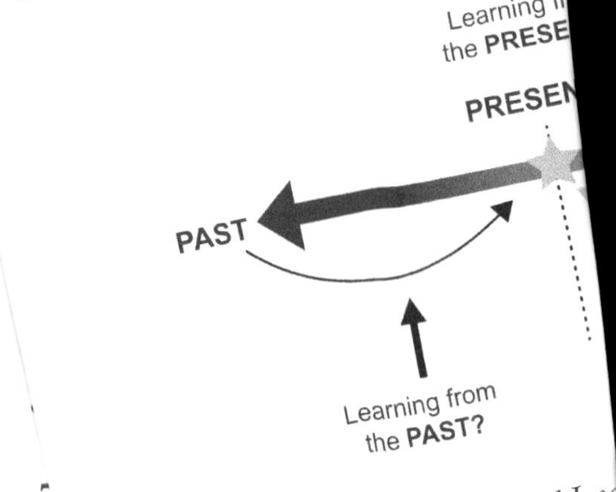

Signals from the Future

Astronomers look for signals from far away galaxies to learn about our universe. However, by the time these signals reach earth, they have been traveling for millions of years, which means that what astronomers observe has happened long ago.
Our ability to see the future is based on the future being embedded in the present in the form of strong ánd weak signals.

Strong signals are typically called trends that are supported by research and data. For example, the trend towards autonomous vehicles is evident, and it is likely only a matter of time before all cars and trucks will be self-driving. Hundreds of trends in society interact to compose the unfolding future. Starting in grade 8, students at Master's study these trends and create what we call S curves. An S curve shows when each trend reaches the adoption stage based on the opinions of experts in a given field. Students then use tools such as a Future Wheel to conduct an impact analysis of their S curve in the mid and long - term futures. They use STEEP vantage points: Social, Technological, Economic, Environmental and Political.

Learning from the **FAR** Future: Invention

Invention is the creation of something new, and within the Imaginal Learning time-frame, the "far out" or "preposterous" future that emerges 20-50 years from now helps inspire what we seek to invent. To understand the "far out" future students engage with weak signal research. Weak signals lie on the fringe of what is possible. Little data currently supports these signals, which is why they are weak, but none-the-less they are being worked on and studied by many experts. Weak signals have a low probability of becoming a reality, but they would have a tremendous disruptive impact if they did. For example, scientists are currently working on 3D printing of human tissue using a person's stem cells, hoping one day to 3D print an entire human organ. Think of the breakthrough this would be to medical science and human longevity!

Another example of a weak signal is nuclear fusion, which is the process that powers our sun. Today, we use nuclear fission, which produces nuclear waste that lasts for thousands of years. But with nuclear fusion, we could use seawater to create a virtually limitless source of energy with no environmental impact. Many researchers are attempting to develop nuclear fusion reactors, and current speculation suggests that the first viable commercial fusion reactor may be available by 2050. If this were to happen, the world would have a clean, limitless supply of energy.

The focus of our Junior High (grades 7-9) program is on Imaginal Thinking and the tools and methods of seeing and learning from the future. This year our grade 9 students are engaged in weak signal research to design life on Mars in 2050. In High School (grades 10-12) the focus shifts to helping our students becoming Imaginal Leaders seeking to make a difference in the world.

Part V: I Have a Dream

What will the future look like? We don't have a crystal ball that magically shows us the future. The question is, can we create the future we want or will we inherit the future someone else has created, perhaps through malevolence or sheer carelessness? Either way the future will come, but will it be by design or default?

The following is excerpted from the Epilogue to my book. I call this my dream for the future.

In 1963, drawing from the vision of the prophet Isaiah, Martin Luther King Jr. gave one of the most electrifying speeches in modern history, in which he laid out his dream for a country where all people were treated equally regardless of race. A dream should be grandiose, it should inspire people, it is not a clearly defined future that can be designed and built using the creation process. Some aspects of the dream are clearer than others, and may approach the status of a more concrete vision.

In a similar spirit, I have a dream for all nations.

To my Fellow Educators, I Have a Dream for You

Let us not wallow in the valley of despair, I say to you my friends. And so, even though we face the challenges of today and tomorrow, I still have a dream, a dream deeply rooted in the fundamental belief that all children are created equal and deserve the best possible education we can create.

I have a dream that educators around the world will rise up, not as a force of discontent, but rather as a voice of hope that the system of education can and WILL BE transformed much like a caterpillar becomes a butterfly.

I have a dream of an army of Imaginal educators willing to pay the price for freedom, freedom from the demands of a system that no longer serves the most precious in our society.

I have a dream of students around the world being set free from the bondages of a system that favors the few and banishes the many to lives of 'also rans'.

I have a dream that in those places where educators have been downtrodden, they will be lifted up to a place of honor and esteem.

I have a dream that the vast majority of students will succeed, that learning will become the JOY it always was intended to be.

I have a dream that all teachers will experience a release of JOY not yet seen by the many who labor in this noble profession.

I have a dream that one day Profound Learning will be experienced from Canada to Argentina, from Nigeria to Ethiopia, from Singapore to the outback in Australia, and throughout all this earth.

I have a dream!

With the eyes of faith, I see a glorious future in which every child is given what he or she needs to succeed in his or her world. I have hope for the future and with faith I pull the future into the now.

With faith we will be able to transform education; we will create a better future for those we LOVE, the children of this world.

I have a dream that one day every valley shall be exalted, and every hill and mountain shall be made low, the rough places will be made plain, and the crooked places will be made straight; "and the glory of the Lord shall be revealed and all flesh shall see it together."

Chapter 7

Academic Pastor: Recovering the Gift of Teachers

David Glesne[1]

"I am afraid that universities will prove to be the great gates of hell unless they diligently labor in explaining the Holy Scriptures, engraving them in the hearts of youth. I advise no one to place his child where the scriptures do not reign paramount. Every institution in which men are not increasingly occupied with the Word of God must become corrupt."
-Martin Luther[2]

A key component of *The Third Education Revolution* is returning education to the church. In chapter 1, Vishal Mangalwadi briefly surveyed the First and Second Education Revolutions, how the universities in the West were birthed by the church, and how education became universalized. These revolutions molded western civilization by grounding education in divine revelation animating the minds and hearts of God's children.

Later, in chapter 4, Pastor Joe Suozzo explained the need for the church to take the lead in education, while Amanda Forbes described 'blended learning' in chapter 5. It is a model of technology-aided learning that allows local congregations to step up in this way. An expert in physics or computer science teaches his subject, the academic pastor helps students integrate specialized knowledge into a holistic worldview and life.

After the Enlightenment, European states took over education from the church. This change began the secularization of the school. Church-based education, which had taken place within a biblical mindset, changed. Education divorced human reason from divine revelation. Cut off from

1 Dr. David Glesne is the Founder-President of Virtues Campus Inc in Minnesota. Prior to that, he served as the Senior Pastor at the Redeemer Lutheran Church in Fridley and Coon Rapids, Minnesota

2 *"History Of The Reformation In The Sixteenth Century,"* by J. H. Merle d'Aubigné, 1846. French edition 1835.
(Es muss verderben, alles was nicht Gottes Wort ohn Unterlass treibt)

revelation, reason could not validate itself. By separating creatures from their Creator, human reason lost the very center of the universe. It could not help students discover the meaning and purpose of their own lives, let alone know how they should live.

Having lost direction and fallen into confusion, ugliness and sorrow, education has fallen captive to the Deceiver of Nations. Divorced from the wisdom of divine revelation, modern education began to deny or de-emphasize God, truth, beauty, and virtue. Jesus' command to "love our neighbor" calls us to disrupt the present tragic and fatal status quo.

Local Church-based College

The Third Education Revolution empowers the local church to reclaim its teaching authority. It does so by partnering with Christian universities and schools who have remained true to their charters.

In our model, students enroll dually in an accredited university and a local church campus. At the church, a small cohort of 6-25 students experience community together as they attend classes under trained and qualified academic pastors. At the same time, the students take online courses taught by the best available teachers. Qualified scholars have designed a curriculum that draws on both reason and revelation, which can be accessed via the internet by students on every continent, even in the remotest village. Students then earn accredited degrees from the partner university.

The heart of the church-based model is the Academic Pastor (AP). He or she plays the essential role of creating and nurturing a culture in the local church in which learning and the pursuit of truth takes place. Who will these academic pastors be? How can we describe their qualifications? What training will they be given? What roles will they serve in the Education Revolution?

At The Virtues Campus, over the past few years, we have begun what may be seen as a pilot program for the international movement now developing. As founder of The Virtues Campus, and a former senior pastor, I will, in the following pages, explain first the practical need for such a movement and how it works in practice, then discuss theological underpinnings

Paul: Teacher of Truth

The vision for the academic pastor comes from the Apostle Paul. Paul was not only an evangelist and missionary, he also served as mentor to young church leaders called to disciple and train believers in cities around the Mediterranean. Paul strongly impressed upon his protégées Titus and Timothy that, as an apostle, he was called to be a preacher and *teacher of the truth* to the Gentiles (I Tim. 2:7; Titus 1:1). God had called him as an apostle because God wants all men "to be saved and come to the knowledge of the truth" (I Tim. 2:3-7; 3:15; II Tim. 1:11; 2:24-25; 3:16; 4:3).

Paul said God wants "all men to be saved." Paul preached the Good News so that men and women might believe and be baptized in Christ's name. This salvation came by grace through a faith that was not blind but rooted in knowledge. So, men and women need a Savior. In his letters to Timothy and Titus, the title "Savior" is ascribed to God (I Tim 2:3; 4:10; 4:10; Titus 2:10; 3:4) and Christ (Titus 1:4; 3:6). Although eternal life was promised long ago, it was now manifest through the preaching of Paul and the successors to whom he entrusted his ministry.

For Paul it was never an either-or. He was both a preacher AND a teacher. This combination of duties is how he understood his calling. The opening words of his letter to Titus define Paul's identity: "Paul, a bond-servant of God, and an apostle of Jesus Christ, according to the faith of God's elect, and the acknowledgment of *the truth which accords to godliness.*"

So how does the innovative approach we have been describing of a local church-based college model, work in practice? What does the Academic Pastor do? I can only speak from my own experience, having served as the original "academic pastor" for the Virtues Campus, in the model we are developing for *The Third Education Revolution*. The relationship between host churches, academic pastors, and partner universities, will vary in different countries and cultural contexts. But I suspect the core elements will be similar. So the model I describe below will provide an example which can be applied with some variation in other national contexts as well.

I. The Role of Academic Pastors

What is The Virtues Campus?

The Virtues Campus brings the university and local church together by offering students an affordable, biblically integrated liberal arts education; integrating Veritas (truth) and Virtue (character) with professional skills and knowledge; fostering civic engagement through service learning; and supporting career development through job-shadowing, which gains field experience. Local church facilities serve as classrooms. Academic Pastors provide teaching and guidance. Congregations and peers offer community. Then, in our case, degrees are awarded through a regionally accredited partner university.

Central Organizational Body

A central organization provides an overall program design. During its infancy, Virtues has developed an infrastructure for the church-based college model. A functioning campus has been housed in two church facilities in the Minneapolis area. In this pilot phase, student numbers have been small while the model secured its footing. But the network is starting to grow. The Virtues Campus is prepared to implement this program in churches that embrace the revolution. It will promote this vision across America, to students, parents, communities, and churches of all denominations.

A central task of The Virtues Campus is to establish a relationship between the local church and the Christian university. It identifies churches willing and able to double as college classrooms Monday through Friday. It also seeks willing academic and institutional partners, and develops and maintains a relationship with them.

The Virtues central office guides and supports the host church in its identification of an academic pastor. Once identified, we will provide ongoing support and training to a cadre of academic pastors and host churches. In addition to linking students to a partner university for online courses, Virtues Inc. develops and/or provides curricula for weekly in-person classes.

Host Church's Commitments

Small churches as well as large churches can serve as host churches. Each church simply needs a sufficiently comfortable classroom area and tools (tables and chairs, internet, power cords, projector and screen, and TV) sufficient for however many students enroll.

The host church must embrace the mission of church-based college, while retaining the freedom to meet the needs of local students. It commits itself to promoting the campus and program to the congregation and community at large. Church-based higher education is encouraged through the church's website and other communication channels.

While Virtues lends guidance and support, the host church is responsible for identifying, recruiting (and dismissing) the Academic Pastor. The AP may be a qualified member of the church staff. Or he or she may hold an advanced degree, accompanied by competencies in biblical knowledge and skills, who becomes a contract employee. In rare circumstances, the lead pastor may serve as AP. The AP serves under the spiritual authority of the host church's pastor.

Financial Benefit to the Host Church

Recently, I was asked to address a group of 20-30 pastors at their monthly pastors' meeting. The person who invited me was a former superintendent of schools who had become an ordained pastor. I asked, "What will the pastors most want to know?" His response was quick and blunt: "They will want to know what it will cost them financially." Budgets matter to churches.

Our program is designed to be funded through student tuition. All tuition is received by The Virtues Campus corporate office. Each campus church then receives a percentage of the tuition based on the number of students enrolled at their campus each term.

Campuses are able to officially open with six enrolled students and are capped at 25 students. If enrollment exceeds 25, a second academic pastor is needed. To maintain the financial stability of the program as a whole, academic pastors are encouraged to target and maintain a campus of 15 students.

In practice, a typical funding structure might look something like this:

Number of Students	Host Church Income
6	$20,500
7 - 9	$24,500
10 - 14	$35,000
15 - 19	$51,000
20 - 25	$66,000

The host church's income provides for a) the academic pastor's salary, b) an executive assistant's salary (if needed), and c) church utility expenses.

Spiritual Benefits to the Host Church

A church-based college provides the local church with a college-aged discipleship ministry that keeps young adults connected to the local church after high school. With current statistics showing that the Church in America loses 70-80% of its youth once they leave for college, this connection is critical for the discipling of the next generation. Serving the wider regional church and civic community, a church- based college provides a purposeful college education for young adults within a 25-30-mile radius. Hosting college classes strengthens the overall teaching ministry of the church, establishing the local church as an educational center in the community.

With classes meeting in their building, discipling the next generation becomes an all-church affair. Members of our congregations often feel helpless about what is going on in academia today. They want to do something. Here is what they can do!

Congregants can provide scholarships that encourage students to attend college in their own church. Christian businessmen can step forward and offer their businesses as job-shadowing sites. Other congregants can serve as tutors in their areas of expertise. Church members can exhibit hospitality by opening their homes to paying students from outside the area and modeling a Christian home for guests. The church as a whole becomes actively involved in discipling the next generation.

Trained Academic Pastors

When the first Virtues campus was birthed in 2015, I became the academic pastor while also serving as president. I had stepped aside from my senior pastor role of a two-campus church to lead this new endeavor. Those years of serving as an academic pastor prepared me to find and train academic pastors.

In America, those who serve as academic pastors either have formal theological training or have gained significant Biblical training. In some other countries, pastors of local churches may need to earn a high school diploma followed by an advanced degree in Applied Theology. As the global educational movement develops and matures, plans are being implemented to develop courses in conjunction with accredited universities.

Beyond biblical and theological training, The Virtues Campus trains workers for all aspects of the work of AP. Training sessions cover program history, design, admissions, curricula, costs, marketing, management, and so on. Because of the Covid-19 pandemic, we recently conducted Zoom training sessions for an AP. Once a campus is birthed and functioning, Virtues provides ongoing support for both the host church and the AP.

Weekly Time Commitment

One of the most commonly asked questions is: "Is the academic pastor position a part-time or full-time job?" We have now had enough experience to have a good feel of the time involved. The weekly time commitment for the AP will vary depending on the number of students enrolled. But generally, the AP's time is allotted as follows:
- 15 hours weekly classroom time, August – May
- 1 – 10 hours, student support through personal mentoring, job-shadowing coordination and community service activities with students
- 1 – 10 hours, administration and marketing (ongoing)

Duties & Responsibilities of Academic Pastors

The central calling of the AP is to be a teacher of truth. He or she helps local churches become wells of knowledge in their communities. But additional competences are also needed. In the day by day leading of the campus, at least four areas of competence are required.

Learning Facilitation Skills

Ours is a form of Learner-Centered education. Usually, a student comes to class having listened to an online lecture or read a chapter, and the AP guides an interactive discussion. He makes sure that students understand and apply what they are reading, watching, or hearing. The preacher does not bring his pulpit into the classroom. Class is not centered around him. He is not there to lecture or preach, but to facilitate the students' self-initiated learning.

The AP facilitates Socratic dialogue. The Socratic Method focuses on the art of asking well-crafted questions to stimulate thinking and draw out ideas and underlying presuppositions. The goal of the Education Revolution is to open minds formerly indoctrinated by secular and critical theories. These minds learn to question, inquire, challenge and investigate even long held assumptions in the pursuit of truth.

The goal of group discussions is to develop critical thinkers. Academic pastors desire to develop Christian minds that judge all things by God's Word. Especially in liberal arts, students learn to apply the Socratic Method - critical thinking - and the truth of God's Word.

Academic pastors also serve as resources for students. Knowing students well, they guide them in choosing courses needed to complete a degree in a timely fashion. They teach good study habits and learning skills where needed. They guide their students to varied resources, engendering an excitement for life-long, inquiry-based learning.

Academic pastors also arrange for guest speakers who hold specialized expertise. These speakers share how their Christian faith integrates with professional knowledge and skills. Here, making connections with government, community and business leaders bears fruit. Our students have been addressed by a former governor of the State of Minnesota, who challenged them to live virtuous lives; a successful businessman who shared how his faith nurtured a Christ-centered business culture; and a candidate running for mayor of Minneapolis, who shared how his faith integrated with a life in government.

The AP can also bring the gifts and expertise of congregational members together with the needs of students. One of my earliest students was taking an online statistics course and hit a wall. She asked if I would help, but statistics are not my cup of tea! So I reached out to a Christian high school math teacher in the community and asked if he would come and tutor her. He happily met with her and helped her work through her difficulties. At the end of the semester, she made the "A" honor roll! We have teachers and subject-matter experts in our congregations who are more than willing to mentor and tutor students meeting in their churches. In the process, the entire congregation becomes involved in discipling the next generation.

Discipleship and Mentoring Skills

It is the experience of a great many university students to be part of large classes and have little or no personal contact with the professor. Unless, that is, you are a troublemaker! In contrast, academic pastors know their students well. The teacher to student ratio is small, so they can personally invest in each student. Discipling and mentoring takes place in many ways. There is interaction before, during, and after daily classes. This keeps the AP current with what is going on in students' lives.

APs also meet with each student regularly one-on-one during the semester. In these face-to-face meetings, they ask how the student is doing academically, emotionally, spiritually, and physically. They listen carefully. They offer encouragement and wise counsel into life situations. The AP prays regularly for his students. He gives guidance from God's Word and wisdom from his own experience.

This mentoring relationship involves holding students accountable to stay on track academically, by setting up study schedules and goals, scheduling activities, etc. APs also hold students accountable in other areas of their lives. This involves confronting a student when necessary. It means speaking the truth in love.

Pastors build a sense of community among students. This involves encouraging and helping facilitate social activities outside the classroom. My wife has a wonderful gift of hospitality, and that gift has blessed Virtues students with warm memories of food, fun, and laughter in our home.

As Titus and Timothy were exhorted by Paul to live exemplary and upright lives, APs share the high privilege of modeling a faithful Christian life. They are teachers of truth. They are also called to live the truth. APs should strive to exhibit a healthy balance between intellectual, physical, spiritual, and social dimensions of life. These day by day interactions encourage students to grow in the grace and knowledge of Jesus Christ. They inspire a love for God and His Word. They cultivate in students the habits of heart and mind. Because the AP is under the spiritual authority of the host church pastor, any breach of trust by the AP is addressed by the church's pastor.

Community Connection Skills

Academic pastors can enhance their students' education by involvement in the wider community. Developing leadership skills includes gaining the confidence to approach leaders in the community. Good relationships with businesses and community leaders provide avenues for community projects, job-shadowing experiences, and future employment possibilities. Job-shadowing helps students build professional networks, gain field experience, and build marketable skills that can be transcribed on a resume. The AP's role is to help students identify an organization or business within the community to conduct a job shadow, visit the student on-site, and provide feedback on the work he or she is completing.

In partnership with the AP, this role may also be filled by someone in the local church with a broad social network and broad influence.

Administrative and Technology Skills

Hybrid online and in-person, or 'blended' learning, employs the latest technology. The AP is responsible for maintaining the infrastructure needed to sustain a college classroom. He or she is responsible for managing the classroom facility, optimizing the learning environment, supplying all classroom needs and equipment, and all matters pertaining to classroom safety. This involves troubleshooting local technology issues. The AP should therefore keep tech skills up to date.

Administratively, the AP plans schedules with the host church, both for the year and each week. Of course, this means coordinating facility usage with church staff.

The AP also manages student and program information. This involves serving as the liaison between the host church and corporate offices. The

AP manages all expenses, ensuring that they stay within budget, and also evaluates the effectiveness of the program.

Benefits to Partner Universities

In these turbulent times, the local church should be an eager partner that not only wants the Christian university to survive but thrive. The benefits to the university which partners with local churches are many.

Instead of the university having, say, 2,000 online students, it potentially may gain tens of thousands of online students, as local churches establish campuses and advocate for such partnerships. The practical key is an arrangement that discounts online courses for students, making such an education financially appealing. It is a win – win proposition. Students win by receiving an affordable education – under $10,000 a year. The partner university may win by gaining thousands more students. In this way, the local church becomes a feeder pipeline for new students, without overloading campus capacity.

In such a partnership, the local church becomes a marketing arm of the university, especially in the homeschool and church communities. As local churches market their local campuses, the partner university also gains visibility.

II Education: Seeking Truth That Transforms

Paul knew that God wants worshippers who love and seek truth. That is why he left Titus on the island of Crete and Timothy in the city of Ephesus.

Crete and Ephesus are microcosms of the Gentile world of the first century A.D, snapshots of the culture and religion of Greco-Roman society. The Ephesians were well-known for enthusiastic devotion to the goddess Artemis, who was worshipped in a magnificent local temple dedicated to her. Artemis was the daughter of Greece's greatest god, Zeus, and his wife Leto, and twin sister of Apollo. Greeks worshipped gods and goddesses whose affairs were related in epic myths.

Crete was the mountainous birthplace of Zeus. He was revered everywhere in shrines built for him on the island, a little smaller than the Big

Island of Hawaii or Puerto Rico. Paul left Titus on Crete to appoint church elders in every city to set things in order (Titus 1:5). As he did so, Paul reminded Titus of what the well-known Greek poet, Epimenides, who lived in Crete 600 years before Christ, had said about the locals' character. He said Cretans were "liars, evil beasts, and lazy gluttons" (Titus 1:12).

Ephesus gives us a picture of the Greco-Roman civilization built upon myth-based religion. Crete offers an image of the morally debased character which a theology, detached from truth, would develop.

Paul left Titus and Timothy in these locales to teach a revolutionary message. He began establishing a network of humble pastors, teachers and preachers of truth, who would gradually transform their civilization. What was so transformative about their teaching?

Paul exhorted Titus to confront makers of wild stories. Paul knew that Greek myths were mere brilliant fiction. Since reason cannot verify myths, they have pragmatic value only if you accept them on blind faith.

Into that myth-saturated world, Paul and Titus spoke of faith based on verifiable fact. They spoke of a God who can be known, who has spoken to man, who entered into history by becoming a man Himself, and lived, died, and rose again. The faith they proclaimed began at an open tomb, not in mere imagination.

Myth-based religion had created Crete's culture of corruption and distrust. Greek gods exhibited the best and the worst of the characters of their creators: courage and cleverness on the one hand; jealousy, covetousness, exploitation, trickery, and distrust on the other hand. As the Greeks trusted their gods - projections of themselves - their behavior came to reflect the behavior of the gods in whom they trusted. (As David Marshall noted in Chapter 2, Socrates himself warned of this danger!) The myth-based Greco-Roman world became morally debased. You could expect a society of lazy gluttons who went into debt by consuming more than they produced. You could expect men to become "evil beasts" by going after women other than their wives. You could expect business partners to be "liars" who betray you for gain.[3]

3 Vishal Mangalwadi, *This Book Changed Everything*
(Pasadena, CA: SoughtAfterMedia, 2019), 23-24

By contrast, Paul and Titus' message was rooted in knowledge. Jesus said, "This is eternal life, to know God" (John 17:3). And again, "You shall know the truth, and the truth shall make you free" (John 8:32). Central to the Christian experience is knowledge. In that sense, Christianity is not what one might call a "faith tradition," but a knowledge tradition.

Truth was seen as discoverable, that is, objective. You could know the truth and the *Truth would set you free. Such was the spiritual and intellectual revolution which tore and then began to rebuild the fabric of the Roman Empire.*

In his remarkable book, *Dominion*, British historian Tom Holland follows the ensuing history of how Christian truth emerged as the single most transformative development in Western history.

Paul's revolutionary message taught that the law of the God of Israel had been written on the human heart by His Spirit. As such, that law can be read and known by all. The truth of that message convulsed both the Jewish and Gentile worlds. With the coming of Christ, the Jews' guardianship of divine law was no longer needed. Christ had charged Paul to proclaim that "The only thing that counts is faith expressing itself in love" (Galatians 5:6). Paul's teaching truly did turn the world upside down (Acts 17:6), rendering his letters the most radically transformative and influential ever written.[4]

In each age, Christian truth confronts forces that seek to discredit and destroy it. So the Christian mind manifested in Paul and his associates in the Roman Empire, the monasteries of Medieval Europe, and in the Protestant Reformation, and its cry of *"Sola Scriptura"*, must counter those forces of dissolution and the lies that inspire them. Our own era brings challenges just as great.

The secularization of education set in motion by the Enlightenment, is now nearly complete. The divorce of reason from revelation has created a post-truth world. Myths (our age calls them stories or narratives) now dominate academia, much of the news media, and social and political thought. Objective facts that don't fit the narrative are canceled.

....

4 Tom Holland, *Dominion: How The Christian Revolution Remade the World* (New York, NY: Basic Books, 2019), 96.

Consequently America is no longer among the 20 least corrupt countries.[5] One might think we were living again in ancient Crete or Ephesus.

The Necessity of a Christian Mind

Churches need academic pastors because our Post Truth Era calls for a passionate commitment to the truth of Christianity.[6] Harry Blamires doesn't mince words about the need, beginning his tract, *The Christian Mind*, frankly:

> "There is no longer a Christian Mind. Unfortunately, the Christian mind has succumbed to the secular drift with a degree of weakness and nervousness unmatched in Christian history. It is difficult to do justice in words to the complete loss of intellectual morale in the 20th Century Church. One cannot characterize it without having recourse to language which will sound hysterical and melodramatic."[7]

Charles Malik echoed Blamires in an address given at Wheaton College in 1980: "The greatest danger besetting American Christianity is the danger of anti-intellectualism. " Malik added:

> "The arena of creative thinking [has been] abdicated and vacated to the enemy."

More recently, in the opening sentence of Mark Noll's superb book, *The Scandal of the Evangelical Mind*, the author states:

> "*The scandal of the Evangelical Mind* is that there is not much of an evangelical mind."[8]

Paul understood that Jesus as the Truth was the cornerstone upon which the Church is built, and that the Church must be the pillar and foundation of the Truth (I Tim. 3:15b). It is this commitment to truth which disrupted

---

5 Corruption Perception Index. In 2019, the USA was ranked as the 23/180 least corrupt country.

6 See Ralph Keyes, *The Post-Truth Era: Dishonesty and Deception in Contemporary Life*, (Manhattan, NYC: St. Martin's Press, 2004)

7 Harry Blamires, *The Christian Mind: How Should a Christian Think?* (Ann Arbor, Michigan: Servant Books, 1978), 3.

8 Mark A. Noll, *The Scandal of the Evangelical Mind* (Grand Rapids, Michigan: William B. Eerdmans Publishing Company, 1994), 3.

the social and ideological fabric of the ancient world. If the church in our day is to counter secularism, academic pastors must recover a Christian mind no less certain of the truth of Christ and his teachings. What does such a mind look like? It will have at least three visible marks: it must be biblically-informed, committed to truth, and broad in scope.[9]

The Nature of a Christian Mind

First, *the recovery of a Christian mind requires a commitment to the truth of God's Word.* What matters is not what society thinks, or what we think, but what God has said. Teachers of truth are wholeheartedly committed to God's Word written as completely true and authoritative for the whole of life.

The importance of this commitment to the Bible as God's Word written is underscored by Harry Blamires when he writes:
> "The Christian mind has an overwhelming sense that the truth it clings to is supernaturally grounded, revealed, not manufactured, imposed, not chosen, authoritative, objective and irresistible."[10]

The teacher of truth teaches a revealed truth, a transcendent truth. It is a truth that comes from above. It is not a truth that our faith creates. It is a truth that God has given us.

Academic pastors, then, are to be grounded in God's Word. They must grasp the major themes of the Bible: creation, fall, covenant, redemption, the relationship between the Old and New Testaments, and the consummation of history.

But the Christian mind is not blinded by submitting to God's truth. There is good and sufficient reason to submit. By analogy, Newton's law of gravity is authoritative and demands submission. But this is because it can be seen to be true. A dish never falls into a higher level. You always snowboard downhill. We submit to the law of gravity because it manifestly fits the facts of life.

---

9 I am indebted for much of the material in this section to Ranald Macaulay, "The Christian Mind," in *What in the World is Real? Challenging the Superficial in Today's World* (Champaign, Illinois: Communications Institute, 1982), 111-124.

10 Blamires, 119

It is the same with the authority of God's Word. We do not need to accept it blindly. As Paul says in Romans 1, God's reality is "evident to all." In submitting one's understanding to God's revealed Truth, the Christian mind is humble. God has not revealed everything to us, either in the Bible or through nature. Therefore, the Christian mind does not claim to "know it all."

Second, *the recovery of a Christian mind necessitates a passionate commitment to truth*. In our post-truth culture, it needs to be stressed that the Christian mind is committed to objective truth.

Objective truth is truth that stands outside one's self, having been revealed through Scripture, nature, and within the human self, made in God's image. God exists objectively as the Creator of the heavens and the earth. Moses really did meet God in a burning bush. Jesus actually was raised bodily from the grave. The statements of Scripture are true in that they correspond to and accurately describe the nature of reality, past and present.

The Christian mind is also passionately committed to the truth of salvation. The objective truth it clings to centers in the saving work of Jesus Christ. So the Christian mind does not merely reason, it is passionate. Christ humbled himself to become a servant to give his life as ransom for many. Let us rejoice in defiance of the gloomy lies of this world! We are not the "frozen chosen," but passionately committed to the objective truth of God's love.

Third, *the Christian mind must be broad in scope*. God's truth covers all reality, after all.

We have been set free by Christ to enjoy the whole of reality. In Christian truth, there is no absolute divide between the spiritual and secular. Government, politics, nature, art, entertainment, prose and poetry, music — all lie within the scope of the spiritual. That is the way God made us, as social, creative, physical, fun-loving, and responsible beings.

Growing up on a farm, I liken the Christian life to opening the barn door and letting young calves out on a fall day. They run out into the brisk, cool air, and across the barnyard, kicking up their legs. They stop, breathe in the fresh air, and run to the other side of the yard. They stop at the water trough and drink. Then they run off again to join the others. What a picture of exhilaration!

That is what God has done for us. Christ has set us free to enjoy all aspects of human experience, the whole of reality, apart from sin. And we are not to feel guilty at this boundless pleasure.

The truth of God's Word is universal. It is true for all people in all places. It is true for all human activities and enterprises: art, archeology, science, family life, politics, medicine, psychology, etc. The Christian mind is to be broad because God's truth spans all reality, as a ceiling spans a room. There is nothing outside His authority.
But caution is needed. While Scripture applies directly to some aspects of experience, it only applies indirectly to other aspects.

In the first congregation I served, we built a sanctuary with rectangular skylights in the ceiling above the altar. On a bright day, the sun's rays shone directly on a rectangular area on the altar area beneath the skylights. However, those same rays would indirectly bring light to the entire room.

So it is with Scripture and the world. God's overarching truth spotlights some areas directly, but other areas indirectly. Where did man come from? What is man? What has gone wrong? What is salvation? Where are we going? Light from God's Word directly illumines such questions, as the light from the skylight shone onto the altar below.

But in other areas, the Scriptures speak indirectly. For example, the Bible does not say much about science. Does that mean science is illegitimate? Of course not. Genesis says that man is to have dominion over the earth, which surely includes exploring the natural world to discover its secrets. God posed questions to Job which science is still exploring millennia later. Scientific inquiry is valid and has improved the human condition. The Word of God shines an indirect light on science, but that also fits within the span of divine truth.

With the Christian mind submitted to the Scriptures and all-encompassing in curiosity, it will inevitably conflict with our culture. Controlled by God's Truth, the Christian mind is, as Paul says, "to judge all things." We are to be aware of what is going on in the world, seeking to understand the nature of society, then discern what is true and what is false, right or wrong. We are to affirm all that is good. At the same time, we are to confront and challenge what is evil. Since there is so much that is untrue in our cultures, confrontation is inevitable; and the teacher of truth must not flinch from it.

As in Timothy's and Titus' day, man's false ideas, "arguments and every high thing that exalts itself against the knowledge of God" (II Cor. 10:5), and hollow and deceptive philosophy (Col. 2:8), are pollutants within the river of experience. They poison, deceive, and destroy. The Christian mind is called to oppose falsehood and untruth with all vigor. And so the idea of developing a Christian mind is not simply an intellectual concept. It requires a passionate commitment to truth - so passionate, in fact, that the inevitable confrontation with evil practices and false ideas will be no less severe than Jesus' own. Yet it is to this that He has called us: "No servant is greater than his master. If they persecuted me, they will persecute you" (John 15:10).

In the footsteps of Paul, Titus, and Timothy, the calling of the AP arises from an awareness that all knowledge and experience can ultimately be understood only in terms of a Christian worldview. His calling is to help students bring every thought captive to Christ.

The Question

What if tens of thousands of churches take up responsibility for teaching America's next generation, by becoming host churches for college classes? What if a network of humble teachers of truth should mentor and disciple millions of young adults in our churches every year? What if ownership of education in the land is taken back by the church? By God's grace, such a movement can spearhead a revolution in education that can tear at the very fabric of secularization and begin to heal a nation.

We encourage you to become part of The Third Education Revolution.

Chapter 8

College-pedia: A New Knowledge Ecosystem

Ashish Alexander[1]

A renaissance of the "Christian mind" must offer the "light of life" (John 8:32) to a generation that cannot distinguish true from false, right from wrong, good from evil, or wisdom from folly. Our lost generation desperately needs a reliable bank of knowledge infused not with ideology, academic fads, or political correctness, but with wisdom, knowledge, and understanding that cultivate the "fear of the Lord." That is the beginning of wisdom (Proverbs 1:7) and that education that chooses not to graduate wise students, is dangerous

The proposed knowledge-bank would make high-quality information freely available. It will become a new ecosystem of learning, which helps students to synthesize all knowledge — sacred or secular — to shape the mind, uplift the spirit and form character. To that end *The Third Education Revolution* aims to create an online encyclopedia. It will cater to the practical, educational and informational needs of the students so that they can find a comprehensive resource to build their world-and-life view of things.

But some may say: "We already have Wikipedia! It's the world's biggest encyclopedia with almost limitless information and it is absolutely free."

Yes, but we shouldn't forget that it was "free" advice that resulted in "*Paradise Lost.*"

The intellectual climate around the world is out of joint. Information is exploding but biases and ideologies are twisting everything in our "library to the world."

1 Dr. Ashish Alexander serves as the Head of the Department of English and Foreign Languages and the Dean of the School of Films and Mass Communications at the Sam Higginbottom University of Agriculture, Technology and Sciences at Prayag Raj, UP, India.

Wikipedia is a remarkable success. Those blessed with prophetic insights into the corruption of our age can learn much from it, especially as they obey their call to change the future.

This chapter builds a case for a new online encyclopedia. First, it looks at the present state of knowledge production and the dangers fomented by confusion about power and truth. Then it discusses the lessons we can learn from Wikipedia's success. Finally it describes the original Christian vision of an encyclopedia. It will, thus, present the case why Spirit-inspired researchers must create a new online encyclopedia to support the many facets of *The Third Education Revolution*. A learner-centered education has to give students easy access to credible facts and fair interpretations.

I - Knowledge, Power and Truth

"History is written by the victors."

On all inhabited continents, this axiom arguably guides all knowledge production. Research theses in our universities are undergirded by it; comic books, popular cinema and Web series are driven by it; a man- about-town can wax eloquent about it. For many people, this ubiquitous phrase strikingly reveals the otherwise-hidden relationship between knowledge and power. Those who have power create knowledge, and vice versa. Putting it the other way: "He who tells the story of the battle is the ultimate victor."

Knowledge is power. The emotional appeal of this saying is particularly compelling for those who have been kept out of knowledge production. In India, for example, where sharp and inviolable distinctions between manual and intellectual labor have been maintained for millennia,[2] uttering this adage seemed a first step towards empowering marginalized people — who knew facts outside the official narrative and offer alternative interpretations of reality.[3]

---

2 India's Hindu caste system divides people on the basis of birth. Those born in higher castes are considered intellectually superior and hence must devote themselves to learning and knowledge production. Manual labor must be carried out by the lower castes.

3 *Debrahmanising History* is the title of an important book that came out earlier in this century, and which argues that Indian history has been interpreted from the perspective of the upper-caste Brahmin intellectuals, and calls for a fresh interpretation of the history of the Indian subcontinent. Contd >>

But the elites still find a way to make the revolution in the production of grassroots knowledge work in their favor. Through an intellectual sleight of hand they re-brand themselves as victims and ensure that their dominance continues. Hardcore Hindu nationalists in India, for example, claim to be victims of Islamic and British colonial aggression, thereby drowning out the voice of their own victims — "lower" castes, Tribals and religious minorities.[4]

In the USA, intellectual nihilism[5] remains seductive for successive generations of college freshmen. They readily accept their professors' claim to be speaking for racial and sexual minorities while advocating the dismantling of "hegemonic" power structures. Academic aristocrats perpetuate their own dominance by asserting that, in challenging the ideological foundations of the Western civilization, they serve the interests of the marginalized.[6]

Even students from disadvantaged backgrounds are swept off their feet by their professors' fine rhetoric and zeal for the crusaders. Such students repeat ad *absurdum*: that knowledge is not pursued for truth or enlightenment but to pull down the so-called oppressive structures. Intellectual sleight of hand, yet again.

---

3 See Braj Ranjan Mani, *Debrahmanising History: Dominance and Resistance in Indian Society* (New Delhi: Manohar, 2005).

4 Immigrant Indians to the USA are largely from the upper castes, those who had means and connections to fly to greener pastures in the "First World." For a long time, they have been the sole representatives of India in the US. Often the elite in their native country, they claim victim status in the West.

5 Gertrude Himmelfarb (1922–2019) highlights the celebration of this nihilism on university campuses in her book *On Looking into the Abyss*. Building on Lionel Trilling's observations in his essay "On the Teaching of Modern Literature", she notes: "…generations of intelligent students under the guidance of their enlightened professors have looked into the abyss [of moral nihilism], have contemplated those beasts [the amoral, subversive texts], and have said, 'How interesting, how exciting.'" *On Looking into the Abyss: Untimely Thoughts on Culture and Society* (New York: Vintage Books, 1994), chap. 1, Kindle.

6 Similarly, in India, for a good part of the seventy years after Independence, the left-liberal perspective in academia perpetuated its dominance by positioning itself as the savior of India's working classes.

Knowledge, thus, is seen increasingly as a function of power relationships. Taking this view to its logical end would mean that knowledge exists only to increase the power of one's own group and diminish that of opponents. Knowledge is but a subjective opinion of the powerful.

This confusion is a fundamental crisis plaguing our academic establishment. No one denies that knowledge and power are related, but to posit an inviolable link between the two is to turn it into the philosophic doctrine of determinism. And it fails. It fails to explain the liberating pleasure of finding facts, confessing one's mistakes and repenting, discovering a solution to a tricky problem, or observing a novel phenomenon.

Power often seems irrelevant to the lover of knowledge. A monk, for example, gives up power and possessions in search of knowledge. Now one may argue that he gives up worldly possessions to gain spiritual power, which eventually gives him a greater control over other people and *their* possessions. This cynical view, first of all, cannot be generalized because many monks sacrificed their lives for truth. Hindu scriptures do celebrate monks who meditated and did penance for hundred of years to acquire occult powers. Many others make humility, service, understanding and wisdom their life goal, thus earning moral legitimacy and respect. Just as a counterfeit bill proves that real money exists, so the corruption of noble ideals proves their nobility. Knowledge is power which is often corrupted into power-lust. But lust does not disprove genuine romance. So the cynics are as blind as the gullibly naïve: a nobler love of knowledge is possible, even if difficult to attain.

"The truth will set you free," said Jesus. Truth, in fact, frees one from the lust for power. The love of truth is thus most safely grounded in the love of God, where knowledge and power both become instruments of grace, not exploitation and trickery. A Christian philosophy of knowledge recognizes both our sin, and the proper nobility of the search for truth. Search for truth is often an attempt to break away from the consensus of the age. It often upsets the powers that be.

Truth Becomes a Mortal Risk

Twice in the Gospel of John, truth is discussed in the context of political hostility to the message and person of Jesus. Truth is presented as a stumbling block to both Jews and Gentiles. In John 8, Jewish leaders vehemently reject the notion that they have in any way been enslaved, while in John 18 Pilate, the Roman governor, dismisses the possibility that the "King of the Jews", a subject people, can teach him anything about truth. Truth is not merely a matter of logically consistent statements that correspond to some factual reality. The two instances from John show that truth is a matter of our correct standing vis-à-vis God. That standing allows us to make accurate assessments about our own selves, our environment and our fellow beings. That is the function of truth. That is what knowledge is for. But Jewish leaders and Pilate are blind to that true notion of truth.

Like the Jewish contemporaries of Jesus, our academics build their "discourse" around emancipation, not truth. The high priests of academia, the custodians of knowledge in our universities, present themselves as champions of freedom, but since they oppose the notion of slavery to sin, their emancipatory projects often end up perpetuating worse forms of slavery. Universities are becoming hotbeds of intolerance where certain ideas cannot be discussed and speakers are often banned from speaking or are shouted down by opponents.

In a recently published book, *Cynical Theories*, authors Helen Pluckrose and James Lindsay point out that those who swear by "Social Justice" are often the perpetrators of academic tyranny. Almost daily, they point out, new stories emerge of people being "canceled" or publicly shamed for comments interpreted as "sexist", "racist" or "homophobic." The reasoning behind the charges seems to grow increasingly tortuous:

> It sometimes feels as though any well-intended person, even one who values universal liberty and equality, could inadvertently say something that falls foul of the new speech codes, with devastating consequences for her career and reputation. This is confusing and counterintuitive to a culture accustomed to placing human dignity first and thus valuing charitable interpretations and tolerance of a wide range of views. At best, this has a chilling effect on the culture of free expression … At worst, it is a malicious form of bullying and — when institutionalized — a kind of authoritari anism in our midst.[7]

Damaging the careers and reputations of university faculty is bad enough.

7 Helen Pluckrose and James Lindsay, *Cynical Theories: How Activist Scholarship Made Everything about Race, Gender, and Identity and Why This Harms Everybody* (Durham, NC: Pitchstone Publishing, 2020), 14–15.

But incarceration and even murder of the intelligentsia is now not uncommon in the non-totalitarian, liberal democratic states.[8] The abandoning of truth as a cultural ideal is having a devastating effect on whole nations. Individual freedoms are shrinking, inter-group conflicts are increasing, and governments across the world seem to grow daily more autocratic. If truth doesn't drive our lives, then force must.

This is a world that has surrendered to the fatalistic notion that pursuit of knowledge is only a hankering after power. Our governments no longer trust our universities because our universities now openly admit they are not in pursuit of truth but power. Knowledge severed from truth has paved the way for all-pervasive nihilism. If universities do not pursue truth — and its corollaries such as wisdom, beauty and goodness — the two options available to them are either to shut down or to serve as the handmaidens of the elites.

One way to circumvent the power of academic elites is to create alternate channels of knowledge flow — to truly democratize access to, and production of, knowledge. One resource that has done that magnificently well has been an online encyclopedia.

II - THE WIKIPEDIA STORY

Since its launch on January 15, 2001, Wikipedia has become the largest and most popular source of information across the globe. As of October 8, 2020, it ranked thirteenth on the list of the world's most popular Web sites,[9] though it often features in the top ten. Commentators have called it the "last best thing on the Internet"[10] because it manages to remain popular despite being a nonprofit entity.

---

8 In India, the world's largest democracy, Dalit, Marxist, Muslim and Christian scholars and intellectuals are increasingly being persecuted by the Hindu nationalist regime. Vigilante groups have a free hand to physically assault the opponents of the majoritarian views. Federal investigative agencies are often the handmaidens of their political bosses.

9 alexa.com/topsites; "List of Most Popular Websites," https://en.wikipedia. org/wiki/List_of_most_popular_websites. Accessed on October 17, 2020.

10 Richard Cooke,"Wikipedia Is the Last Best Place on the Internet", *Wired.com*, February 17, 2020, https://www.wired.com/story/wikipedia-online-encyclope-dia-best-place-internet/

Jimmy Wales, an Alabama-born entrepreneur, co-founded Wikipedia along with philosophy graduate Larry Sanger, who also served as its editor-in-chief. Their brainchild now has 6.2 million articles in its English version and over 54 million across all languages. It claims to attract 1.5 billion unique visitors every month.[11]

The mission of the site "to put the sum of all human knowledge in the form of an encyclopedia in the hands of every single person on the planet for free"[12] is widely lauded and appreciated. In her 2006 article on Wikipedia in The New Yorker, journalist Stacy Schiff gave a further glimpse into the vision behind Jimmy Wales' Wikipedia:

> In his view, misinformation, propaganda, and ignorance are responsible for many of the world's ills. 'I'm very much an Enlightenment kind of guy,' Wales told me. The promise of the Internet is free knowledge for everyone, he recalls thinking.[13]

Wales obtained a degree in finance and was pursuing his Ph.D. in the subject when he decided to develop an online encyclopedia. During the dot-com boom of the 1990s, Wales had already co-founded a for-profit company called BOMIS. That company tasted some success hosting content primarily catering to "men's interest." Wales and Sanger first teamed up to found another internet encyclopedia, Nupedia. It was conceptualized on the model of traditional encyclopedias, where experts would write in a peer-reviewed fashion. However, progress was slow and tedious over its first year.

It was then that they decided to use wiki as technology and common Internet users as content providers. Wiki software had been developed by Ward Cunningham, allowing people to make changes in real time to the content they saw online.[14] It turned passive consumers of information into active editors and creators of knowledge. Readers could engage more actively with topics of their choice, start their own entries, and edit and

---

11 *Wikipedia.org.* https://en.wikipedia.org Accessed October 17, 2020.

12 "The Encyclopedia in Cyberspace: Wikipedia Makes Every Man an Editor." *The New Atlantis*, no. 7 (2004): 146–48. Accessed October 14, 2020. http://www.jstor.org/stable/43152159.

13 Stacy Schiff, "Know It All: Can Wikipedia conquer expertise?", *The New Yorker*, July 24, 2006, https://www.newyorker.com/magazine/2006/07/31/know-it-all

14 *Wiki* is the Hawaiian word for quick.

revise them in a collaborative manner. Wikipedia, the new online encyclo-pedia, became an instant hit; and within a year, it had almost a thousand times more articles that Nupedia had during a similar time span.[15] Wales reportedly invested $100,000 he had earned from BOMIS to develop this enterprise.[16] In 2003 he registered it as a non-profit which it remains to this day. Administrative costs — for example, monthly payment for band-width — are met by donations and fund drives.[17] Since contributors are not paid, how and why do they contribute? An article marking the first anniversary of Wikipedia noted: "Many participants are attracted to the notion that they are contributing to a completely free resource that can be used worldwide."[18] This faithful community has grown over the years and, for some people, it is the most spectacular achievement of the founder of Wikipedia. It demonstrates that there are enough people in the world who care about producing reliable knowledge that must be made readily available to the wideworld.

While currently the English Wikipedia enjoys over forty million users, the count of "active users", those who contribute and edit, stands at a little over one hundred thirty-two thousand.[19] This faithful community of anon-ymous volunteers is the force behind Wikipedia. They take knowledge creation seriously, and enjoy it.

---

15 Cooke, "Wikipedia Is the Last Best Place".

16 "Bomis," *Wikipedia.org*, https://en.wikipedia.org/wiki/Bomis. Martin Hickman and Geneviève Roberts, "Wikipedia under the microscope over accuracy," The Independent, February 13, 2006, https://www.independent.co.uk/news/media/wikipedia-under-the-microscope-over-accuracy-466444.html.

17 Peter S. Vogel, "In 2011, Google cofounder Sergey Brin and his wife Anne Wojcicki (23andMe cofounder) used their Brin Wojcicki Foundation to grant US$500,000 to the Wikimedia Foundation. The Wikimedia Foundation kicked off its 8th annual fundraiser on November 16, 2011, and raised $1.2 million the first day." "The Mysterious Workings of Wikis: Who Owns What?", *E-Commerce Times*, October 10, 2012. https://www.ecommercetimes. com/story/76351.html.

18 Michael Singer, "Free Encyclopedia Project Celebrates Year One," Siliconvalley. internet. com, January 16, 2002, https://web.archive.org/web/20030316082912/ http://siliconvalley. internet.com/news/article.php/ 3531_956641. Accessed on October 14, 2020.

19 Across its 303 languages, Wikipedia has over 92,045,028 registered users and more than 308,167 active users. "Wikipedia," *Wikipedia.org*, https://en.wikipedia. org/wiki/Wikipedia. Accessed on October 17, 2020.

In his 2005 TED Talk, Jimmy Wales said: "The type of people who were drawn to writing an encyclopedia for fun tend to be pretty smart people"[20] and Wikipedia and its founders deserve credit for making that possible.

NEUTRALITY: AN ANTIDOTE TO NIHILISM?

It is natural, however, that "pretty smart people" from diverse backgrounds and unknown to one another sooner or later find themselves in conflict. They may be opinionated and sometimes belligerent. They will wish to add their own slant to the entries they created. So how does Wikipedia handle the problem of bias? The editorial policy that drives these volunteers is the ideal called NPOV, or Neutral Point Of View. In the talk mentioned above, Wales clarified that Wikipedia has chosen to do away with the notions of truth and objectivity and has opted for neutrality:

> [T]he biggest and the most important thing is our neutral point of view policy. This is something that I set down, from the very beginning, as a core principle of the community that's completely not debatable. It's a social concept of cooperation, so we don't talk a lot about truth and objectivity. The reason for this is if we say we're only going to write the "truth" about some topic, that doesn't do us a damn bit of good of figuring out what to write, because I don't agree with you about what's the truth. But we have this jargon term of neutrality, which has its own long history within the community, which basically says, any time there's a controversial issue, Wikipedia itself should not take a stand on the issue. We should merely report on what reputable parties have said about it. So this neutrality policy is really important for us because it empowers a community that is very diverse to come together and actually get some work done.[21]

An encyclopedia by definition must resist bias. But no encyclopedia can claim to have achieved absolute neutrality, nor perhaps it is desirable in all cases. Neutrality, that is, giving space to both sides of a controversial topic, can often become an escape from responsibility of making a fair judgement. British journalist Martin Bell, for instance, thinks that neutrality sometimes obscures the element fairness:

20 Jimmy Wales, "The Birth of Wikipedia," TEd.com, TEDGlobal 2005, July 17, 2005, https://www.ted.com/talks/jimmy_wales_on_the_birth_of_wikipedia/transcript.

21 ibid

> There is a distinction to be drawn between fairness and neutrality.
> Fairness is the bedrock of good journalism … But neutrality? Neu-
> trality is a snare and a delusion. It makes no judgements. It stands
> aside as an equal distance between good and evil.[22]

A twenty-first-century online encyclopedia is not merely a storehouse of information. The ever-alert Wikipedia contributors update the entries in real time and thus the encyclopedia functions as a media outlet as well, confirming or debunking any alleged development in a particular area. Many people do turn to Wikipedia to check the entry the moment, let's say, a celebrity dies or any corporate takeover is announced.

The more complex developments, however, can seriously test the limits of neutrality. In many such cases, neutrality can even be an eyewash. If someone were to argue that he or she presents both sides of the story and gives relevant facts to support both sides, one may still ask, "How do you select facts and prioritize their presentation?" Besides, in a highly charged intellectual environment in which knowledge is reduced to being a cudgel to beat your opponent with, what role does a "neutral" encyclo-pedic entry play?

The entry on the controversial topic "Intelligent Design" (ID) might il-lustrate the difficulties that an encyclopedia like Wikipedia runs into. How should one approach a genuine scientific controversy such as the origin of life? Did life emerge in a random accident or does a living cell exhibit deliberate design? Wikipedia editors often discard scientific neutrality and promote anti-theistic bias, which is evident in their entry on ID.

In an article he wrote in 2018, Jewish writer David Klinghoffer, a Senior Fellow of the Discovery Institute (DI), announced that Wikipedia was the "winner" of DI's tongue-in-cheek "Censor of the Year" award, for their alleged "lies" about Intelligent Design.[23] The "masked mob" who edits the entries had made it almost impossible to counter negative descriptions

---

22 Quoted in Jenny Taylor, "From Prophetic Press to Fake News," in *This Book Changed Everything*, vol. 1 The Bible's Amazing Impact on Our World. Vishal Man-galwadi, (Sought After Media, 2019), 265.

23 David Klinghoffer, "Wikipedia Earns Censor of the Year Tag for Botching Evo-lution, Intelligent Design," CSN News, February 12, 2018, https://www.cnsnews.com/commentary/   david-klinghoffer/wikipedia-earns-censor-year-tag-botch-ing-evolution-intelligent-design.

of Intelligent Design. In an earlier article, Klinghoffer had written about Larry Sanger's opinion on the Wikipedia entry on ID. Sanger admitted that he didn't agree with ID himself, but even he found that the Wikipedia entry on that topic was "appallingly biased". He lamented, "I completely despair of persuading Wikipedians of the error of their ways." Klinghoffer noted, "a masked mob of pseudonymous trolls has taken over and the public's 'latent demand' (which Sanger said there was for neutrality) is permanently blocked from being satisfied."[24]

The opening sentence of the entry on intelligent design has been a topic of frenzied discussion on Wikipedia "Talk" page. Klinghoffer quotes it in his articles as follows:

> "Intelligent design (ID) is a religious argument for the existence of God, presented by its proponents as "an evidence-based scientific theory about life's origins", [sic] though it has been discredited as pseudoscience."

That was in 2018. In 2020, the opening line has changed to the following:
> Intelligent design (ID) is a pseudoscientific argument for the existence of God, presented by its proponents as "an evidence-based scientific theory about life's origins".

From "religious argument" to a "pseudoscientific argument", the pejorative introduction has only intensified the bias. Wikipedia editors and contributors pretend that they are only reflecting the mainstream scientific review, though if one were to compare the opening line with that in another encyclopedia, such as *Encyclopedia Britannica*, he or she would see that it is possible to introduce a complex and controversial topic without conveying explicit bias.[25]

Wikipedia has decided to discard its tradition of neutrality on moral controversies where the secular mind is most confused. These include

24 David Klinghoffer,"Wikipedia Co-Founder Blasts 'Appallingly Biased' Wikipedia Entry on Intelligent Design" *Evolution News*, Dec. 12, 2017, https://evolution-news.org/2017/12/ wikipedia-co-founder-calls-wikipedia-entry-on-intelligent-design-appallingly-biased/ Accessed on October 18, 2020.

25 "Intelligent design (ID), argument intended to demonstrate that living organisms were created in more or less their present forms by an "intelligent designer,"" says Encyclopedia Britannica. https://www.britannica.com/topic/intelligent-design Accessed on October 18, 2020.

questions of gender identity and same-sex marriage. Recently it was reported that Wikipedia has been gagging its editors who support traditional marriage.[26]

This religious bias is expressed everywhere. Take for example the Wikipedia entry on Scottish missionary to India, Alexander Duff (1806–1878). Duff made an indelible mark on India's higher education. He promoted Western education in English medium in India when literacy level in the country was abysmally low. Hindu social reformers were already campaigning for English education. Duff founded one of the most important colleges in Calcutta: Free Church Institution (later known as the Scottish Church College).

Incidentally, his two colleagues, John Wilson in Bombay and John Anderson in Madras founded two other pioneering colleges in those cities respectively. These colleges made it possible for India to get its first three universities of Calcutta, Madras and Bombay. These universities did not teach. They were created to examine students and grant degrees. In spite of a few exceptions, most students studied in institutions pioneered by missionaries such as Duff. Colleges that followed Duff's example graduated the leaders who built modern India.

The Wikipedia article, however, presents Duff, a builder of modern India, as a failed missionary. His educational initiatives led to very few conversions. But how should missionary influence be judged? By number of converts? Or also by the change in social attitudes and philosophic outlook of the culture? Duff was primarily a missionary who wanted all humans, including Indians, to seek and worship the true God. He believed that it was sinful for Hindus to see their "low-caste" neighbors as untouchables, or consider human suffering a just reward for past Karma. He wanted us to believe that all men were created equal and that God had commanded us to love our neighbors as ourselves. Did Duff really fail? Yes, casteism and untouchability, female infanticide, child-marriage and polygamy outlived Duff's English-medium education. But one could counter argue that Hebrew slaves' march towards Promised Land outlived Moses. In any case, prominent Indians such as Mahatma Gandhi agreed with Duff and other

---

26 See Anugrah Kumar, "Wikipedia bans editors from expressing support for traditional marriage," The Christian Post, October 18, 2020, https://www.christianpost.com/news/wikipedia-bans-editors-support-traditional-marriage.html Accessed on October 18, 2020.

missionaries that high-caste Hindus needed to see the lower-caste as God's children, and that modern India needed to be rebuilt on the biblical belief in human equality.

Consequently, independent India did embrace Duff's biblical beliefs as its official laws and policies. Wikipedia's religious bias judges Duff as a failure because Hinduism has proven itself to be very "resilient." It's faith in myths continues to overshadow our quest for truth. The question is: Should Wikipedia's readers rejoice in the "resilience" of our sacred traditions of caste, Karma, and public killing of cow traders? Or should they learn to acknowledge the continuing mission that Duff began?

Given the logic within which Wikipedia operates, it is futile to expect it to break free from its own biases. On many contemporary topics, Wikipedia admits an entry if its subject is spoken of in the established mass media. The statements made in the entry must be verifiable, which means that there should be hyperlinks connecting a particular statement to a familiar news source. This often means that newspaper articles become the "reputable parties" that determine how an entry will be referenced, how it will be presented, and whether it will remain on the site at all or not. Let's imagine there is an open meeting where a Christian public figure is speaking on matters of sexual purity such as abstinence, heterosexual marriage and monogamy. Four or five newspapers decide to cover that sensational event. These newspapers, which promote sexual promiscuousness in their columns and advertisements almost daily, choose to send their finest reporters. These reporters have all been trained in universities that celebrate sexual perversion. The message of responsible sexual behavior in the public meeting would appear on the pages of those newspapers but only after being filtered through the biases of the reporters and the newspapers. So now the Wikipedia article would have enough references to paint the Christian preacher as homophobic. Thus, the policy of "neutrality" and appeals to "reputable parties", in reality, paint a very biased, intolerant picture where a wise man or woman is not even allowed to present their case.

An online encyclopedia that reflects cultural biases in its entries, it is no antidote to nihilistic despair that attends the knowledge-is-power equation. The Enlightenment ideal of neutrality is ill-equipped to meet the challenges of postmodernism, relativism and nihilism.

III - ENCYCLOPEDIA: A CHRISTIAN IDEA

The preceding section should not be read as a tirade against Wikipedia. It does not impute any deliberate conspiracy to the great encyclopedia of our time. The crisis of Wikipedia is in-built. Wikipedia is not able to make good its own principle of neutrality because it must operate under the spirit of the age, the zeitgeist. "Neutrality" is determined by the current academic trend. Wikipedia, then, is inescapably caught up within its own deterministic universe, unable to carry the weight of either truth or neutrality.

So our call for a new online encyclopedia is not meant to disparage Wikipedia. The site is a great success story. It is an inspiration that shows that it is possible to build a huge online library with minimal resources, smart use of technology, and with input from a volunteer community that comes together for the sheer joy of knowledge creation.

Most people do not know that the first efforts at building a modern encyclopedia were Christian in their nature and origin. Exactly four hundred years ago, in 1620, English essayist, politician, philosopher and scientist, Francis Bacon (1561–1626), published his masterful work on scientific method *Novum Organum* (The New Tool, or Method). Bacon had been fascinated with the idea of credible knowledge. How do we learn what is actually true? How do we know we are not merely repeating the errors of our predecessors? What is the basis of true knowledge?

Bacon found a clue to the answer to these questions in Mathew 22:29, "Ye err, not knowing the Scriptures nor the power of God." He included this verse in *Organum* to sum up his argument that we can acquire knowledge because it is God himself who wishes us to be knowledgeable. And for that purpose science[27] and religion are designed by God to work in unity:

> But truly, if one thinks about it, natural philosophy, after the word of God, is the strongest remedy for superstition and the most proven food of faith. Therefore it has deservedly been granted to religion as its most faithful handmaid; for one manifests the will of God, the other his power. He was not mistaken who said: 'ye do err, not knowing the scriptures and the power of God', mixing

---

27 Science, that is, human knowledge gained through reliable tools and methods for observation, classification and interpretation.
Bacon uses the term natural philosophy.

and uniting the revelation of his will and the thought of his power in an indivisible bond.[28]

About quarter of a century earlier, he had chosen this same verse—"Ye err, not knowing the Scriptures nor the power of God"—as the epigraph for his meditation on heresy, which began as follows:

> This canon [Mt 22:29] is the mother of all canons against heresy. The cause of error is twofold: ignorance of the will of God, and ignorance or superficial consideration of the power of God. The will of God is more revealed through the Scriptures: *Search the Scriptures*; his power more through his creatures: *Behold and consider the creatures*.[29]

For a quarter of a century, it seems, this verse was unpacking its radical potential in Bacon's subconscious mind. This insight from the New Testament convinced him that errors that plagued all spiritual and material knowledge can be rooted out by delving deep into the mysteries of the scripture and nature, that is, the power of God. The key words are, of course, *search* and *consider*. Revelation of God in the Bible and in nature had to be freshly studied by clearing the thicket of traditional human opinion. God himself commanded Adam to observe nature and classify that observation as knowledge. One effect of the Fall, however, was that man's attention was shifted from creation of God to creation of his own fancies.[30] He marveled not at God's creation, giving Him the glory, but revelled in the idols[31] — that is theories and constructs — of his own mind. And over time an accretion of human opinions killed individual initiative to break newer grounds. Knowledge was reduced to merely an agreement with the prevailing opinion. In Bacon's time the Aristotelian paradigm ruled the Western scholarship. Bacon attacked the syllogistic theory of Aristotle and proposed the inductive method as a better alternative. A new paradigm

28 Francis Bacon, *The New Organon*, ed. Lisa Jardine and Michael Silverthorne (Cambridge: Cambridge University Press, 2003), 75.

29 Francis Bacon, "Of Heresies," *The Works of Francis Bacon*, ed. James Spedding, Robert Leslie Ellis, Douglas Denon Heath, (Cambridge: Riverside Press), 14: 94.

30 "After you had turned to view the works which your hands had made, you saw that all things were very good, and you rested. But man, turning to the works which his hands have made, saw that all things were vanity and vexation of spirit, and has had no rest." Bacon, *New Organon*, p. 24

31 Not to be confused with Bacon's idea of Four Idols.

of knowledge thus emerged that encouraged observation of phenomena, experimentation and tabulation of data as primary means towards building knowledge, as opposed to the Aristotelian system of deductive reasoning. And a new method made it necessary to rethink the project of knowledge production. Bacon's ambitious project *The Great Instauration* or The Great Renewal (of all human knowledge) paved the way for reimagining human knowledge systems. Significantly, Bacon also suggested that study of creation through science also draws man closer to God:

> [I]n physics likewise I maintain this — that a little natural philosophy and the first entrance into it inclines men's opinions to Atheism; but on the other hand much natural philosophy and a deeper progress into it brings men's minds about again to religion.[32]

One understated but fundamental aspect of Bacon's thinking was theism. Tacit belief in the goodness of God allowed him to trust the capacities of the human mind. Aware of reason's role in distorting reality, Bacon proceeded with confidence toward his project of knowledge creation because God wishes to reveal truth to the seeker. Despite its limitations, the human mind is able to comprehend the universe, and overcome effects of the Fall, because God is good. Knowledge is not a trick played by a capricious pantheon of demigods but the revelation of a loving Father. Human knowledge is never to be divorced from its anchor in the goodness of God.[33] Despite all its brilliance, the Indian mind — Hindu, Buddhist or Jain — could not envisage an encyclopedia, the integration of all knowledge, precisely because the Indian worldview did not believe that the human mind can know truth or that human words can articulate truth. This is because there was no verbal revelation by a benevolent God that gave the confidence that the mind was made in God's image and could integrate knowledge in a systematic way. This idea of integration of all

---

32 Bacon, "Of Atheism", *Works*, 93.

33 "Hence the teaching which cleanses the mind to make it receptive to truth consists of three refutations: a refutation of philosophies; a refutation of proofs; and a refutation of natural human reason. When we have dealt with these, and clarified the part played by the nature of things and the part played by the nature of the mind, we believe that, *with the help of God's goodness*, we will have furnished and adorned the bedchamber for the marriage of the mind and the universe. In the wedding hymn *we should pray that men may see* born from this union the assistants that they need and a lineage of discoveries which may in some part conquer and subdue the misery and poverty of man." Bacon, *The New Organon*, p. 19. (emphasis added)

knowledge—which was later given the name *pansophia* by Comenius, and which became the fundamental philosophy of encyclopedia—was rooted in the goodness of God as seen in the Bible.

Thus Bacon's new scientific method called for a new project of knowledge creation. His confidence in human ability to know, and his firm conviction that knowledge draws men closer to "religion," formed an intellectual atmosphere in which people like Alsted breathed.

Johann Alsted (1588–1638) was a German theologian who was consumed by the idea of presenting all learning in philosophy in the form of an encyclopedia. His aim to gather and integrate knowledge was similar to that of Bacon, namely, to provide complete knowledge to humankind and undo the effect of the Fall on learning. Pursuit of knowledge, in his Christian worldview, was a divine discipline. Alsted was also influenced by the French logician and philosopher, Petrus Ramus (1515–1572), another scholar who opposed Aristotle and called for undoing his power over philosophy. Unfortunately he was killed in the St. Bartholomew's Day massacre in 1572. However, Alsted agreed with Ramus and Bacon that God's truth is consistent, and that biblical special revelation and natural general revelation combine for the benefit of humanity. An encyclopedia would testify to that conviction.

Classical, Medieval and Renaissance thinkers had also conceived of a "circle of subjects" to aid learning but the patently Christian vision of Francis Bacon and Johann Alsted marks a watershed. While Bacon's scientific method made the need of an encyclopedia urgent and inevitable, Alsted showed how this need might materialize.[34] Alsted's encyclopedia, published in 1630, was a thoroughly Christian enterprise: "The Puritan students of England and New England read it, and the Catholic students of France found it valuable."[35] Alsted's Czech student John Amos Comenius

---

34 "Johann Alsted's *Encyclopaedia* of 1630 was one of the first to use this word in a title; but it is telling that while respecting the legacy of the Greek concept, Alsted enlarged its compass, explaining that his weighty (and wordy) four-folio-volume work offered the 'methodical systematization of all things which ought to be learned by men in this life. In short, it is the totality of knowledge.' Especially after Francis Bacon's call for a quest for 'new' knowledge, the problem of an expanding and exploding encyclopedia was apparent." Richard Yeo, "Lost Encyclopedias: Before and After Enlightenment." Book History, 2007, 10:49.

35 Robert G. Glouse, "Johann Heinrich Alsted and English Millennialism," Cont >

(1592–1670) was likewise consumed by a passion to integrate all knowledge. Inspired by Alsted's initiative, Comenius attempted to revolutionize education. His vision of *pansophia* (lit. temple of wisdom) mentioned above was a bold attempt to integrate all knowledge. Comenius believed that since God knows everything being omniscient, it must be possible to integrate all knowledge and teach all knowledge to everyone. It does not seem amiss to quote Wikipedia on the breadth of his ambition:

> Comenius introduced a number of educational concepts and innovations including pictorial textbooks written in native languages instead of Latin, teaching based in gradual development from simple to more comprehensive concepts, lifelong learning with a focus on logical thinking over dull memorization, equal opportunity for impoverished children, education for women, and universal and practical instruction.

So Christians like Bacon, who initiated a new method; Alsted, who synthesized knowledge; and Comenius, who began to build a new pedagogical architecture, gave birth to the modern world of fierce commitment to seeking all truth, integrating all knowledge and disseminating truth to the masses.[36] Their vision, however, could not be fully realized because of Europe's Thirty Years' War (1618–48). But these men, with an all-encompassing vision of knowledge, laid the foundations of an intellectual rebirth of the West. The idea of integration of knowledge had taken a deep root in the minds of most Christian scholars of that time. Isaac Barrow (1630–1677), an English theologian and mathematician, who was also the teacher of Isaac Newton, once said: "He will be a lame Scholar, who hath not an insight into many kinds of knowledge, that he can hardly be a good Scholar, who is not a general one."[37]

Alsted's encyclopedia inspired a variety of European thinkers to create such a storehouse of knowledge and information. A French Catholic priest Louis Moréri published his encyclopedia *Le Grand Dictionnaire historique* in 1674. It was the French Enlightenment thinkers, however, who wrested the initiative to create the most popular encyclopedia of the

---

35 *Harvard Theological Review*, 62 (20) (April 1969), 194

36 Samuel Hartlib and William Ames in England were other significant links in this chain of great integrationalists. In the USA, Jonathan Edwards carried on this integration of knowledge.

37 Cited in Yeo, p. 49.

period. But while the biblical worldview inspires man to integrate natural and supernatural knowledge, Enlightenment encyclopedists used natural reason to attack the supernatural authority of God. The next great encyclopedia to appear was the *Encyclopedia Britannica*, and it is no surprise that it germinated in the Puritan-soaked haven of learning, that is, in Scotland.[38]

What has happened to Christian thinking and scholarship since? Mark Noll observes that "serious academic research guided by explicit Christian norms has been thin on the ground for at least two hundred years."[39] The breadth and scope of Christian intellectual vision has been shrinking for over two centuries; it has ceded much ground to secular philosophies and allowed the old thicket of opinion to again dominate the intellectual landscape. Political correctness now ensures that only "acceptable" and politically correct "woke" views are considered as knowledge. Theory, with capital T, now dominates academia. Facts are no longer important; "story" is. Time is ripe for another encyclopedic moment.

A global network of professors, scholars, professionals and writers must come together to undo the grip of Critical Theory on our knowledge systems and stitch together an alternative compendium of knowledge. Every topic under and over the sun should be discussed fairly, with a focus on the search for truth. We are faced with the information explosion but there is hardly a consensus on the purpose and value of all this information. There is no moral or any other compass that guides our relationship with knowledge. Our children are as likely to be lost in a library as they would in a jungle, if they do not understand that we as a species are searching for truth. As other contributors to this volume have repeatedly pointed out, education is part of the holy mandate of the Church. Experienced and knowledgeable members of every denomination and every Christian congregation contribute not just change into the offering basket, but vital knowledge to brothers, sisters, and unbelievers around the world. Church — in a broader sense of the word — is the ecosystem in which comprehensive learning will take place; in which new methodologies will be developed and perfected, new encyclopedic works will appear and a new pedagogical framework will be established.

---

38 The next chapter by Giftson Selladurai gives a very informative account of the rise and fall of *Encyclopedia Britannica*.

39 Mark A. Noll, *Jesus Christ and the Life of Mind*, Eerdmans, 2011, p. 43

The desire to integrate, classify and preserve knowledge was long a Judeo-Christian concern. God revealed Himself in nature and, from the days of Adam, who named each animal species (a job which biologists have yet to complete!), humankind rightly feels obliged to gather, tabulate and disseminate knowledge. A renaissance of Christian scholarship must express itself in an encyclopedia that is committed to Truth, Goodness, Beauty and Wisdom. "Neutrality" as we have seen is itself a bias which hides biases: it cannot help seekers of truth. A Christian encyclopedia must present all sides of a controversy fairly — but should not simply declare which is right; it must establish the truth. Wikipedia provides a wonderful proof that creating an online encyclopedia need not be hugely expensive or involve rocket science. The global body of Christ has the capacity to develop something better. What is needed is the passionate urgency to "fill the earth with the knowledge of truth."

Chapter 9

God's Mandate Becomes the e-Mandate

Giftson Selladurai[1]

1. The Great Commission

Having had the privilege of being born in a nation where one of Jesus disciples, Thomas was sent as a first missionary and being born in a rural city just 400kms from a place where he was martyred, our city had a huge influence and impact by lots of missionaries during the 1800s and 1900s. Infact, even my parents and grandparents came to know the true living God through the faithful obedience of many missionaries to "The Great Commission" of Jesus Christ.

Every night during our family prayer, my dad used to pray these words - "Lord please use my children mightily for your Kingdom purposes". We as a family grew up listening to this prayer every night. I didn't understand the meaning of it for many years even after having a personal salvation experience with Jesus. Every time I read the following verses from Matthew 28:18-20 it used to haunt me.

> *"18 Then Jesus came to them and said, "All authority in heaven and on earth has been given to me.*
>
> *19 Therefore go and make disciples of all nations, baptizing them in the name of the Father and of the Son and of the Holy Spirit,*
>
> *20 and teaching them to obey everything I have commanded you. And surely I am with you always, to the very end of the age." [2]*

I used to think the only way to be used mightily for God's Kingdom purposes is to take the bible and go around the world and preach the Gospel.

---

1 Giftson Selladurai, a first generation entrepreneur, is the co-founder and current CEO of Ruah Tech, an IT solutions company, that has its office in three countries globally and is headquartered in Melbourne.

2 Matthew 28:18-20 NIV - https://www.biblegateway.com

I was prepared for it because I had believed it was the meaning of the prayer my dad had been praying every night over his children. My father was one of the C-level executives in a fastly growing private national bank in India. He was very devoted to his work. His sincerity and hard work made him to be appreciated by everyone around him. We as a family supported lots of prayer and missionary movements that were reaching the unreached. Seeing my dad be a witness in the workplace and the call to preach the Gospel as mandated in the verses Mathew 28:18-20 used to confuse me a lot. Not to mistake, I had a great passion for reaching the unreached. The book, "Taking the Gospel Across the Borders" by Rudy Lack used to be my favourite[3]. But somewhere deep within, I felt my mandate was beyond travelling to Nations and preaching the Gospel.

Growing up as a teen, the Great Commission was very close to my heart, but sadly I had understood it wrong. The wrong understanding also posed lots of questions regarding my future, ambitions and passion. But they all changed dramatically in an unexpected moment.

Shortly after finishing my undergraduate during 2008, one evening I received a YouTube video sent by my friend, and it had the title "Reclaim 7 Mountains of culture".[4] The title created a lot of curiosity that I immediately watched. It spoke about influencing the 7 mountains of culture by Loren Cunningham, Founder of YWAM. It shifted something within me. Something sprung deep within me, as if I was having a sneak peek of what Heaven would look like. I kept watching the video again and again. I ordered some books related to these and started to know more regarding what I just watched. This set a burning fire in me to understand and pursue the true mandate that Jesus has placed on my life and God's heart for the church.

This verse, 1 Corinthians 12:11 became so real and meaningful to me after understanding the mandate of Jesus Christ through fresh eyes.

All these are the work of one and the same Spirit, and he distributes them to each one, just as he determines.

3-https://www.amazon.com/BREAKTHROUGH-Taking-Gospel-Forbidden-Borders/ dp/3906589048

4-https://www.youtube.com/watch?v=dUvoFJbnaak&ab_channel=ProtectorofMidgard

Yes, God through His Spirit distributes different gifts and roles to each of us towards fulfilling the greater mandate which is His great commission. With more than 2000 years of the power of the gospel at work, the question to ask is, "What does His mandate look like in the 21st Century?" Please read Matthew 28:18-20 once again. We know how to disciple individuals, but the mandate is about the whole nations. How do we fulfill this mandate? How do we disciple nations?

I would like to propose, it's indispensable that our perspective of God's mandate to the church should become **e-mandate**. It's time we harness the power of technology in fulfilling the great commission. Further sections of this chapter will elaborate what this e-mandate looks like, what we can learn from history, the challenges that are ahead of us and the need to fulfill HIS e-mandate in our generation.

2. Gospel through Technology

Technology has always been at the helm of cultural change in any civilisation. As scary as every leap feels, we can be confident that as human beings created in God's image, innovation and creativity is at the heart of God's DNA in us.

The moment we mention the word "Technology", millennials and many others immediately think and relate it to the Internet. But technology is broadly defined as a set of techniques, skills, methods, and processes used in the accomplishment of certain objectives.[5]

Now this makes us wonder how the Gospel has travelled through history with the use of Technology, and the undeniable need for Technology to play a key role in our e-mandate of discipling nations. Saint Irenaeus said, "The Glory of God is man fully alive ".[6] The question to ask is, what does a fully alive man look like in the 21st century with all the innovations that are faster paced than life itself.

The evolution of technology and education cannot be separated. Throughout history mankind has used prime technologies available to educate the current generation. Right from the ancient times when language was

---

5 https://en.wikipedia.org/wiki/Technology

6 https://en.wikiquote.org/wiki/Irenaeus

formed and stones were used as a platform to transcribe, to the print media in the 15th century, to the electronic media in the 18th century, we are now at the cusp of what is called the "future tech", which comprises Artificial Intelligence, Augmented reality and Robotics where the 'merging' of man and machine seems inevitable.

Modern technology has disrupted accessibility of information and made communication seamless across continents. Remote villages and backward cities that can no longer afford university buildings and expensive scholars are filled with hope through the world wide web (internet) that has opened the portals of education to every household.

With Technology pacing leaps and bounds faster than any growth mankind has ever seen in a short duration of time, traditional universities and educational institutions should be re-invented to carry the e-mandate and great commission of Jesus Christ. Let us see the origin of traditional universities. It's empowering to look back into history and know that it was the Church and the Christian mind that pioneered the idea of University. Will the church lead *The Third Education Revolution* in the forefront and take up the mandate of Jesus Christ as its e-mandate?

3. Traditional University vs Online University

The first brick and mortar university, was founded in Bologna, Italy in 1088. The Latin phrase *universitas magistrorum et scholarium* indicated an association of teachers and scholars.[7] The British empires and sooner other European empires started to use this educational model around the world. Just as Islamic invasions ended India's Buddhist learning in the second millennium, the barbarian conquests virtually ended Europe's classical education in the first. Though never completely lost, education was so depressing that the fifth to the ninth centuries are sometimes called Europe's dark ages. Illiteracy was the norm in most of the world, until the missionary movement began transforming our world.[8]

Church has played a key role in education throughout history. The famous Harvard University established by the puritans within the first decade

7-https://dailyhistory.org/How_did_universities_develop%3F

8-https://www.amazon.com.au/Book-that-Made-Your-World-ebook/dp/B004Z70982

of arriving in America is a good example to relate how Bible inspired universities taught secular subjects. It's the biblical worldview that turned information into meaningful knowledge and wisdom. Till date almost every nation spends billions of dollars towards education through various programmes and by building Universities and colleges.

Just a decade ago, the Australian Government came up with an initiative called "Building the Education Revolution - Primary Schools for the 21st Century"[9] The program, totalling $16.2 billion has three elements:[10]

• Primary Schools for the 21st Century ($14.2b): providing new and refurbished halls, libraries and classrooms.
• Science and Language Centres for 21st Century Secondary Schools ($821.8m): providing new and refurbished science laboratories and language learning centres.
• National School Pride program ($1.28b): providing new and refurbished covered outdoor learning areas, shade structures, sporting facilities and other environmental programs.

It's interesting to note that most of the funding was for the establishment and maintenance of the brick and mortar schools and learning centres.

Doesn't this make our education very expensive? Is there an alternative way to promote education in the current times we live in. Innovation and positive disruption are inevitable as time progresses. With all the advancement of technology at hand, we are ripe for a new education revolution.

The first new and fully online university was founded in 1994 as the Open University of Catalonia, headquartered in Barcelona, Spain. In 1999 Jones International University was launched as the first fully online university accredited by a regional accrediting association in the US. Between 2000 and 2008, enrollment in distance education courses increased rapidly in almost every country in both developed and developing countries.[11] The internet boom has created unparalleled and fast tracked options to educate anyone anywhere in the world.

9-https://www.anao.gov.au/work/performance-audit/building-education-revolution-primary-schools-21st-century

10-https://en.wikipedia.org/wiki/Building_the_Education_Revolution

11-https://en.wikipedia.org/wiki/Distance_education

4. Embracing the Technology Revolution - A Case Study:

I would like to take you through a journey with the history of encyclopedia britannica and what lessons we can learn from someone who became a casualty for missing the technology revolution in their times.

Since the first publication of the Encyclopedia Britannica in late 1700s, it has been seen as a huge reliable book for reference of knowledge.

The first edition of the Britannica was published one section at a time, over a three-year period, beginning in 1768. The three-volume set, which was completed in 1771, quickly sold out. Encouraged by this success, the publishers issued the second edition in 10 volumes (1777-84)[12]

In the 1980s Microsoft approached Britannica to collaborate on a CD-ROM encyclopedia, but the offer was declined. Senior managers at Britannica were confident in their control of the market and that their healthy profits would continue. At this time complete sets of the encyclopedia were priced between $1,500 and $2,200, and the product was considered part of a luxury brand with an impeccable reputation handed down from generation to generation.

The management did not believe that a CD-ROM could adequately compete or supplement their business. Microsoft responded by using content from Funk & Wagnalls Standard Encyclopedia to create what is now known as Encarta. In 1990 the Britannica's sales reached an all-time high of $650 million, but Encarta, released in 1993, soon became a software staple with almost every computer purchase and Britannica's market share plummeted. Britannica countered by offering a CD-ROM version of their product, although it could not generate the print version's $500–600 in sales commissions. Britannica decided to charge $995 for just the CD-ROM, while bundling a free disc with the print version, hoping that including the CD-ROM would persuade buyers to stay with the brand. In 1994 an online version was launched, with subscriptions for sale for $2,000. By 1996 the price of the CD-ROM had dropped to $200, and sales had dropped to $325 million—about half of their 1990 levels. Only 55,000 hard copy versions were sold in 1994, compared with 117,000 in 1990, and sales later fell to 20,000.

12-https://web.archive.org/web/20061020084752/http://corporate.britannica.com/com- pany_info.html

Facing financial pressure, Britannica was bought in 1996 by Swiss financier Jacob Safra for $135 million, a fraction of its book value. Safra introduced severe price-cutting measures to try to compete with Encarta, even offering the entire reference free of charge for a time (around 18 months, from October 1999 to March 2001) on the Internet. Currently, Britannica co-operates with Taiwan companies to provide a Traditional Chinese-English bilingual version encyclopedia on the internet according to the 2002 edition. It is the first bilingual product of Britannica.

Former editor-in-chief Robert McHenry believes that Britannica failed to exploit its early advantages in the market for electronic encyclopedias. Britannica had, for example, published the second multimedia encyclopedia titled Compton's MultiMedia Encyclopedia as early as 1989 (the first one being the Academic American Encyclopedia published by Grolier), but did not launch Britannica CD until 1994, a year after Microsoft launched their Encarta encyclopedia. McHenry believes these failures were due to a reluctance among senior management to fully embrace the new technology, caused largely by the overriding influence of the sales staff and management. The sales personnel earned commissions from door-to-door selling of the print encyclopedias, which McHenry believes led to decisions about the distribution and pricing of the electronic products being driven by the desires of the sales personnel rather than market conditions and customer expectations. After ending the publication of its print edition, which at the end supplied only 1% of the company's revenue, it hoped to transition to a CD or online version. Sales of both of these were disappointing and the inability to compete with Wikipedia.[13] Sales of the CD ended with the 2012 "Ultimate Edition".

Britannica, though a giant and pioneer for centuries missed to capitalise on the technology wave and eventually lost the battle to wikipedia which was quick to understand the market need by harnessing the power of the internet. Jorge Cauz, former president of Encyclopedia Britannica says this in his own words,

> "I had been following Wikipedia since the launch of its parent project, Nupedia, in 2000. At the time, I thought Nupedia was going nowhere, because it was trying to do exactly the same thing that Britannica was, and I knew how much editorial staff and budget it took to do that. Nupedia didn't have them. When Nupedia

---

13-https://hbr.org/2013/03/encyclopaedia-britannicas-president-on-killing-off-a-244-year-old-product

adopted the wiki technology and became Wikipedia the following year, it seemed to me like an act of desperation. Needless to say, its success was a surprise, not only to me, but to everyone I've talked to about it. As Wikipedia's articles, contributors, and visitors skyrocketed in number, and Google's search algorithm continued to reward the site with top placement, I understood that this was another game changer for Encyclopedia Britannica"

5. Future Tech & Education

Winston Churchill famously said "Those that fail to learn from history are doomed to repeat it". Like the Encyclopedia Britannica, the body of Christ will be repeating a huge mistake if the church doesn't onboard the technology revolution to train, educate and disciple young minds.

The internet boom had opened doors for remote education like none. The 1980's were the birth years of the modern internet. Before this era, the internet and online education were just research experiments. The vision for the internet was primarily based in university computer labs. But online education does find its earliest entrants in the 1980's with the first online college courses and online degrees as distance education embraces the idea of online learning. During this era, the internet reaches Europe and Asia. Infrastructure is laid down, providing for faster and more expansive internet operations and effectively opening the door for the total commercial and popular permeation of web use in the decade that would immediately follow. The early pioneers of online learning entered the league around this time, with the first accredited online college as well as the development of learning management systems (LMS) starting during the 1990s.[14]

The first version of Google search engine was developed during 1998 and this started to shift gears for online learning, research and quest for gaining knowledge online. It was just around this time wikipedia also began to gain popularity. Around 2004 Mark Zuckerburg launched Facebook, which was originally intended as a collegiate social chat site. As more and more people started using the internet to communicate and to expand their knowledge, around 2006, Khan academy was founded by an American who showed a new possibility to the world in education. Apple launched the first iPhone in 2007 and takes education straight into our hands. Youtube started "Youtube EDU" during 2009 to raise its market share in this

14-https://thebestschools.org/magazine/online-education-history/

online education space and liberty university, a private, Christian college, first launched its online degree program. More than 5.5 million students around the world enrolled in at least one online college course. All these developments were happening parallely in less than a decade and it was setting a platform for a new type of education - that is set to become the new norm in the education system. Online education has had a major impact not only on how we pursue formal education, but on how we teach, learn, and perceive knowledge.

The last decade has seen more advanced technological shifts than in any decade. The rise of Artificial Intelligence (AI) which is a merge of man and machines shows lots of impossibilities can be made possible. Initially Artificial cardiac pacemaker was considered as the highest integration of machine with man, but the recent research progress and demo by neuralink which is developing high bandwidth brain-machine interfaces[15] is truly astounding to see the boundaries of impossibilities stretched. Neuralink claims to create a future to cure blindness, deafness, paralysis, memory, stroke. Apple Inc has been working on re-visualising the world we live in today, through its augmented reality technologies.[16] Augmented reality is a thin line between our imagination and the real world. Apple, Facebook, HTC and many other companies are keen to explore AR which transforms how we work, learn, play, shop and connect with the world around us. Augmented Reality is the perfect way to visualise things that would otherwise be impossible or impractical to see.

On the other hand, the extensive use of the internet with all its advancements and the benefits around 4G, NBN, free wi-fi, satellite communications and more has equally thrown its challenges with cyber security issues around data breaches and hacking. Engineers are working round the clock to keep data secure from intruders. The recent rise of Bitcoin and Blockchain tells us the frustration people have in government controlling the currency supply and the desire to see a decentralized way towards currency trade, which they call crypto currencies. Technology keeps improving and keeps making our lives better and easier if its true potential is harnessed within the boundaries.

15-https://neuralink.com/

16-https://www.apple.com/au/augmented-reality/

With all the above rapid growth and leap of technology, how is the church going to react towards its growth and progress? It still amazes me how the same preachers and pastors who once opposed TVs and Social Media's like Facebook and Instagram are now delivering sermons and conducting prayer meetings through the same mediums. It's just that they have become mature to understand that technology by itself isn't necessarily evil but it's how we handle the progress of technology and are now seeing them as tools in our hands to build God's Kingdom. Can you see how important it is to see God's mandate as e-mandate to fulfill HIS great commission?

6. The Challenge Ahead:

Having known Dr Vishal Managalwadi personally over the last 7 years, I have been inspired to see *The Third Education Revolution* take shape and become a powerful movement. Along with a group of friends, who are committed to see God's move in the marketplace, we had the privilege of hosting Dr Vishal twice for our 3 day conference at Bangalore and Chennai over the last decade. This led to a journey of learning more from him as to how this revolution can take the world's best education to the poorest child in the remotest jungle or desert. Obviously, this cannot be done by investing in school and college buildings and hiring qualified teachers. We have to harness the available technology to achieve this goal.

But this poses one serious challenge. How much is the body of Christ willing to take up this vision in making churches as education centers? Can we fulfill this e-mandate with the possibility of using technology? To build a brick and mortar college in America costs an average of $100 million which educates approximately 5000 students a year. But with current technology at hand, that kind of investment would easily reach 500 million students across the globe beyond geographical borders. Does the wider christian leadership have such a big vision to see the future?

A recent research done in America by The Learning House and Aslanian Market Research[17] in 2014 says that more than 80% of public universities and half of private colleges offer at least one fully online program. When every university and education centers are on-boarding the technology revolution, it is imminent for the church to pace itself towards it. It is encouraging to see some minor initiatives by various para church organizations

17-https://www.learninghouse.com/wp-content/uploads/2017/09/2014-Online-College-Students-Final.pdf

towards online education, but we are way behind given the urgency of the hour and it needs a global revolution to shake the church from its slumber.

Five years back, I started a technology company along with my twin brother. We named it Ruah Tech[18] as we always believed in our e-mandate to educate, innovate, and empower young minds who are inspired to play a key role in impacting the world around us. As an organization we have always given importance to innovation and creative ideas, as we believe we have our Heavenly Father's DNA of innovation within us. Over the last many years, we have been building many innovative products and solutions. As I write we have our presence in every cutting edge technology like Augmented and Virtual Reality, Blockchain, Cyber Security, and Artificial Intelligence. We strive to be at the cutting edge of Technology. We are very grateful to the excellent team God has given us, filled with passion and purpose and we look forward to leading the technology front of such a revolution.

We need many entrepreneurs, business leaders, pastors, preachers, academic teachers, research scholars, and more to be part of this e-mandate.

7. Envisioning a Third Education Revolution:

Every action towards building God's Kingdom begins with a dream and every revolution begins with a single act of defiance to settle for anything normal outside of fulfilling His great commission.

How does it look when pastors are prepared to be educated as academic trainers and every church building becomes the center of education and excellence during the week outside the worship days. How does it look when every person in church congregation including women and children have access to the world's best education system through online portals of learning, while the importance of "how the bible was the source of inspiration that created the world we live in" is taught in parallel. Such an education revolution is possible.

With all the challenges in the education system around us and the infiltration of unrighteousness in every sphere of society, the enemy makes us feel daunted by the great work ahead of us. Many times we feel like how the frustrated prophet Habbakuk cried out, "when will you do justice to

---

18-https://ruahtech.com/home/

us Lord?" But the comfort and promise to us is in God's beautiful reply in the verse Habakkuk 2:14.

> *For the earth will be filled with the knowledge of the glory of the Lord as the waters cover the sea.*

This *Third Education Revolution* will become the modern version of Elijah not only schooling prophet Elisha but training simultaneously many more elisha's across the rural places through online education, and Jesus's teaching on parables to his chosen twelve disciples being live streamed to millions of his followers across the world. Or better still, Paul's defence of the gospel to the jews at the synagogue, explaining and proving Jesus as the messiah, being exposed to all his universal critics on a world's stage.

If the Cultural mandate of discipling all nations has to be met, it has to be embraced as an e-mandate that will pave the way for such a revolution. And as the fast pacing technology itself, we might find it surprising how rapidly through such electronic mediums, this gospel is being taken to the ends of the earth.

May the church rise up to take its place to fulfill Jesus' prayer in bringing God's kingdom on earth as it is in Heaven.

Chapter 10

C.S. Lewis College

Gayne John Anacker[1] & David M. Bastedo[2]

As noted by others in this volume, the responsibility for education ultimately belongs to the family and, by extension, to the church, which nurtures and sustains faithful families. The secular state has become an increasingly hostile supplier of this most essential service, the development of the moral and intellectual lives of our children. This hostility extends from grade school on through the university level.

Our concern is for the full range of education needed in a healthy society and, particularly for education at the university level. Today Secularization (a religious worldview by the way) has severed higher education from logic and reason. Academics specializing in their individual fields warp reality and edit history. Students often lose their way in the secular milieu of warped ideas from myopic professors. What is needed to address this hostile environment? One particular need is often overlooked. *Who has been trained to speak authoritatively of the entire sweep of Western civilization?* Given the West's growing secularization, we increasingly need Christian leaders who are prepared to respond to challenges with a strong and broad knowledge of the roots and major turning points of the civilization that has shaped our world. C.S. Lewis College intends to meet just this need. C.S. Lewis College will train Christian leaders to become deeply familiar with the cultural treasures of Western civilization. In doing so, we will celebrate the 'transcendentals — goodness, truth, and beauty — and teach the virtues, which are the heart of genuine character.

1 Dr. Gayne Anacker is a Trustee of the C.S. Lewis Foundation, which he also served as Vice President for Academic Affairs for over 20 years. In 2020, he retired from his position as Professor of Philosophy and Director of the University Honors Program at California Baptist University. He also served this institution as Dean of the College of Arts and Sciences for 15 years.

2 David Bastedo is the President of C.S. Lewis College an arm of the C.S. Lewis Foundation. He is currently Professor of Anatomy at San Bernardino Valley College in Southern California.

We are inspired by the life and legacy of C.S. Lewis. As a young man, Lewis enjoyed a remarkable classical education. He was renowned for his scholarly accomplishments. He was genial and jovial, and he loved the company of his friends. He enjoyed a good debate. He was acclaimed for his literary achievements in the realm of imagination. And, last but most important, he was a joyful follower of Jesus Christ.

In honor of our namesake, we aim to found a robustly Christian college of the liberal arts, enabling young people to study and discuss classic texts; enjoy ideas and the arts together; seek goodness, truth, beauty, and virtue; practice hospitality; and worship the living God who is the Source of all good things. This is the vision that animates the founding of C.S. Lewis College.

How Did We Get Here?

Our vision began in 1972, in the mind of Dr. J. Stanley Mattson. He was concerned to provide an answer to the shrewd challenge (prescient in light of our present crisis) presented by Harry Blamires in his 1963 book *The Christian Mind*. Blamires, a former student of Lewis at Oxford, opened his book with this startling declaration: *"There is no longer a Christian mind"* (emphasis added). When serious scholars of any academic discipline meet—whether on campus or at conferences—a cacophony of diverse and sometimes radical voices could be heard. Scholars of many persuasions planned programs, selected speakers, and smothered participants with promotional materials. Christian scholars, however, were nowhere to be seen, let alone heard. Blamires said that
> "Today there is no public pool of discourse fed by Christianly committed thought on the world we live in" (p. 13).

In light of this challenging situation, Mattson asked this hypothetical question: if Christians were to be allowed "a place at the table" alongside secular leaders in order to discuss the course of civilization and how future challenges might be met (as we had been hotly demanding), *would we have anything to say?* Mattson agreed with Blamires that we might not have much to say. That spring, he convened a retreat at Covenant Presbyterian Church in Simsbury, CT, inviting friends and scholars who shared his concern. The consensus of this retreat was that Stan should, with the help of those gathered, launch an interdisciplinary, "merely Christian" community of higher learning. At the time he was a 36-year-old Assistant Professor of

History at Gordon College, Wenham, MA. He would soon leave Gordon to begin the decades-long quest to found the institution that we now refer to as C.S. Lewis College.

Stan Mattson founded the C.S. Lewis Foundation in 1986. By then a plan had emerged to found a college in which to model strategies to engage the secular world of ideas and arts from a robust and creative Christian perspective, following Lewis's example of 'friendly persuasion." A year later, Dr. Mattson and 20 others met for five days at St. Andrew's Priory in Southern California to develop the conceptual framework for the college. Among others, Christian philosopher Dallas Willard (University of Southern California) and Paul Ford, Roman Catholic theologian (and noted Lewis expert) participated.

Attendees hammered out the foundation's "mere Christian" statement of faith, which the college would share. They determined that the college would be a Christian "Great Books College," with a school of visual and performing arts, to be named in honor of Lewis.

Starting in 1988, the Foundation began producing its signature triennial Summer Institutes in Oxford and Cambridge, England, now known as the Oxbridge conferences (10 institutes so far, and counting). These conferences have varied in length from nine to fourteen days. The first two were held in Oxford, the third was held in Cambridge, and all the rest in both cities and universities (since Lewis lived and worked in both). These events were intended to build a constituency for the founding of the College, as well as to model and test the curriculum, pedagogy and ethos to be implemented therein.

From 2009-2011 a major effort was made to bring the College into operation as a residential, undergraduate school. Those efforts ultimately fell short, but an enormous amount of concrete planning was carried out, ready to be capitalized upon at a later date.

In 2013, the College was legally incorporated in the state of California as a Christian not-for-profit institution of higher education for the public benefit. In 2019 an application was made to the IRS for 501(c)3 tax exempt status; receipt of this status is anticipated any day.

Over the years hundreds of people have contributed prayer, labor, and treasure to realize the vision of this college. We are deeply grateful for this generous support, and continue to seek funds to select and establish a campus, and commence operations. For now, it is our privilege to share the exciting vision for transformative education that has developed.

Ultimately, we envision both an undergraduate program and multiple graduate degree programs. The CS Lewis Foundation, the parent organization to the college, has determined that the most effective way to commence the operations is with a graduate degree, the Master of Arts in Humanities, offered through a low-residency program with internet-based enhancement. The college is now completing concrete plans to initiate operations of its low residency Master of Arts degree in Humanities. This program will transform specialized Christian academics into broad range thinkers.

For full-time students, this 48-unit degree will be a 25-month program. In six semesters spread over these 25 months, students will encounter a bracing list of classic readings, spread across the entire sweep of Western civilization, in the areas of theology, philosophy, history, literature, and the arts. The reading list for the Master's degree is found at the end of this chapter.

After successfully launching this Master's Degree, the college will begin to enact the plan for its undergraduate program. The under-graduate program best envisions and more completely documents the mission of CS Lewis College. We begin by utilizing the undergraduate program and its distinctions as a means of expressing all that the college intends to become. Following the description of the undergraduate program, a more complete description of the unique elements of the Master's degree will follow.

The Undergraduate Program

Five qualities characterize our model for undergraduate education, and reveal the philosophy of education which we believe will most strengthen the Church in our day.

Distinctive 1: *"Merely Christian"*
Following Lewis' lead, the College will be, at its core, a "merely Christian" institution, celebrating the common commitment to Jesus Christ that is shared by the Orthodox, Roman Catholic, and Protestant Christian tradi-

tions. The College community — students, staff, faculty, trustees — will be drawn from all historic branches of Christian faith. College curricula will also reflect this "mere Christian" commitment. This diversity within unity will enrich the community of faith and strengthen bonds between traditions while ensuring that we do not lose sight of the *"cornerstone" of Christian thought* — Jesus Christ.

Distinctive 2: *"Great Books"*

C.S. Lewis College will be a Great Books college. Four elements describe this concept:

a) Instead of textbooks, students study the pivotal texts of Western civilization (and some non-Western classics) — the work of the great thinkers whose ideas shaped civilization.

b) There will be no daily lectures. All classes will be discussion-based. Students will carefully study assigned readings, then come together in seminars and tutorials to thoughtfully discuss the significance of the readings.

c) At the undergraduate level, there will be one major, Great Books. All students will read everything. Why? Think of the Western intellectual tradition as a "great conversation," in which one author presents a new idea, and the next author replies to it, attempting to extend, elaborate, turn it to a new direction, or refute it in whole or part. In order to truly understand what is said, a student of the Great Books must "hear" the entire conversation, from beginning to end, without jumping in half-way or skipping parts. *Thus, all students will read everything.*

d) There will be no departments, and no specialist teachers. Great Books college tutors are not there to profess specialized expertise, they are there to help students read difficult material. Tutors model how to learn. Further, a Great Books program treats the Western intellectual tradition as an organic whole, not separating the literature, science, theology, philosophy, history, and art from one another. Teachers, along with students, must study the whole tradition. While our faculty will come with standard academic specializations (physics, languages, music, mathematics, literature, philosophy, theology, etc., sharing their expertise), over the years, and with appropriate preparation along the way, *all teachers will teach everything.* This approach models active search for understanding, rather than passive reception, and celebrates the unity of truth and the interconnectedness of knowledge.

This Great Books approach to education honors students by placing upon them the primary responsibility for education. By preparing thoroughly *prior* to class, they will be able to discuss ideas in a well-considered, well-supported, and accurate manner. Students thus take on themselves the primary work of education. Growth comes best when students commit to the hard work of puzzling through difficult ideas, or at least grasping *why* they struggle to understand. Then seminar discussion requires students to clearly formulate their views, or to articulate clearly their lack of clarity, so others can help.

Those of us who are guiding the development of the College have taught by these methods in other programs, and have observed this philosophy of education in action in other Great Books colleges. When the Great Books method is fully adhered to—students responsible to study carefully, then discuss, classic works under guidance of the tutors—the result is a stunning education for students who are motivated to develop themselves through what we believe is the demanding program of general education in the world.

Distinctive 3: *"Faculty-governed"*
Since our college is centered on a powerful course of instruction, we take care that the school is administered by those who teach that course. Some two thirds of its Executive Council, the chief administrative body, will consist of teaching faculty.

Distinctive 4: *"Broad Cultural Engagement"*
The College aims to prepare its graduates to engage the broader world of ideas and the arts. In pursuit of this, we plan to locate our campus close to a major secular university. This will enhance the academic experience by sharing intellectual, cultural, and artistic events, as well as shared conversation deriving from those interactions. For students to be effective agents of change, they must understand the culture as well as the books that helped create that culture.

For the students' later effectiveness as advocates of a Christian understanding, their study of the Great Books needs to be balanced with fluency in the cultural context of the present.

Distinctive 5: *Visual and Performing Arts Programs*
Art is a key element of Western civilization. The College will address this key mode of understanding and communication in two ways. First, the primary Great Books degree program will include a year-long tutorial on

the visual arts, which will cover both artistic creation as well as the historical/critical analysis of art. The aim of this special training is to assist our students in learning to "read" this vital element of culture.

Second, at the appropriate time, the College intends to establish a School of Visual and Performing Arts, offering bachelor's degrees in music, theatre, dance, visual arts, graphic design, and film. The general education component of these programs will consist of the Great Books, taught in the standard Great Books modality. The strong performance/studio orientation of these degrees will allow students to make progress in their respective art forms as they enjoy the foundation of Greet Books learning. The performance/studio orientation of these degrees will allow students to layer artistic skills upon a foundation of Great Books learning. This focus on the creative arts is intended to help the Church gain a voice in this critical sphere.

Together these distinctives will produce graduates who understand, first, how to *learn*, and second, how to broadly *understand* Western civilization and its various trajectories (good and bad), in order to allow the healing truth of Christian faith to repair a culture which is in desperate need of reformation.

Academic Order

Academics involve both content and class structure. The content of the College's instruction will consist of a Reading List, containing books and articles to be carefully studied over the course of the four-year program. The Reading List will be created by fellows of the college, but it will be similar to the reading lists of existing Great Books colleges and programs. The greatest western authors will be studied: the Bible, Homer's *Iliad* and *Odyssey*, Pythagoras, Sophocles, Aristophanes, Plato, Aristotle, Marcus Aurelius, Euclid, Galen, Ptolemy, Eusebius, Irenaeus, Athanasius, Augustine — not just theology, philosophy, literature, and history, but mathematics and natural sciences, up through Newton, Einstein, and non-Euclidean geometry (Lobachevsky).

(The students will also be creating and analyzing visual art, and will learn the structure of music by analyzing pieces by Bach and Mozart.) By studying the best ideas in the civilization's history, our students will be challenged to become their best.

These texts will be studied and discussed in seminars, tutorials, and laboratories. In all formal class meetings, the rule will be to engage — as friends — in conversation, discussion, and debate concerning the assigned texts, according to a protocol of civility and seeking truth.

Seminars
Seminars will meet once a week for three hours, every semester, all four years. Seminars will include 17-20 students and 1 or 2 Fellows (tutors). Every student will be enrolled in his or her year-appropriate seminar. It will be in these seminars that the broader sweep of readings will be discussed, synthesizing insights from the Bible, literature, philosophy, theology, history, and political and economic theory.

While the seminars will be conducted under the guidance of fellows, student discussion will be central. This is their opportunity to grapple with great ideas and try to make sense of them and their relevance in the modern world.

Ideas will be offered, with supporting evidence from the text. Questions of interpretation will be raised and similarly grounded. Challenges will be made and rebutted, all with evidence from the text. A delightful and educational interplay will arise between the students' soaring ideas sparked by the authors' genius and, on the other hand, the requirement that every contribution to the discussion be rooted in the text as well as supported by evidence from the text.

The effect of reading such literature, read with respect and discussed with rigor over four years, will form minds in a superior educational experience.

Tutorials
Tutorials are small groups (10-15 students with a single tutor) designed to facilitate the study of texts and material that require close, line-by-line examination. These classes will meet twice-weekly, for a total of three hours per week. The subjects studied will include theology/ philosophy (worldview), mathematics, music, visual art and languages. The worldview, mathematics and languages tutorials will run throughout the four years; the music and visual arts tutorials will be limited to a single year each.

Tutorial classes allow students to demonstrate mastery of subjects requiring careful attention to detail and subtle reasoning. Often students will take turns going to the board to work through a mathematical proof, translate a sentence, realize a figured bass (music theory), or draw a diagram of the meaning latent in a paragraph. When one student gets stuck, others will offer help.

Laboratories

These classes, meeting all four years, will be structured like tutorials and designed to allow students to work through experimental ideas (reading key scientific texts) and activities that are critical to understanding the natural sciences. They will often involve the replication of key historical experiments.

Educational Objectives

C. S. Lewis College will seek to send forth graduates who are excited to be followers of Jesus Christ and called to engage the culture and the world in ways that are loving, redemptive, dynamic, winsome and effective. To meet this calling our graduates must be competent, wise, virtuous, learned, and imaginative. The College is intended to imbue graduates with six general qualities and capabilities:

Objective #1: A Unified Ethos:

The College's five distinctives combine to create an intense, focused educational experience in which collegiality and camaraderie will flourish around a core of Christian worship. To bring together keen students with dedicated faculty members, all carefully studying the greatest works that have ever been written, diligently struggling with and debating vital ideas, will create a bracing intellectual atmosphere. Substantive conversations will no doubt flourish at meals, in the residence halls, and in the café at 11:00 pm after seminars (dozens of freshmen re-hashing their Plato reading!). This is what happens when intellectually alive students are given a common vocabulary and a shared reservoir of ideas and concepts by which, together, to come to terms with the world, especially in light of the challenge of integrating Christian faith throughout their life of thought. It is this ethos of vital intellectual and spiritual engagement and interchange that is such a superlative setting for the cultivation and development of the more specific intellectual and character objectives which the College covets for its students. The creation of this spiritual/intellectual ethos is indeed the primary objective of the College because it nurtures, stimulates, and supports the growth of all the other objectives.

<u>Objective #2: Basic Intellectual Virtues:</u>

Certain habits of the mind are critical to enabling one to perform capably in a wide array of professional settings and becoming a dynamic, life-long learner. The College's Great Books program will cultivate these basic intellectual virtues - including the ability to:
- Engage in sharp analysis and rigorous reasoning;
- Read carefully and tenaciously;
- Craft subtle, sensitive interpretations; and
- Grasp, assess and evaluate comprehensive theories about important matters.

These basic virtues will help form a critical perspective on one's own views, the ability to subject one's own beliefs to objective reflection. This sense of perspective is what Socrates advocated when, according to Plato's *Apology*, he states that "the unexamined life is not worth living." Socrates' dictum may deserve careful scrutiny itself but, clearly, Socrates assumes that there is objective truth related to the life one is living, and that that truth ought to be sought.

So C.S. Lewis College will cultivate basic virtues that equip students as critical thinkers. But make no mistake.: the objective will not be merely to enjoy self-reflection, but to use the intellectual and moral freedom thus achieved, to recognize and embrace what is true. Critical reflection that does not aim at the apprehension of truth is ultimately either solipsism or narcissism- intellectual failures all too common in the contemporary academy. Thus, the ability to challenge one's own beliefs is not about oneself, but rather about the discovery of that which is good, true and beautiful. C.S. Lewis College will prepare students for the exciting task of fully examining all ideas in order to embrace truth.

<u>Objective #3: Wide Knowledge of the World:</u>

The College's program will, over the course of four years, yield students whose minds are well-furnished with:

- Knowledge of the sweep of ideas in the Western intellectual tradition, including not only theology, philosophy, literature and history, but also key concepts and breakthroughs in the historical development of the Natural Sciences;

- Exposure to some classic ideas from non-Western cultures;
- Appreciation of the role and history of art in various forms (music, drawing, painting, sculpture, architecture); and
- Awareness of the diversity and richness of human experience and culture.

Objective #4: Communication skills:

The curriculum will lead to the development of effective communications skills, in two most essential dimensions:

- Writing: Students will be taught to craft well-structured expository and argumentative essays; and
- Oral communication — In every class students will learn to articulate their views. After four years of explaining, arguing, defending, rebutting and reformulating ideas, students will be adept at expressing their thoughts subtly and clearly.

Objective #5: Intellectual Appetite:

In approaching the authors of the Great Books with humility and respect (even those authors with whom one may largely disagree), our program will cultivate the essential virtues of learning (accuracy, honesty, diligence, humility, etc.) and the thirst for understanding. It will seek to instill a proper sense of wonder, a keen sense of curiosity and a hunger for knowledge and wisdom.

Objective #6: Moral and Spiritual Virtues:

Finally, there are the capstone moral and theological objectives that students will come to know, namely:

- The demands of goodness and justice;
- The virtues by which one lives well;
- The fabric of Christian faith, by which all the rest becomes truly intelligible and by which faith we are enabled to achieve what is otherwise impossible; and
- A life of virtue, animated by the Holy Spirit, forged in an intentional community overseen by the Office of Student Life, enabling the development of a full life that demonstrates the love of God, having been equipped to live effectively as followers of Jesus Christ in the contemporary world.

Our College motto, *Dedicated to the pursuit of truth in the company of friends*, will characterize the overall life of the College. It is truth that we are after, and nothing less; truth in the world of ideas and truth in the fabric of our lives together.

But does this exciting program provide the basis for meaningful employment? Certainly. The scope and rigor of a Great Books education produces graduates possessing impressively wide knowledge, sharp analytical abilities, creativity and well-honed writing and speaking skills. Most employers desire employees who are able to read carefully, figure things out and communicate clearly. And perhaps most important: they want workers who are dedicated and who possess the personal discipline and character to make reliable, well-adjusted, honest and diligent workers — employees who can be relied upon and who can work well with others. This statement well describes the persons who will be drawn to the study of the Great Books and persevere in the program, having mastered the skills and virtues required to make them highly desirable employees. They will also find themselves to be effective in more specialized studies. Further, their consequent work within specialized fields, whether as teachers or computer programmers or managers, will be all the more valuable by virtue of their having acquired such a powerful liberal arts education.

Why is C.S. Lewis College Needed?

There are several reasons why the Great Books curriculum is desperately needed:

First: our culture is in danger of losing a vision for the whole. Our universities and colleges have become so good at creating specializations that we have begun to lose the ability to see the big picture, to address the big questions of life that can only be meaningfully examined from a truly integrated approach to serious learning.

Second: our increasing specialization has made it very difficult for educated people to speak to one another from within the "silos" of their separate domains of learning. This loss of effective communication cripples the society in addressing problems.

Third: if a civilization has lost its way, only those who are schooled in its entire path are likely to discern this effectively. Even more: solutions for problems are likely to be heard and heeded only if those offering the solutions "speak the language" of the civilization in terms that it will understand.

Finally, to the extent that academic specialization maintains its grip on higher education, Christian faith will continue to be in eclipse within the culture. This is because the detailed, specialization-based criticisms of faith will continue to be heard, but the macro-level power of Christian faith as an explanatory account for the whole range of life and existence can never be deployed adequately within the "specialized" academy

In light of these concerns, it is essential that some particularly strong students be trained in the breadth, richness and rigor of the civilization's whole range of learning. In short, we need those whose *specialization* is the *breadth* of the civilization's learning. This is particularly critical from the standpoint of Christian faith, which shines like a priceless gem when seen from the vantage point of a comprehensive worldview.

Master of Arts in Humanities

The M.A. in Humanities program of C.S. Lewis College will provide an academic experience for Christians who have already completed academic undergraduate degrees but desire to understand themselves and our world better from a Christian perspective. The central component of this study is "The Great Books". However, as the C S Lewis College Statement of Faith affirms, the Bible is the divinely inspired written Word of God, is entirely trustworthy, and is the final authority in all matters of faith and practice. It follows then, that God's Word is the final authority over man's wisdom.

The Bible has been the light that has guided most of the important builders of the modern world. The deepest understanding of the impact of the Bible on the modern world, however, comes through the careful study of the key writings that have defined the civilization in which the Bible emerged (and in which—like a bolt of lightning—it soon became by far the greatest influence on the subsequent development of the civilization). For example, to enjoy the deepest understanding of the remarkable revolution in morality that took place in the West deriving from the Bible's teaching on the moral virtues, you first need to understand the ancient Greek notion of moral virtues found in the writings of Homer, Plato, Aristotle, and Epicurus, as well as Rome's Cicero.

The study of these key writings also provides one of the most rigorous educations, since mastering these pivotal writings requires the careful cultivation of numerous intellectual virtues.

For these reasons, C.S. Lewis College is eager to lead students through the careful study of selected Great Books: The following is a tentative list of the readings organized by each of the six terms of study.

Semester 1
Aeschylus – *The Oresteia*
Bible – *Deuteronomy, Mark*
Augustine – *The Confessions, On The Trinity*
Plato – *Euthyphro, Apology* Aristotle – *On the Soul* Aurelius – *The Meditations*
Homer – *The Odyssey* Plato – *The Republic*
Sophocles – *Oedipus the King*
Aristotle – *Metaphysics, Poetics*
Boethius – *The Consolation of Philosophy*
Anselm – *Monologion, Proslogion, On Truth*

Semester 2
Dante – *The Divine Comedy*
Bible – *Genesis, Isaiah, Romans*
Athanasius – *On the Incarnation*
Bonaventure – *The Journey of the Mind to God Beowulf*
Spenser – *The Faerie Queene*
Shakespeare – *King Lear*
Chaucer – *The Canterbury Tales* Descartes – *Meditations*
Hume – *An Enquiry Concerning Human Understanding*
Lewis – *The Great Divorce*

Semester 3
Aristotle – *Ethics*
Voltaire – *Candide*
Shelley – *Frankenstein*
Madison – *The Federalist Papers, The Constitution of the United States*
Kant – *Groundwork of the Metaphysic of Morals*
Mill – *Utilitarianism*

Semester 4

Cervantes - *Don Quixote*
Bible – *Jeremiah, John, Galatians, I Peter*
Swift – *Gulliver's Travels*
Lewis – *Miracles*
Tocqueville – *Democracy in America*
Herbert – *The Temple (Selections)*
Austen – *Pride and Prejudice*
Marx – *Economic and Philosophical Manuscripts*
Dickens – *Tale of Two Cities*
Dickinson – *The Complete Poems (Selections)*
Twain – *Huckleberry Finn*
Ibsen – *A Doll's House*

Semester 5

Dostoevsky - *The Brothers Karamazov*
Bible – *Joshua, Judges*
Maximus the Confessor – *Four Hundred Chapters on Love (selections)*
Edwards – *The Nature of True Virtue*
Shakespeare – *Henry V*
Nietzsche – *Thus Spoke Zarathustra; The Gay Science*
Conrad – *The Heart of Darkness*
Buber – *I and Thou*
Freud – *Civilization and Its Discontents*
Lewis – *The Abolition of Man*
Habermas – *The Philosophical Discourse on Modernity*
Solzhenitsyn – *One Day in the Life of Ivan Denisovich*

Semester 6

O'Connor – *Wise Blood*
King, Jr. – *"Letter from Birmingham Jail"*
T. S. Eliot – *Four Quartets*
Beckett – *Waiting for Godot*
Lewis – *The Space Trilogy; Till We Have Faces*

The formal study of language will be integrated into this program. The details are still being finalized.

While this array of names and titles may seem overwhelming, it is good to remember that every work comes from a particular understanding of life and reality — a particular worldview. It is central to this program to understand ways of life, understandings of goodness and visions of ultimate reality represented in each specific reading. In addition to the sheer intellectual and analytical skills students will develop as they read, digest, discuss and understand these masterpieces, they will also progressively develop the ability to recognize conflicts within an age or between ages, recognize trends and advancements (or retrogressions) in thinking, note cultural turns or major deviations, and periods of reform. *This sort of study attunes students to the intertwining threads of the fabric of the culture.*

Note that the Bible, as the greatest of the Great Books, is present throughout the program. It is God's true light, that illumines all else that we study. (It is also largely responsible for the West becoming the West.) Those of us privileged to live in the "bright shadow" of God's revelation cannot overestimate what we owe to him. It is our rational, academic duty and joy to come to understand everything according to the knowledge and wisdom He grants us in his Word.

Such a program prepares students to become leaders with a deep understanding of the impact of Christianity on the world and culture. Graduates will recognize patterns, understand the origins of ideas, see the value of Christian faith within the fabric of Western civilization, articulate the value of freedom of speech, explain why belief in the inherent goodness of human nature is foolish, show how atheism undermines belief in objective morality, and challenge other popular intellectual errors.

The program will be managed as befits a program for highly-motivated students. The College is committed to face-to-face encounters as ideal for quality education. Digital interaction can supplement classroom meetings, and we are grateful for modern conveniences. But there is no replacing face-to-face encounters between people in training students to fully appreciate goodness, truth and beauty.

The program is called "low residency" because the total contact time is about 50% of the total "seat time" in a full-residency program. We actually think this intensive contact time is more efficient than a regular weekly class time, since the (essential) preparation guarantees that class time will be more effective, while the intensity of the week-long residencies compounds the learning that takes place. The low-residency structure will keep costs down while facilitating significant face-to-face education. While living at home, students will study independently, under the supervision of tutors, reading and writing papers, more than would be the case in a full-residency program.

Students will come together in special gatherings called "residencies," five in total over the 25 months of the program. Residencies will be held in carefully chosen locations, with ready opportunity for cultural interaction and experience of Nature.

The students will be arranged in cohorts of 8 to 16, and ideally a cohort will be together throughout the program. Each of the five residencies will involve a week of intensive seminars, tutorials, worship services, artistic and cultural events, and excursions. This face-to-face contact will allow students to get to know each other well over two years. They will dine together, share cups of coffee, take bus rides to excursions, and chat in the dorms.

Between residencies, students will read the assigned material, electronically submit assignments as required, write papers, and meet with tutors online in individual sessions and synchronous class meetings (Zoom or similar). In addition to assigned meetings, we expect that students will engage regularly with one another in study groups and other collegial contact — texting, emailing or video conferencing.

A final significant component of the program is the Distinguished Lecture Series. Six times a year, a distinguished Christian scholar will be invited to address the entire College on a topic germane to the studies of the program and its setting in Western civilization, and the broader world. The lectures will be video-recorded and available for individual viewing, but there will also be a live, synchronous question-and-answer period for deeper probing of the subject. These lectures and Q & A sessions will be integrated into digital or face-to-face class sessions for enhanced under-standing and evaluation of comprehension.

This Distinguished Lecture Series will bring the power of world-class scholarship into a program primarily focused on the careful reading of difficult texts and the painstaking crafting of academic papers.

The M.A. in Humanities program of C.S. Lewis College will provide an academic experience for Christians as they become imbued with the virtues and values of a Christian education in pursuit of goodness, truth and beauty. *The Third Education Revolution* will find one of its most willing partners in C.S. Lewis College. The College and its Master of Arts in Humanities program will develop believers who can reason carefully and come to understand the rich academic and cultural heritage of the West - a foundation which comes from the heart of Christ and his church.

Chapter 11

The Business of Educating the Poor

Jason E. Benedict[1]

Summary

The convergence of demographic, technological, economic, financial and socio-political trends in sub-Saharan Africa has created a unique window of opportunity for the Global Church to invest in education. This is an unparalleled evangelism and discipleship opportunity but also a significant business opportunity.

Africa's swelling population is expected to double to over 2 billion by 2050. There is a surplus of demand for education on every level from preschool to post graduate. Africa's emerging middle-class has proven its willingness to pay for education. Increased urbanization and changes in technology are solving logistical challenges that have hindered educational development in the past.

Foreign direct investment into this sector has increased dramatically over recent years. Every indication is that returns will be attractive. So far much of the investment is from the non-western world, and from ideologies that are hostile to the Kingdom of God. We should change that!

Our willingness to engage in this opportunity will have far-reaching consequences. Over a billion Africans will need to be educated in the next 30 years, and someone will rise to the occasion. Let it be the Body of Christ!

The Opportunity

Nelson Mandela, known to many as Africa's favorite son said, "Education is the most powerful weapon which you can use to change the world." Jesus the Son of God equated education and discipleship when he said,

1 Dr. Jason Benedit is an entrepreneur, business strategist, author, missionary, theologian and international trainer.

"A disciple is not above his teacher, but everyone when he is fully trained will be like his teacher." (Luke 6:40 ESV). Jesus went on to give his disciples a mandate to "make disciples… teaching them to obey everything I have commanded you." (Mt 28:19).

The convergence of several trends are creating an unprecedented opportunity for education in Africa. The Church's resolve in responding to this crucial challenge will have long lasting repercussions not only in Africa, but for the rest of the world. It is not an exaggeration to say that a billion souls hang in the balance.

Five Trends Are Particularly Vital:

1. Demographic: The world is becoming more African: the continent's population is young and exploding. Africa's 1.3 billion people represent the youngest population in the world. The under-15 population in Africa is equal to that of Europe and the Americas combined. Over half of Africans are under university age and, with the highest birth rate in the world, the population of sub Saharan Africa (SSA) is set to double over the next 30 years.[2]

While birthrates in the rest of the world have decreased to replacement levels or are declining rapidly, birth rates in Africa remain relatively high. According to UN statistics more than half of global population growth over the next 30 years will come from Africa. Statistician Hans Rosling points out that the global school age population of the world is becoming more African. While Asia currently has a youth (under-15) population that is 2.5 times as large as that of Africa, The African population is quickly catching up to that of Asia. "For every 4 children in Asia who pass their 15th birthday, 3 are being replaced by another Asian baby and 1 is being replaced by an African baby", and the ratio of African to Asian births is increasing.[3]

---

2 UN. (2017). *UN Population Report.* Retrieved January 29, 2019, from UN Population Report, https://esa.un.org/unpd/wpp/Publications/Files/WPP2017_Key-Findings.pdf

3 School, T. G. (2015, December 01). Retrieved January 28, 2019, from the Video Titled: Why the world population won't exceed 11 billion | Hans Rosling | TGS.ORG by Think Global School YouTube Channel: https://www.youtube.com/watch?v=2LyzBoHo5EI&list=FLlWYuD5_mJXPJj3a-hZopVA&index=1

Between now and 2050 there will be 1.35 billion school age children in Africa. These children should all be educated but they probably will not be. This number of 1.35B would need to be adjusted to 904M to account for global enrollment norms[4] and to arrive at the approximate number who will be seeking education.

When one compares Gross Enrollment Ratios (GER) in Africa[5] to the global averages it appears that 157M of Africa's school age and university age population is currently un-served, with the biggest gaps occurring in secondary and tertiary education. The educational capacity of Africa is currently around 221M students over the next thirty years, but African schools will need to accommodate at least 904M students by 2050. Therefore we can estimate a need to increase educational capacity by 682M students to meet global enrollment norms.

Education Capacity Needs in Africa Present - 2050	
Current Education Need*	464,000,000
Current Education Capacity	221,800,000
Seeking Education Present – 2050	904,000,000
Needed Education Capacity	682,200,000
*All segments all levels. This is not 100% enrollment, but only the capacity to meet global norms by segment (primary, secondary, tertiary).	

The idea that this vast need will remain totally un-served is farfetched. Where there is a demand, a supply will arise to meet it. The question is: who will meet this demand or grasp this opportunity? If the global Church does not serve to meet this need then someone with a competing ideology will likely do so, at least in part.

---

4 Worldbank. (2017). School enrollment, primary (% net). Retrieved January 29, 2019, from https://data.worldbank.org/indicator/SE.PRM.NENR

5 Caerus Capital LLC. (n.d.). *The Business of Education in Africa*. Retrieved January 14, 2019, from https://edafricareport.caeruscapital.co/thebusinessofeducationinafrica.pdf, p 22.

than inflation, projected long-term revenue growth, high barriers to entry, and education being a defensive investment (resistant to recession).

A review of press releases with respect to private equity investments in African education reveals that much of the current investment is coming from the Arab world and India. For example, GEMS, a Dubai-based firm, recently spent $25M USD to acquire Kenya's prestigious Hillcrest Schools[14].

  5. Urbanization: Today 40% of Africans live in urban centers and this is projected to increase to 64% by 2050[15]. Urbanization affects educational demand, efficiency and scale of delivery. In other words: greater urbanization produces more eager educational consumers who are in turn easier to reach and serve.

ICT (Information and Communication Technology)

Another factor influencing the demand for education is the increase in mobile phone technology and internet access. Africa's total bandwidth increased 20-fold from 2009 to 2014[16]. Africa is still the only continent on the other side of the "digital divide,"[17] but internet usage is now above 35% and growing rapidly. Much of this is on mobile devices. There were 444M unique mobile subscribers in SSA in 2017 and that is expected to grow to 634M by 2025. There are 250M smartphone users now but an additional 440M will have been added by 2025[18].

14 Juma, V., Ngugi, B., Otieno, B., Irungu, G., & Okoth, E. (2019, January 09). Dubai school takes over Hillcrest for Sh2.6 billion. Retrieved from https://www.businessdailyafrica. com/news/Dubai-school takes over-Hillcrest-for-Sh2-6-billion/539546-4927236-8uf1ab/ index.html

15 UN. (2014). *World Urbanization Prospects - 2014 Revison.* Retrieved January 28, 2019, from https://esa.un.org/unpd/wup/publications/files/wup2014-highlights.pdf. 7

16 Caerus Capital LLC. (n.d.). *The Business of Education in Africa.* Retrieved January 14, 2019, from https://edafricareport.caeruscapital.co/thebusinessofeducationin-africa.pdf. 29

17 Where the majority don't have access to the internet.

18 GSM Association. (n.d.). Sub-Saharan Africa 2018 - GSMA Mobile Economy. Retrieved 2018, from https://www.gsma.com/mobileeconomy/sub-saharan-africa/

This growth in ICT will have a great impact on how education is delivered in the next 5-10 years. Learning Management Systems (LMS) are already being judged on their ability to function in a responsive/mobile friendly way. Innovation in mobile technology will bring distance education closer to many on the continent. For example: UNICAF, Africa's largest online university platform, just completed a $28M funding round (Goldman Sachs) in a bid to provide online degree programs to 100,000 learners by 2023[19].

According to a study conducted by Caerus Capital[20], the educational segments with the most business potential for the private sector, in order of financial viability, are:

Segment	5 year investment opportunity	Notes
Contact Higher Education	$2.2B	
Mid-priced Premium K-12	$2.2B	
Distance Higher Ed	$0.7B	Tertiary online
Teacher Training	$0.4B	
Supplementary Education	$0.6B	Tutoring, ESL, Certification, Test prep, etc.
Pre-Primary	$1.2B	Daycare/pre-school

As we have seen, the scale of intervention needed to meet the educational opportunity in Africa is immense. It would be impossible for the Church to meet this demand using a donor-based mission school model. That is why this opportunity should be approached from the perspective of kingdom business.

19 Unicaf. (2018, November 14). Africa's Largest Online University Platform Raises $28 Million to Meet Unprecedented Demand for Higher Education. Retrieved from https://www. prnewswire.com/news-releases/africas-largest-online-university-platform-raises-28-million-to-meet-unprecedented-demand-for-higher-education-300750189.html

20Caerus Capital LLC. (n.d.). *The Business of Education in Africa*. Retrieved January 14, 2019, from https://edafricareport.caeruscapital.co/thebusinessofeducationinafrica.pdf. 16

An enterprise model that allows for profitability and sustainability is more likely to marshal the needed human and financial capital. Additionally, the overlap between economic opportunity and the strategic Kingdom potential is considerable. Consider the following:

- **Teacher Training:** It is essential that we train godly teachers! The student, when fully trained, becomes like the teacher (Luke 6:40). In North America the humanist architects of secular education achieved their secularizing objectives by first taking over the teacher training institutions. By investing in teacher training in Africa the global body of Christ has an opportunity to disciple the disciple makers.

- **Premium K-12:** These are the children of professionals, influencers and the elites of society. They are more likely to have access to tertiary education and are likely to be the decision makers of tomorrow. I have personally witnessed this: In 2004 I was part of a team that facilitated the development of a premium primary school in the Sahel region of Africa. This school was self-sustaining from tuition revenues paid by upper middle class and wealthy Muslim families. The curriculum was Christian and we were essentially paid to disciple ruling class Muslim children – tomorrow's leaders.

- **Higher Education:** Society's leaders are drawn disproportionately from university graduates. Again this segment is financially viable and holds great potential for Kingdom impact. We can shape leaders who will influence every sphere of society: religion, education, business, the sciences, arts, media, government and more.

An educational segment that I have omitted from the list above is Low Cost K-12.

This is the largest single segment in terms of needed investment ($8.2 B USD)[21] but this segment has less business viability for investors. Nevertheless it is arguably one of the largest opportunities for Kingdom impact because of the sheer number of students that could be influenced.

I believe this segment (as with the others) presents an opportunity for innovative African churches to begin to provide education on a large scale. Many African churches provide primary education. Efforts should

---

21 Ibid

be made to mobilize and facilitate this on a large scale. Technology should greatly aid in this effort.

The magnitude of the educational opportunity (some might call it a crisis) in Africa is such that it will need to be approached on many fronts. It will take an all-out effort by educators, business people, policy makers and church leaders.

Key Considerations and Strategies

Jesus told us to count troops before going to battle. Likewise, we must consider several challenges before stepping into this field.

Awareness: by and large the western church is unaware of this opportunity, while the non-western international community is already moving. We need to mobilize, but we must also serve African churches as full partners; more precisely: as leaders, in the endeavor.

Finance: Education in Africa will require patient investors with considerable risk tolerance, especially with regards to regulatory risk. Nevertheless it is estimated that Internal Rates of Return for private equity can be as high as 25-30%[22]. We need to develop ways to sensitize believers in the investment community to this opportunity.

Talent: We need to recruit organizations and individual believers with a passion for education to engage the opportunity. Places to begin could include: international ministries that emphasize education, Christian universities with schools of education, and mission organizations with a considerable footprint on the continent that may not recognize the opportunity.

Technology: Education globally is being changed by technology, which will also drive the future of Africa. The church should lead in educational innovation for the continent. Anyone wishing to venture into this business sector needs to understand that technological acumen will be a key success factor.

---

22 Sulaiman, T. (2013, April 08). Closing Africa's education gap: Private equity does the maths. Retrieved from https://www.reuters.com/article/us-africa-summit-education/ closing-africas-education-gap-private-equity-does-the-maths-idUS-BRE93709Z20130408

Regulatory environment: In many African countries the bureaucracies surrounding education are considerably more formidable than those surrounding business and commerce. It has become significantly easier to do business in several parts of Africa. Hopefully this trend will extend to educational bureaucracies as well in the near future.

Possible Strategies

I see four general strategies by which the Church can invest in educating young people in Africa, each with its advantages. In each of them those called to participate should have a *multiple bottom line* approach and work towards both profitability and our Kingdom objectives of training students in a biblical worldview. The magnitude of the opportunity is such that, ideally, we would have multiple organizations or parties (Kingdom business teams, mission organizations, denominations, etc.) tackling each of these segments, or pursuing one or more strategies(or hybrids). In other words: the size of the opportunity is such that it will require many people working simultaneously to make a dent.

Start Small and Develop a Prototype: Find an existing institutional partner in one or more spheres of education. (That is, pre-school, K-12 partner, higher as well as supplemental education and teacher training). Then work with this partner to develop a scalable prototype; then growing - through either replication or acquisition.

Acquire and Merge (Roll Up) Approach: This is a speed to market approach. Raise a multi-million dollar PE fund(s) for the purpose. Identify top-performing institutions across one or more product categories. Put together a world-class team that will work to achieve economies of knowledge, scale and scope across the network

Mass-Mobilization of African Churches as Educational Providers[23]: The African church has a long tradition in education. In this model we develop a support infrastructure with economies of learning, replicable systems and technologies that would make it easier for churches across the continent to turn their churches into school campuses. Each church would start a low-cost K-12 that would run during the daytime and a low-cost college

---

23 Vishal Mangalwadi in his book *Truth and Transformation* makes an interesting proposal for church based tertiary education. Mangalwadi, V. (2009). Truth and transformation: A manifesto for ailing nations. Seattle, WA: YWAM Pub.

or technical school that would run in the evenings. This would increase the utilization of church facilities, accomplish mission and provide an additional revenue stream for churches.

Study Abroad: Far-sighted Africans have long sent their children abroad for study. The main educational destinations have traditionally been Europe and the United States. A new trend is for Africans to send their children to India and China for study. This education is an export for the host nation. We would like to move more of this educational value chain back to Africa. Nevertheless research should be done on the feasibility of establishing kingdom businesses that support study abroad by funneling students into institutions that offer a biblical worldview. Similarly part of the solution could be for educational institutions with a biblical world-view (i.e. Christian universities in the West and Asia) to establish satellite campuses in Africa.

Postscript by Vishal Mangalwadi

Jason Benedict is right: Africa's growing middle-class would gladly pay the church to educate their children in partnership with an accredited university or school.

But what about the poor?

The Third Education Revolution seeks to re-plant education in the theological soil of the Priesthood and Kingship of ALL believers — not just the rich believers who can pay.

The church must make the world's best education available to the poorest by challenging competent and compassionate Christians to build educational banks which micro-finance poor churches and students.

A visionary Academic Pastor (AP) should mobilize his community to build a class-room next to their sanctuary, even if it is a mud hut. Educational banks could finance a digital TV, smartphone, internet connection and other educational equipment. The church should repay the loan in regular installments.

The AP will then recommend a needy child for a student-loan to buy a laptop and pay tuition. His parents, extended family or a church elder would sign the Loan Agreement with the bank. The signatory will take responsibility to repay a mutually agreed installment.

Suppose the family circle responsible for a student has no steady source of income. The child has no local supporter who can commit to repay even a modest sum. In such cases a scholarship fund could step in as the sponsor. However, where possible, the AP should encourage a student's immediate or extended family to start a business. A family member could be loaned finances to start a simple business like selling boiled peanuts or making lemon pickle.

A student or family member who handles talents responsibly will, over time, qualify for larger loans. The church would inject into such cultures of chronic poverty what Max Weber called *"The Protestant Ethic and the Spirit of Capitalism."*

Chapter 12

The Revolution's Intellectual Nucleus

Hans Joachim Hahn[1]

1. Introduction

Secular education that dominates the world today is much more than schools, colleges, universities, research institutions, publications and media. It is a whole worldview that links educational institutions and publications. It is the "spirit of the age." That's why a new institution cannot transform secular nihilism or paganism. An outpouring of the Spirit of life is needed to bring resurrection to a valley filled with dead and dried bones (Ezekiel 37). *The Third Education Revolution* will happen when visionary prophets, captive in Babylon as was Ezekiel, find the grace to prophesy to our culture of death.

European universities transformed education in the West and around the world during the last millennium. The university came out of the womb of Christian monasteries and cathedral schools. From Padua to Paris, from Oxford and Cambridge to Halle or Heidelberg, St. Gallen, monastic schools grew into universities because of their commitment to truth, accuracy and diligence in learning. Christian Scholars such as Nikolaus Copernicus, Galileo Galilei and Johannes Kepler did not challenge the Bible when they refuted the traditional view of the Geocentric worldview. Rather: these and other scholars were inspired by the Bible to study God's creation and to rely on empirical observation more than on philosophical theories. Thus Francis Bacon, who was cited in the earlier chapter quoting Matthew in order to encourage empirical science, was also fond of quoting Solomon: "It is the glory of God to conceal a matter, and the glory of the king to find it out." (Prov.25:2).

---

1 Hans-Joachim Hahn is an Ass. Professor of Economic Ethics, is coordinator of Professors´ Forum and the co-founder of Truth and Transformation in Europe

The Medieval Church was committed to the traditional Ptolemaic World-view, and also to maintaining power. That was the main reason why a few pioneering scientists (most famously Galileo) courted disgrace and even persecution in promoting their discoveries.

But commitment to truth molded the spirit of the modern university. The imprint of this Christian love of truth can be found, for instance, on the inscription at the Cavendish Laboratory of Physics, which the great James Maxwell helped found, and where the electron, neutron and the structure of atom were discovered. It quotes Psalm 111:2: "The works of the Lord are great, sought out of all them that have pleasure therein." Maxwell, who formulated the classical theory of electromagnetic radiation, was himself a dedicated student of Scripture and advised: "Let us follow the light."

One can find evidence of the same inspiration in the Crest of Harvard University:

VE-RI-TAS (Latin veritas = truth), displayed in three books: The Book of God's Word, the Book of God's Works, and the Book of Human Reason created in God's image.

The golden inscription on the Main Building of Freiburg University in southern Germany reads, "Die Wahrheit wird euch frei machen" (the truth shall set you free), John 8:32.

Truth is revealed in more specific Christian forms in the Scepter of Heidelberg University in Germany: It shows Christ as the Teacher with four students sitting around him:

These "disciples" represent the original faculties of Theology, Law, Philosophy and Medicine, listening to the Teacher who is the Truth.

In his Inaugural lecture as Professor of Theology in 1947 – only two years after the end of WW II and the Nazi-Regime – Edmund Schlink, later Rector of Heidelberg University, asked:

> "What would it mean in this situation, if in all fields of thought we would hear the voice of Christ? What does this Christ have to teach us, this wrecked and crucified man? What does this teaching of Christ, the son of God who died for the world and rose again, mean for our disciplines?"[2]

Characteristic of Schlink's own work and how he influenced the revitalization of Heidelberg University, was the encouragement he gave to interdisciplinary research. This encouragement was already evident in his inaugural lecture as professor, in which he used the scepter of the university as a symbol for a relationship between "Christ and the disciplines." The image of the twelve-year-old Jesus teaching four figures that represent philosophy, law, medicine and theology, reflects the vision of the Medieval philosopher Bonaventure, according to which the crucified and risen Christ is the true teacher of every aspect of truth. In light of this vision, Schlink believed that Christian theology ought to be in critical dialogue with all the disciplines of the modern university.[3]

Consider the original meaning of university. The Latin term "universitas" is composed of two words: "unus" (one) and "versus," "versitas" (*directed to or directedness*); thus the combined term means "*directed toward one.*" This is the relationship between truth and education that the scepter of Heidelberg university illustrates: The Teacher of Truth standing in the middle of the disciplines. In contrast the present Postmodern University might better be described as "Multiversity," lacking any clear center.

---

2 Edmund Schlink,"Das Szepter der Univerſität Heidelberg: Christus und die Fakultäten" [The Scepter of Heidelberg University: Christ and the Faculties] in: *Aus Leben und Forschung der Universität 1947/1948*, ed. W. Kunkel (Heidelberg: Springer, 1947), 31–50 (reprinted in AB 125–46)

3 *Edmund Schlink Works*, Edited by Mattew L. Becker, Volume 1, © 2017,Vandenhoeck &Ruprecht GmbH & Co. KG Göttingen ISBN Print 9783525569289 – ISBN E-Book 978364756028
http://www.ciando.com/img/books/extract/3647560286_lp.pdf

2. The Mandate of the Christian Professor

Professors have always served as role-models. Indeed, "professor" referred originally to "someone who stands for and professes knowledge-based convictions" (*profiteri, professus* = confess openly). A professor is thus given a mandate to pass on knowledge with conviction (acquired by research, test and experience) to students.

Yet, as the post-modern university has become a stronghold of relativism which denies God´s revelation, Christian scholars have been increasingly marginalized, isolated and even discredited by the secularist mainstream. Philosophical atheism has become the paradigm for research and thought, and many Christian scholars have withdrawn their faith into the private areas of church or home. Open academic debate of Christian vs. other worldviews rarely occurs: most Christian scholars wouldn't be up to such a challenge because they have not been trained and lack confidence. They do not experience unity of conviction between research and teaching. A professor of economics may serve on his church's board and sing in the choir on Christmas while, at school, he teaches a reductionist view of "homo oeconomicus," man with mere material needs, the extent and limit of which economics determines. In today's Academy such subjects are divorced from both ethics and religion. The Christian professor finds himself a victim of this reductionist approach to science which effectively excludes his faith and values from education.

In a German university most believers in God's creation don't dare attempt a career as Professor of Biology these days. We know of only one who is tolerated because he stands at the top of his field of microbial ecology, and because the president of his university protects him.

The so-called 'Enlightenment' led to what Francis Schaeffer called "sep aration of Nature and Grace." In other words, rationalism led us down a dead-end road. It barred generations of scientists from experiencing a healthy identity and intellectual integrity. It pushed many into agnosticism or atheism.

Thankfully a growing number of scholars in various fields no longer accept this status quo. They have unmasked the methodological or philosophical naturalism of the modern academy as an obsolete premise. This natural-ism fails the test in both honest academic investigation and the test of life.

Here are two examples from my field of Economics:

1) In an interview with the German daily magazine WELT, Dennis Snower (professor of macroeconomics and former president of the Kiel Institute of World Economics) stated:

> "All of the most important experiences of my life had to do with human relationships. Everything in my life that matters to me is incompatible with selfishness. Economics fails utterly to explain my life. I am doubting the very foundations of my discipline; our science is actually nonsense. This insight was hard for me to take." (*Die Welt* online, 29.9.2012; translated by H.J. Hahn)

2) Tomas Sedlácek teaches Philosophy and History of Economics at Charles University in Prague. He is a chief macroeconomic strategist at the Czech commercial bank CSOB, member of the National Economic Council of the Czech government, and author of the bestseller "Economics of Good and Evil." At the Christian Leadership-Summit in Leipzig in January 2013, Sedlácek expressed a view he has not been shy about stating:

> "By denying ethics and religion, present mainstream Economics has become the biggest religion in itself – with economic Growth as its new God. We created the economic system because it brings us freedom and growth. But by separating it from ethics and religion we have become slaves of the Economy."

Sedlácek suggests that we return to a style of economics oriented around values, humanity and God, as was the Sabbath economy of the Old Testament.

These are just two examples of scholars who are breaking out of the system of materialist secularism which has enslaved scholars over the past decades. Such thinkers stand for an uncompromising search for truth in their fields, as Christian scholars should. In their commitment to the truth as followers of Jesus the Lord, Christians have a unique perspective from which to practice true science in research and teaching.

3. How I Came to Work with Professors

As a student in the early seventies I sensed this spirit of antagonism against the Christian thought. At the same time I encountered the deep skepticism and despair in many prestigious writers and intellectuals of the Twentieth

Century – French existentialists like Sartre and Camus, and British and Irish writers like George Orwell, Samuel Beckett, Harold Pinter, and John Osborne. I cited the latter four men as examples of "the quest for man's identity in modern English drama" in my written exam in English literature. Themes like hopelessness, loss of purpose and loss of self speak loudly out of Beckett's dramas from "Waiting for Godot" and "Happy Days" to "Krapp's last Tape."

In "Waiting for Godot," the two vagabonds do not know whether Godot will ever come. Still they wait, filling their boring days with sad and ridiculous conversations. In "Happy Days" a couple is trying futilely to communicate; she: buried in a pile of sand, he: in a dog house with his feet looking out. In every scene the pile of sand grows higher, the character's motions weaken, and their conversations degrade. In "Krapp's last Tape" an old man is trying in vain to establish his identity by remembering events from his life by listening to a tape recorder. As the tapes with recordings from his past proceed, his voice grows angrier, the halts more furious and his frustration more desperate: the man proves pathetically unable to find out who he is by remembering his past.

As a follower of the Lord Jesus, I was struck by such colorful descriptions of life without God. I admired the honesty of these excellent writers and at the same time felt deep concern for my fellow students who no longer read the Bible or attend church, since the university had ruled out Christianity as an option worth re-considering. Yet they listened to such intellectual leaders and adopted nihilist worldviews and values. I began to see what this might mean for Western society in the future. God used these impressions to call me into full-time service with Campus for Christ in Germany in 1974. They had just started working with students and I felt that their vision of reaching today's students to reach tomorrow's world was the right response to this spiritual and intellectual challenge.

After 20 years of evangelism and discipleship with students God gave me a new calling: to work with professors. Students look up to their teachers who shape and disciple the leaders of tomorrow. Teachers pass on their worldviews and values to the next generation. This led me to start the Professors´ Forum.

4. The German Professors´ Forum

The Professors´ Forum has brought together Christian instructors and scholars from all fields and denominations since 1996. Part of our purpose is to bring individual professors out of isolation and show them that they are not alone. Similar initiatives have started in Poland, India, the US and other countries, some of which will be described later in this chapter.

In Germany we started organizing annual symposiums in which Christian scholars would lecture on popular topics in their fields from a Christian worldview. In the beginning, in order to build a Christian academic identity, we mostly invited Christians to speak. Among the topics we addressed were:

- "Is University Education Off-Target?",
- "Programming of the Infantile and Juvenile Brain",
- "The Professor as Role-Model",
- "Are We Fed-up with Democracy?",
- "Europe at the Crossroads", and
- "Where is the Family Headed?"

After ten years we started a new platform of academic debate in Regensburg. We invited non-Christian as well as Christian lecturers to address the same topics from their respective worldviews. After presentations they would debate for 20 minutes, then we would open up the floor for audience participation.

Four professors had prayed together over several years in Regensburg and decided to start this new strategy at their university. One of these professors, Christiane Thim-Mabrey, felt led to organize events following the model of the first symposium that our team had organized independent of their initiative. They made their symposium a part of their university's public program. Because of her involvement in the university senate the rector even gave an official welcoming speech.

A two-day symposium usually hosted three or four Christians and as many non-Christian lecturers (atheists, agnostics, etc.), with thirty or forty members of the audience. Time for interaction and free evenings for socializing in pubs or restaurants helped create an atmosphere of friendship that few had experienced in academic events before.

The well-known atheist philosopher Bernulf Kanitscheider attended several times and told us that he learned something new each time. Over a glass of wine in the evening we would discuss apologetic topics and share our personal testimonies with him and other non-believers.

In one symposium we hosted the popular astrophysicist and philosopher Harald Lesch, who runs a nationwide program on TV which explains the science of the cosmos and natural science to the public. After he offered an impressive presentation on the mainstream narrative of evolution of life and religion, a non-Christian professor of philosophy asked: "Dear colleague, you reported this as if you had been present when it happened. Are the findings and results really as certain as you have just led us to believe?"; at which Lesch replied, "Well, I have to admit there are several skeletons in the closet, but I do not have the time here to address them."

In the first symposium in Regensburg we tried to persuade Bernd Michael Rode, a famous Austrian professor of chemistry and atheist, to join us as a speaker. He had worked on proving the evolution of life without divine help in his labs in Innsbruck. As a heavy smoker he kept railing against Germans who were so obedient in implementing the new ban on smoking in pubs and restaurants that you could hardly find a pub for smokers anymore. He gave this as a reason not to participate in our symposium. It was clear that we had to find a smoker-pub in Regensburg if we wanted him on board. After a long search we made a find, and the symposium was saved for his participation. He liked our meetings so much that he came again, and even brought some of his students along.

In addition to the symposium Christiane Thim-Mabrey, the hosting professor in Regensburg, set up a complementary summer-school for students who were interested in studying worldviews. Students would study the lectures of the previous symposium under the guidance of two professors and learn to analyze their own worldviews. During the next symposium these students would sit in the front rows, each assigned to one of the lecturers to find out which worldview they represented and whether they were consistent with it. After completing this worldview-course they would get a paper from the university.

Some of the topics discussed in Regensburg included "Atheistic and Judeo-Christian Faith: How Is Natural Science Being Shaped?", "Scientific Statements and Socially Responsible Decisions", "Science, Reality and

Human Action", and "Knowing and Unknowing – the Limits of Knowledge in the Sciences."

We have not yet seen dramatic conversions at these events. However, the word has spread in the academic community that Christian scholars can run relevant academic symposiums, that they can debate agnostics and atheists face-to-face in a respectful and friendly atmosphere.

In an attempt to build the next generation of Christian professors, we decided to set aside a day for post-graduates called "Meet the Prof." This enables young Christians who are considering an academic career to meet with professors who are believers and who successfully combine faith and science in their lives and teachings. Lectures, testimonies, small groups, and individual sessions provide opportunities to learn, interact and network.

The Professors' Forum is also working on an internet-and social media strategy to increase the number of active Christian professors who will join us in the Third Educational Revolution. (Our website is www.professorenforum.de)

5. Chrześcijańskie Forum Pracowników Nauki, Poland

This forum began a similar journey in 2001: Andrzej Zabolotny, my colleague in Campus for Christ Poland, asked me to share what I had done with professors, since he also wanted to move from student ministry to working with teachers. We met in Berlin for several hours, shared and prayed together, and off he went to implement in Poland what we were trying to do in Germany. Since then he has been rallying Christian professors for summer conferences to build a strong Christian witness in Polish universities. They alternate Science-Ethics-Faith conferences with Bible studies and hiking retreats to build community.

But perhaps it is best to let Andrzej speak for himself:

> "Science-Ethics-Faith conferences have been organized by Polish Forum of Christian Scientists since 2005. They are interdisciplinary international meetings which create a space for free exchange of ideas on the relationships between these three important areas of human experience and activity. Some people believe that science and faith stand in inevitable conflict, some see harmony between

the two,while others claim they are totally separated.We believe that Christianity offers a reasonable and rational perspective on science, and offers important contributions to ethics, knowledge and practical human life."

"Our first two conference on Science, Ethics and Faith beginning 2005 carried no set theme. But from 2009 on, we have arranged discussion around such themes as Human Dignity; Science: Limitations and Opportunities; Science and Faith: Challenges of the Future; The Impact of Ideologies on Science and Social Life; and God's Action in the World from an Interdisciplinary Approach.

"The texts of the conference presentations and lectures are published in book format and also available at the Polish Christian Faculty Forum website www.chfpn.pl."

"Our Forum has also invited individual professors and groups of scholars from the US and other countries to give public apologetic lectures and presentations in Polish universities, demonstrating that science and the Christian faith are complementary, rather than mutually-exclusive and conflicting."

6. Scholars Collective, India

In India, the situation is quite different: Due to the colonial past and a long Hindu tradition, Christian scholars face unique challenges for which they are finding creative ways to handle. Ashish Alexander is one of the leaders of a group of Christian academics. He writes as follows:

A Bird's eye View of the Indian Intellectual Landscape
by ASHISH ALEXANDER

Christian scholars in India, broadly speaking, face a two-pronged challenge, from "nationalists" and from the "secularists."

The period directly after India's independence from the British in 1947 was marked by a liberal version of nationalism, combining the Gandhian and Nehruvian philosophies. Both Mohandas Gandhi and Jawahar Lal Nehru belonged to elite Hindu communities but were significantly shaped by Western thought, and had spent formative years in the West imbibing the civilizational influences of the Western world. The two men enjoyed a teacher–disciple relationship. But while Gandhi, a modern Hindu sage, was more traditional, anti-industrialist in his outlook, Nehru, a socialist, was an outspoken champion of industrialization and mega projects. However, both held moderate religious views, and in the case of Nehru, the first Indian prime minister, those views were subservient to a commitment to a "scientific temper." The academic environment that their influence fostered held to a moderate Hindu, liberal-left bent. Radical left and Hindu extremism were relegated to the margins.

The ideological framework for academic pursuits was defined by (i) India's struggle for freedom from the British and also (ii) the conflict between capitalism and socialism. This posed a certain challenge to a Christian scholar because he or she must always be careful to not appear aligned either with the British colonialism or American capitalism. The myth of collaboration between missionaries and British imperialists had taken deep root in the Hindu psyche. A Christian always lived in the awareness of this collective unconscious of the nation. He or she must always be watchful what to say and how to say it. Non-Christian scholars did not have to really worry about any such things. A moderate Hindu could, for example, say that things were better during colonialism or that American capitalism is a better economic system without anyone questioning his patriotism. A similar comment from a Christian might be damning, for him individually as well as for the Christian community.

Secularization of academia, in the name of modernism, also contributed to the marginalization of meaningful Christian engagement. Atheistic presuppositions were deemed to be scientific, a phenomenon not unlike what the Western academic world was experiencing.

Squeezed between these two dominant trends of nationalism and left liberalism, a Christian scholar was in for still more crushing times. With the end of the Cold War in the late 1980s and early 1990s, and the decline of the Congress Party of Gandhi and the Nehru dynasty, ideological configurations in India shifted drastically. The liberal version of nationalism gave way to a more rigid, religiously defined Hindu nationalism.

The rise in the political fortunes of Hindu nationalists took place when postmodern tendencies in the West were fast eroding the liberal humanist order. As liberal professors in the West became relativists and deconstructionists, many of their Indian counterparts joined the movement for Hindu revivalism. This further marginalized Christian scholars, who internalized their exclusion from the centers of knowledge production. Deep down, they also internalized colonial guilt and increasingly lost their Christian voice. Many sought to survive by holding onto the vestiges of left liberalism, which in some ways was intellectually more rigorous than the Hindu nationalist academic order.

A lingering sense of colonial guilt, self-censorship and nationalistic rhetoric all worked to convince Christians that they may not have much to contribute in the current academic scenario. Or if they did, not many will buy what they have to say.

It is against this background that a few friends began to discuss the possibility of an intellectual fraternity that will help develop an Indian Christian mind. Scholars Collective is a step in that direction.

Scholars Collective is an emerging consortium of Indian Christian scholars and researchers from different institutions that exists to share resources, and provide feedback, mentoring and academic support to Indian Christian scholars in various disciplines.

Birthed in the chaotic times of a global pandemic, this new movement has gradually gained the support of some eminent academics. Recently, two of the finest scholars who have spent their lives studying Indian history have generously given their time and shared their wisdom and resources with the group.

The collective is already a vibrant community with members making their own WhatsApp group, common e mail, YouTube channel and a fledgling Web site. It is to this group that individual members turn for feedback on academic papers and even blog posts; to enquire about books and articles; and, share personal struggles as scholars.

Scholars Collective understands that its preliminary task is to instill a sense of confidence among Indian Christian scholars. No Christian learning or teaching can happen if scholars do not strongly believe in their own work.

We also believe that the Gospel of Jesus Christ has had an immensely positive influence on the Indian subcontinent. It has touched all areas of human knowledge in modern India because the pioneers in all such spheres were either Christian missionaries themselves, or Indian Christians, or Indians of other faiths who were mentored by Christians.

Christian contribution in the area of education and health care is well known and well documented. However, Christians have also been pioneers in shaping the intellectual landscape of modern Indian through their groundbreaking work in literature and journalism. British Baptist missionaries in Bengal published *Digdarshan* and *Samachar Darpan*, in 1818 — the first periodicals published in Bengali. Hana Catherine Mullens (1826–1861) wrote India's first novel *Phulmani O Karunar Bibaran (Story of Phulmani and Karuna)*, again in Bengali, in 1856. Rev. Baba Padmanji (1836–1901) wrote the first Marathi novel *Yamuna Paryatan (Journey of Yamuna)* in 1857. Journalistic writing and reformist novels paved the way for India's intellectual renaissance.

To fight hunger and poverty, Christian initiatives in the field of agriculture are also worth mentioning. William Carey (1761–1834), the father of modern missions, helped establish the Agriculture and Horticulture Society of India in 1820. Generations later, in Allahabad, the founding of an agriculture institute by Sam Higginbottom (1874– 1958) inaugurated scientific farming in India. It was the first institute in Asia to start a department of agriculture engineering, in 1921.

This great legacy of Christian work in India has slowly been fading away even from the consciousness of Indian Christians themselves. The way we remember our national history, the way it is disseminated through established channels and even the way it is codified, shows the need to engage afresh with knowledge production in our country. An exclusive focus on political or nationalist history has overshadowed the contribution of Christian missionary movement in the making of modern India. Kenneth Ingham, Professor Emeritus of History, University of Bristol, introduced his book *Reformers in India* thus:

> 'The growth of Indian nationalism has tended to obscure the contribution of external forces to the development of India. In the field of social progress emphasis has been placed upon the activities of the Brahma Samaj, the Arya Samaj, and more recently the Congress Party, rather than upon the work of Europeans in India. But the history of Christian missionary achievements is older than any of these indigenous movements, and prepared the

way for them to a degree far greater than the number of Christians in India might now suggest. Conversions to Christianity were proportionately few, but the influence of missionaries upon social conditions was outstanding.'

The "nationalist" bias has led to a blind spot in Indian history. The national history of India is largely silent when it comes to the influence of Christianity on India's "social conditions." Historian John C. B. Webster in his recent talk at Scholars Collective webinar refers to this silence:

> This silence is due in part to a general preoccupation with political history in history textbooks and the tiny Christian minority has not played an overly conspicuous role in Indian political history. However, it is also due to a general ignoring of Dalit, Tribal and women's history, where Christianity's role has been far more significant. Such people, and this includes the entire Northeast, have been ignored as outside what has been called the "mainstream" of Indian history, even though they have provided much of its backbone.

This silence envelopes many Indian Christians and their works also. Pandita Ramabai (1858–1922), the well-known high-caste woman convert to Christianity from Maharashtra has largely been forgotten. Uma Chakravarty, who wrote a notable intellectual biography of one of modern India's greatest figures asks

> Why has the life and work of Ramabai and, more importantly, her critique of society been marginalised from mainstream history? … Ramabai's critique of Brahmanical patriarchy and her decisive break with its oppressive structure through conversion to Christianity were too much for those riding the high tide of history and for whom nationalism was synonymous with Hinduism, Ramabai became at best an embarrassment and at worst a betrayer.

She further observes:

> …[T]here has been an easy conflation not only of nationalism with Hinduism but more importantly of Christianity with colonialism. There is a latent assumption that in opting for Christianity Ramabai and others had accepted the religion of the rulers and had therefore become 'compradors' and were complicit with the colonial presence. … There is no reason to accept such assumptions without an analysis, which has hardly been undertaken, of the many

facets of Christianity in India. It is unlikely that such lacuna is likely to be filled in the near future given the obsession with 'colonial discourse' which is currently dominating historical scholarship.

The biases, the silences, the obsessions, that govern Indian academia need to be addressed, something which Scholars Collective hopes to do in the time to come.

Finally, from the US, Robert Osburn, PhD and Senior Fellow, Wilberforce International Institute reports about the concept of Christian Study Centers which have been launched near major universities, offering programs to help in the Christian formation of students.

7. Christian Study Centers And The Third Education Revolution

ROBERT OSBURN, PhD[4]

"Christian thought is the open-ended adventure into searching the unsearchable and scrutinizing the inscrutable."
Richard John Neuhaus, October 1998 <u>First Things</u>

Over the past four decades over thirty university-based Christian study centers have been launched next to major universities such as Yale, Dartmouth and a number of state universities. They sponsor lectures by Christian scholars, offer programs to help in the Christian formation of students and otherwise champion a vision of education shaped by the monumental heritage of 2000 years of Christian thought. In 2008 leaders of some of these centers organized the Consortium of Christian Study Centers, in order to both deepen and widen the influence of such centers in academic life.

Christian study centers can be valuable allies in *The Third Education Revolution* by helping to shape future professors who hold a distinctly Christian vision for their disciplines. They not only validate the role of Christian scholarship in this revolution, but also ensure that its research agenda is both true to a biblical vision and the best principles of scientific inquiry.

---

4 Senior Fellow, Wilberforce International Institute

In what follows I offer five answers to the question: "What is a Christian study center?" Those answers help us to identify ways that Christian study centers can contribute to *The Third Education Revolution*. First we must consider the core responsibilities of such centers of which I see three: *interpretive, transformative* and *protective*.

First: the *interpretive* duty. To those in the church, Christian study centers explain the agendas of higher education while answering the following question for many academics:, "What does the Christian faith have to do, if anything, with my academic calling?"

Along with an interpretive task (Church to Academy, Academy to Church) Christian study centers have a *transformative* task: fostering changes in the academy, in part by enabling academics to become agents of transformation. These agendas are related in a vicious cycle: The transformed academy will foster the development of change agents, who will change academics.

A final task of the Christian study center, beyond its interpretive and transformative tasks, is *protective*. Mark Noll wrote about the deeply ingrained anti-intellectualism that, in an earlier generation, so profoundly crippled evangelical academic engagement. Rather than cocooning Christian students, Christian study centers teach students to both discern error and embrace the good, the true and the beautiful. In order to impact Babylon, a Daniel has to master Babylonian learning without surrendering to its deception. Christian study centers protect by creating discerning minds.

Embedded in those general duties, then, are five more specific goals:

1) Interpret the Academy to Church

Historically, most American evangelicals have either ignored the academic world, or attacked it as a threat to faith. While many Christian leaders (such as James Dobson) recommended that Christians retreat to Christian colleges, the reality is that academics have a profound influence on the shape and direction of culture. Prior to his conversion, the Apostle Paul had orchestrated public opinion against early Christian believers as a foreign student studying under the leading Jewish academic of his day.

Approximately 25% of the world's current political leaders have been trained in US universities and colleges. So helping Christians to appreciate the role of Academia in the development of nations is an important task of a Christian study center.

2) Interpret Christ in Terms that Academics Understand

Numerous studies reveal that most academics consider Evangelical Christians to be the greatest single threat to society, and unworthy of serious consideration in Academics. Such skeptics have helped to push Christian faith out of the public square. Since most academics have embraced perspectives that deny the significance of God, they simply do not realize that Christian faith is deeply committed to rational thought. When Paul addressed the Athenians on Mars Hill in Acts 17, he appealed to their prior understanding and respected authorities ("even some of your own poets have said..."). Throughout the Book of Acts, Paul repeatedly argued from the first premises of his audiences, whether Greek or Jew, commoner or intellectual, and presented evidence of many kinds to back up his points. Jesus called himself "the Truth" as well as "the Way" and "the Life," and said that the truth "will set you free" (John 14:6; 8:32). Christian study centers not only help churches to value the task of academics, but they also help secular academics to better appreciate Christian contributions to thought and social development.

3) Give Christians within the academy a place where they can develop discernment and cultivate their appetites for God and good thought

With fear and trepidation, thousands of parents each year offer up their children to what was until recently considered the "marketplace of ideas". Unfortunately many children from Christian homes either <u>die</u> spiritually on campus or dive under spiritual cover. 75% of African students who come to study in the USA, upon arrival claim to be at least nominal Christians. Upon return years later, the same percentage claims no relationship to Christian faith.

In our Christian study centers well-designed, thoughtful courses in Christian studies provide students not only with answers to skeptical professors, but also with a framework for confidently affirming the trustworthiness of biblical revelation and learning how to utilize God-given reason.

Rather than being "taken captive by false ideas", students and others learn how to thoughtfully dialogue and debate ideas.

4) Channel the transformative impact of Christian ideas into the lives of those who shape culture.

As students and scholars come to recognize the transforming power and truth of Christ and His word, they are prepared to engage culture, rather than to flee it or collapse into it. They learn, for example, of the profoundly Christian ideals that revolutionized society in northern Europe and North America.

While our societies are currently in rebellion against those ideals, others, such as the thousands of foreign students in our midst, are learning that Christ stands ready to heal their nations. Thoughtful, biblical training of future leaders in our universities can reap dividends in the future of nations. This quest is mostly a driving force behind *The Third Education Revolution*, and Christian study centers are perfectly situated to help train these future transformative leaders.

5) Assist in the transformation of the academy itself.

The humanities (history, literature, arts, philosophy, etc) have long formed the intellectual core of our universities. Owing to the rise of postmodern deconstruction and critical theory, Western universities are facing not only financial, but also intellectual crises. Our universities are desperately in need of both genuine community and a commitment to students' ethical development. As Christian study centers help to "take captive every thought to make it obedient to Christ", they do so with a yearning to assist in the renewal of our universities so that they may once again be thoughtful communities in search of truth and wisdom.

Five centuries ago, Martin Luther wrote:

> "I believe that there is no work more worthy of pope or emperor than a thorough reform of the universities. And on the other hand, nothing could be more devilish or disastrous than unreformed universities."

Luther's prophetic words resonate in our 21st century ears. Many Christian study centers are ready to interpret the university to the church and the church to the university in order to provide shelter for Christian students while helping them develop discerning minds and good intellectual and spiritual appetites, and to help transform the university and thus, nations around the globe. We must pray that Christian study centers will help foster a 21st century version of the reformation of our universities that Luther sought.

These forums of professors, scholars, study centers and professionals need to be networked to forge an intellectual nucleus for *The Third Education Revolution*. They will help create the college-pedia discussed in the previous chapter. They will serve as the Subject Matter Experts to create the online curricula. They will undertake research and writing projects and guide script-writers and directors to produce works of art and media needed to reform our age. The movement must finance academic research and writing. It must support creative talent to communicate truth.

Chapter 13

A 100 Year Vision

Samson Selladurai[1]

"If your plan is for one year, plant rice. If your plan is for ten years plant trees. If your plan is for one hundred years, educate children". ~ Confucius

Just before His ascension to Heaven, on a mountain in Galilee, Jesus commissioned His disciples to go forth and make disciples of all nations. When understood through the lenses of both theology and history, this "Great Commission" implies that those who wish to fulfill Jesus' final command should formulate a comprehensive, cohesive, multi-generational plan to educate future generations, then put it into practice.

Born into a family with a number of school-teachers on both maternal and paternal sides, I recognized the value of education early on. Tamil Nadu, the south Indian state in which I was born, went through an educational revolution during the 1950's and 1960's[2] (a government aided push for free education), which changed the socio-economic climate of the state by raising its literacy level. Global executives like Sundar Pitchai, CEO of Google, Indra Nooyi, CEO of Pepsico, and Shiv Nadar, founder of HCL technologies, all of whom studied at some level in Tamil Nadu, are a testament to that value. In South India, many Protestant missionaries also built schools alongside churches, leading to the transformation of the villages and towns where they were built. My schooling at Santhosha Vidhyalaya, a missionary-founded school in south Tamil Nadu, further convinced me that education changes not just one person but entire communities.

---

1 Samson Selladurai is the co-founder and Director of Ruah Tech, an IT solutions company, that has its office in three countries globally and is headquartered in Melbourne.

2 Kamarajar Contribution towards education, accessed 25th November 2020, http://read-learn-share.blogspot.com/2013/09/kamarajar-contribution-to-wards-education.html

After undergraduate studies in India, I moved to Adelaide, Australia for my Masters, and have resided there ever since. Now an entrepreneur, working with church, governmental and business leaders across Australia and India, I have grown convinced of the need for an intentional multi-generational educational vision, building on and expanding the vision those missionaries brought to South India.

The character of Him who spoke the world into being must be understood so as to see why a long-term perspective is essential. In the following pages, first we will look at how God planned ahead - not just for a couple in a garden, but for their extended family, blessing them to be fruitful and multiply. The goal was that descendants of Abraham would carry knowledge of the glory of God from family to family and generation to generation, teaching their children's children the ways of God, until the "knowledge of the Lord covers the earth, as the waters cover the sea" (Habakuk 2:14). From the Garden of Eden in Genesis to the garden city in Revelation, God's intent for the human race has not changed. Then we will examine two modern examples of how education with a long-term vision has shaped the culture of a nation, for better and for worse.

GOD Thought: An Extended Family

From Scripture we see that the Triune God created a family to represent Him, and to extend His heavenly culture to the ends of the earth. So intending, He created Adam and Eve in His image. What was God's purpose for the first humans? To steward the Garden of Eden and expand the culture of Heaven by "being fruitful and multiplying and subduing the earth."

By "subdue," did He refer to a project of environmental exploitation and degradation? On the contrary, God told Adam to name the animals and "whatever Adam named them, that was their name" (Gen 2:19) giving the world a glimpse of the human mission in regard to the natural world. Adam was commissioned as the world's first zoologist. Knowing animals requires knowing what each species eats. Studying food, requires study of soil, climate and nature etc. That is why Adam and Eve's children began agriculture and animal husbandry. Adam and Eve had many sons and daughters (Genesis 5:4). They were responsible to pass on to their children the knowledge they had accumulated so that their descendants may fulfill God's purposes on the earth.

The Bible does not specify if Adam and Eve took that job seriously, but in the life of Cain, at least, God's purpose was frustrated. Paul wrote that "God chose us before the creation of the world." (Ephesians 1:4) Humanity was not God's Plan B. We are His original design: He intended that His people have authority to steward the earth.

God was thrilled with His new extended family and visited the Garden daily to commune with the couple and see how they would fulfill His heart's desire. When Adam and Eve gave in to Satan's temptations, and were evicted from the garden, God's plan was disrupted, but only for a time. God continued to work to fulfill His sovereign purposes, repeatedly seeking out people to participate in His plan of redemption. This plan revealed God's limitless love for humanity when He sent His Son to the world. Jesus took the sins of us all to a cross. He conquered sin and its consequence, death, thereby reconciling man with God. He made us God's children (Rom 8:15) as Adam and Eve had once been (Luke 3:38).

An Unconditional Blessing

God's blessings to Adam and the Patriarchs not only reveal His generous heart for humanity but also the role He intended for us within His long-term redemptive plan. Each time He blessed a person, God gave a command with the whole earth in mind. To Adam God said "Be fruitful and multiply, fill the earth and subdue it; have dominion" (Gen 1:28), To Noah He said "Be fruitful and multiply and fill the earth" (Gen 9:1), To Abraham He said "I will make you into a great nation, so that you will be a blessing...I will make you exceedingly fruitful, all nations will be blessed through you" (Gen 12:2, Gen 17:6), To Jacob He said, "Be fruitful and multiply" (Gen 35:11) and in Ephesians 3:10 the Apostle Paul wrote, "His (God's) *intent* was that now, *through the church*, the manifold wisdom of God should be made known."

Again and again God told those that He had called: "I am blessing you, my representatives, to be a blessing to the world." But in no case is the full blessing immediate. Whether to humanity as a whole, Israel as a nation, or the Church, blessings are intended for generations to come.

God's covenantal promises (Gen.3:15) that began in Adam descended over generations to a man called Abraham, who was told he would become father of many nations. When God blessed Jacob, He invoked the same blessing He gave to Jacob's father Issac and his grandfather Abraham. God said: "The Land I gave to Abraham and Isaac, I give to you and to your offspring after you" (Gen 35:12), again revealing that He is interested in multiple generations and that He wants Jacob to pass on the same legacy to His children.

After four hundred years in Egypt, one of Abraham's descendants came upon a mysterious bush in the wilderness, on fire but not consumed. Through that bush, God revealed Himself as Yahweh, the God of Abraham, Isaac and Jacob. So again, it is clear that our divine mandate to disciple nations is inherently multi-generational. The God of Abraham, Isaac and Jacob is the Lord of generations. So we should aim at educating our children and our children's children after them, in the ways of the Lord, seeing our purpose in life is not merely individual salvation, but the redemption of the nations.

In his book "*Walk in Generational Blessings*," Joseph Mattera writes, "As Christians we are not just called to grow and multiply churches, but collectively influence entire cities, giving them a blueprint of how a Christ-dominated nation would look under the rule and reign of God."[3] So having received the royal blessing to be fruitful and have dominion on earth, it is impossible to work towards transformation of the nations unless we intentionally plan to educate those who will come after us.

A Global Mandate

The First Adam sinned; the patriarchs proved unequal to the task; the nation of Israel, led by Moses, rebelled; and generation after generation of kings and priests also failed to carry God's blessing and glory throughout the earth. But at the central point in history, Christ entered the world. Here was the "second Adam", a new Moses, a true Israel, a perfect Prophet, Priest and King.

Jesus reiterated the original divine plan when He told His followers, "Go and make disciples of all nations" (Matt 28:18). Jesus' commission meant that his soldiers have to make God's enemies his footstool. The rebels have to surrender to God acknowledging that Jesus is Lord. That is the entry point into the blessings of God's kingdom.

---

3 Joseph Mattera, *Walk in Generational Blessings*, 2012, p 30

In his letter to the Corinthian Church the Apostle Paul writes: "We are ambassadors for Christ" (2 Corinthians 5:20). In Jesus' commission God doubled down on the royal blessing given to Adam and the patriarchs. His purpose was to seed all earthly cultures with the leaven of Heaven. Such a mandate cannot be achieved in a lifetime but requires generations of God's children building upon one another's legacies. The Bible tells how the fate of God's chosen nation depended upon the faithfulness of its leaders in imparting the law of God to young people:

> "Take to heart these words that I give you today. Repeat them to your children. Talk about them when you are at home or away, when you lie down or get up. Write them down, and tie them around your wrist, and wear them as headbands as a reminder. Write them on the door-frames of your houses and on your gates." (Deuteronomy 6:5-9)

> "Be careful never to forget what you yourself have seen. Do not let these memories escape from your mind as long as you live! And be sure to pass them on to your children and grandchildren." (Deuteronomy 4:9-10)

This command to teach the grandchildren was so vital that God told the Jews to lay down stones so that a key moment in history would be exhibited to later generations as reminders (Joshua 4:6). When we read the Old Testament we see how Moses, a powerful leader, left a legacy through Joshua, how Elijah the prophet left a legacy through Elisha, and then how David prepared materials, furnishings and human capital to enable his son Solomon to build the temple of God.

God's long-term, multi-generational plan to redeem humanity is thus made abundantly clear in Scripture. As Jesus said, the Kingdom of God is like a seed that grows (over time) into a tree in which the birds of the air can nest. The Bible was written in three languages over some 1300 years, yet this theme reveals a single Mind with a clear objective.

From my experiences in Australia and India, let me offer two examples which show that a long-term educational strategy is the best – a program in Australia which was recently started and has begun to yield good results, and another one begun in India almost a century ago which is reaping abundant but often bitter fruit.

Policy Influence in Australia

Lachlan Macquarie Institute in Australia (LMI), with which I was affiliated after I completed my Master's degree in Adelaide, helps to show how we can plan to change culture over generations.

The Australian Christian Lobby (ACL) was founded in 1995 with a vision to influence Australian public policies and politics towards truth and justice based on the Scriptures. The lobbying accomplished a great deal in defending conservative Christian values. However, after more than twelve years of lobbying, the management saw that they were reactively snuffing out bush fires of current controversies. They needed to plan at least a generation in advance, partly by raising leaders in public policy for the future. Clearly the Culture War, the battle of ideas and sexualization of the masses through the LGBTQ+ agenda were only going to increase, and there was little holiness or light of the divine in the halls of public power. Like Paul the Apostle, ACL wanted to raise up leaders who could both 'reason' and 'defend' the truth. They knew that education was the means by which this nation could be won back to truth. This long-term mission inspired the leaders to found the Lachlan Macquarie Institute (LMI).

Since its inception in 2011, LMI has held biannual programs combining a healthy dose of Scripture, social analysis, Christian apologetics, lawmaking, political science and philosophy. Teachers include professors from Australia's leading universities, elite public policy analysts, media experts and notable church and business leaders. Regular guest speakers include former and present parliamentarians and cabinet members.[4]

LMI is designed to help participants gain both a theoretical understanding of basic theology, worldviews and public policy, and some practical experience in working with political leaders. All this is done in a 16-week residential program located on the outskirts of the capital. The goal of this initiative is to raise "wise leaders" who are effective in building their nation in the light of the Great Commission mandate. Already many alumni are making an impact working both directly and indirectly in the public sector.

During my time at the LMI, I enjoyed a short internship with a Member of Parliament, met other public servants and began to understand how the federal government functions and how policies are enacted. Among

---

4 Lachlan Macquarie Institute website, accessed 22 sep 2020 <www.lmi.org.au>

the highlights of my training was meeting (with others) a former prime minister and a former deputy prime minister.

In 2017, Australia legalized Same Sex Marriage and changed the traditional definition of marriage.[5] It is shocking that in less than four decades, a radical worldview could dismantle the age-old institution of marriage. It's time we think ahead, taking a multi-generational approach to tackle the cultural challenges of our time wherever we are.

The education I received at LMI as a young adult shaped my worldview, purposes in life and the need to engage in conversations in the public sphere so as to leave a better nation for future generations. In fact, LMI helped me to zero in on my calling of working with leaders in Church, Business and Government to bring about holistic social transformation. Soon after my experience with LMI we hosted a conference in Australia in 2014 and another two in India in 2015 and 2016, each time hosting more than a hundred Christian leaders in those three domains plus Christian missions. These conferences have helped forge alliances between political parties to work towards common objectives. Prayer groups have been formed, and leaders have arisen to fulfill their calling in their respective spheres of influence. If our nations are to be baptized in the ways of the Lord, and discipled into truth, we need a 100 year vision, and now is the time to get going.

Changing the Spiritual Guard in India

The impact of an even more comprehensive long-term vision among radical Hindus is now bearing a different kind of fruit in my homeland. With its population now nearing 1.4 billion, a burgeoning working middle class and relatively young population, India naturally attracts the attention of businessmen and politicians alike. Opportunities for young, hard-working and intelligent minds are many. Whoever educates this population will, for decades, influence the course of the country, and, as India grows in power, the world.

An Indian organization that has made the most effective use of multi-generational planning is the 'Rashtriya Swayamsevak Sangh,' or RSS. The RSS has founded multiple organizations across various sectors, including the

5 AAP, 2017 Australia Legalises same sex marriage, SBS News, accessed 22 september: https://www.sbs.com.au/news/australia-legalises-same-sex-marriage

Bharatiya Janata Party (BJP) or National People's Party, which presently rules India under the leadership of Prime Minister Narendra Modi. In my view, if there is one organization in the world today that has successfully implemented the vision of a "Cultural Mandate", it would be the RSS. Their vision is detailed with clarity, their commitment seems unwavering, and their long-term view extends well beyond the common socialist Five-Year Plan.

The RSS was founded in 1925, close to a century ago, when the concept of a Hindu Rashtra (Sanskrit for 'nation') was seen as far-stretched. But the long-term plans of the RSS proved remarkably successful.

The parent body has a clear vision. They see education as the key to dominating the Hindu heartland. This is evident in the 12,363 formal schools, 12,000 single teacher schools and numerous Seva Kendras (service centers) run across the country by the Akhil Bharatiya Vidhyarthi Parishad[6] (ABVP) (All India Student Council), an affiliate of RSS.

Today the RSS wields so much influence across the fabric of the nation that many fear that the integrity of India's secular constitution hangs in the balance. This right-wing Hindu "extremist" organization was banned by the first prime minister Jawaharlal Nehru due to their opposition to the secular constitution of India,[7] the national Tricolor flag, and the fact that a former RSS member had assassinated Mahatma Gandhi, "the Father of India." In 1949 this ban was lifted. The RSS organized itself furiously and has grown exponentially.

RSS includes more than twenty para organizations for women, youth, farmers, workers, nurseries, schools and institutes, the World Hindu Council, and of course the National Peoples' Party (BJP), all growing steadily and working towards the vision of a Hindu nation. These organizations are directly influenced by RSS, their ideological mentor. At present, RSS claims to run fourteen *samkalps* (training institutes). These Institutes train

----

6 Rohini Mohan, 2016, 'Indianise, nationalise, spiritualise: The RSS education project is in expansion mode' Scroll, accessed 22 september, <https://scroll. in/article/815049/indianise-nationalise-spiritualise-the-rss-education-project-is-in-for-the-long-haul>

7 Rashtriya Swayamsevak Sangh, accessed 22 september, <https://en.wikipedia. org/wiki/ Rashtriya_Swayamsevak_Sangh>

young minds as future bureaucrats to staff key positions managing the affairs of the nation in Law, Judiciary, Administrative, Revenue and so on.

Currently, around "60% of successful bureaucratic candidates were associated" with RSS Samkalps (Training institutes). Out of 1,078 candidates shortlisted to serve the government in key roles in 2020, 646 had undergone coaching at RSS Samkalps at some stage.[8]

Today, the RSS largely controls the media, the legal system including judges, and the civil administration. They have begun to brazenly criticize and even persecute minorities like Muslims and Christians, especially in the past five years.[9] With RSS gaining political and ideological power, the threat that it will alter the Constitution more in line with the principles of the *Law of Manu* (Hindu law) is real. What would that look like? Some want to revive the guru-disciple system of education. Development, diversity and freedom of India would be harmed by a return of the caste system and the increased influence of upper caste Hindus. It remains to be seen what RSS influence might mean for women, the lower castes and 'untouchables.' Some of them want to replace Mahatma Gandhi with Godse (his assassin) as the Nation's icon! I hope this turns out to be nothing more than gloomy speculation. However, that is India's trajectory under the RSS as was Germany's direction under Nazism.

In her book *How to Lose a Country: The 7 Steps from Democracy to Dictatorship*, writing from modern Turkey, Ece Temelkuran describes a similar downwards scenario.[10] Temelkuran says that the descent begins with the creation of a movement with an extremist agenda, followed by dismantling judicial and political mechanisms. The end result, she writes, is "a world where the humiliated greets the perpetrator as his savior." An open-minded reader will notice that the patterns of the signs she warns of, can mostly be observed in India as well.

---

8 Sameer, 2020, '60 percent of civil servants associated with RSS run Samkalp', The Siasat Daily, accessed 22 september, <https://www.siasat.com/60-percent-of-civil-servants-associated-with-rss-run-samkalp-1918054/>

9 Antichristian violence on the rise, accessed 25th November 2020, <https://www.ucanews. com/news/anti-christian-violence-on-the-rise-in-india/88960#>

10 Ece Temelkuran, How to Lose a Country: The 7 Steps from Democracy to Dictatorship, 2019

When one observes how the RSS has managed to indoctrinate even intellectual elites who are generally skeptical of extreme views, while the Body of Christ has often remained visionless, divided, and selfish, focusing on its own needs rather than raising future leaders, we can only blame ourselves for the results. For example: the percentage of Christians in India from the 1950s to the last official census in 2011 has remained about the same at 2.3%. Although there are various reasons for this, it can be largely attributed to the fact that we lack long-term vision. When Jesus said "I am coming soon," He was in essence telling us "occupy until I come" but we seem to have forgotten our role in His kingdom and have lost our focus along the way.

When the God of Abraham, Isaac and Jacob commands His people to teach their children and children's children His global mandate; when He proclaims that His mercy extends to "a thousand generations" for those who love Him, why is it that we as Christians fail so completely in long-term thinking? Why don't we raise our children to be the light of the world as leaders, doctors, scientists and entrepreneurs to the glory of God? Might not the future of India be different if 29 million Christians think ahead and raise at least their own children with a long-term plan and a clear purpose within this overarching divine calling? Needless to say, loving our neighbors must include loving our neighbors' children as well.

India is the land where the Apostle Thomas landed 2000 years ago. Here great missionaries like William Carey, Alexander Duff, Sam Higginbottom and the Jesuits transformed the subcontinent through education. The Learning Reformation they inspired, created intellectually equipped Indians who could think for themselves and fight for their rights and freedom.

William Carey pioneered print technology, published India's first newspaper and built the largest press in India not to mention his contributions to astronomy, biology and language. Carey also fought the ancient evil of *sati*, killing widows when their husbands died. By the end of Carey's life India had been greatly transformed. Asian historian Hugh Tinker summarizes Carey's impact[11] on India this way:

> "And so in Serampore, on the banks of the river Hooghly, the principal elements of modern South Asia — the press, the university, social consciousness — all came to light".

11 Scott Allen, William Carey, A Missionary Who Transformed a Nation, accessed 25 Sep 2020 <https://www.missionfrontiers.org/issue/article/william-carey>

Vishal and Ruth Mangalwadi's book *The Legacy of William Carey: A Model for the Transformation of a Culture* describes Carey's influence in modern India in depth.[12]

Higginbottom founded what is now called, in his honor, the Sam Higginbottom University of Agriculture, Technology and Sciences (SHUATS), which played a role in the Green and White Revolutions that transformed agriculture and animal husbandry in India.

The impact of such reforms can be seen after many centuries. The fact that most politicians in India are graduates of institutions built and founded by missionaries, is a testament to their influence. Why then do only a few such graduates retain a Christian worldview? Should we not re-imagine a world in which we carry God's mandate to transform and disciple nations down through the generations? Compared to the ideological juggernaut of RSS which barrels through India today, and the work of early missionaries, modern Christianity falls far short. We as the body of Christ seem to lack the long-term vision to transform India. Let us remember the far-seeing words of Christ, who said, "You shall do greater works" and commanded us to "Go and disciples the nations!"

Why the Third Education Revolution Requires a Long- Term Vision

The great cathedrals of Europe were built with a plan for centuries. Historians say that most cathedrals took at least a century to construct. Imagine the vision responsible for carrying out such projects over several generations by the common man, "the most muscular and bodacious folk art the world has known," as Anthony Esolen put it:

> "Imagine what is was to 'own', with the rest of your townsmen, a structure that pierced the skies with its grandeur, yet that also welcomed you in; and that stood as an eloquent witness when you were born, when you married, when you had children and when you died."

These cathedrals were places of education too. Some of history's greatest universities were born in these cathedral schools. The prophetic word given by Isaac and Jacob to their sons and grandchildren (Gen 27:29; 49;

---

12 Vishal Mangalwadi, Legacy of William Carey: A Model for the Transformation of a Culture,1999,<https://www.amazon.in/Legacy-William-Carey-Transformation-Culture/dp/1581341121>

48:14-16) were similarly visionary. Should not Christians in India, Australia and around the world also seek to bless our children, and the world through them, with a similar view of the far horizon?

When Old Testament prophets received a word from God and spoke to the nation, they often did so with the long-term future in view. When God told Jeremiah "Your nation's sons and daughters will be taken captive", the Jews knew that they would face this destiny as a nation. It was painful, but they held onto the hope that, after turbulent times, their sons and daughters would return and their great-grandchildren would play in the streets. Why have we perverted the promises of God and made them about "me, myself and I?"

How wonderful it is when parents (both biological or spiritual) raise children with a vision to bring God's Kingdom to their spheres of influence. Children mentored by such visionaries stand on the shoulders of past generations. Will it be said of us, too, that we contended for the truth to win nations because we believed God's promises and planned generations ahead? With such daring dreams, anything is possible.

Sex trafficking and racism, ideologies like atheism and postmodernism, the spirit of death as embodied in euthanasia and abortion, the demons of power and selfishness, can only be combatted with a long-term vision.

Jesus compared the Church (His royal family) to a leaven "that permeates the yeast" over time, to salt that changes the flavor of the meal, to a light that shines through darkness and to a seed that slowly grows into a tree, giving roost to many birds. God was in essence saying, "Don't worry if things begin small. Give it time, and watch how the culture of this new kingdom I am building will cover the Earth." After all, Isaiah had promised that of the increase of God's kingdom there would be no end. (Isaiah 9:7) with one generation building on the legacy of the last. And then the voices in heaven shout, "The kingdoms of this world become the kingdom of our God" (Rev 11:15).

The mandate lies in our hands. Let us go and make disciples of all nations – and of their children's children.

II

The Rise and Fall of Western Education

Chapter 14

The Pietist Origin of the Modern University

Gottfried Sommer[1]

Martin Luther's Educational Reforms

Professor Martin Luther wrote more about education than any other sixteenth century Reformer. Besides writing letters, Luther also published tracts, sermons, catechisms and commentaries on the subject of reforming education. He persuaded secular authorities to authorize the use of church property for schooling.

Luther's movement for reform succeeded because he got the masses excited about knowledge. One of his important contributions was to move his own university at Wittenberg to study other classical languages and literature aside from Latin. That set the stage for his younger and learned colleague Philip Melanchthon to be recognized as the *praeceptor Germaniae*, the "teacher of Germany." Unlike other Renaissance humanists, the reformers took learning to the common man.

In *Two Reformations* (2003), Heiko Oberman explains that Martin Luther changed the knowledge industry because he realized that God acts in history. Scholasticism had reduced education to Aristotelian speculation about the existence of God. But God is more than an actor in pre-history. He addresses man personally through his living Word.

As early as 1509 Luther had begun to critique both branches of medieval scholasticism: *antiqua* and *moderna*. Careful study of the Bible forced him to rethink the relationship between theology and philosophy. "The paradigm shift from God as *Being* to God as *Person*" freed Luther to get out of contemporary intellectual boxes and consider issues that other scholars could not tackle.

---

1 Dr. Gottfried Sommer is a theologian with a Ph.D. in Church History and an IT Instructor.

Luther's study of the Bible did not lead to rejecting reason as a means of knowledge. He used it primarily to fight against the seductive arts of Satan. Luther's eschatology motivated him to "throw everything forward" in order to snatch as many people as possible from Satan's seduction. His *Letter* to the German nobility explains why a university that is focused on the "plague" of Aristotle "serves only to increase sin and error" and needed to be reformed:

> "What else are the universities, . . . but places where loose living is practiced, where little is taught of the Holy Scriptures and Christian faith, and where only the blind, heathen teacher Aristotle rules far more than Christ? In this regard my advice would be that Aristotle's *Physics, Metaphysics, Concerning* the *Soul,* and *Ethics,* which hitherto have been thought to be his best books, should be completely discarded along with all the rest of his books that boast about nature, although nothing can be learned from them either about nature or the Spirit. Moreover, nobody has yet understood him, and many souls have been burdened with fruitless labor and study, at the cost of much precious time. I dare say that any potter has more knowledge of nature than is written in these books. It grieves me to the quick that this damned, arrogant, villainous heathen has deluded and made fools of so many of the best Christians with his misleading writings. God has sent him as a plague upon us on account of our sins."[2]

Luther's language was harsh. That, however, does not mean that he was intolerant of pagan books. He recommends Aristotle's works in which the philosopher observes nature without speculating about the nature of God:

> "I would gladly agree to keeping Aristotle's books *Logic, Rhetoric,* and *Poetics,* or at least keeping and using them in an abridged form, as useful in training young people to speak and to preach properly. But the commentaries and notes must be abolished, and as Cicero's *Rhetoric* is read without commentaries and notes, so Aristotle's *Logic* should be read as it is without all these commentaries."[3]

Luther drew a sharp distinction between the Scholastic theologians of glory and his own *theology* of the cross. However, the discontinuity wasn't absolute, Bielfeldt explains:

2 Luther, 2015

3 Luther, 2015

> "Luther did not reject reason or philosophy *in toto* but, rather, a particular and limited employment and understanding of it that supposed reason, through its own resources, could provide access to God's nature and actions. . . Indeed, in his rejection of Aristotle . . . Luther shows himself to be a competent philosophical thinker."[4]

Luther often cited Greek and Latin classics. In one standard addition of his works, one finds more than 700 references to Aristotle or his works, 300 to Cicero, 250 to Virgil, followed by Horace and Terence with some 200 each, and more than a hundred each to Ovid, Pliny the Elder, Plato, and Aesop. On the next layer, Luther cited Seneca, Demosthenes, Suetonius, Juvenal, Homer, Plautus, and Epicurus more than 50 times, followed by Plutarch, Quintilian, Lucian, Livy, and Martial.[5]

Philip Melanchthon: Teacher of Germany

While Luther refuted the humanist Erasmus on many points, Phillip Melanchthon unified Luther's theology with Erasmus's Humanism to oppose Scholasticism. No modern day fundamentalist, Melanchthon published the work of numerous ancient pagan writers, including Cicero, Plutarch, Virgil, and Ptolemy. He shared Erasmus' concern with grammar, rhetoric, and social reform.[6] He prepared a "wealth of pedagogical material" on every subject under the sun:

> "Manuals for instructors in Greek and Latin, texts on dialectic, rhetoric, moral philosophy, arithmetic, and etymology; commentaries on Aristotle's Politics, Ethics, and De anima."[7]

The education revolution launched by Protestant Reformers bore much fruit. Melanchthon's advocacy of education increased by a third the number of students going to university in the region around Frankfurt (Hesse). Matriculation rates in Latin schools also soared.

The Reformers' goal of educating an elite class of leaders in humanistic studies was largely met. They began to change Germany because the majority of top-tier public officials were graduates of the University of

---

4 Bielfeldt, 2015

5 Springer, 2007

6 Jackson, 2013

7 Overfield, 1984

Marburg. This school was founded because of the reforms Melanchthon promoted.[8]

The University of Königsberg (1542) was founded by Margrave Albert von Hohenzollern under Melanchthon's influence. He also served as an adviser to the University of Jena, founded by John Frederick of Saxony in 1548. Melanchthon aided both Ulrich von Württemberg in the reorganization of the University in Tübingen, and Joachim I. von Brandenburg in reforming the University of Frankfurt on the Oder.[9] Luther and Melanchthon did not champion what is now called "the Simple Gospel." They are rightly recognized as proponents of the integration model of Christian education. In shaping education, they relied on the Bible but utilized and corrected the theories of non-Christians like Plato, Aristotle, and Virgil.[10]

The Medical Faculty of the University of Wittenberg

Development of the medical faculty in Wittenberg shows how open educational reform initiated by Luther and Melanchthon could be. Melanchthon encouraged the medical faculty to learn from ancient physicians, especially from the Corpus Hippocraticum and the works of Galen (c 129 AD - 210 AD). However, their medical practices ought to be subjected to observation and experimentation.

This intellectual openness freed Melanchthon to respect groundbreaking findings of the Flemish anatomist Andreas Vesal (1514-1564). Vesal had discovered fundamental errors in Galen's views on anatomy by dissecting corpses. He suspected that Galen studied anatomy by dissecting animal bodies. Melanchthon's textbook *"Liber De Anima"* (1553) incorporates Vesal's corrections of ancient medical beliefs. This anti-authoritarian, observation-based approach to medicine was radically new for the sixteenth century.

Melanchthon evaluated fifteen of Galen's writings. He went on to connect the anatomy of the body with the soul. He believed that the Creator showed himself in nature, especially in human anatomy. Natural philosophy (now called science) does not answer deeper theological questions

---

8 Wright, 1987 in Jackson 2013

9 Meyer, 1975

10 Jackson 2013

about the nature and acts of God. So even the best natural history could not replace the revealed gospel. It had to remain subordinate to God's revelation.

Jürgen Helm demonstrated that anatomical knowledge at the Protestant university in Wittenberg was not fundamentally different from that at the Catholic university in Ingolstadt. What made it modern was its new approach to submitting the conclusions of human authorities to experimentation and observation. Daniel Sennert (1572-1637), for example, became a professor at the University of Wittenberg in 1602. He combined ancient atomic science with the teachings of Paracelsus, especially his use of chemical drugs in the art of healing.[11]

German Universities and the Emergence of Modern Science

Innovations at the University of Wittenberg affected reforms at the University of Halle (1694) and Göttingen (1736) which became role models for other universities. The University of Leipzig developed the modern tradition of scientific and cultural life. It published scientific periodicals and fine literature; combined vibrant theater with music while pursuing philological sciences. The developments that define a modern university blossomed in Halle, especially when Christian Thomasius moved there from Leipzig.[12]

Researchers like Ian Hunter have described the challenges of transforming medieval into modern universities.[13] The Lutheran "Second Scholasticism" faced sustained attack. By the end of the 17th century, two fractions emerged out of the turmoil.

On one side were the Pietist theologians deeply concerned about the poor emphasis on the spiritual life of university students. On the other side were philosophers concerned about their constricted intellectual development. Both strongly criticized the then-dominant academic life.

11 Schlöder, Schochow, Steger 2015

12 Döring 2015

13 Hunter 2000

"Desacralization" of Philosophy

In 1699 Christian Thomasius attacked Aristotelian metaphysics prevalent in universities at that time. He cautioned law students at the University of Halle against six philosophical errors:

> (1) That God and matter were two co-equal principles.
> (2) That God's nature consisted in thinking.
> (3) That man's nature consists in thinking and that the welfare and happiness of the whole human race depends on the correct arrangement of thought.
> (4) That man is a single species and that what is good for one [person] is good for another.
> (5) That the will is improved through the understanding.
> (6) That it is within human capacity to live virtuously and happily.[14]

Following Luther's example of making the Bible available in German, Thomasius fought for using the common vernacular in science. He opposed sorcery and witch trials, opposing the latter for 30 years. The last witch trial took place in Prussia one year before he died. This shows an important aspect of the genius of Thomasius and makes clear that it was not Enlightenment, but a pious Christian professor of law, who refuted this unjust practice, which was rooted in superstition.[15]

Pietist Theologians in Opposition to "Lutheran Scholasticism"

German Pietism was a robust movement that sought to combine heart and mind, and opposed Lutheran scholasticism. Some people find it hard to believe that Pietism fashioned the modern university because they confuse it with Radical Pietists such as Gottfried Arnold. He quit the University of Giessen in 1698 because he thought that "it was impossible to be a real Christian in such a secular and pagan atmosphere. University education corrupted youths and led to vanity."[16]

Philip Jakob Spener, the founder of Pietism, saw himself as a successor to the reforming efforts of Martin Luther. In one of Pietism's central texts,

---

14 Hunter 2000

15 Tomasoni 2009

16 Gehrz, 2014

Pia Desideria, Spener follows "a medical model of diagnosis, prognosis and therapy."[17] What was the diagnosis? Spener perceived that the academic life of his time did not follow practical Christian ideals. Therefore he called on lecturers and students to be examples of a sacred Christian life, focusing on one's relation to God:

> "Those who are wanting in love of Christ and who neglect the practice of piety do not obtain the fuller knowledge of Christ and more abundant gift of the Holy Spirit. Hence to obtain a genuine, living, active, and salutary knowledge of divine things it is not enough to read and search the Scriptures, but it is necessary that love of Christ be added, that is, that one beware of sins against conscience, by which an obstacle is raised against the Holy Spirit, and that one earnestly cultivate piety."

Students should receive from universities not only certificates of academic achievements but also of spiritual maturity. Spener urged lecturers to be academic pastors who guide students, taking into account their individual talents and the needs of their regions:

> "It would also be helpful if the professors would employ their skills to observe which studies might be useful and necessary to each student according to his intellectual gifts, his homeland, his professional goals, and the like. Some should pursue polemics with more zeal in preparation for their profession, because it is necessary that the church always have adequately equipped men to contend with enemies of the truth; rather than allowing every Goliath fearlessly to taunt the ranks of Israel, it must have some Davids who can step forward and face the Goliaths."

In addition to academic literature, the student ought also to read edifying literature by German mystics. Spener cited Luther to recommend one:

> "If you desire to read the old, pure theology in German, you can obtain to the sermons of the Dominican friar, John Tauler. Neither in the Latin nor in the German language have I found a purer, more wholesome theology or one that agrees more with the Gospel."

Spener recommended a practical, even ascetic piety:

> "Just because theology is a practical discipline and does not consist only of knowledge, study alone is not enough, nor is the mere

17 Williams 2014

accumulation and imparting of information . . . It would also be desirable if students were given concrete suggestions on how to institute pious meditations, how to know themselves better through self-examination, how to resist the lusts of the flesh, how to hold their desires in check and die unto the world . . . Our dear Luther expressed this opinion:" A man becomes a theologian not by comprehending, reading, or speculating but by living and indeed dying and being damned.'"

The goal of biblical exegesis is to put what has been worked out, into practice. Exegesis should be a community affair:

". . . each student may be permitted to say what he thinks about each verse and how he finds that it applies to his own and to others' benefit. The professor, as the leader, should reinforce good observations. If he sees, however, that students are departing from the end in view, he should proceed in clear and friendly fashion to set them right on the basis of the text and show them what opportunity they have to put this or that rule of conduct into practice."

The student body should learn to encourage one another to put the Scriptures in practice, making the Christian walk both a collective and an individual endeavor. They should offer "brotherly admonitions" to one another to follow the godly rules, with the professor playing a role in accountability as well.

August Hermann Francke, Educational Reformer

August Hermann Francke was a close friend and ally of Spener. Around the time they first met, Spener had taken up a coveted post as senior court chaplain to the Saxon Elector, Johann Georg III, in Dresden. However, he could not stay long because of their constant clashes. Spener considered the court culture excessively secular.

By 1685, Francke had earned his Masters in Hebrew Grammar and Philology at the University of Leipzig. There he founded the Collegium Philobiblicum, where pupils studied both the language and the teachings of the Bible. When he met Spener, he testified to a conversion experience that he described as a "hard-won struggle."[18]

---

18 Whitmer, 2015

Having spent some "quality time" with Spener, Franke returned to Leipzig in 1689, and began to lecture in German instead of Latin. His lectures, which were extremely popular, unabashedly criticized the way in which theology was being taught. He attacked the culture of abstract disputation and emphasis on scholastic philosophy. This offended several orthodox Lutheran theology professors. They launched formal investigations against him and his friends, banned the student meetings, and refused to allow him to teach.

With help from Spener, in 1691 Francke received a pastorate in a suburb of Halle, 50 kilometers northwest of Leipzig.

Soon Spener was invited to serve as the Hohenzollerns' court chaplain in Berlin. There he learned of Friedrich I's plans to found a new university in Halle. Spener ensured that Francke was offered a chair in Greek and Oriental Languages when the new university opened in 1694.

Upon commencing his duties in Halle, Francke founded the "Orphanage". This was not just a home for orphan boys and girls. Around that core were established a school and a community of teachers and researchers, including famous philosophers and mathematicians like Ehrenfried Tschirnhaus.

The "Orphanage" nourished a research community with a wide range of interests in books, gardening, medicinal herbs, and a collection of "curious things," including a variety of scientific instruments such as burning mirrors and an air pump. This community provided a world-class education to the poorest children. The Orphanage partnered with the Berlin Academy of Sciences run by Gottfried Wilhelm Leibniz, one of the most famous German philosophers of all time. Francke's visionary leadership attracted the attention of Tsar Peter I.[19]

Francke was deeply concerned about the condition of German universities because almost all church and secular offices were filled by university graduates. But universities were not exactly known for their piety:
> "The universities have been such places where everything wild, bold and raw was exercised under the name of an Academic Freedom. And by such false freedom they have become a pool of all shame and abominations . . . seduced and seducing people, drunkards, thugs and other such horrible people . . . have been taken out of

---

19 Whitmer, 2015

these holes and put into public office, i.e. not only into the secular, but also into the spiritual offices..."[20]

Halle University

In 1680, a Huguenot named Michel Milié dit la Fleur founded a language and retreat school, from which emerged Knights' Academy. That was the seed that grew into the University of Halle. When Leipzig expelled philosopher Christian Thomasius, he began lecturing in Halle in 1690. Aristocratic listeners came to hear him. On July 1, 1694 was founded the "first free-spirited university in Germany", the University of Halle.

Halle took academic freedom as essential for innovative teaching and research. The leitmotif of the university was: "Science in the Service of Life." This joining of intellectual and spiritual pursuits raised the young Pietist school to the top tier of German universities. Thomasius and Francke ensured that Halle began as a reforming university. In the first 50 years, it was primarily focused on law. Thomasius lectured in German, so he is considered one of the fathers of German-speaking science. Dissertations, however, continued to be written in Latin. Rivals warned that a student who went to Halle would come out an "atheist or pietist."[21]

The theological faculty was pietist from the beginning, because Prussia accepted pietists who were harassed elsewhere. The Prussian court that hired Philipp Jakob Spener knew that he had been a provost and consistory councilor in Berlin since 1691. He had formulated a concept for reforming theological training and also knew suitable candidates. Their goal was to establish a training program in Halle that was professionally and practically oriented but not denominationally polemical and theologically controversial. Francke came to Halle as professor of Greek and Oriental languages. He attracted Lutheran criticism because he subjected Luther's translation of the Bible to critical review in a monthly journal of philological-exegetic comments on Bible verses.[22]

---

20 Fries, 1894

21 Kathe, 1998

22 Kathe, 1998

The Faculty Reforms Medical Science

Halle's medical faculty began with four teachers. Between 1693 and 1700, only 144 students out of 2884 enrolled in medicine. Anton Amo from the Gold Coast (Ghana) became the first African student to be enrolled at a European university in 1727. Dorothea Erxleben became the first woman in Germany to gain her thesis in medicine at Halle. With the addition of the famous physician Friedrich Hoffmann and of Johann Junker, who began teaching at the Orphanage from 1716, the medical faculty became an internationally renowned center of practical training.

The relationship between the institutions Francke had founded, and the Halle medical faculty, was strong from the beginning. The university provided nursing facilities as well as medical care even when the medical faculty had only two professors, Hoffmann (1660–1742), and Georg Ernst Stahl (1659–1734), among the most famous physicians of their day.

At the beginning of the 18th Century, the medical laboratories were supervised by Johann Junker, while Hoffmann conducted medicinal research and published papers. These medicines were exported as far as India and South Africa.[23]

Halle's medical faculty contrasted dramatically with Lutheran universities that largely relied on the ancient physician Galen. Hoffmann diagnosed and treated from observation, based on his own theories.[24] His approach began to be called "mechanistic," though he never saw it as a conflict with his faith.[25] Stahl, by contrast, doubted that a mechanical perspective could express the complexity of human life, emphasizing the interaction of soul with body.[26] That such contrary positions existed together at the same university shows something of the academic freedom at the first Pietist university.

---

23 Zumkeller, 2001

24 Stitziel, 1996

25 Stitziel, 1996

26 King, 1964

A New Epistemology: Observing with Outer and Inner Eyes

In reforming academics, Leibniz, Tschirnhaus and Francke dealt with issues which Johann Amos Comenius, the Czech pedagogue who is described as the "Father of Modern Education", had touched on in his work. Comenius, mentioned in an earlier chapter for his "encyclopedic" interests, was a refugee from Europe's Thirty Year Wars. His vision was to use education to bring about Europe's spiritual, moral, and social re-generation. This goal, inspired by Francis Bacon, was explained in several essays. He also communicated his optimism in a collection of plays for students called *Schola Ludus*, or School as Play.

Comenius traveled extensively through war-torn Europe. In London he was a part of the celebrated Hartlib Circle, a network of scientists and thinkers that the great early chemist Robert Boyle seems to have referred to as the "Invisible College." There he published his system of natural philosophy. His 1633 treatise *Natural Philosophy Reformed by Divine Light* suggested that God had spread pieces of light throughout creation. These needed to be reassembled "not through an encyclopedic systemization" but intuitively — through an "inner eye" of faith. "Comenius noted that he derived his physical system directly from the book Genesis."[27] His insights played a decisive role in the founding of the world's first scientific institution, the Royal Society of Science in London.

Comenius' thinking influenced Francke's approach to finding truth. The Orphanage was not an ashram where monks closed their eyes to meditate on their breathing or on a *mantra*. Theologians such as Francke saw education as a means of training the "outer" and the "inner" eye to observe properly. So in addition to maths and physics, teachers under his guidance taught this approach to students.

> "Orphanage student teachers explored strategies for making a pious system of natural philosophy accessible as a set of practices, including teaching young people how to observe, gather information, and reassemble it responsibly."[28]

27 Whitmer 2015

28 Whitmer 2015

Observing with the Outer Eye: Using 3-D Models

As a child, Georg Friedrich Meier was a pupil of Christoph Semler, a mathematician and local preacher, and a teacher in the Orphanage School. In his autobiography Meier, an empirical philosopher, described Semler as "a lover of mathematics" who built models of the heavens and the routes the planets took, Jerusalem, the Tabernacle, and Solomon's Temple, all kept in the Orphanage's "cabinet of curiosity."

Semler let his students help him build models in his home, which they found both fun and intellectually profitable:

> "In his house he also had a mechanical manufactory. He worked on building earthly and celestial globes and we children helped him with this. He instilled in us, playfully, a love of mathematics this way."[29]

Semler designed other machines meant to help students learn to observe by suspending them "outside of and above the heavens." His comet machine displayed "all the comets that have been seen at some point and can be shown according to a specific hypothesis." His *lucerna astronomica* "show[ed] solar eclipses, the phases of the moon and present[ed] all asteroids in a very lifelike manner." Additionally, Semler built an instrument he said allowed young people to practice seeing the earth as a non–earth dweller might. "Using the small instrument, *Astronomia Selenitarum* will be presented," Semler noted, "or how we would see the world if we were on the moon." Since the moon "turns against the earth all the time," he continued, "if there were people who lived on the side of the moon that faces the earth, they would constantly see the earth." Although the frequency with which they would see the earth would depend on where they live on the moon, "it would appear to their eyes four times larger than the moon appears to us." These 3-D models, observable with outer eyes, were intended to trigger *Klugheit* — wisdom or insight.

Francke's view of the inner eye came from the New Testament. The Apostle Paul wrote to the Ephesians (1: 18) "I pray that the eyes of your heart may be enlightened . . ."

The ability to grasp truth thus rests on both the mind (knowledge, understanding) and the body (experience and the senses). Such a biblical

29 Whitmer 2015

approach to knowledge set Halle at the forefront of epistemology at the dawn of what is now called the "Enlightenment." The fellows of this remarkable intellectual community debated theories of emotions consistent with a mechanical worldview, seeking to reconcile empiricist and rationalist approaches to knowing the world.

Observing With the "Inner Eye"

Comenius' system confronted educators with fundamental questions about interpretation. Should some views be rejected entirely? Or is one obliged to find some good in all perspectives? Was reason the primary tool of synthesis, or should moral principles and spiritually-informed intuition direct this process?

Debating such questions led to major curriculum revision. As strange as it may seem to modern secular pedagogues, it was such theological churning that led Halle University to re-imagine the importance of teaching mathematics (relative to history and ethics, for example) in the Orphanage.

It is difficult to translate German word *Anschauung*. It connotes a visual process of experiencing with the senses and understanding with the mind via intuition. The word combines intuitive perception, contemplation, and conception. It refers to the cultivation of attention and various forms of experiences one needs to embrace and properly understand something.

Anschauung combines sensory observation with cognitive and emotional imagination. It means to see with outer as well as inner eyes. This term very well expresses the holistic epistemology of these pietist intellectuals, and how they sought to "love God" with heart, soul, mind and strength, by exploring His Creation with every facet of their being. Whitmer explains:

> "Comenius also described the eye of inward seeing as the spirit of understanding. He believed it could be awakened by demonstrations and required light, the cultivation of attention (the strategic application of reason), and objects, which stimulated the senses."[30]

Francke advocated careful reading and engagement with thoughtful authors. Equally important, he advised students to spend time and energy "in rapt contemplation" so that the Holy Spirit would "open [their] eyes to see the wonder in God's law." One could contemplate devotional images as

30 Whitmer 2015

a spiritual exercise, which would also generate "illumination" (*Erleuchtung*). He spoke of such matters in his sermons and writings, stressing how "the eye in people" can generate wisdom.

Christian Thomasius is sometimes branded as a "pre-enlightenment" philosopher. He challenged the dominance of logic in medieval education. Because of his biblical worldview, he questioned the mind's power over matter and stressed the importance of careful observation and intuition. The university in the 21st Century continues to struggle with issues that Halle debated around 1700 AD.

If the body is simply a machine, how do we perceive things or make decisions?[31]

Pietist theology inspired university education because Thomasius believed that what a person desires or loves, affects what he learns. So one must ensure that one's desires are oriented toward the good:

> "In his opinion, the only way to do this was first to 'attain the state of Christian faith' through an authentic conversion experience. Thomasius wanted more of what he called 'rational love' in the world, but he believed it had to start with an 'honest passion' located in the body, which then impacted the mind — sometimes producing forms of illumination or enlightenment."[32]

Intellectual Diversity, Not Indoctrination

The Pietist university did not seek to brainwash or narrowly indoctrinate students. It drew on eclectic learning from all available sources of information. Diversity or eclecticism was the fashion in Halle when Francke started to build the university's foundations. Christian Thomasius and Johann Buddeus were prominent practitioners. In an introduction to philosophy in 1688, Thomasius defined eclecticism as follows:

> "I call eclectic philosophy not what depends on the teaching of an individual or on the acceptance of the words of a master, but whatever can be known from the teaching and writing of any persons on the basis not of authority but of convincing arguments."

31 Whitmer 2015

32 Whitmer 2015

Researcher Thomas Ahnert shows how closely linked Thomasius' ideas were with certain tenets of Pietist theology. They attached much importance to the "believer's heart over the authority of institutions, formulaic professions of faith, and subtle doctrinal argument."

Thomasius was soon joined by Buddeus, who also championed the merits of eclecticism. One of Buddeus's most influential contributions was his *Elements of Instrumental Philosophy*. Teachers in Francke's *Pedagogium* were asked to read it before taking on their teaching duties.
Francke and Buddeus remained in close contact for most of their adult lives.[33]

Halle's Influence on the Development of the Modern University

In his essay "Puritanism, Pietism and Science", Robert K. Merton offered strong praise for the influence of Pietism on the development of modern science:

> "Wherever Pietism spread its influence upon the educational system there followed the large-scale introduction of scientific and technical subjects. Thus, Francke and Thomasius built the foundations of the University of Halle, which was the first German university to introduce a thorough training in the sciences. The leading professors, such as Friedrich Hoffman, Ernst Stahl (professor of chemistry and famous for his influential phlogiston theory), Samuel Stryk and, of course, Francke, all stood in the closest relations with the Pietistic movement. All of them characteristically sought to develop the teaching of science and to ally science with practical applications."

One of Francke's disciples, Gehr, influenced the University of Königsberg, which began promoting study of the natural and physical sciences in the modern sense of the seventeenth century. The University of Göttingen likewise became famous for the cultivation of science education, as did Heidelberg University (which was Calvinist in orientation) and the University of Altdorf. Heubaum summarized these developments by asserting that progress in the teaching of science and technology occurred mainly in Protestant and, more precisely, in Pietistic universities.[34]

---

33 Whitmer 2009

34 Merton 1936

The Decline of Halle Pietism and its University

Critics don't deny that the innovations described above made the Pietist university at Halle Europe's first modern university.
But it is embarrassing for the worldview of many modern skeptics to credit the Bible as the source of such path-breaking innovations. So they credit the Enlightenment, not Pietism, as the force that transformed the medieval university.[35] They also point to the theological decline of Pietism following these heady early years.

Indeed, a conflict between theology and philosophy broke out after the University appointed Christian Wolff as full professor of philosophy and mathematics in 1706. Wolff's early interest in mathematics was overtly religious. He wanted to learn the mathematical method because his goal was to achieve certainty in theology. In 1710 Wolff began teaching metaphysics, logic and morals.[36]

Tensions arose in 1712 when Wolff declared philosophy to be the "science" to which theology must submit. Pietist theologians reacted by resisting Wolff's philosophical lectures. He labeled the Pietists as uneducated and anti-philosophical. Joachim Lange, who had joined the theological faculty in 1709, warned his students against Wolff's lectures, warning of "atheism." In 1721 an open break occurred between Wolff and the theological faculty after he gave a controversial ceremonial speech. In his lecture Wolff argued that non-Christians are able to live according to the correct political and moral maxims without proper theology. Theologian Joachim Breithaupt accused Wolff of following Leibniz and making human reason his ultimate intellectual authority.[37]

The Pietists persuaded Frederick William I to expel Wolff from Halle in 1723. But on the accession of Frederick the Great (1740), one of the new king's first acts was to recall Wolff. He re-entered Halle on 6 Dec. 1740 in triumph. Rationalist theologians displaced the Pietists and took control of Halle, rendering the university the center of rationalist theology in German Protestantism.[38]

....

35 See for example, Becker, 1984.

36 Beutel, 2001

37 Beutel, 2001

38 Encyclopaedia Britannica 2016 and Cross, Livingstone 2005

How Germany Lost Truth

Wolff's return was a triumph for rationalism, but proved a great loss for Europe. Immanuel Kant (1724 - 1804), a teenager in 1740, would later demolish that rationalism. Rejection of both revelation and reason left European universities without any means of knowing truth.
From the beginning, Thomasius had realized that the schools and institutions Francke and others founded would not produce their intended fruit. One cannot generate true piety or make young people morally upright without a genuine conversion. The Spirit of God must write His law upon human hearts. Francke and other theologians accused Thomasius of "examining questions he was not competent to discuss." Unfortunately, Francke used political power to silence his critic, rather than refuting him by means of strong arguments and evidence.

Thomasius taught at Halle until the end of his life. But in the end the rationalism championed by Leibniz and systematized by Christian Wolff, dealt the death blow to Halle's precocious and sincere search for goodness and truth. Germany and Western civilization needs a new epistemological reformation to re-establish the cultural authority of truth.

Bibliography:

- Becker, George, (1984) *"Pietism and Science: A Critique of Robert K. Merton's Hypothesis"*, American Journal of Sociology Volume 89, Number 5, March, pp. 1065-1090

- Beutel, Albrecht (2001). "Causa Wolffiana. Die Vertreibung Christian Wolffs aus Preußen 1723 als Kulminationspunkt des theologisch-politischen Konflikts zwischen halleschem Pietismus und Aufklärungsphilosophie. In Köpf, Ulrich (Eds.), *Wissenschaftliche Theologie und Kirchenleitung*, 159-2002. Mohr Siebeck.

- Bielfeldt, Dennis, "Heidelberg Disputation," in The Roots of Reform, ed. Hans J. Hillerbrand, Kirsi I. Stjerna, and Timothy J. Wengert, vol. 1, *The Annotated Luther* , pp. 69–70. Fortress Press.

- Cross, F.L. and Livingstone, Elizabeth eds. (2005), "Christian Wolff ", *The Oxford Dictionary of the Christian Church*, 1772. Oxford University Press.

- Döring, Detlef (2015), *Studien zur Wissenschaftsund Bildungsgeschichte in Deutschland um 1700*. Harrassowitz.

- Encyclopædia Britannica (2016). *Rationalism.*

- Fries, Wilhelm (1894), *August Hermann Franckes großer Aufsatz*, Verlag der Buchhandlung des Waisenhauses.

- Gehrz, Christopher (2014), Does Pietism Provide a "Usable Past" for Christian Colleges and Universities? In *The Pietist Vision of Christian Higher Education Forming Whole and Holy Persons*, InterVarsity Press

- Grim, Harold J. (1975), Martin Luther. In Towns, Elmer L., *A History of Religious Educators* (1975).Books, Paper 24. http:// digitalcommons.liberty.edu/ towns_books/24

- Hunter, Ian. "Christian Thomasius and the Desacralization of Philosophy." *Journal of the History of Ideas*, Oct., 2000, Vol. 61, No. 4 (Oct., 2000), pp. 595- 616

- Jackson, Christopher D. "Educational reforms of Wittenberg and their faithfulness to Martin Luther's tought" *CEJ*: Series 3, Vol. 10, No. 1, p.71-87

- Kathe, Heinz (1998). Die Universität Halle in den ersten fünfzig Jahren ihres Bestehens. In Ralf-Torsten Speler (Ed). *Die Universität zu Halle und Franckens Stiftungen* (pp. 11-23). MartinLuther-Univ. Halle-Wittenberg.

- King, Lester (1964) "Stahl and Hoffmann: A Study in Eighteenth Century Animism" *Journal of the History of Medicine and Allied Sciences*, Vol. 19, No. 2, 118-130

- Luther, Martin (2015) "To the Christian Nobility of the German Nation Concerning the Improvement of the Christian Estate," in *The Roots of Reform*, ed. Hans J. Hillerbrand, Kirsi I. Stjerna, and Timothy J. Wengert, vol. 1, *The Annotated Luther.* pp. 448–449. Fortress Press.

- Merton, Robert K. (1936) 1968. "Puritanism, Pietism and Science." in *Social Theory and Social Structure.* 628-60, New York: Free Press.

- Oberman, Heiko A. (2003). *The Two Reformations.* Yale University Press

- Overfield, J. H. (1984). *Humanism and Scholasticism in Late Medieval Germany.*

- Raabe, Paul (1996). August Hermann Franckes Waisenhaus. Wirtsch-aftliche

Autonomie und staatliche Förderung einer pädagogischen Herausforderung. In Dietrich Benner, Adolf Kell (Eds.) Bildung zwischen Staat und Markt, *Zeitschrift für Pädagogik*, Beiheft 35). 171-184

- Schlöder, Schochow, Steger (2015). „Die Medizinische Fakultätder Universität Wittenberg 1502-1817 — Stand der Forschung *Sudhoffs Archiv*, 2015, Bd. 99, 2015
- Spener, Philip Jacob (1964), *Pia Desideria*, ed. Theodore G. Tappert, Fortress Press

- Springer, C. (2007). Martin's martial: Reconsidering Luther's relationship with the classics. *International Journal of the Classical Tradition*, 14(1/2), 23–50.
- Stern, Leo (1954). „Christian Thomasius – der geistige Begründer der Universität Halle." In: *Wissenschaftliche Zeitschrift der Martin-Luther-Universität Halle-Wittenberg*. Gesellschaftsund sprachwissenschaftliche Reihe 4,4, pp 493-495.

- Stitziel, Judd (1996). God, the Devil, Medicine, and the Word: A Controversy over Ecstatic Women in Protestant Middle Germany 1691-1693, *Central European History*, Vol. 29, No. 3 (1996), pp. 309-337

- Sträter, Udo (2010). *"eine wunderliche conjunction Planetarumzu Halle"* – *oder: Wie eine Reformuniversität entstanden ist*. Universitätsverlag Halle-Wittenberg.

- Tomasoni, Francesco (2009). Christian Thomasius Geist und kulturelle Identität an der Schwelle zur europäischen Aufklärung. Waxmann Verlag

- Williams, David C. (2014). Pietism and Faith-Learning Integration in the Evangelical University In *Christopher Gehrz The Pietist Vision of Christian Higher Education Forming Whole and Holy Persons*, InterVarsity Press

- Whitmer, Kelly Joan (2009). "Eclecticism and the Technologies of Discernment in Pietist Pedagogy" in *Journal of the History of Ideas*, Volume 70, Number 4 (October 2009), 545-567. University of Pennsylvania Press

- Whitmer, Kelly Joan (2015). *The Halle Orphanage as Scientific Community*, The University of Chicago Press Chicago and London

- Wright, W. J. (1987). Evaluating the results of sixteenth century educational policy: Some Hessian data. *The Sixteenth Century Journal*, 18(3), 411–426.

Chapter 15

How the Bible Educated America to Live in Liberty

Stephen McDowell[1]

The Christian idea of man teaches us that all men have great value, but that men are sinful, in a fallen state, and in need of a redeemer. We cannot save ourselves. We need the regenerating power of the Holy Spirit to work in us, to translate us into the kingdom of God. Once we become a new creation we must grow in our salvation — we must be sanctified in His truth so we can extend His kingdom in the nations. Biblical education should be central in transforming the mind and reforming nations.

In the fourth and fifth centuries, as Christianity changed from a grassroots movement to a top-down movement, the church began to embrace a pagan philosophy of education, on the assumption that only certain people can know the Bible. These stewards of truth, the clergy, would then explain that truth to the common person. This practice led to bondage, as many people were cut off from the truth. The Protestant Reformation changed this. It sought to reclaim the Christian idea of education; that is, everyone should know the truth themselves. Everyone should have access to the Bible, God's revealed truth. This idea motivated many people to translate the Bible into the common language of the people, both before and especially after the Reformation. In cases where a people group had no written language, Bible translators gave them one.

America's early settlers and founding fathers were keenly aware of the relation between education and liberty. Thomas Jefferson explained:

> "If a nation expects to be ignorant and free, in a state of civilization, it expects what never was and never will be."[2]

---

1 Stephen McDowell is the co-founder and President of the Providence Foundation, an author and internationally renowned speaker.

2 *The Writings of Thomas Jefferson*, XIV: 384. Letter to Colonel Charles Yancey, January 6, 1816.

Benjamin Franklin noted that ignorance produces bondage:

> "A nation of well informed men who have been taught to know and prize the rights which God has given them cannot be enslaved. It is in the region of ignorance that tyranny begins."

America's founders generally agreed that each individual should know God (the Truth), that everyone should have access to the Bible, God's source of truth to mankind. This idea motivated early settlers to found schools and colleges, and to translate the Bible into languages of Native Americans.

The Massachusetts school law of 1647, which provided directions for educating youth, begins,

> "It being one chief project of that old deluder, Satan, to keep men from the knowledge of the Scriptures."[3]

One of the original rules of Harvard College, established in 1636, states:

> "Let every Student be plainly instructed, and earnestly pressed to consider well, the maine end of his life and studies is, to know God and Jesus Christ which is eternal life, (John 17:3), and therefore to lay Christ in the bottom, as the only foundation of all sound knowledge and Learning."[4]

Puritan minister John Eliot worked for decades to give the Algonquin Indians a written language and then to publish the Bible in their language (1661-63). This was the first Bible printed in America.

Education in America for the first few centuries was centered in the home because most saw it as the right and responsibility of parents to govern the education of their children. A statue to the Pilgrim Mother in Plymouth, Massachusetts, bears the inscription: "They brought up their families in sturdy virtue and a living faith in God, without which nations perish." The American home passed on the faith and virtue necessary for liberty. To the vast majority of early Americans the most important aspect of education was to impart Christian character, to shape the inner man.

---

3 Richard Morris, editor, *Significant Documents in United States History*, Vol. 1, p. 19

4 "New England's First Fruits in Respect to the Progress of Learning in the College at Cambridge, in Massachusetts Bay," *America, Great Crises In Our History Told by Its Makers, A Library of Original Sources, Vol. 2*, Chicago: Americanization Department, 1925, pp. 155-156.

Upon this foundation they taught a worldview deeply rooted in the Bible that provided instruction for all spheres of life.

The Biblical philosophy of education upon which America was built was of utmost importance in producing the most free, prosperous, and charitable nation in history. As has been said, the philosophy of the schoolroom in one generation will be the philosophy of government (and economics, business, law, liberty) in the next. Biblical education produced an exceptional nation that embraced many godly ideas and rights, including: freedom of worship; freedom of assembly; opportunity for all to labor and benefit from the fruit of their labor; freedom to elect representatives and have a voice in government; freedom of thought and expression of ideas; freedom to own property; freedom to obtain ideas, start businesses and create wealth; limited jurisdiction of civil government; equal standing before the law for all people; no class distinctions; and the central role of the family.

That is not to say early Americans did this perfectly, nor were they without sin and shortcomings. It took time for many of these ideas to benefit all men – those enslaved being the most obvious group. However, the liberating principles expressed in America's founding documents – the Declaration and Constitution – did ultimately prevail. Slaves were liberated, the position of women was elevated, and equality before the law spread to all men. The United States led the way in overcoming evils that had plagued mankind since the fall of man in the Garden of Eden.[5] Christian education was the primary reason for this.

While they strove to provide Biblical education, they were discovering and applying more and more truth over the generations. Consequently, the fruit that came forth from their efforts, while generally good, contained some thorns as well. And in the past century, as secular education has supplanted Christian education, those thorns have increased.

All Education Is Religious

All education is religious. This is why state education is so dangerous; it passes on the predominant religion of those in control. Some people say

5 See Stephen McDowell, "The Bible, Slavery, and America's Founders," Chapter 12 in *Building Godly Nations*, Charlottesville: Providence Foundation, 2003, for the issue of how biblical truth motivated early Americans to work to end slavery.

education is neutral, and therefore religion must be kept separate from education, which in America today translates to mean that any mention of God or godly values must be extirpated from our public schools. But all education imparts a worldview and basic presuppositions about life which are rooted in religion. The issue is not keeping religion out of education (which is impossible); the issue is what religion forms the foundation of education.

Modern secularists rightly decry any attempt to compel in matters of worship. However, the modern state compels everyone to be educated, and hence, is compelling in the arena of fundamental beliefs, in faith or religion. Throughout most of history, nations have controlled and compelled in the area of faith. Many people who came to America did so to escape this, and set an example that ended state-compelled worship.

In his Statute for Religious Freedom, Thomas Jefferson said "that to compel a man to furnish contributions of money for the propagation of opinions which he disbelieves is sinful and tyrannical."[6] This was one argument used to end state established religion in early America. Throughout the nineteenth century this idea spread to many other nations in the western world. However, at about the same time the western world stopped compelling worship, they began to compel education.

While the modern humanist is appalled at forced worship, given that education is compelled, and given the inherently religious nature of education, he is really compelling in the area of religion. This is why we need an updated version of the Virginia Statute for Religious Freedom today; that is, we need a Statute for Educational Freedom.

The Religious Nature of Modern State Education

In most nations today, the state or government is in control of education. The foundational philosophy of modern state education contrasts greatly with education that is Christian. Biblical education is rooted in the absolutes of God's Word. Man-centered, state education has a completely different foundation, which includes these components:

---

6 "Statue for Religious Freedom, Virginia, 1786, *Significant Documents in United States History*, Vol. 1, 1620-1896, Richard B. Morris, Editor, New York: Van Nostrand Reinhold Company, 1969, p. 119.

1. Relativism

Relativism has been defined as the conviction that "there is no such thing as truth or right, but only the varying beliefs of varying cultures, each apparently justified in its own terms; no fixed norms, but merely shifting opinions."[7]

Christians believe that the basis of truth is found in God's Word. It is what the Bible proclaims. Jesus prayed to the Father: "Your word is truth" (John 17:17). His Word is not just true, but it is truth (a noun). The Bible is God's Word and the source of Truth to all men. A Christian worldview proclaims that there is truth, there is right and wrong, there are absolutes that we can know.

The secularist has a much different view of "truth." From a humanistic perspective there is no absolute truth. All so-called truths are relative. The relativist says:

> "Whatever I want to believe, I may believe. Whatever I think is true is true for me, and whatever you think is true is true for you. If you believe in a God as the source of truth, that's okay, but I don't believe in God or absolute truth; and you shouldn't force your view upon me or upon society."

Relativism is the predominant view of those in academia, the media, and western governments. But such a view is completely illogical. When someone says "there is no absolute truth," a simple question will reveal the absurdity of this position. Merely ask them, "Are you sure?" If they answer no, they have jettisoned their epistemology, acknowledging that they do not know for certain that there are no absolutes. If they answer yes, then they have affirmed the position that there are absolutes.[8]

---

7 Will Herberg, "Modern Man in a Metaphysical Wasteland," *The Intercollegiate Review*, vol. 5 (1968-69), p. 79; quoted in Ronald H. Nash, *The Closing of the American Heart*, Probe Books, 1990, p. 62.

8 After someone admits there are absolutes, the next point to consider is the source of those absolutes. For Christians, it is the Bible. For humanists, it is man, either as an individual or corporate man with the state expressing "truth" to society. A Christian worldview teaches there is absolute truth, where God is right about every-thing, and He reveals the truth that man needs to know in His Word. Relativists will condemn Christians who believe in right and wrong as narrow-minded >> contd

A pagan view of "truth" has captured the thinking of most of the world. Relativism is the dominant view of Americans today, even those Americans who claim to be Christians. The Barna Group conducted a poll in the spring of 2002. In a survey of adults and teenagers, people were asked if they believed that there are moral absolutes that are unchanging, or that moral truth is relative. 64% of adults said truth is relative to the person and situation. Among teenagers, 83% said moral truth is relative; only 6% said it is absolute. Among born-again Christians 32% of adults and 9% of teens expressed a belief in absolute truth. The number one answer (as to what people believe is the basis for moral decisions) was doing whatever feels right (believed by 31% of adults and 38% of teens).

Early Americans, who were mostly Christians, held to the Christian idea of truth, which was reflected in their laws and constitutions. They believed that there is a fixed law that applies to everyone and is always true. God reveals His law in nature (the laws of nature) and by special revelation in the Bible (the laws of nature's God). The phrase Jefferson used in the Declaration of Independence —"the laws of nature and of nature's God"— had a well established meaning.[9]

An early civics textbook, *First Lessons in Civil Government* (1846) by Andrew Young, reveals the Founders' Biblical view of law:

> The will of the Creator is the law of nature which men are bound to obey. But mankind in their present imperfect state are not capable of discovering in all cases what the law of nature requires; it has therefore pleased Divine Providence to reveal his will to mankind, to instruct them in their duties to himself and to each other. This will is revealed in the Holy Scriptures, and is called the law of revelation, or the Divine law.[10]

>> 8 - and bigoted. They say, "You should not see things as right and wrong. It is wrong to do this." What they are really saying is that they do not want to face the reality of the Creator God — Who is the source of all right and wrong — and His standard of righteous living. They want to live life on their own terms. Hence, their theology, or worldview, follows their morality.

9 See Stephen McDowell, *Building Godly Nations*, chapter 11, "The Changing Nature of Law in America," Charlottesville: Providence Foundation, 2004, pp. 183 ff.

10 Andrew W. Young, *First Lessons in Civil Government*, Auburn, N.Y.: H. And J.C. Ivison, 1846, p. 16.

This is in great contrast to the secular or socialist view of law, as revealed in the French Declaration of Rights (1794):

> "the Law … is the expression of the general will.… [T]he rights of man rests on the national sovereignty. This sovereignty … resides essentially in the whole people."[11]

To the humanist, man is the source of law, of right and wrong. But if whatever man declares to be lawful is the standard for society, then everyone's fundamental rights are threatened, for a majority, or ruling dictator, can declare anyone to be an outlaw. Tyrants have done this throughout history, and tens of millions of people have been killed under this worldview.

The Christian view of law proclaims that all men have God-given inalienable rights, and the Bible states what those rights are. No man can take them away. All men are subject to God's higher law, rulers as well as common people. No man is above the law, nor is man the source of law. Hence, the rule of law originated in the western Christian world where the Christian idea of law prevailed. This Christian view of law produced the unique nature of American constitutionalism and law.

2. Positivism

Positivism is a second underlying principle upon which modern state education rests. According to educator Ronald Nash, positivism is "the belief that human knowledge cannot be extended beyond what can be discovered by use of the scientific method."[12] Nash writes:

> Many people believe that science is the only area of human study (other than mathematics and logic) that is true. Anything else can only be a matter of opinion. If some belief cannot be tested by the scientific method, it cannot be true; belief in it cannot be rational. Of course, it is interesting to ask if that claim (the positivists's own thesis) can be tested by the scientific method. Obviously, it cannot.[13]

---

11 Thomas Paine, "Declaration of Rights," *The Writings of Thomas Paine*, Collected and edited by Daniel Conway, New York: G.P. Putnam's Sons, Vol.3 , p. 129-130.

12 Nash, p. 65.

13 Nash, p. 66.

Scientists, as the keepers of truth, have become **the** voice of reason and of what is objectively true, for many in our nation today. They have become priests for those who worship at the shrine of science.

3. Humanism

The third tenet upon which modern state education is built is humanism, or better described as secularism–naturalism–humanism.[14] Secularism is the belief "that human life can be lived and understood, in its own terms, without regard to any higher order of reality, that is, without regard to God."[15] The claim of naturalism is that "nothing exists outside the material, mechanical, natural order"[16] (which of course cannot be proved). Both secularism and naturalism are aspects of humanism. In reality, humanism is a religion in which human beings assume the place of God. Humanism is the belief that man is god; man decides what is right and wrong.

Relativism, positivism, and humanism form the foundation of state education today. These are the tenets of the religion that predominates in public schools in the western world. This is in great contrast to the foundation of education in the western world, which had its roots in Christianity.

A Liberal Arts Education

Many Americans who go to college today receive a liberal arts education. In our primarily secular schools this means imparting a worldview deriving from secular humanism. Paul warns us to not be taken "captive through philosophy and empty deception, according to the tradition of men, according to the elementary principles of the world" (Colossians 2:8). A man-centered, worldly philosophy brings captivity. In contrast, an education "according to Christ" brings liberty.

In times past, a liberal arts education meant that you were educated to live in liberty. Education gave youth the character and ideas necessary to live free. It is not easy to live free. Liberty is not the default state of fallen man. Sinful man naturally devolves to a life of bondage.

14 Nash, pp. 67-70.

15 Nash, p. 67

16 Nash, p. 68

Early Americans understood this, so they not only taught their children at home, but also began to establish schools and colleges shortly after arriving in the wilderness.

We are in a war today – not a war of guns and bullets, but a war of worldviews. One of our greatest enemies is statism, putting government in place of God, often because we deny God (atheism) or put man in his place (secular humanism). Every expression of statism – secularism, socialism, communism, Marxism, democratic socialism – regards civil government (or man via civil government) as the ultimate authority, and as such is the source of law and morality. The state (and man as its head) defines what is right and wrong, what is lawful and unlawful, what is moral and immoral. The state becomes the de facto god of the society, or in the words of Roscoe Pound, President of Harvard Law School in the 1920s, "the state takes the place of Jehovah."[17]

Secular education has produced a new generation of leaders who, instead of advancing liberty and universal flourishing, have attacked God and His Word, the source of our blessings. Secular humanists have sought to remove God and the Bible from education (the source of Truth), have devalued life by promoting abortion on demand, have worked to redefine the biblical family (the foundation of free nations), and have promoted homosexuality, transgenderism, and other immoral behavior as normal.

In addition, they have sought to remove any mention of God from government and have enacted many laws contrary to the Bible and the U.S. Constitution.

America's secular education is making a huge change in the thinking and action of many Americans, even those who are Christians. As mentioned previously, one of the tenets of secularism—relativism—has so permeated the worldview of Americans that only one-third of them believe moral absolutes exist, and among teenagers only six percent said moral truth is absolute. Surprisingly, this same percentage holds for those identifying themselves as born-again Christians. Only 32% of adults and 9% of teens expressed a belief in absolute truth.[18] A decline of biblical thinking (and

17 Roscoe Pound, *The Spirit of the Common Law*, quoted in Stephen McDowell, Building Godly Nations, Charlottesville: Providence Foundation, 2003, p. 197.

18 Barna Group Poll, Spring 2002.

action) occurs when Christian parents fail to understand the great importance of education. Nineteenth century theologian Robert L. Dabney said:

> The education of children for God is the most important business done on earth. It is the one business for which the earth exists. To it all politics, all war, all literature, all money-making, ought to be subordinated; and every parent especially ought to feel, every hour of the day, that, next to making his own calling and election sure, this is the end for which he is kept alive by God – this is his task on earth.[19]

Noah Webster wrote:

> "The education of youth [is] an employment of more consequence than making laws and preaching the gospel, because it lays the foundation on which both law and gospel rest for success."[20]

Both statist and Christian educators may take issue with Webster's statement. Statist educators certainly believe education is more important than preaching the gospel, but to them education should be devoid of religious instruction, as they see this as a hindrance to developing good citizens. Some Christian educators would say that nothing is more important than preaching the gospel; education must be secondary to this. But Webster is presenting an important principle; that is, from a biblical perspective, education is a primary component of preaching the Gospel. Jesus said we disciple nations by teaching all He commanded. Discipling believers, especially our children, is a central command of the Scriptures.

The biblical education of early America produced men and women of character with a worldview that gave birth to this free nation. Without biblical education there would be no America, no godly law, and no freedom to propagate the Gospel. Nor would we have had the economic prosperity to pay for the spread of the Gospel throughout the world without such an education. Biblical education produced a free and prosperous America, and only biblical education can preserve our freedom and prosperity.

....

19 Bruce N. Shortt, *The Harsh Truth about Public Schools*, Vallecito, Cal.: Chalcedon Foundation,2004, p. 356.

20 Noah Webster, "Education of Youth in America," *American Magazine* (March 1788): 212. Quoted in K. Alan Snyder, *Defining Noah Webster, Mind and Morals in the Early Republic*, New York: University Press of America, 1990, p. 114.

As stated earlier, this does not mean that early Americans were without fault, nor did they perfectly apply God's principles in their education, government, and nation. But they did align the nation more closely to God's Word than any other nation in history. Because of this, they experienced more of the good fruit of obedience than any other nation. Certainly, other nations have incorporated aspects of God's truth into their laws and institutions, and prospered and advanced accordingly. In addition, some nations have copied the principles of God's Word while not necessarily embracing the Spirit. Obedience to the principles has produced some positive results. For example, Japan in the past 70 years has prospered materially, with little growth of Christianity, but that is due to their copying the biblical economic principles that worked in America.[21]

How have we come to this point of decay in America? Princeton Seminary Professor (1906-29) and a founder of Westminster Seminary in Philadelphia John Gresham Machen explained:

> "If liberty is not maintained with regard to education, there is no use trying to maintain it in any other sphere. If you give the bureaucrats the children, you might just as well give them everything else."[22]

We have given our children to secularists to train and disciple them, which would be like the ancient children of Israel giving their children to the Philistines to educate them. When we teach our youth that they are merely animals (grown up worms evolved from bacteria) and that morality is based upon the ever-shifting views of a selfish people, we should not be surprised when they act like animals and throw off any moral constraints. After all, Jesus taught that we will be like our teachers (Luke 6:40).

Whoever controls children controls the future. Marxists understood this and sought to control education, indeed still do. God has given the responsibility of educating children primarily to the parents, not the state.

....

21 For more on this see Stephen McDowell and Mark Beliles, "Principle of Christian Economics," Chapter 12, *Liberating the Nations*, Charlottesville: Providence Foundation, 1995.

22 Robert E. Fugate, *Key Biblical Principles for Civil Government*, Omaha: Thy Word Is Truth Publishers, 2007, p. 47.

Unfortunately, Americans have rendered unto Caesar (civil government) the things that are God's, contrary to Christ's command to render unto God the things that are God's. In particular, with devastating consequences, we have lent Caesar control of our children and our property (and much more). Statism has become the golden calf of America and much of the modern world.

What is the solution to America's problem? It is restoring biblical education to America.

Biblical Education

The Bible has much to say about education. Parents and grandparents bear the duty to teach their children and grandchildren all of the Word of God, using all opportunities as they walk through life (Deuteronomy 6:4-7). Jesus told us that we disciple men and nations through teaching all of His Word (Matthew 28:18-20).

Education is how we sow and then reap the soul. The parable of the sower and the soils (Mark 4) shows that the kingdom of God is like a seed. When we repent and submit ourselves to Christ we are instantly converted, but the establishment of God's character and kingdom within is a gradual process. Like the growth of a plant or tree, a seed is planted; nourishment, care, and sunlight are provided; eventually a mature plant comes forth bearing fruit (pruning is important, too). This same principle applies in establishing God's truth in the nations of the world. Transformation occurs gradually and Christian education is central to that process.

What would be necessary for us to restore true liberal arts education? What does the education that produces liberty look like? What are its components? Certainly such education will look very different from most modern education. Let me suggest five principles.

1. Education is primarily the responsibility of the family, then delegated to others.

Parents have the right and responsibility to govern the education of their children. They bear responsibility to train children in biblical character and worldview (Ephesians 6:1-4; Proverbs 1:8; 22:6). Parents should disciple their children. As they are faithful in doing so, they will have an impact, not only on their children's lives, but on society at large, at times affecting nations. Consider one such example.

From an early age, Susanna would pray daily for God to guide her and make her life count. Born the last of 25 children to a minister and his wife, she loved God from youth and had a burning desire to live her life for Him. As a young woman she dreamed of starting a spiritual fire that would burn through London, the United Kingdom, and "to the uttermost parts of the world."

Susanna was always looking for an opportunity to fulfill that dream and was always asking God what He would have her do. How should she start that fire? Should she become a missionary, a teacher? Or did God have another plan for her? At a young age she married a minister and, like her mother, began having children—nineteen in all. She devoted most of her time and effort to being a good wife and mother.

Even in the midst of hardship after hardship, Susanna continued to pour herself into her children and inspire them for good. When her children were five or six, she would set aside one whole day to teach each of them how to read. She taught the alphabet phonetically and then had her children read the Bible.

Susanna never traveled the world or directly started those great spiritual conflagrations. But Susanna's dream became a reality in her thirteenth and seventeenth children, Charles and John Wesley, who spread the Gospel and inspired worldwide reforms, giving birth to the Methodist movement. Their education, centered in the home, still impacts the world today.

Susanna's life gives meaning to the saying, "You can count how many seeds are in an apple, but you cannot count how many apples are in a seed." The potential for an entire forest resides in one seed. God wants His seed (His Truth), not the seed of secular humanism, to be planted in those who will bear fruit in our nation.

God's seed gave birth to America and passed on the heritage of liberty to the generations. Biblical education laid a foundation for America's liberty, prosperity, virtue, and justice. Early American education followed the pattern given to the covenant nation of Israel. First, it was centered in the home where the seed of transformation is developed. Our Founding fathers were primarily educated at home. One third of the men who gave us the Declaration and Constitution had no, or little, formal schooling; they were home schooled and trained to be self-taught. Such was the case for the Father of our Country, George Washington. Others started schooling at home and then supplemented this with tutors or at schools (mostly in someone's home). Most of these tutors in early America were ministers, since they were the best educated. Thomas Jefferson, James Madison, and Noah Webster were a few founders who received such an education. Only one in four of the Founders went to college, and these colleges were thoroughly Christian.

The Education of John Quincy Adams

The education of America's sixth president, John Quincy Adams, provides a great example. Adams' father and mother, John and Abigail, taught him at home until around age eleven. As a 10-year-old, John Quincy knew French and Latin, read the writings of Charles Rollins and other difficult works, and helped manage the farm with his mother while his father was away serving the nation. Letters from John Quincy to his father at this time reveal the level of literacy and the reasoning skills his parents imparted to him. In one letter he wrote, "I wish, sir, you would give me some instructions with regard to my time, and advise me how to proportion my studies and my play, in writing, and I will keep them by me and endeavor to follow them."[23]

In a letter to his father on June 2, 1777, at age ten, John Quincy wrote:
> "Sir, If you will be so good as to favor me with a blank-book I will transcribe the most remarkable occurrences I meet with in my reading, which will serve to fix them upon my mind."[24]

At age eleven, John Quincy traveled with his father to France, yet Abigail used her letters to continue the education she had so well begun at their home in Braintree, Massachusetts. In June of 1778 she wrote:
> You are in possession of a naturally good understanding, and of spirits unbroken by adversity and untamed with care. Improve your

---

23 *Life, Administration and Times of John Quincy Adams, Sixth President of the United States,* by John Robert Irelan, 1887, p. 16, quoted in Verna M. Hall, compiler, *The Christian History of the American Revolution, Consider and Ponder,* San Francisco: Foundation for American Christian Education, 1976, p. 605.

24 Irelan, p. 16, in Hall, *Consider and Ponder,* pp. 605-606.

understanding by acquiring useful knowledge and virtue, such as will render you an ornament to society, and honor to your country, and a blessing to your parents. Great learning and superior abilities, should you ever possess them, will be of little value and small estimation, unless virtue, honor, truth, and integrity are added to them. Adhere to those religious sentiments and principles which were early instilled into your mind, and remember, that you are accountable to your Maker for all your words and actions.[25]

In the same letter she encouraged John Quincy to pay attention to the development of his conduct by heeding the instruction of his parents:
> "for, dear as you are to me, I would much rather you should have found your grave in the ocean you have crossed…than see you an immoral, profligate, or graceless child."[26]

This home-centered, morality based education that taught biblical methods of reasoning enabled John Quincy to go on to a remarkable career. When he was 14, he received a United States Congressional diplomatic appointment as secretary to the ambassador of the court of Catherine the Great in Russia. He served as foreign ambassador to England, France, Holland, Prussia, and Russia. He was a U.S. Senator, Secretary of State, and the sixth President, after which he served 18 years in the U.S. House of Representatives, during which time he was a leader in the antislavery movement. Biblical education produced this man who served his country and the cause of God.

2. Schools as an Extension of Family Education

Following the biblical model, home education can be supplemented by tutors and schools. In ancient Israel, the Levites provided these schools. In early America the first schools were started by Christians, and ministers were usually the teachers. These schools were started by the church to teach people to read the Bible. Making provision for everyone to be able to read the Bible was the primary impetus for common schools, which were established in the 1640s in Massachusetts.

---

25 Irelan, pp. 20-22, in Hall, *Consider and Ponder*, p. 607.

26 Ibid.

The Connecticut School Laws of 1650 began like those of Massachusetts:
> "It being one chief project of that old deluder, Satan, to keep men from the knowledge of the Scriptures."[27]

A 1690 law declared:
> "This [legislature] observing that…there are many persons unable to read the English tongue and thereby incapable to read the holy Word of God or the good laws of this colony…it is ordered that all parents and masters shall cause their respective children and servants, as they are capable, to be taught to read distinctly the English tongue."[28]

They understood that the devil wants to keep people ignorant, because if they are ignorant he can keep them in bondage.

Colleges were started to train ministers in a knowledge of the Bible. The first college, Harvard, was started in 1636 by the Puritans of New England, not long after they began to carve out a home in the wilderness, because they wanted "to advance learning, and perpetuate it to posterity, dreading to leave an illiterate ministry to the churches, when our present ministers shall lie in the dust."[29] One of the original rules of Harvard stated:
> Let every student be plainly instructed, and earnestly pressed to consider well, the main end of his life and studies is, to know God and Jesus Christ which is eternal life, John 17:3, and therefore to lay Christ in the bottom, as the only foundation of all sound knowledge and learning.[30]

Yale University was started in 1701. The Regulations at Yale College in 1745 began:
> All scholars shall live religious, godly, and blameless lives according to the rules of God's Word, diligently reading the Holy Scriptures,

27 "Connecticut Blue Laws," *Annals of America*, Vol. 1, Chicago: Encyclopedia Britannica, Inc., 1976, p. 203.

28 Edward Kendall, *Kendall's Travels*, New York: I. Riley, 1809, Vol. 1, p. 299-305.

29 "New England's First Fruits," (1643) in *The Pageant of America*, Ralph Henry Gabriel, ed., New Haven: Yale University Press, 1928, Vol. 10, p. 256.

30 "New England's First Fruits in Respect to the Progress of Learning in the College at Cambridge, in Massachusetts Bay," *America, Great Crises In Our History Told by Its Makers, A Library of Original Sources, Vol. 2*, pp. 155-156.

the fountain of light and truth; and constantly attend upon all the duties of religion, both in public and secret.[31]

The motto of Princeton University, which was started by Presbyterians in 1746 as a product of the First Great Awakening, was "Under God's Power She Flourishes."

In 1754, Rev. Samuel Johnson was chosen as the first President of Columbia College (called King's College up until 1784). In that year he composed an advertisement announcing the opening of the college. It stated:

> The chief Thing that is aimed at in this College is, to teach and engage the Children to know God in Jesus Christ, and to love and serve him, in all Sobriety, Godliness and Righteousness of Life, with a perfect Heart, and a willing Mind; and to train them up in all virtuous Habits, and all such useful Knowledge as may render them creditable to their Families and Friends.[32]

So the biblical model followed by early Americans began with education in the home where the parents discipled their children. Home instruction was often supplemented by tutors and Christian schools; then young adults were apprenticed by their parents or others to learn vocational skills; a few went on to higher education at colleges. All were given the tools for self-study.

3. Education to a Calling

Training at home and in schools helped young people fulfill their unique calling or vocation, where each contributed to the advancement of the liberty and prosperity of the nation. Early American teachers understood the idea of biblical vocation; that is, that God gives talents and skills that we are to use to advance His purposes through every aspect of our lives, especially in work. Jesus told us to "Occupy till I come" (Luke 19: 11-27) or according to one translation, "Do business with this [minas, representing our talents, skills, and abilities] until I come back" (v. 13). We are to work as partners with Him to take dominion over the earth (Genesis 1:26-28) by using the talents He has given us. Our work is a vital part of God's

---

31 "Regulations at Yale College," *Annals of America*, Chicago: Encyclopedia Britannica, Inc., 1976, Vol. 1, p. 464.

32 *The Pageant of America*, Ralph Henry Gabriel, editor, Vol. 10, p. 309.

plan for us and the nations. We occupy through our occupation. We are to fulfill our biblical duties in every sphere of life whether the family, church, media, government, marketplace, education, or science.[33]

This model of education helped form a new and unique nation, the most free and prosperous the world had yet seen. Biblical education produces good fruit.

4. A Biblical philosophy, methodology, and curriculum

The first thing we can do to restore biblical education to the nation is for families to assume the responsibility to govern the education of their children, and next, establish schools to assist in training youth. Third, we must encourage students to seek a God-given vocation. A fourth component of biblical education is that each facet – the philosophy (why), methodology (how), and content (what), of education – should be biblical.[34]
A biblical ideology motivated early Americans to teach their children at home, start schools and colleges, and make provision for those unable to obtain an education at home. The concept of education for all is a Christian idea and developed first in Christian civilization. Our system of state education is based upon this idea of education for all; unfortunately, the way we attempt to provide universal education does not follow the biblical model. Our current system is state-controlled and mandated; it teaches a humanistic philosophy of life and increasingly denies God and truth.

The Bible was the central text for early American education. John Locke observed in 1690 that children learned to read by following "the ordinary road of Hornbook, Primer, Psalter, Testament and Bible." [35] Hornbooks were the most widely used tool for teaching reading in seventeenth century America. A hornbook was a flat piece of wood with a handle, upon which a sheet of printed paper was attached and covered with transparent animal

---

33 See Stephen McDowell, *Transforming Nations through Biblical Work*, Charlottesville: Providence Foundation, 2018, and *Building Godly Nations*, Chapters 1 and 14 for more on biblical work.

34 To learn more about these 3 elements see *Liberating the Nations, Building Godly Nations*, Providence Foundation Biblical Worldview University course on *The Principle Approach, and Jim Rose, A Guide to American Christian Education for the Home and School: The Principle Approach*, Camarillo, Cal.:American Christian History Institute, 1987.

35 *The Pageant of America*, Vol. 10, p. 258

horn to protect it. A typical hornbook contained the alphabet, sometimes colored, an invocation of the Trinity, and the Lord's Prayer.

Another important educational book was the New *England Primer*, first published in Boston around 1690 by devout Protestant Benjamin Harris. It was the most prominent schoolbook for about 100 years, and was frequently reprinted through the 1800s. It sold over three million copies in 150 years.

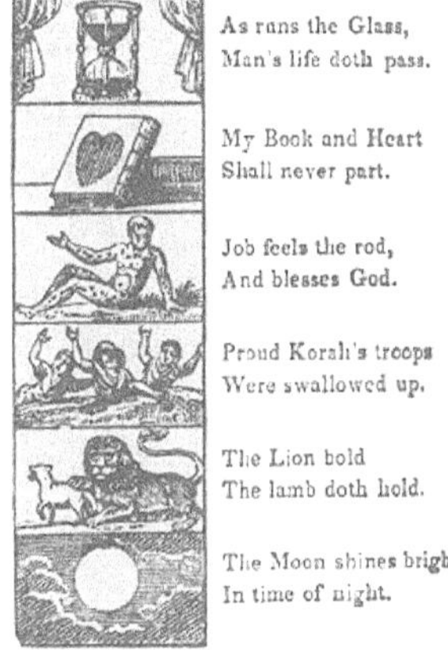

New England Primer.
This edition of the Primer differed somewhat from
the 1777 version but still used Biblical imagery.

In a 1777 *Primer*, the alphabet was taught by means of the following rhyme:
    A In Adam's Fall - We sinned all.
    B Heaven to find - The Bible Mind.
    C Christ crucify'd - For sinners dy'd.
    D The Deluge drown'd - The Earth around
    E Elijah hid - By Ravens fed.
    F The judgment made - Felix afraid.
    G As runs the Glass - Our Life doth pass
    H My Book and Heart - Must never part.[36]

Noah Webster's "Blue-Back Speller" was first published in 1783 and sold over 100 million copies during the next century. It was the most influential textbook of the era and was written to instill into the minds of the youth

---

36 *The New England Primer*, Boston: Printed by Edward Draper, 1777

"the first rudiments of the language and some just ideas of religion, morals, and domestic economy." The book's premise was that "God's word, contained in the Bible, has furnished all necessary rules to direct our conduct." It included a moral catechism, large portions of the Sermon on the Mount, a paraphrase of the Genesis account of creation, and numerous moral stories. Students would read such things as:

- "God will forgive those who repent of their sins, and live a holy life."
- "Examine the Scriptures daily and carefully, and set an example of good works."
- "Those who enjoy the light of the gospel, and neglect to observe its precepts, are more criminal than the heathen."[37]

Noah Webster also produced the monumental work, *An American Dictionary of the English Language*. Webster spent over 20 years working on this first exhaustive English dictionary. First published in 1828, Webster's Dictionary gave biblical definitions and used thousands of Scriptural references. In contrast, dictionaries today, even those bearing Webster's name, give humanistic definitions and indoctrinate youth in a non-biblical worldview. Consider, for example, the word *immoral*. In his original 1828 dictionary, under the definition for immoral, Noah Webster writes:

"Every action is immoral which contravenes any divine precept, or which is contrary to the duties men owe to each other."[38]

To Webster, divine precept was the standard to judge immorality. Today, the standard is quite different, as reflected in the definition of *immoral* in modern dictionaries. *Webster's New World Dictionary* defines *immoral* as "not in conformity with accepted principles of right and wrong behavior."[39] The standard for immoral behavior today has become what the consensus of the population thinks. Man, rather than God, has been declared the judge of right and wrong conduct. Other prominent textbooks from early America, like McGuffey's *Readers*, Murray's *Reader*, Butler's *General History*, and Young's *Civil Government* were thoroughly Christian as well.

---

37 Noah Webster, *The Elementary Spelling-Book*, New York: D. Appleton & Co., 1880, pp. 101, 121, 115.

38 *An American Dictionary of the English Language*, 1828, republished in facsimile edition by Foundation for American Christian Education, San Francisco, 1980.

39 *Webster's New World Dictionary of the American Language*, David B. Guralnik, editor, Nashville: The Southwestern Company, 1969.

5. Biblical education advances God's kingdom with good fruit

A primary purpose of education is to build Christian character, to shape people both internally and externally. Noah Webster gave a biblical definition for *education*:

> "Education comprehends all that series of instruction and discipline which is intended to enlighten the understanding, correct the temper, form the manners and habits of youth, and fit them for usefulness in their future stations."[40]

The focus of education should firstly be the inner man. The fruit of education, as reflected in Webster's definition, is the same fruit that the Word of God will produce within an individual. Paul wrote that "all Scripture is inspired by God and profitable for teaching, for reproof, for correction, for training in righteousness; that the man of God may be adequate, equipped for every good work" (2 Timothy 3:16). Webster's definition implies that education will build the total man (inside and out) and prepare him to fulfill his destiny ("fit them for usefulness in their future stations").

A central purpose of education is to build godly character. Whoever controls education in a nation controls the formation of character. Whoever controls the character of the people controls the form of government. America began as a constitutional republic because the Christian character necessary to support such a government was formed in Americans in homes and churches.

Biblical education will not only affect individual lives but will impact all of life. It is a primary way by which we accomplish our godly mission to bring His kingdom to earth[41] and to disciple the nations.[42] Where biblical education is implemented in the earth, God's kingdom advances. Where state education is put into effect, man's kingdom comes.

---

40 Definition of *education* in Webster's 1828 Dictionary.

41 Jesus taught us to pray, "Thy kingdom come, Thy will be done, on earth as it is in heaven" (Matt. 6:10).

42 Jesus commissioned us to disciple the nations: "All authority has been given to Me in heaven and on earth. Go therefore and make disciples of all the nations … teaching them to observe all that I commanded you" (Matt. 28:18-20).

Christian education gave birth to America. Almost everyone was biblically literate and understood the principles of liberty. Thus, early Americans could effect a Christian revolution and give birth to the American constitutional republic. Education in biblical truth produced a free society. Signer of the Declaration Benjamin Rush wrote in 1806 that:

> The only means of establishing and perpetuating our republican forms of government, … is, the universal education of our youth in the principles of Christianity by the means of the bible. For this Divine book, above all others, favors that equality among mankind, that respect for just laws, and those sober and frugal virtues, which constitute the soul of republicanism.[43]

As we have abandoned Bible-centered education, America has declined from a republic to a socialistic democracy. The Protestant reformer Martin Luther recognized the great power of education. He said:

> I am afraid that schools will prove to be the great gates of hell unless they diligently labor in explaining the Holy Scriptures, engraving them in the hearts of youth. I advise no one to place his child where the Scriptures do not reign paramount. Every institution in which men are not increasingly occupied with the Word of God must become corrupt.[44]

Nineteenth-century theologian A.A. Hodge was even more direct:

> I am as sure as I am of the fact of Christ's reign that a comprehensive and centralized system of national education separated from religion, as is now commonly proposed, will prove the most appalling enginery for the propagation of anti-Christian and atheistic unbelief, and of anti-social, nihilistic ethics, individual, social, and political, which this sin-rent world has ever seen.[45]

The home is primarily where education for liberty occurs. The ability to affect society can grow exponentially with each succeeding generation, as evidenced by Jonathan and Sarah Edwards. Jonathan Edwards was a leader in the First Great Awakening and was one of America's greatest theolo-

---

43 Benjamin Rush, *Essays, Literary, Moral and Philosophical*, Philadelphia: printed by Thomas and William Bradford, 1806, p. 113.

44 Robert Flood, *Rebirth of America*, Philadelphia: Arthur S. DeMoss Foundation, 1986, p. 127.

45 A.A. Hodge, 1886, *Outlines of Theology*, Banner of Truth Trust.

gians. He and his wife faithfully trained their eleven children in accordance with their biblical duty.

Their children, in turn, passed on to future generations the vision for advancing liberty and building up their nation. A study was done of 1400 descendants of Jonathan and Sarah. Of these, 13 were college presidents, 65 were professors, 100 lawyers, 30 judges, 66 physicians, and 80 holders of public office including 3 senators, 3 governors, and a vice president of the United States.[46] Their training not only benefited their children, but thousands of their descendants, and the nation at large. The seeds we plant today through the education of our children (and others) have impact beyond measure in the future. Remember the great potential that comes from even a single seed.

Biblical education will produce kingdom fruit. As stated earlier, a primary purpose of education is to build Christian character, to shape the man both internally and externally. Biblical education will not only affect individual lives, but it will also impact all spheres of life.

John Witherspoon was a Kingdom educator who trained young men to be "Kingdom men." He was the man who shaped the men who shaped America. Witherspoon was a Presbyterian minister who came from Scotland in 1768 to serve as President of the College of New Jersey. During Witherspoon's tenure there were 478 graduates of what became Princeton University. Of these, at least 86 became active in civil government and included: one president (James Madison), one vice-president, 10 cabinet officers, 21 senators, 39 congressmen, 12 governors, a Supreme Court justice (Brockholst Livingston), and one attorney general of the United States (William Bradford).[47]

Nearly one-fifth of the signers of the Declaration of Independence, one-sixth of the delegates of the Constitutional Convention, and one- fifth of the first Congress under the Constitution were graduates of the College of New Jersey.[48]

---

46 William J. Petersen, *Martin Luther Had a Wife*, Wheaton, Ill.: Tyndale House, 1983,

47 Mary-Elaine Swanson, *The Education of James Madison, A Model for Today*, Montgomery: The Hoffman Education Center for the Family, 1992, p. 53.

48 Ibid.

Here was a man who literally discipled his nation. Those today with a vision for biblical education, and an understanding of the components of kingdom education, may, likewise, have an opportunity to disciple the nations.

The history of America shows that biblical education is central to the advancement of liberty and prosperity in history. Biblical education will produce kingdom fruit. Christian ideas have transformed the world. Consider the recent history of Korea.

The Story of Korea

The people of North Korea have lived in bondage for over 70 years, with no freedom and little material wealth. How have they been kept in such bondage for so long?

The people living in the Korean peninsula had a common history until the end of World War II. They embraced the same religion and cultural influences. Christianity was first introduced to Korea toward the end of the nineteenth century when missionaries from the United States carried the Gospel to them. In 1907 a great revival swept throughout the land. Three years later the Japanese invaded the country and began to persecute the people, especially those who were Christians. Many Christians fled to the countryside and established many "prayer mountains," where they hid out. Many of these prayer mountains remain today.

At the end of World War II, a decision was made for the defeated Japanese troops south of the 38th parallel to surrender to the Americans, while those north of this line surrendered to the Russians. Under the Americans, South Korea gained freedom, while communism grew in the North. The Korean War started in 1950 when communist forces from the North invaded the South. It ended a few years later with the permanent division of the nation along the 38th parallel, the North governed by communists, the South by those who over time embraced more and more liberty.

As freedom increased in the South, Christianity flourished and many churches were started, some growing to enormous size. The largest church in the world is in Seoul, South Korea – there are 750,000 members in the church started by Dr. Paul Yonggi Cho. The largest Presbyterian church in the world is also in Seoul, with 70,000 members.

These Christians carried their faith into all spheres of life. They started many Christian schools and colleges, including a Christian law school. They started many businesses, seeking to build them upon biblical principles. They became involved in government, having such an influence that today about 40% of the national legislature is Christian. The economy has grown greatly and liberty has flourished.

This is in great contrast to North Korea. During the time of great advancement and change in the South, the North has barely survived under the oppression of communist dictators. The people cannot produce enough food to feed themselves. They have no freedom of any kind — religious, civil, political or economic.

The contrast between North and South Korea is astonishing; it is as different as day and night. A satellite picture of the Korean peninsula at night clearly reveals the stark contrast.

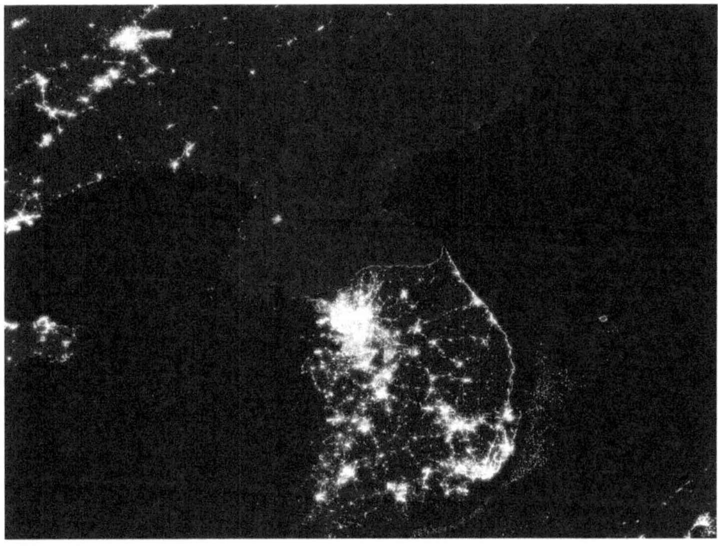

In this image South Korea is lit up from lights all over the nation (which shows just one aspect of her great prosperity), but the North is in complete darkness as they do not have enough electricity to power the nation, nor the prosperity to buy all that is necessary to light the nation. What has made the difference? Liberty.

Liberty is the primary reason for the great disparity between these two nations. Liberty is the cause of progress for mankind. Liberty causes more cultivation, more invention, more labor, and more wealth.

Liberty produces prosperity.[49] Freedom rather than natural resources is the key to prosperity. Yet, even more important is to understand the source of liberty. Where does liberty originate? From Christianity. Christianity produces liberty, which in turn produces prosperity.

So how then has North Korea been kept in such darkness and bondage? They certainly have not lived in liberty, because Christianity has been kept from the people. Why have they not risen up and thrown off the tyrant, especially with modern means of communication?

Some years ago, I heard a South Korean minister (who currently pastors a large, primarily Korean church in metro New York City) relate the story of how he had years earlier taken numerous secret trips into the North to find an answer to these questions. He discovered that when children are still infants the government takes them out of the home and puts them

---

49 Note: when I use the word prosperity, here, and in reference to America being the most prosperous nation in history, I do not mean solely material riches. Christianity produces wealth and riches. Riches are perishable assets. Anyone can obtain riches, and many people and nations have done so in ungodly ways. Wealth is having the skills, spiritual knowledge, and Godly character needed to live a productive and kingdom-centered life. Those who possess wealth can obtain riches; those who have riches but no wealth cannot keep, increase, and pass on riches (they – individuals or nations – will end up losing them). Biblical prosperity encompasses wealth and riches. A prosperous nation is one where everyone has the opportunity to use their God-given and human-developed talents to produce needed goods and services for mankind, and in so doing advance the kingdom of God. Prosperous nations are those that have all the blessings the Bible says comes to those who obey all of God's word. Nations that embrace some biblical economic principles will prosperous to some degree, but without embracing all of His principles, prosperity will be limited. China has obtained many riches in recent decades. This is partly due to their embracing some free market principles, which are biblical. Yet, they reject many other biblical principles, so their prosperity is limited – two thirds of their population still live in poverty, and those who have increasing material wealth do not have social, civil, emotional, and spiritual wealth. For more on this see Stephen McDowell, *The Economy from a Biblical Perspective*, Charlottesville: Providence Foundation, 2009.

into government schools to "train" (rather indoctrinate) them. Youths are taught the philosophy of the communist government: that society is of first importance and citizens must sacrifice for the good of all, which in practice means working for the prosperity of party leaders. Government leaders are the supreme voice. Whoever controls the children controls the future, and pagan thinkers want to control the future, so they seek to control education. Indoctrination through state schools is why the North still lives in darkness today and shows the power of education in shaping the course of nations.

Renovating the Age and Passing the Baton

God has called us to transform the nations. The Father of the American Revolution, Samuel Adams, declared that education in the principles of the Christian religion is key to reform. He wrote in a letter October 4, 1790, to his cousin John Adams, then Vice President:

> Let divines [ministers] and philosophers, statesmen and patriots, unite their endeavors to renovate the age, by impressing the minds of men with the importance of educating their little boys and girls, of inculcating in the minds of youth the fear and love of the Deity and universal philanthropy, and, in subordination to these great principles, the love of their country; of instructing them in the art of self-government, without which they never can act a wise part in the government of societies, great or small; in short, of leading them in the study and practice of the exalted virtues of the Christian system.[50]

To transform America and re-establish her as a beacon of liberty and prosperity, we must recover her original model of education, and then pass it on to the next generation. Psalm 78:1-7 reveals to us as parents and educators that we are to pass on to our posterity all of the vision, mission, principles, character, and truth that God has made known to this generation. We are to do this in such a way that they will then, in turn, teach their children, who will teach their children,

> "that they may arise and tell them to their children, that they should put their confidence in God and not forget the works of God" (v 6-7).

---

50 William V. Wells, *The Life and Public Services of Samuel Adams*, Vol. 3, Boston, 1865, p. 301.

We are in a race — not a hundred yard dash but a relay race. We will not win the race by merely running fast. We must pass the baton (that is, find faithful men who will teach others, 2 Timothy 2:2). Our generation was not given the baton, but had to grope around and find it in the weeds. After finding it we had to learn what the race was all about, where the track was, how to run, and how to pass the baton. We also must train our posterity to run in the race, how to receive the baton, and how to pass it to the next generation.

We can do great things for God in this generation, but if we fail in this, we have failed to fulfill God's purpose for this generation.

Biblical education is the means of passing the baton (the kingdom) to the next generation and equipping them to pass it to their posterity. The extent to which we educate in a kingdom manner determines the extent to which His kingdom will come on earth. Establishing biblical education in the nations is, therefore, of utmost importance.

Chapter 16

The University's Failed Worldview: Secular Humanism

Karla Perry[1]

I sat riveted to the scene playing out in my classroom at Old Dominion University. Chagrin flashed upon the history professor's face. At the university's request, she implored her class to not engage in plagiarism. She should not have been surprised that her pleas had fallen on deaf ears. For months she had driven home the idea that truth, and with it, history, was unknowable. The entire point of her *Introduction to History* was that we were entering a discipline we could not master with any degree of confidence. She professed to doubt that we could uncover truth in the past because truth did not exist to be discovered or, at least, was too illusive to serve as the goal of historical inquiry. But now she encountered the natural consequences of her worldview.

Our teacher laid out the policies and disciplinary policies relating to plagiarism. She then opened the floor for discussion, as was her style. The room exploded with voices as students offered what they saw as valid reasons for engaging in plagiarism. I watched as moral outrage overtook her. Appalled at their excuses, she began to lecture the class on the moral wrong that is plagiarism. I remember scribbling notes as she talked. I recognized the failure of a worldview that lacked grounding in truth. How could students be impressed upon to not steal intellectual work if there is no standard for truth? If history is unknowable, and unattainable, what does intellectual property even mean?

I had entered the university eager to learn. Having been raised in a Christian home and afforded a Christian education, I saw the purpose for education as not simply gaining a good career, but becoming an educated

---

1 Karla Perry is a worldview revitalizer and author of The Reformation of America. She and her husband, Joseph, pastored in Virginia Beach, VA for eleven years. Karla is a co-founder of The Serve Initiative; an organization designed to equip and empower believers for the work of reformation.

person, ready to contribute to society. I sought out rigorous courses because I wanted to learn and become what is known as "learned."

In almost every class I met similar disappointments. While I had a few professors who were fine educators, many others seemed hampered by the secular humanism that had influenced them so deeply. Their ideology handicapped their ability to provide an education that can build the souls of their students. I valued the moments when their expertise shone through the fog of philosophical error.

The English Department proved no better. On my first day in *Advanced Composition*, the professor announced, with great bravado, that there are no facts. She dared anyone to contradict her. As a rebel for the truth, I raised my hand. Her eyes caught mine and asked for an example. "Today is Tuesday," I blurted out. To which she replied, "It is here." "Give me another one", she challenged the class. She was met with silence. My hand shot up again. "The earth is round," I offered. Her response came swiftly: "Did you measure it?" She then abandoned the dialogue and dove into the syllabus for the course, containing truths about time and location that she seemed to wish us to hold in common and abide by.

Literature teachers informed us that books had no meaning. "The author is dead", declared the professor teaching the philosophy of the French philosopher Jacques Derrida. She organized her class into groups to study, or rather deconstruct, Charlotte Bronte's classic novel *Jane Eyre*.

Each group chose a different perspective from which to examine the novel. We were not supposed to seek the author's intended meaning (*exegesis*), but impose our own meaning upon the text (*eisegesis*). Since there is no truth and no standard by which to judge perspectives, my reading of the text is as valid or invalid as yours. Much to my dismay, my group voted to use lesbian literary criticism theory to analyze the book. At the end of the project, each group gave a presentation from their chosen literary criticism, producing multiple variant readings of *Jane Eyre*. It is thus that post-modernism destroys not only objective truth, but even great literature.

One student in my *Jane Eyre* group had a Christian background. I heard her musing that, if what our professor was saying was "true", it would mean that the postmodern literary criticism we were learning should be applied to the Bible. I told her we ought not to do that, and she repeated that it would be appropriate to do so, given what we were learning. She also had no qualms about reading lesbianism into *Jane Eyre*. I provided the dissenting opinion in our report, but the other students were eager to uncover an imagined romantic interest between Jane and her best friend.

Such experiences, repeated many times, prompted me to study worldview to understand the foundations of a healthy society. Clearly, I was not going to find that in the decaying secular humanism which is deeply woven into the curriculum of modern American universities.

Secular Humanism assumes that the natural world is all there is, but borrows from Christianity the search for human equality and harmony. It recognizes that the natural world is real, and that humanity can achieve progress. While lacking an anchor in truth, it carries a modicum of Christian thought removed from its supernatural and revelatory source.

Francis Schaeffer astutely observed in *How Should We Then Live*:
> "[Secular] Humanism has no final way of saying certain things are right and other things are wrong. For a humanist, the final thing which exists — that is, the impersonal universe — is neutral and silent about right and wrong, cruelty and non-cruelty. Humanism has no way to provide absolutes. Thus, as a consistent result of humanism's position, humanism in private morals and political life is left with that which is arbitrary."[2]

My fellow students were consistently living out a worldview in which plagiarism was not morally wrong. The students had surpassed their teacher in carrying out the logical conclusion of the worldview in which their education was steeped.

Secular Humanism is not, as some assume, a neutral worldview. James Sire observes in *Naming the Elephant*:
> "Every declaration about a worldview is based on a worldview. A worldview is inescapable."[3]

---

2 Schaeffer, Francis *How Should We Then Live?* (Illinois: Crossway), 1976, 2005 p. 128

3 Sire, James *Naming the Elephant: Worldview as Concept* (Illinois: Intervarsity Press), 2004 p. 113

To keep a discipline neutral, it is removed from its foundation of truth. The subject is taught without regard for where it came from. For instance, science is cut off from the Christian worldview that birthed it. History professors have no grounding to validate the study of history. Within the worldview of secular humanism, every subject is taught from a system of thought that strips away its origins. We are now seeing the decay of disciplines which cannot maintain their integrity without a firm foundation of truth. Truth, not neutrality, should be the goal of a healthy education.

In *Abington v. Schempp* in 1963, it was argued that reading the Bible in public schools violated the principle of government neutrality. Supreme Court Justice Potter Stewart noted, in his dissenting argument:

> "A refusal to permit religious exercises thus is seen, not as the realization of state neutrality, but rather as the establishment of a religion of secularism."[4]

Judge Stewart understood that secularism is just as much a religion as is Christianity. For the government to choose one over the other constituted an establishment of religion, not a religiously-neutral act. Secular humanism is an empty shell of the Christian worldview.

It can be seen as the illegitimate child of the church's affair with the Enlightenment. It is more Christian than it admits, but far less Christian than a worldview must be to support the integrity of a nation.

Professor Alan Bloom, a liberal Jew, noted in his groundbreaking book *The Closing of the American Mind*:

> "Secularization is the wonderful mechanism by which religion becomes non-religion. Marxism is secularized Christianity, so is democracy, so is utopianism; so are human rights. Everything connected with valuing must come from religion. One need not investigate anything else, because Christianity is the necessary and sufficient condition of our history."[5]

Secularism can only work to the degree it does because it is based on ideas which came from Christianity. It cannot support the idea of human

---

4 Cox, William F., Jr. *Tyranny Through Public Education* (Allegiance Press), 2004 p. 357

5 Bloom, Alan. *The Closing of the American Mind,* (New York: Simon & Schuster), 1987, 2012 p. 211

rights without borrowing, on the sly, the biblical idea that God makes each person in His image. The Israeli philosopher of education, Aharon Aviram observes:

> "The Enlightenment, as an empiricist, materialist and determinist conception, was incapable of providing support for the two premises that constitute a vital foundation for human life; freedom of the individual and the human hope that life has some meaning beyond the level of material phenomena."[6]

Aviram explains at length that, abandoning the "eternal and immutable", resulted in "contrived depthlessness", leading us back to religious revival. Aviram argues that this would be detrimental to the universities and that the best solution lies in developing a post-postmodern world of which he considers Frederick Nietzsche a pioneer.[7] Thus he proposes doubling down on post-modernity to solve that which ails the post-modern world.

We must not imagine that a non-religious and neutral education has no ill effect upon knowledge. Education was never meant to be stripped clean of divine truth. That path only grows darker and more confused the further one passes down it. Righteous education brings students into greater levels of truth, responsibility and freedom to live in healthy nations which have been biblically discipled. We cannot learn about our world and our responsibilities in a religiously neutral framework. In fact, it is not accurate to even call it a framework as it has been divided up piecemeal to such an extent that education has lost nearly all cohesion. Cut off from roots in Truth, our students lose even the basics of civics. Bloom observed:

> "When a student arrives at the university, he finds a bewildering variety of departments and a bewildering variety of courses. And there is no official guidance, no university-wide agreement, about what he should study. Nor does he usually find readily available examples, either among the students or professors, of a unified use of the university's resources. It is easiest simply to make a career choice and go about getting prepared for that career."[8]

---

6 Aviram, Aharon. *European Journal of Education*: The Humanist Conception of the University: A Framework for Post-Modern Higher Education. 1992, Vol 27, No. 4 (1992) p. 397-414

7 Ibid.

8 Ibid, p. 338

Universities thus become mere sites for learning a career, having lost a sound worldview that joins disciplines into a coherent whole. The university is meant to join "unity" to "diversity," but both are being lost to a standardized philosophical muddle. Bloom again observed:

> "In short there is no vision, nor is there a set of competing visions, of what an educated human being is. The question has disappeared, for to pose it would be a threat to the peace. There is no organization of the sciences, no tree of knowledge."[9]

Without a basis for truth we cannot say what it means to be an educated human, or even what is human as opposed to animal or artificial intelligence. How can universities guide students to become learned if they have no idea what that goal even means?

More disturbing still, Bloom concludes:

> "These great universities — which can split the atom, find cures for the most terrible diseases, conduct surveys of whole populations and produce massive dictionaries of lost languages — cannot generate a modest program of general education for undergraduate students."[10]

In fact, Bloom believed that a student seeking a career path can accomplish that goal in under two years, and that most of what else is taught in the modern university is not worth the time and money expended.

Bloom was not the first to recognize that something was sick in the state of education. In 1963, Catholic historian Christopher Dawson wrote in *The Crisis of Western Education*:

> One of the chief defects of modern education has been its failure to find an adequate method for the study of our own civilization. The old humanist education taught all that it knew about the civilization of ancient Greece and Rome, and taught little else. In the nineteenth century, this aristocratic and humanist ideal was gradually replaced by the democratic utilitarianism of compulsory state education, on the one hand, and by the ideal of scientific specialization, on the other.

---

9 Ibid, p. 337

10 Ibid, p. 340

The result has been an intellectual anarchy imperfectly controlled by the crude methods of the examination system and of payment by results. The mind of the student is overwhelmed and dazed by the volume of new knowledge which is being accumulated by the labor of specialists, while the necessity for using education as a stepping-stone to a profitable career leaves him little time to stop and think. And the same is true of the teacher, who has become a kind of civil servant tied to a routine over which he can have little control.[11]

An adequate method for learning exists, but it has been abandoned due to the allure of "neutral" secular humanism. Instead of seeking an un-obtainable pseudo-objectivity, we should rely on a worldview developed from truth. The Christian worldview helped in forming the foundation for modern science in the first place. The Christian worldview first suggested that all people should be afforded an education - not just the elite.

To abandon that worldview, or whittle it down to its bare bones and then to build upon it the foreign idea that 'man is the measure of all things,' is to twist it in such a manner as to make it useless. In fact such decon-struction leads to the bog of post-modernity, where understanding of the nature of man has been buried. A post-Christian humanism has lost the foundation of its knowledge and its confidence that we can know truth. A broken worldview can only produce a broken nation. This is why edu-cation requires reform that sets it free from secularism and restores it to its Christian origins.

It would be a mistake to consider the prevalence of secular humanism in our educational institutions as a grand conspiracy. George Marsden writes that a conspiratorial explanation "is simplistic."[12] Many factors throughout American history have affected our educational system. To a large extent secularization of the schools is not something done to Christians, it is something we participated in creating. We abdicated our role as educators of a nation by agreeing with a theology that divides secular and sacred. We were also pushed out of education because we were no longer able to communicate our values in a rapidly secularizing system.

---

11 Dawson, Christopher. *The Crises of Western Education*, (New York: Catholic University of American Press), 1961 Ch. IX.

12 Marsden, George. The Soul of the American University. *First Things*. January 1991.

But pointing fingers gets us nowhere: the important question is "What should we do now?"

Marsden argues in his brilliant essay "The Soul of the American University" that our options are: either to become a valuable part of a more pluralized educational setting where all voices are allowed, or to create our own educational system. The former option would require us to reform the present (increasingly anti-Christian) education establishment in which it would be one of many competing ideas. The latter option demands an entirely new system that makes Christian education relevant to more than those few individuals who seek Bible degrees. The goal will be not to create a sub-cultural Christian education, but a vibrant education that is the envy of the world.

Indeed, that is our goal. We seek to serve the world through education, providing the cohesion only found through the application of divine revelation.

It is important to remember that professors generally teach what they believe to be true (to the extent that they believe in truth).

Having enjoyed a Christian K-12 education, I experienced a dramatic cultural clash in college. I developed a contempt for my professors, imagining them to have sinister goals. I began to battle them in class with an evangelistic fervor that lacked the kindness of God which may have led them to repentance. Despite my strong Christian school education, I was not prepared to face the challenge I met daily in class.

I have a keen sense of truth. I recognized errors around me, but lacked the worldview training I needed to properly respond to these challenges.

I dove deeply into apologetics, as it was all the support I knew to seek. In the process I discovered the works of Francis Schaeffer and others who strengthened my worldview. It took years before I understood that my professors were trapped in their worldviews and were merely communicating the world as they saw it. They wanted me to see it that way too, not to deceive me, but because, "in the futility of their thinking", as Paul put it, that was the best they understood.

Proverbs 4:19 says, "The way of the wicked is like deep darkness; they do not know what makes them stumble." (NIV). We cannot blame the darkness for being dark. We should not act as if those in the darkness could see clearly enough to act rightly. We see the effects of errant philosophy, but those discipled within it cannot recognize the error of their ways until they are brought into the light. Our attitude should be like Jesus who, as he hung on the cross, said: "Father forgive them, for they do not know what they do."

The only way for Christians to be an intellectual light in response to such philosophies is to be educated in full light of the truth. When we go to secular universities, we must carry a robust Christian worldview to engage false ideas without succumbing to them.

Even most Christian high schools do not provide the worldview training needed. After all, high school teachers and textbook writers studied in the same universities. The worldview of the elite taught in Academia has trickled down to pop culture, and even permeates the church. Pulling out of culture into Christian schools and Bible Colleges does not equip a nation. Our goal should not be a Christian culture isolated from the world, but rather an education that flows out of the Christian worldview, bringing truth that transforms society.

When we pull out of the world, we leave the world to disciple the nation in every area we have abandoned. Instead of teaching our nation, we allow the world to disciple us. Instead of being the lawyers, doctors, scientists, engineers, authors of textbooks, journalists and others who transform the world, we are being passively transformed by secular leaders.

The revolution we propose does not encourage Christians to retreat from education. The Christian faith should again be a gift of education to the nations of the world. The revolution that this volume represents aims to regain that unity in the diversity of subjects that universities were designed to promulgate. It means discipling in that truth and applied theology which have created the modern world and can stabilize nations. It means restoring education to a biblical worldview, liberating it from secular humanism and other philosophical dead-ends. For truth sets free - nations as well as individuals.

Chapter 17

The Fall of American Education

David Marshall[1]

One day, subbing at a Middle School on the eastern edge of suburbia outside Seattle, I found about twenty biographies of "The Prophet Mohammed" in pencil, hanging on the walls. Each seemed entirely laudatory: all praise, and no criticism was offered in those I read.

Odd. I had never seen student essays praising Jesus or Buddha in public classrooms. How many of the essayists were from Christian homes? America is not, after all, a majority-Muslim country, certainly not in the forested foothills of the Cascade Mountains. Was it even legal to "establish religion" by asking students to uncritically praise the founder of one faith, rather than to write objective history?

As an historian of religion, I knew that Mohammed had been accused by serious scholars of many acts worthy of criticism: raids and wars, torture, assassination, enslaving, marrying a young child, stealing his adopted son's wife, then threatening his other wives with hell if they complained when he brought her into the harem. But none of those were mentioned.

On later teaching assignments, I found a textbook called *History Alive* that appeared to be the source of those flattering stories about Mohammed. It also explained why there were none about Jesus, although it was He - not Mohammed - who truly brought "history alive".

This chapter tells how truth has been exchanged for untruths in American schools. Karla Perry has already told part of that story from a former student's perspective. I would like to offer a teacher's view, concentrating on the corruption of education in two American cities: Boston and Seattle. We will meet some famous people in this chapter: not just Mohammed, but

---

1 Dr. Marshall is author of a dozen books, including *True Son of Heaven: How Jesus Fulfills the Chinese Culture*, and *Letter to a 'Racist' Nation*.

also Howard Zinn, Matt Damon, Kendi Ibram and Robin DiAngelo. We will see how campus ideologies may flow into radical activism: a bombing at a race in Boston, a district in Seattle that "seceded," for a few weeks, from the United States.

In the last chapter Perry described how Secular Humanism and Relativism undermined both the search for truth, and even coherence among some of her fellow students. It even ruined great Christian literature like *Jane Eyre*. In this chapter I would like to show how other bad ideas spoil education: Islamophilia, Marxism, Critical Studies and Neo-Racism. We will see how that destruction may spill off campuses into violence in our most prosperous cities.

1. Howard Zinn at a Christian College

In 1956 a new professor began to teach at Spelman, a Christian college for girls in Atlanta, founded by ex-slaves with a Bible. Howard Zinn, an atheist from Brooklyn and probably a member of the Communist Party, may have seemed an odd choice for a Christian school. But Zinn was a World War II veteran, held a PhD in history from Columbia University and had studied under top historians. In any case, Zinn was sympathetic to the struggle of African-Americans for their rights. Karl Marx himself had been a racist, among his other faults. Zinn was savvy enough to recognize that old-fashioned Marxism required a little contextualization (as missionaries call it) to work in the American classroom.

Some forty years later, Howard Zinn's famous book, *People's History of the United States*, was given a pop-cultural nod when the young genius played by Matt Damon in the film *Good Will Hunting*, (Damon happened to be Zinn's real-life neighbor in Boston), told the psychiatrist played by Robin Williams:

> "You wanna read a really good American History book? Read Howard Zinn's *A People's History of the United States*. It will knock you on your ass!"

Peoples' History did, indeed, knock the reputations of Columbus and other American heroes on their backsides, before their statues were toppled by mobs in the summer of 2020.

The introduction to the book's 34th anniversary edition accurately claims: "Howard Zinn fundamentally changed the way millions of people think about history." The toppling of those Columbus statues might be explained by three facts: (1) Zinn began his book by depicting Columbus as a bloody oppressor; (2) readers tend to begin with the first chapter, even if they make it no further; but (3) few have read Mary Grabar's rebuttal, *Debunking Howard Zinn*, which shows that Zinn misread the story of Columbus and grossly misrepresented much of what he said about American history in general - from the founding of the Republic to World War II.

Yet arguably, Zinn was most dangerous in what he got right. In an earlier chapter I already talked about what secular humanists borrowed from the "third teacher".

It would never have occurred to Roman historians like Suetonius, Polybius or Plutarch to tell the story of America from the perspective of the oppressed. Columbus was an explorer and conqueror, which would have inspired most ancient historians to celebrate his life, all the more if some blood that was shed, even as they celebrated the lives of Alexander and Caesar. Zinn takes the perspective of slaves, the working class, Chechen immigrants to Boston, and native peoples whom Columbus exploited, while ignoring facts to the contrary. Historian Tom Holland argues in his magisterial *Dominion* that concern for the marginalized, was taught to the western world by Jesus of Nazareth. Even Will Durant seemed to recognize this fact.

But Zinn is more like Marx than like Jesus. Zinn stands up for the underdog, but fails to also rebuke the sins of the underclass or to recognize that even Pharisees and Centurions sometimes act nobly or speak with insight. He echoes the class blindness of the elite by distracting the marginalized from their own sins, ensuring that, after the revolution, power will merely transfer to a new crew of despots, when pigs walk on hind legs and attack dogs police the boundaries of *Animal Farm*.

We should not read history naively, but this is history with an attitude and an agenda. It is a litany of actual horrors that ought to be faced - at least when Zinn gets his facts right. But it is post-truth history which must not be mistaken for Truth.

And some of Zinn's "facts" are false. He says that Mao's government in 1949 was "the closest thing to a peoples' government" China had ever had. As a China scholar, I tend to think it was the most tyrannical Chinese regime since that of Zhu Yuanzhang, founder of the Ming, or that of Qin Shihuang, founder of the Qin, two centuries before Christ. Zinn implies that American military spending remained the same after the breakup of the USSR. In fact: it was reduced dramatically, from almost 11% of GNP during the Vietnam War, to 6% in the 80s (and now near 3.5%). Zinn claims that violent crime continued to increase despite a big prison population. Actually it had already declined by the time of the edition I read (1996), and petered out further until the Covid riots "defunded" (or defanged) the police in many cities. Zinn does not seem to have noticed improvements in the environment, either: I now swim across the water from Bill Gates' house in a clean Lake Washington - which was badly polluted when I was a child.

Some of Zinn's sins of omission edge close to lies. According to him, if the US supports a government, it engages in "imprisonment of dissenters, torture and mass murder"; if Americans oppose it, worse crimes are not fit to be mentioned. South Vietnam jailed "thousands" of political prisoners; no one, it seems, suffered such a fate in North Vietnam, nor is genocide in Cambodia worth troubling the reader with. The life expectancy of a black man in Harlem is less than in Sudan. But surely, when he wrote, Zinn knew that the cause of most early deaths in Harlem was not simply "poverty" - men were not dying of starvation - but AIDS, murder, suicide and crack cocaine - pathologies that are not solved by social spending, or by outrage against the ruling classes.

Zinn did not explicitly say that letting Stalin, Mao and the cruel Kim Dynasty have their way with the Koreas would have been better than contesting their will: he simply did not face the question, as Truman had to. In complaining about tough choices that adults have to make in a complex and difficult world (and for Zinn American leaders never made the right choice) and offering no real solutions, Zinn acted as forerunner to mobs who think that attacking police will fix Portland; and politicians who smile awkwardly and predict a "Summer of Love", or shrug and say: "People will do what they do" when mobs deface public statues.

Howard Zinn taught his disciples to commit the sin of the Children of Israel: ingratitude. Blind patriotism is wrong, but who can stand to be around someone who is always criticizing? Zinn did, after all, rake in millions of dollars by attacking free enterprise and the free institutions which rendered those attacks lucrative.

In an earlier chapter I noted that "a teacher is a dangerous thing", and quoted Clement of Alexandria, who said: "Truth is one" but that it had been torn to pieces by ideologues. Zinn tore a thin scrap off the Gospel which the world's greatest teacher taught, and clothed America's youth in that tattered cloth.

Jesus looked at categories (short tax collectors, old widows, Samaritans, serial wives) and saw individuals. Zinn and his followers look at individuals and see categories: Black, White, Rich, Poor, Male, Female, Trans, Gay. True prophets teach us to challenge the stereotypes of all scapegoating, not just those of one class or race. Following Karl Marx, Zinn taught students to locate evil in the group, not in individual choices.
Jesus praised the rich and chastised the poor by the same standards that he praised the poor and chastised the rich. Zinn merely flipped the bigotry of rich snobs and haughty kings, judging people by who they are, not what they do.

Jesus healed, fed, protected, and liberated those in need, and taught his disciples to do the same. He was the Shepherd who laid down his life for the sheep. Zinn parlayed his obsession with class into riches, with feminism into love affairs with students, and with racism into undermining a historical black college. One could say that, while Jesus turned water into wine, Howard Zinn turned ideological whining into gold.

It is Howard Zinn's shallow, ungrateful heresy, however, that is sweeping through American schools and bringing chaos to her streets.

2. The Boston Bombers

On April 15, 2013, 23,000 athletes from around the world gathered outside Boston to run the 117th Boston Marathon. Four hours into the race, two bombs exploded near the finish line, 17 seconds apart. Hundreds of people were injured, with three dying, and seventeen losing limbs. A citywide manhunt ensued for two Chechen refugees, the brothers Dzhokar and Tamerlan Tsarnaev, who later said they were upset over American invasions of Afghanistan and Iraq. During the manhunt, a young officer for MIT named Sean Collier was shot and killed by the brothers. A Watertown officer, Dennis Simmonds or "DJ," was struck with an explosive device, which caused his death a year later.

The story of these sibling terrorists intersects with that of the actor Matt Damon, his brother Kyle, and the teachings of Howard Zinn, in surprising ways. Both Damons and Tsamaevs attended Cambridge Rindge and Latin High School, a few minutes walk from Harvard. (Both schools are part of the legacy of the city's Puritan founders which Stephen McDowell describes in his chapter.) Dzhokar Tsarnaev and Kyle Damon were both on warm terms with a teacher named Larry Aaronson, who lived a few houses away from the two immigrants and remembered the murderer kindly:

> "He had a heart of gold, he was a sweetheart, he was gracious, he was caring, he was compassionate."

Aaronson taught at Cambridge Rindge and Latin High School for some 40 years, using his position as a Social Studies teacher the same way Howard Zinn used his job in Spelman: to radicalize students. Aaronson was, in fact, a protégé and friend of Zinn. When the latter passed away, after quoting the "knock you on your butts" line from *Good Will Hunting*, Aaronson explained how he taught history, and the effect his lessons had:

> "The world-famous historian, retired BU professor, playwright, poet, novelist, and 'radical' peace and civil rights activist, died Jan. 26th, the same day President Obama delivered his State of the Union message. Howie was 87, active until the day he died, struck down by a massive heart attack. His famous history book, *People's History of the United States*, has sold well over 2 million copies, and counting. Last Dec. 11th, 'The People Speak,' produced in part by Matt Damon and Ben Affleck ('88 and '90) appeared on the History Channel. Before moving to Cambridge in the mid-70's, Matt Damon grew up next door to the Zinns. Both households equally sharing progressive politics, they became life-long 'family.' September '81, Kyle Damon, Matty's older brother, enrolled in my US History class. It was Kyle's freshmen year, my 'rookie' year at The Pilot, the very first year *A People's History* appeared. This was pure serendipity, all to the delight of their mom. Soon after I was invited over for dinner with the Zinn's. The rest is history . . ."

Aaronson bragged that he was "one of the very first teachers" to teach Zinn's "revisionist history" in a public American high school, and did so "extensively" for two decades. Aaronson believed his approach had a profoundly positive effect on young minds:

> "I submit there is a direct correlation between the introduction of Zinn's book and the extraordinary awakening of student leadership in Cambridge Rindge and Latin during the 80's and lasted until early 90's. The change in the political activism in the school was palpable."

Aaronson encouraged activism, from passing out condoms to combating racism and "gender stereotypes." What all those programs share in common with Zinn's book is a focus on those previously marginalized. In that sense, Aaronson, too, was unknowingly a disciple of Jesus. But better disciples, like Charles Dickens, Booker T. Washington or Martin Luther King spoke for the poor while recognizing that all humans possess both dignity and sin. To Marxists the racial or sexual proletariat hardly need repent, because evil is located in the "owning" classes, the One Percent, White People or the Police. In that sense Marxism is merely the mirror image of traditional Brahminism, which simply locates good and evil in different castes.

One morning, in a giddy mood, Aaronson posted on Facebook:

> "MAY DAY!!!! MAY DAY!!!! MAY DAY!!!! It's blessed May Day! Shall this be a call to socialist revolution for social justice???"

Aaronson concluded by asking the big question:

> "How will we be able to get this curriculum into our public schools?"

Aaronson wasn't worried about his own school, where he had been teaching radicalism for years and from which he elsewhere rejoiced that "literally hundreds" of grads were working "in the public sector" for "social justice." He was wondering how to revolutionize the thought life of your child, too.

Aaronson may have been a caring teacher who held what he perceived as the best at heart for his students. But the coincidences are striking.

Two Chechen brothers are given refuge in the United States. Muslims, according to available accounts they are welcomed at an elite school which brags of its diverse student body, and treated kindly by both staff and students.

A social studies teacher (personal friend of Howard Zinn and neighbor to these boys) adopts Zinn's approach to radicalizing students at his school. He teaches the history of an America that relentlessly oppresses Blacks, Native Americans, immigrants and workers. (Zinn ignores the Pilgrims' more humane approach in Massachusetts itself, as Grabar shows.) Aaronson not only preaches activism; he credits his own neo-Marxist teaching with an upsurge in radical activity among students, as Zinn had at Spelman.

But May Day is not symbolized by the color red for nothing.

Perhaps the Boston Bombers were "radicalized" by the invasions of Afghanistan and Iraq, as they say. Perhaps we will never know the full truth. But how could one not learn to hate America from books like *Peoples' History*? Ingratitude towards the country that welcomed them so warmly could only have been encouraged by a Zinnian education. And Marxism strongly justifies violence. The full chain of influences that led those two young immigrants to try to blow up hundreds of innocent people, is unknown. But among Larry Aaronson's pupils, the Boston Bombers proved the most active of activists.

3. Ibram Kendi Comes to Boston

Boston University has just passed the baton of radical indoctrination to the Critical Theorist Ibram Kendi, who was invited in the summer of 2020 to direct the new Center for Antiracist Research. Kendi's Christian parents got to know one another at InterVarsity's Urbana '70. His father was told by James Cone, the "scholarly father of black liberation theology," that a Christian should be defined as "one who is striving for liberation." Having been raised in Christian schools in Queens, and now Professor of History at an elite university founded by Methodists, Kendi harms America more out of ignorance than spite, I argue in an Open Letter addressed to him at *The Stream*. But the harm grows deeper by the day.

Let us now travel west, to the school where I encountered Mohammed, the famous Capitol Hill Autonomous Zone (Chaz), and to the grassy quad where I got my BA and MA, and meet the one person whose sermons on the evils of traditional American society seem even more popular these days than those of Dr. Kendi.

4. History Alive

You jump in your car (much as Matt Damon does at the end of *Good Will Hunting*) and head west. About 30 miles from Seattle and the end of I-90 you notice a granite mountain to the right that you may recognize from the old "Twin Peaks" TV show. You're in the Snoqualmie Valley. The text, *History Alive*, teaching students to praise the Prophet Mohammed, was used in two middle schools in this district. From it children learn two clear lessons that even Howard Zinn did not dare teach: Islam good, Christianity bad.

"Islam Good"

In a long chapter that describes Mohammed's teaching and movement, children are told that he "enjoyed a reputation throughout (Mecca) for his honesty. People called him al-Amin, which means 'the Trustworthy.'" His mission, it seems, came straight from the top:

> "God told Muhammed to teach others about treating people with compassion, honesty, and justice."

Islam was not only a "way of life", but the basis for "creating a just society". The book in which Mohammed's revelations were collected is outstanding for its "poetic beauty".

Mohammed:

> "Taught that people must worship one god, that all believers in God were equal and that the rich should share their wealth. He urged (Meccans) to take care of orphans and the poor, and to improve the status of women".

Unfortunately not everyone appreciated Mohammed's idealist teachings, but their attacks only proved the nobility of the Muslim religion:

> "Some Arabs called Muhammed a liar. Some tortured his weaker followers. Despite this treatment, the Muslims would not give up their faith..."

Mohammed established the first Muslim community in Medina:

> "Muslims pledged to be loyal and helpful to each other. They emphasized the brotherhood of faith over the ties of family, clan and tribe. Mohammed also asked his followers to respect Christians and Jews."

Mohammed even nobly "forgave his former enemies" after conquering Mecca.

> "He reminded Muslims to treat each other well and to be faithful to their community. Shortly after his return to Madinah, Muhammed died."

In this account, the founder of Islam is portrayed as a font of virtues: an honest, tolerant, brave and compassionate poet, kind to the poor and to women. The man seems all virtue and no vice.

Maxime Rodinson tells a starkly different tale in his biography of Mohammed:

> "Alliances were made with tribes in the vicinity of Medina . . . with no hesitation in resorting to the torture of prisoners as an example . . . They negotiated with the Jewish leader, Usayr ibn Razim, and ended by persuading him to go to Medina with an escort of thirty of his own men, to reach an agreement with the Prophet himself. On the journey all the Jews were killed by surprise. Mohammed congratulated the leader of the band on his return . . ."

In fact, according to Muslim sources, Mohammed conducted more than two dozens raids on neighboring cities and tribes, and murdered 700 males in a Jewish clan in Medina that allegedly cherished subversive thoughts. He enslaved and tortured enemies, raped the widow of an enemy just killed in war, and married a nine-year-old girl.

But school children only learn positive things about Saint Mohammed. In a Zinnian world, Islam is perceived as marginalized and therefore portrayed as inherently noble.

By contrast, the authors had nothing good to say about the religion that is the foundation of western civilization.

"Christianity Bad!"

Students who wonder who Jesus was are not given a whole chapter of hagiography, as with Mohammed, but the following three sentences:

> "The Christian religion is one of the most important legacies of ancient Rome. Christians are followers of Jesus Christ, who was put to death on a Roman cross in the first century C. E. Christians

believe that Christ was the son of God, that God sent him to Earth to save people from their sins, and that he rose from the dead after his crucifixion."

The pernicious influence of Christianity on Europe is covered later in the book. Describing a "boom in art and learning" in Renaissance Italy, students read nothing about the Church that founded universities and hospitals in imitation of a Teacher and Healer. Interest in learning was supposedly spurred rather by "humanism," which "balanced" religion with "an emphasis on individual dignity and an interest in nature and human society."

"Humanists separated the state and its right to rule from the church. In doing so, they helped lay the foundation for modern thinking about politics and government."

So "religious faith" in its Christian (but not Islamic) mode should be seen as negligent of human dignity and incurious about nature and society. Never mind that the theme of much Renaissance art was explicitly religious. Never mind that this is where Francis of Assisi appeared, whose poetry and life was as clearly inspired by the life of Jesus as can be. Students also learn nothing of the faith of Alfred the Great, Alcuin, Roger Bacon, Robert Grosseteste, St. Anselm, Thomas Aquinas, Jean Buridan, or John Scotus. Christianity needs to be "balanced" by healthier concerns and informed by our pagan past, from which Europe allegedly derived the ideas of "the importance of and dignity of each individual", emphasis on "human life and culture" and even the teaching of grammar, rhetoric, history, poetry and ethics. (Though Christians had in fact been teaching these things for centuries by this time.)

In short: nothing good came from Christianity; everything useful had to be imported from classical sources.

The authors credit "humanist ideals" with the development of individualism and freedom. But such liberal ideas were opposed by foul, reactionary Christianity:

> "The humanists' new ideas sometimes brought them into conflict with the Church. The Church taught that laws were made by God and that those who broke them were sinful. It encouraged people to follow its teachings without question in order to save their souls.

For the church, life after death was more important than life on Earth. In contrast, humanists believed that people should use their minds to question everything . . . Some directly challenged teachings that were dear to the Church. An Italian humanist, Giodano Bruno, paid for his ideas by being burned at the stake."

What an ugly picture these authors paint of Christianity! They give the Gospel no credit for anything good that happened in the Medieval world. "Don't question our dogmas, or you will go to hell! Don't doubt, or we will burn you at the stake!" In contrast, Islam taught kindness, honesty, respect for others, women's rights, and no doubt how to separate paper, plastic, and metals into clearly-marked recycle bins.

History Alive did not seem (so far as I found) to credit the Christian faith for a single positive development. By contrast, it hovered over Mohammed like a teenage paparazzi with a crush; naively affirmed almost every Muslim claim about him; credited Islam for numerous goods; and politely refused to mention mass-murder, torture, rape or war-mongering when led by the lips and sharp sword of the "prophet."

After reading my description of *History Alive*, a distraught young woman posted on my blog:

"I'm a high school senior who took A.P. World History last year. We watched a documentary produced by PBS about the rise of Islam and the Islamic empires that followed. I am not exaggerating when I say it literally refused to acknowledge any intolerant act ever done by Muslims, except al-Hakim's burning of churches, but he was dismissed as being insane and the exception. The worst, most horrible thing about the film was the portrayal of the Ottoman Empire's confiscation of children from Christian subjects for the Jannisaries.

"I cried during the documentary – Christians were portrayed as terrible, backwards people and Muslims universally good. I hate it that teachers act like they need to inform us students that we shouldn't hate Islam whenever the subject comes up, often aiming this admonition exclusively at Christian students, when the school has many secular students who hate Christianity. They're never told to remember all the evil atheists of history – never."

The biggest problem with such propaganda is not merely that it is "unfair" to one religion and to students like this girl, and naively credulous towards another. (Though I would be ashamed if even communism were painted such unremittingly dark colors, or Christian history were portrayed as unsullied brightness.) Neither is it merely that America has not been conquered by an Islamic power, so why should we cram Muslim catechisms down the throats of our children? Nor is the fundamental problem merely that it is un-Constitutional to establish one religion, and disestablish another, by means of the public schools. (Though lawyers should look into such cases carefully.)

The core problem with Zinn, Aaronson, and the authors of *History Alive* is that they are propagandists, not true historians at all. What they say is often simply not true, while they fail to teach vital historical facts that are verifiably true.

The influence of the "rabbi who must not be named," whom I earlier called The Third Teacher, is thus systematically swept from history in many schools. The revolution Aaronson yearned for has occurred. Dolores Umbridge now runs Hogwarts. But as Zinn and Aaronson also wished, the chaos did not stay on campus.

French Academician Rene Girard described how episodes of scapegoating work. A victim is identified: some group of people that stands out from the crowd (in 2020, the police). A terrible sin is ascribed to them (poisoning wells, witchcraft, systemic racism). Lynch mobs do violence to create a new society. But to justify itself, society must "conceal its origins in collective violence," whether by Mohammed, Mao, or Black Lives Matter, even while it scapegoats the actual founders and preservers of civilization.

5. Chaz

Capitol Hill is Seattle's well-healed "gay district," adorned with multi-million-dollar mansions, lively night life, an Asian art museum, and beautiful views. Seattle is one of the world's best-educated and wealthiest cities, with tech titans having set up shop just down the hill. The neighborhood reeks of privilege.

Yet when I visited it in May, 2020, a "big beautiful wall," or at least a rough set of little barriers, had been erected around the center of the district.

Graffiti was sprayed across walls next to a police station:
"Kill cops!" "Shoot the Police!" "Blue Lives Murder!"

A board set on a chair on the street as you left the zone warned pedestrians:
"In a world without cops, we must never again become the cops ourselves."

In fact, the vast majority of those killed by police in Washington State are Asian, Hispanic, Indian, or White. But local radicals hung up a poster of 29 Blacks alone who succumbed in police custody. Researching these and other cases, I found that the vast majority of "victims" of police shootings of any color, were little more innocent than Mohammed. Most were career criminals, were beating, shooting, or threatening lovers or neighbors, or were out-of-control due to drugs or mental illness (a few even demanded to be shot). The vast majority were well-armed, with guns (mostly), knives, swords, clubs, chain saws, or speeding vehicles.

Chaz is the long toss of a brick from the Jesuit-run Seattle University, where Robin DiAngelo studied sociology and history, and was class valedictorian in 1991. Kendi and DiAngelo are the twin stars of the Woke Revolution of 2020, with more than 15,000 and 24,000 reviews of their books on Amazon, respectively (at last glance).

One subway stop north of Capitol Hill lies the University of Washington, where DiAngelo studied "Whiteness in Racial Dialogue." I well know the Liberal Arts Quadrangle or "Quad," a rectangle of cherry-shaded grassy calm surrounded by departments of art, music, history, sociology and James Bank's Multicultural Education, where DiAngelo took her PhD. Such academic oases are the eye of the ideological storm that is wreaking havoc on the western world today.

Sociology lies to the left as you enter the Quad. The great Rodney Stark, one of the top sociologists of religion in the world, taught in this department for 32 years. Stark told me he "wrote my way back" to Christian faith:
"It became more and more plausible and likely, and here I am."[2]

Donald Treadgold headed the History Department in my day: a Cold Warrior who never brought his faith up in class or when he guided my research

2 David Marshall, *Faith Seeking Understanding: Essays in Memory of Paul Brand and Ralph Winter*, "A Conversation With Rodney Stark," 137

in Marxist history and language. But the eminent historian Herb Ellison told me that, when he was a student questioning his faith a generation before, Treadgold's encouragement helped him find his way on a campus that was already often hostile to Christianity.

Over the years, the ideological atmosphere has ratcheted up considerably. For instance, the UW's Secondary Teacher Education Program (STEP) is described by Nick Wilson, a prospective teacher:

> "A 12-month immersion in doctrinaire social justice activism. . . light on academic rigor, in which the faculty quite consciously whips up emotions in order to punch home its ideological message."

That message is "identity politics", and any student who thought the course should focus on training how to teach was, Wilson noted, assumed to support discrimination and inequality:

> "This is how the social justice elements in STEP get ratcheted up each year by a small, noisy group of committed student activists who intimidate their peers and professors into agreement and silence. Indeed, the program prides itself on its innovative and extreme measures to incorporate social justice activism into the academy with an almost theological confidence that this panacea will finally resolve all the problems in contemporary public education."[3]

UW-Education prof Wayne Au writes textbooks with the conscious goal of seeding "Marxist and socialist ideas" in high schools and even primary schools. Au also now serves as "acting Dean of Diversity and Equity" for the UW-Bothell campus. My former anthropology professor, Dr. Stevan Harrell, an atheist and leftist but a kind and excellent teacher, admitted in his retirement speech that the intolerance of many of his fellow academic leftists was tearing his field apart. Stuart Reges, who designed a computer science introductory course which tens of thousands of students have taken and has received high ratings, was "Demoted and Placed on Probation," he claims, for suggesting that men and women think differently, and that may help explain why men are more interested in computer science.[4]

....

3 Nick Wilson, *Quillette*, April 5th, 2019, "What They Don't Teach You at the University of Washington's Ed School"

4 Stuart Reges, *Quillette*, "Demoted and Placed on Probation," January 11, 2020

I speak of my own alma mater because I know it best. But that is a microcosm of what has become of "public" and private campuses across America, not only from Boston to Seattle, but from San Diego to Miami and back up the coast to the other Washington.

Georgetown University professor John Hasnas relates in the Wall Street Journal that, in twenty years of searching for academic talent, every faculty search began with the administration calling for more women and minorities. No expense, no effort, was too great to bring more minorities and women on board, but the ideology of new teachers should all belong to one brand:

> "In my experience, no search committee has ever been instructed to increase political or ideological diversity. On the contrary, I have been involved in searches in which the chairman of the selection committee stated that no libertarian candidates would be considered. Or the description of the position was changed when the best résumés appeared to be coming from applicants with right-of-center viewpoints. Or in which candidates were dismissed because of their association with conservative or libertarian institutions."

Serious Christian faith appears even less welcome on campus than unorthodox political views. George Yancey, who now teaches sociology at Baylor University, found in 2011 that a large minority of sociologists openly admitted they would be biased against hiring an "evangelical", and still more against a "fundamentalist" for a faculty position. (He tells me the 2011 data remain the most up-to-date he knows of, but one can be sure matters have not improved since.)

To be fair, many tremendous professors still teach in America's universities, and most high school teachers are dedicated and sincere. One can learn a great deal from a well-informed atheist, Muslim or Marxist. And some fields are less infected. My sons recently graduated from the UW in engineering and business respectively, and never complained of ideological brow-beating.

But vast regions of higher education, especially those focused on the nature of man (whom Christ came to save) are now spiritual wastelands where faith goes to die. And hatred of western civilization and its foundations, along with the intolerance of Cancel Culture, have spilled out not only to high schools and neighborhoods like Chaz, or to the streets of

Boston, but to western society as a whole.

Your Weather is Canceled

Consider the case of Cliff Mass. Dr. Mass is of Jewish descent, and likely the best weatherman in the Northwest. Mass teaches Atmospheric Science at the University of Washington but that is not where he got into trouble. He also ran a popular weather program at public radio station KNKX.

In early August, 2020, Mass took a stroll through Downtown Seattle in the wake of riots, and was heartbroken by what he saw: drug dealing; "the open sore of homelessness"; the mentally-ill; the drug-addicted living in filth; stores boarded up to protect them from mobs. He vented on his popular blog:

> "Seattle's brownshirts have hidden within protest groups, attempting to destroy businesses both to deliver a political message of fear and to loot their contents. Dozens of police have been seriously injured by bottles and fireworks, or partially blinded by lasers. Even in my neighborhood, graffiti calling for the killing of police have been sprayed at a prominent location. These are not protests complaining about official wrongdoing. This is wanton destruction, and no city can remain healthy if such anti-social activities are allowed to go unchecked."

Mass asked:

> "How could a major world-class city, home to some of the most important businesses and academic institutions on the planet, allow itself to be crippled and demeaned this way? How could city and state leaders allow the undermining of the foundations of physical safety and rule of law that are the basic prerequisites of any functioning society?"

The next day the station manager and program manager fired Mass from his radio show, claiming that Mass had compared protestors as a whole to Nazis. (Falsely: he clearly said the brownshirts had "hidden within" protest groups, which I find rather kind to many of the protestors).

Yet as Mass later pointed out, several leaders at KNKX had themselves compared *non-violent* political opponents to Nazis:

> "KNKX management believes it is ok to use Nazi, brownshirt and

fascist analogies if one is attacking Trump and Republicans, but a terrible offense and cause for expulsion if one uses these same analogies for violent rioters who are destroying the fabric of civil society with wanton property damage, malicious personal violence, and intimidating political leaders with different viewpoints."

Our institutions thus grow more corrupt. Public school teachers judge again by color of skin, gender, class or origin, not by content of character. Society overlooks a beam of violence in one eye, while gouging out the other to remove a speck. Some instructors deny free speech, lie to children about history, proselytize instead of teach, and crowd even the mildest contrary voices out of the Public Square.

Jesus came to save human beings. This is why Christians should be especially concerned with the corruption of the Humanities and Social Science, fields which study culture, our past, the nature of man and how the human mind works.

God bless those called to study or teach in such schools. We should support and pray for them. American campuses have become a hostile mission field, even a boot camp for revolution. (I think with nostalgia of my Philosophy of Marxism professor who brought black armbands to class when a UW student radical died in Nicaragua: the good old days, when practicing revolutionaries were a small, eccentric minority, part of a well-rounded education!) In the present climate, it is critical that the Church not only build independent educational structures, but give students the highest-quality education, so we don't have to hire another Howard Zinn, Ibram Kendi, or Robin DiAngelo to come among our young people like wolves among sheep.

Howard Zinn and his disciples have made the case for a *Third Education Revolution* better, perhaps, than anyone.

Chapter 18

Intolerance In Postmodern University

Pablo Munoz Iturrieta[1]

Preceding chapters by Karla Perry and David Marshall show that Western universities have crucified truth. Should it then surprise us that liberty is now being buried with the truth? Is a resurrection possible?

Is Academic Freedom Necessary for the University?

If teachers are afraid of losing their jobs, promotions or funding for their research projects, can they even discuss the loss of intellectual freedom in their institutions? How can knowledge grow without academic liberty? Intellectual liberty keeps the university alive and civil. It makes the university an instrument of reforming society.

Academic freedom of inquiry faces at least three challenges today: a dogmatic Christian worldview; postmodern obsession to deconstruct the values of Christian Civilization under the guise of "political correctness", "diversity" and "inclusion", as well as the intrusion of corporate interests that control what is said, published and taught. How do we balance the search for truth with the fear of error? That act is challenging but it makes the university a civilization's brain.

The first potential threat to liberty is the clash between academic freedom and the obligation to comply with the established tenets of the institution one serves. The freedom of an inquiring mind needs protection and it is a part of the university's traditional wisdom.

One has to remember how Western universities gained its unique liberties to think and express ideas that challenge established beliefs. The conflict

1 Dr. Pablo Munoz Iturrieta holds a doctorate in political philosophy from Carleton University, and is the author of four books on philosophy of knowledge, religious freedom, a critique of gender ideology, and the problem of education today.

is resolved when we realize that the Bible is the source of our culture's respect for both the priest (the conservor) and the prophet (the innovator). The prophet may appear to be tearing down the norms, but in reality he is a restorer of the real foundations. He takes us back to the life-giving roots that matter.

The second threat comes from putting "diversity" above quality. Many universities in the United States and Canada now require an "equity, diversity and inclusion statement" as a condition of employment, while also clarifying that priority in hiring will be given to "under-represented" and "historically oppressed" minorities. This "inclusion statement" acts as a de facto "litmus test" - which determines whether an applicant will be hired or not. Academic freedom is thus violated in the name of tolerance, inclusion and diversity, since these principles have nothing to do with academic research. Having a racially diverse academic staff does not ensure that biology classes are "world-class". Having only "world-class" academics regardless of race, can help schools lift their students above mediocrity.

The third threat comes from the commercialization of the university. Corporations seek to capitalize on discoveries made on campus, with or without ethical considerations. Media that puts sensationalism above a long-term sense, cater to foundations, lobbies and interest groups. These push agendas-without-wisdom to control university policies, chastise or expel professors, and control what is taught and published. Some of them wrap their agendas in the seductive language of Human Rights and Social Justice in order to shut down free discussion. Lavishly funded LGBT activist groups, for example, publish a "Corporate Equality Index" and a "Healthcare Equality Index" in order to pressurize universities and medical schools to teach and offer experimental and dangerous sex reassignment therapies, and to punish even those who may be more careful thinkers. Just imagine: universities using abuse to silence serious thought!!

What is Academic Freedom?

Academic freedom is misunderstood when it is reduced to "freedom of expression". Consider a recent controversy in Canada:

Bill C-16, given royal assent in 2016, introduced terms such as gender identity and gender expression. This legislation was correctly viewed by many as an infringement on freedom of expression. The bill sparked a national debate because the legislation made it a crime to question gender identity and expression, penalizing citizens who did not use specific pronouns when referring to persons of certain perceived identities. This meant that a biology professor had to "acknowledge" that a student's "gender" may not only differ from their biological sex, but that their sex is not in fact divinely assigned. It also meant that a psychology professor could not refer to a "gender identity disorder" anymore, or dare question the idea of a "non-binary gender spectrum." If anyone in the Academy affirm a biological truth that contradicts this ideology, he/she could be accused of committing a hate crime and be expelled from the university by recommendation of the "diversity and inclusion office", experts can be stripped of their license to practice (in the case of a psychologist), and face heavy fines - even imprisonment - from the Court of Human Rights.

Clinical psychologist and University of Toronto professor Dr. Jordan B. Peterson testified before Parliament during preliminary hearings. He continued to oppose the Bill vocally, even after it had received Royal Assent from Queen Elizabeth II and became Canadian law. In a video lecture series Peterson hit out at political correctness. He criticized what he saw as a campus culture in which left-wing radical political activists ran rampant. Peterson argued that legislation requiring one to use pronouns like the singular "they" or "ze" and "zir," violated free speech. His videos on this subject became a worldwide hit with millions of views and eventually brought Peterson international fame: he was named by a New York Times Opinion piece as "the most influential public intellectual in the Western world".[2]

Fearing legal and political retaliation, the University of Toronto went after Professor Peterson. The school asked him not to speak on the issue anymore and to delete his YouTube videos. This was a clear infringement of his academic and political freedoms. Moreover, the Human Resources department at the University of Toronto made anti-bias and anti-discrimination training mandatory for its staff - which Peterson saw as coercive and politically motivated.

Dr. Peterson opposed these measures in various public arenas: in Parliament where he challenged arguments from the parliamentary committee, on social media platforms and at free speech rallies within the university, even as his position sparked a campus battle. Many saw the problem solely

2 Brooks, 2018

as "infringement of speech". But freedom of personal expression was only part of the story.

The concept of Academic freedom has developed over the last hundred years into a significant ethical value. It involves four essential elements: freedom of teaching (which includes freedom from prescribed orthodoxy from the lectern); freedom of research and publication; freedom to express one's views of the educational institution in which one works; and freedom to exercise one's rights as a citizen without sanctioning by the university. Academic freedom has been understood mainly as an individual right of the professor, but also as a collective right of academic staff, and as an institutional right of universities against government or judicial intrusion.[3] One can argue that this right is a necessary component of academic life. It safeguards teaching and research against political pressure, special interests, corporations, religious authorities, the media, donors, board members and ideologically motivated groups.

In the late nineteenth and early twentieth centuries, scholars from American universities were subject to attacks by commercial interests. A well-known case is the firing of A. Edward Ross in 1909. He was an economist at Stanford University and criticized the exploitation of cheap immigrant labor. That offended the Stanford family. Their fortune had been built on such labor and abuse of workers' rights. Mrs. Leland Stanford ordered the university president to fire Professor Ross and he complied.[4] This event led to the creation of the American Association of University Professors and the "1915 Declaration of Principles on Academic Freedom and Academic Tenure".

The cases of Ross and Peterson illustrate the need to protect academics from pressure on universities to sanction them for public utterances or for their research. Academic freedom is vital because universities help fulfill the common good of society. Every mature society should allow citizens' freedom to discuss matters of public importance without fear.

As for "institutional" academic freedom: some scholars and judicial decisions have maintained that First Amendment protection, which originally safeguarded professors against external interference from the

....

3 239 Turk, 2014, p. 8

4 240 Finkin & Post, 2009; Veysey, 1965

state, should be understood only as institutional autonomy. The problem with this approach is that, if a professor's right to academic freedom is violated by university administrators or governing boards, the university will be insulated from judicial scrutiny. Thus, there is an inherent tension between institutional and individual academic freedom when faculty and administration are at odds. On the one hand, the academic freedom of a professor must be protected, but, on the other hand, courts have to be careful not to violate the freedom of a university "to determine for itself, on academic grounds, who may teach, what may be taught, how it shall be taught and who may be admitted to study". Thus, without proper balance, institutional freedom may threaten academic freedom and the individual rights of professors.

Let us now consider three alleged threats to academic freedom in turn.

Is an Openly Christian University a Threat to Academic Freedom?

The university is a unique fruit of the Judeo-Christian civilization.[241] The life of the mind was institutionalized in university because Christians believed that the dialectics of fruitful debate would enable the community of teachers and scholars to find answers to human problems.

The secular university does not believe that God has the solutions to our penultimate needs. Yet, seeking God's will on every issue remains a central question for every child of God.

Seeking what is true, right, good and wise (i.e. God's will) in every matter makes theology the queen of all sciences. Knowing God then becomes the key to understanding the complexities of the world and to live one's life wisely.

Christian civilization respected the institution of the university because it sought to interpret the world by settling every dispute in an appropriate relation to the divine.

The university was born out of the church's womb because Christians wanted God's will done on earth. Divine revelation emboldened the Christian mind to set for itself the great task of creating an institution that taught "universal knowledge". The Christian university extended the boundaries of knowledge and diffused the knowledge gathered.

The university cannot give us light unless it is guided by a set of ideals formed within a free civilization. John Newman made this point effectively in *"The Idea of the University"*.[5] The Post-Christian university replaces the search for "universal knowledge" with shallow theories, superficial fads and ideological dictates. These transient social trends uproot reason from the soil of ultimate truth. Manipulated mobs then dictate that the universities ought to obey their demands without asking whether they are reasonable or whimsical. Not well-reasoned wisdom, but mobs have begun to exercise authority on university campuses.

A good example of this connection between the university and Christian civilization is the fact that, having lost faith in the Christian Scriptures, all subsequent Western literature seems to lose its deepest meaning. Karla Perry's chapter described how her literature class twisted *Jane Eyre* from a brilliant boy-girl love story about a shy Christian of deep faith, into a banal text for proto-lesbian propaganda. I also have encountered students with little to no familiarity with even the most widely known Bible narratives. When schools refuse to teach the Bible, the students come out of the school without the basic information needed to make sense of the great ideas, literature, art and music needed to understand Chaucer, Shakespeare, Dickens, Tolstoy or Emily Dickinson.

If one is clueless about the Bible, he or she may as well forget about the tragic whale tale, *Moby Dick*, or the more recent works of C. S. Lewis, G. K. Chesterton, or J. R. R. Tolkien. If new generations of students are unable to recognize biblical symbolism and allusions that suffuse great western literature, the Great Books will necessarily suffer misreading. As David Marshall points out in his chapter, having become incapable of understanding its Great Books, Western university is replacing them with recent books of questionable quality, imbued with leftist ideology.[6]

The university and the humanities are linked. Christian civilization is connected to the humanities like Vine to the Branches. Uproot one and you kill the other. To discard Great Books is to scrub history. You cannot replace the civilization that gave life to the humanities and pretend to preserve them intact.

---

5 242 Newman, 1959, p. 7

6 see also Little, 2017

Christian universities birthed academic freedom in order to research, teach and publish because one of Christ's most powerful teachings was: "You will know the truth, and the truth will set you free" (John 8:32). The search for truth is an integral part of the Christian life. As Hans-Joachim Hahn and Gottfried Sommer have shown in their chapters the Church's moral obligation to seek truth produced European universities. They were communities of intellectuals dedicated to finding answers to life's difficult problems. The Church saw that the university needed Intellectual freedom to seek and teach truth. Once the university discards pursuit of truth as its mission, the "free speech" on campus becomes a means of robbing others of their freedom to seek wisdom.

All professions have codes - not just of ethical conduct but regarding research and the limits of a given science. If an academic from the physics department tried to "deconstruct" mathematical theories since they are thought too hard for some members of the population, or have been used to "oppress" minorities in the past, and proposed to remove numbers from physics, that academic will deserve to be fired. To do math, physics, or chemistry, certain parameters must be respected and, in that sense, may be considered "dogmatic," unless one can prove that a different paradigm may explain the facts better. In a way, professional norms are similar to the constraints placed within a Christian university, *which may be essential to its proper function*. As Gerald Gerbrandt explains, policies that require hiring of Christian faculty are defensible, given reasonable expectations that a faculty member work at his discipline within a larger tradition and community.[7]

How about theological norms which, for a Christian, stand on the solid ground of divine revelation? Is there academic freedom if a Christian university demands a Christian understanding of reality? This is a thorny issue, as the university as an institution does enjoy institutional freedom, while the professor is also entitled to individual freedom. Yet again we must take into account the goal of the university: the diffusion and extension of knowledge. Or as Joseph Koterski puts it, the "academic instruction of students, or docility to inconvenient truths, or service to a particular community that a religiously affiliated university was founded to provide".[8] Theology not only possesses its own methodological standards, but it is also grounded in the truth of divine revelation, and to depart from this

---

7 Gerbrandt, 2014, p. 177

8 Koterski, 2009, p. 43

is to depart from theology altogether. To teach theology within some church-sponsored universities requires accepting the truth of revelation and, in some cases, also the specific teachings of a given church.

From a Christian perspective the university should protect its spirit so that freedom serves a higher goal. In the secular university today academic freedom is envisioned as utterly unrestrained, and there is a tendency to criticize any position that might order freedom to the service of any other interest. Yet this abstract vision of academic freedom empties it or cuts it off from higher goals. Besides, there is a moral, and perhaps legal, distinction between private Christian and public universities. Whether they should do so or not, private Christian universities have the right to support work that agrees with the principles of their founders. Public universities are paid for by the taxpayer, and therefore have no moral right to turn themselves into madrassas for promoting sectarian ideologies.

A Christian university is entitled to establish and publish standards. Frederick Schauer, speaking about the First Amendment and academic freedom as an institutional right, notes that "granting individual academics enforceable rights against their academic supervisors would inevitably restrict the academic authority of the institution itself".[9]

Even though he is not speaking about the tension between a Christian university and academic freedom, his words remind us that universities must set standards. If a university is to be called Christian, it must be invested with the authority to implement and achieve its goals.

One way to ease the tensions that may arise within a Christian university is to frame the academic work of the institution as an endeavor to bring faith and reason together for the service of the larger Christian community and society at large. If this is the goal, Christian doctrine and way of life need not be seen as a censorial imposition of doctrine. We need academics who will give us reasons to live by our faith today, and who lead by example. In fact, as Ronald Dworkin argues, it is inevitable and right that academics be hired depending on whether they conform to the norms and policies of the university.[10]

....

9 Schauer, 2006, p. 907

10 Dworkin, 1996

It is also important to distinguish between rights, privileges, and obligations. Academic freedom is a privilege that imposes moral obligations on those on which it is bestowed. It is certainly a right, but a right that is ordered to the pursuit of the truth within a given academic's area of competence. When an academic is hired, he is given the privilege of acting as part of the institution as one who pursues truth, so he is obliged to use that right properly. Secularists may conceive of academic freedom as an atomized, nakcd liberty "from" all constraints. But freedom is more properly seen as being "for" something else, a means to a higher end. The right to search for truth engenders an obligation to devote one's life to research, and to communicate glimpses of truth that enlighten the mind. A Christian academic, then, may also obey Jesus' command through his/her study and teaching: "Love God and love one's neighbor as oneself" (Matthew 22:37.40). (We have met some Christian academics who seek to do just that - also in the networks that they have formed.)

Political Correctness and Academic Freedom

In many modern institutions, such ideologies and values as feminism, deconstructionism, social justice, "bottoms-up" history, post-colonial studies, gender theory, intersectionality, identity politics, minorities studies, diversity, multiculturalism, sustainability and global citizenship collectively constitute a guiding ideology. What once was considered "academic heresy" is now the norm, a norm not open to intellectual challenges. Political correctness has thus become one of the most significant factors infringing upon academic freedom.

In January 2009, the president of the American Association of University Professors, Cary Nelson, debated Peter Wood, president of the National Association of Scholars, on "The Meaning of Academic Freedom." Professor Nelson said that he supports the scientific method in pursuit of knowledge. However, what constitutes evidence is "contingent." "Knowledge" is culturally constructed. It is not transcendent. This viewpoint reflects the postmodern spirit that has permeated Academia.

The contending ideologies within Postmodernism are Marxism and Historicism, creating all the intellectual byproducts mentioned at the start of this section. According to modern Historicism, the only objective truth is that one can't know objective truth, so all is relative. Marxism, however, underwent deep theoretical transformations inspired by the writings of Antonio Gramsci and the Frankfurt School. After World War II and revelations about Lenin and Stalin's crimes in the Soviet Union, academic Marxists began migrating from traditional, economic Marxism to a Cultural Marxism, or even dropping the Marxist name so as to avoid public criticism of their failure to criticize communist atrocities. Academics who embraced this type of Marxism reinterpreted economic class struggle as sexual class warfare, represented by the oppression of women by men, and the struggle of sexual minorities, such as the LGBTQ2S+ collective, defined in neo-Marxist terminology as a class oppressed by the "heteronormative patriarchy."

Postmodernism in both its Historicist and Marxist versions has undermined education on three fronts: the quality of the teachers graduated from schools of education, the capability of the students, and curriculum. Yet Postmodernism has spilled out of schools to permeate the media, politics, national security, the justice system, and corporate culture through race and gender diversity policies and quotas, giving rise to what is known today as "Cancel Culture."

As mentioned earlier, the postmodern goals for the Academy are not to search for truth and the freedom to make that search possible, but representation and diversity. One consequence is that most administrative boards require an "equity, diversity and inclusion statement" as a condition of employment. When it comes to hiring new faculty, they give priority to "under-represented" and "historically oppressed" minorities. This "inclusion statement" becomes in practice a "litmus test." As we have seen, it violates academic freedom in the name of various postmodern doctrines. Sex and gender are redefined by often ill-informed theorists as superficial phenomena produced by oppressive social forces, and disconnected from biological reality. Thus, academic theories threaten academic freedom.

But the problem doesn't stop there. Universities are patrolled by a ruthless new thought police, "diversity and inclusion" offices, placed within the university in an effort to enforce postmodern dogmas. This results in "an ethical chaos where intolerance masquerades as tolerance and where individual liberty is crushed by the tyranny of the group," as Camila Paglia observes.[11] This led to the creation of "safe spaces" and subsequent policies in violation of academic freedom, such as the introduction of "safe space marshals" who monitor intellectual behavior in the classroom. This

---

11 Paglia, 2017, p. ix

is fundamentally at odds with the rigorous intellectual exchange that is central to the idea of the university.

In 2017, Lindsay Shepherd, a teaching assistant for a first-year Communications seminar at Wilfrid Laurier University, screened in class a televised debate on gender-neutral pronouns. The debate, which had appeared on the public station *TV Ontario*, featured Dr. Jordan Peterson and a transgender activist professor, both from the University of Toronto. She showed the debate to illustrate the sometimes-controversial politics of grammar. But after an anonymous student complained to the Office of Diversity and Inclusion "thought police", Shepherd found herself reprimanded for violating the school's Gender and Sexual Violence policy. In a subsequent meeting with university officials, she was accused of creating a "toxic" and "problematic" environment that constituted violence against transgendered students, and was also falsely told that she had transgressed Canadian law.[12] From an academic perspective one can argue that there was no topic timelier than the "pronouns" political controversy, a topic that deserves to be discussed within the university. And in fact Shepherd had taken a neutral stance on the matter and offered a balanced presentation of both positions.

The Shepherd case sharply reveals the competing ideas regarding the "purpose" of a university. Prior to the Postmodern Age we find few examples of a school of thought that proactively tried to shut down anyone who disagreed with their tenets. In the theologically-centered university of the Middle Ages there was robust controversy. Dominicans, Franciscans, Averroists, Nominalists and others had a place and a voice in spite of their profound theological disagreements."Disputations" were the standard form of examination. Students did not just memorize answers in order to regurgitate them down on paper in examination halls. Students thought about different issues and debated each other in front of examiners. Lawyers use it every day in every courtroom.

Now Postmodernism has set itself up as the one and only voice permitted in the public sphere. Every other voice is "canceled." As Nathan Rambukkana, one of the "canceling" professors on the Shepherd case put it: "Not all perspectives are valid." Shepherd argued that ideas, however controversial, deserve mention in the classroom. Rambukkana, however, insisted that some ideas are "problematic" and cannot be raised without

12 Hopper, 2017

being clearly labeled as such.[13] For Rambukkana "problematic" meant challenging the postmodern dogma.

As an institution the university, as a place of learning and a rigorous forum for seeking answers to human problems, holds a unique role in shaping the common good of society. As such, the university has its own set of norms and customs. One of them is that students and academics should be encouraged to explore particularly difficult subjects, to take risks regarding emerging areas of research, and to debate some of the most contentious and pertinent issues of our time. Is there a place for the claims that postmodernism makes? Certainly those claims should be put to the test by academics in different fields.

The creation of safe spaces contradicts the purpose of a university, even if defenders of that concept aim at providing those formerly without a voice, an opportunity to be heard and study, free from (alleged) harassment or abuse. There cannot be a safe space from disagreement because the Academy is, by definition, a place for rigorous disagreement.

The postmodern attack on what was once called Christian civilization perhaps best explains the similar attack on academic freedom because the two are connected. As Postmodern ideas seek to erase Christianity from the public square, the idea of what the university should be, seems to fade. Unless one bows to the ideological demands of radical feminists, social justice warriors, critical theory and gender ideologues, there is no room for dissenters in the chambers of knowledge.

The most pressing question here is whether or not "political correctness" and academic freedom are compatible. Probably not. I heartily hope that academic freedom prevails.

Financial, Political and Cultural Pressures

Academic freedom is threatened - not just by postmodern ideas and the politically-correct enforcement of those ideas, but also by the commercialization of the university by corporations that seek to capitalize on the economic value of discoveries made on campus, and by foundations that exercise political and cultural pressure to reverse university policies, chastise or expel professors and control what is taught and published.

13 Hopper, 2017

If a university's mission is compromised by finance, greed or power, sooner or later academics working in it will not only adapt to survive, but will rationalize this adaptation. This will mean the end of academic freedom as such. We only have to remember the role German universities played under Hitler, when academies justified forced sterilization and murder of the mentally ill[14]. This is happening again under a new cover in our debates on abortion, embryonic stemcell research and euthanasia. In these cases, Academia may serve the interests of powerful corporations and foundations with only pragmatic interest in truth or ethics. Consider the relationship between Planned Parenthood, through the Guttmacher Institute, and Columbia University following a memorandum in 2005 to share ideas and staff. Academics must either pay the price of freedom and speak up, or else use their platform for biased research of which the only purpose is to satisfy the demands of the best suitor.

Universities have, since their inception, been considered nonprofit institutions, so that they would not succumb to the demands of power or wealth. Even though governments and corporations depend greatly on the knowledge produced by the Academy, it is crucial to keep a wall of separation so that academics may maintain freedom to research without pre-determined results being demanded of them, or to serve interests that produce biased knowledge.

Yet as Sheldon Krimsky points out, starting in the 1980s universities have developed intellectual property offices in order to capitalize on the economic value of discoveries made on campus. Some have even become equity partners in corporations that fund university research.[15] Recent events have deepened this conflict of interest. For example, AstraZeneca and Oxford University made a deal to produce a vaccine for COVID-19. Reports of disappointing results are bound to hurt the Bottom Line, posing a threat to the interest of investors who rushed to fund a vaccine that promises millions in gains. This may put undue pressure on academics and their freedom to honestly make findings public.

The agreement between the Charles Koch Foundation and Florida State University is another clear example of such intrusion. In this case the university gave the foundation authority to decide selection criteria used

------

14 Gallin, 1986

15 Krimsky, 2014, p. 233

to fill faculty positions in economics, and to veto candidates of whom it disapproved. In other cases, contracts allow a corporation to determine whether the results of research should be published. Such conflicts of interest badly undermine academic freedom, institutional processes for the assignment of professors, reviews, research, education practices and publication. Mark Barnes and Patrick Florencio note that, under these circumstances, researchers "could be influenced by an awareness that their own institution's financial health may be affected by the results of their research if their institution holds a significant stake in the drug or device being tested",[16] as with Oxford University and AstraZeneca. Inevitably, academic honesty will be questioned as a consequence.

The intrusion of tobacco companies in academic research is also well known. These companies financed a large number of studies intended to discredit research on cancer conducted by the International Agency for Research on Cancer. They even co-sponsored studies, literature reviews and scientific conferences to debunk competing studies showing a causal link between smoking and lung cancer and other medical conditions. Such corruption has been documented also in relation to the asbestos, lead, beryllium, chemical, bioengineering, and pharmaceutical industries.

Since new forms of university-industry partnership began to emerge, often justified by the political ideology of privatization, David Blumenthal reports that university scientists have noticed change in their relationship with colleagues. There is now a general unwillingness to discuss research methods and results because of corporate contracts that restrict researchers from sharing information or that give corporations the right to see this information first for potential future patents.[17]

Foundations and NGOs also exercise pressure in a way that limits academic freedom. Unlike corporations which seek to profit from knowledge produced within the academy, foundations and NGOs use their platform to impose an ideological agenda. The most striking example is the influence of ideology on medical practice.

Johns Hopkins Hospital is the teaching hospital and biomedical research facility of the Johns Hopkins School of Medicine. At one point the insti-

---

16 Barnes & Florencio, 2002

17 Blumenthal, 2003

T.
kins
The F
group, is
advance "tr
legal changes.
Index" and the
versities to implem
schools to offer sex re
very low in the Equalit
condemn the research con
Human Rights Campaign wer
sity from the "elite classification.
announced that it would start perfc
even if research showed that surgery

Conclusion: Can We Recover Academ

I have tried to make it clear that academic fr
freedom of speech, or the mere liberty to elabora
mind. Academic freedom is a condition for finding
of truth justifies the privilege and special protection
granted.

18 Money, 1955

19 McHugh, 2004

20 Mayer & McHugh, 2016

Academic freedom needs protection in vie
social good of knowledge. That is why
larger aim than freedom of speech, prot
the US Constitution. Academic freedo
a university in supporting the commo
Taking this into consideration, three
freedom were considered.

The first case concerned the Ch
about a university prescribing a
dational for research. It may se
freedom without deference t
A Christian university is not
an endeavor to bring togeth
demics embrace this ideal
freedom. While academic
inherently limited. Perha
this. Nevertheless, a Ch
freedom, for only the
possibility of truth,
university works fo
and disseminating
to find. Academic
but not in itself
means for the e

The paradox i
sent, a genui
ademics wh
century S
Christiani
to make
in you"
not so
to oth
to c
and

w of an even greater go... he
academic freedom has an n
ected by the First Amendment
n is fundamental to the mission
n good of society.
ossible or actual dangers to academic

ristian university. Some may complain
ertain way of life and worldview as foun-
m to critics that one should exercise one's
prescribed doctrines or fear of penalty.[21]
only entitled to frame its academic work as
er faith and reason, but many Christian aca-
wholeheartedly and do not find it a restraint to
freedom is all about protecting reason, reason is
s it takes honesty and humility to acknowledge
istian university should be committed to academic
ruth will set us free. Freedom is a condition for the
d truth is the goal of freedom. Thus, the Christian
the good of Church and Society by searching for
nowledge, ideas, and answers, which require freedom
freedom is thus an indispensable condition for inquiry,
he goal of the university. We should never mistake the
d.

s that, faced with a postmodern ideology that allows no dis-
ely Christian university might be the only safe haven for ac-
seek to work free of ideological intrusion. In the nineteenth
ence sought to expel theology in the name of reason. Today,
ty welcomes science in the name of faith: "Always be prepared
a defense to anyone who asks you for a reason for the hope that is
(1 Peter 3:15). From a Christian perspective, academic freedom is
me privileged sphere where one expresses personal beliefs unrelated
er ends. Academic freedom brings with itself the huge responsibility
ontribute and *"love your neighbor as yourself,"* through research, teaching
publication and, in so doing, fulfill the mission of the university.

21 Baker, 2014, pp. 131-132

The second case concerns postmodern ideas within the Academy. The paradox today is that academics need protection - not just from external forces but also from the totalitarian dictates of postmodernist academics and administrators fulfilling the role of a "thought police." The biggest losers are students, who are living in a unique historical situation. As Norman Doidge points out, students have been taught two contradictory ideas about morality and this has left them disoriented and uncertain, without guidance, and deprived of the riches of the Great Books canon they don't even know exists. The first idea is that morality is relative, that there is no absolute right and wrong in anything; everything is a social construction by which we exercise power over others. The second idea is that students go to university to learn "critical knowledge" and to study the greatest books ever written. Instead, they are fed ideological attacks on those books. As a consequence the uncertainty and void left by moral relativism is paradoxically filled by a type of ideological zeal that makes some students hyper-judgmental, censoriously pushing a "Cancel Culture" that always knows what is wrong about others, and how to deal with it.[22]

The rejection of Western Civilization by postmodernists has left standards of objectivity, truth, and rationality largely abandoned and has opened the door to an education agenda whose primary purpose is to achieve social and political transformation which are of questionable value.

The third and final case involves corporations and foundations that threaten the independence of research and the autonomy of universities. Commercial partnerships sometimes attempt to impose an agenda undermining the principles and independence of Higher Education. Autonomy is central to the university's ability to fulfill its social mission. Once it becomes dependent on corporate funding, academics will inevitably be caught in the conflict between the corporations' private interests, the ideological interests of foundations and the responsibility of the academy towards the public. One mark of academic research is independence, which alone ensures research of high quality, legitimacy and integrity. The new "shared governance model" makes it difficult to restore such independence.

Perhaps the solution will come from collective faculty revolt against all that threatens academic freedom. Perhaps the current state of our public universities is hopeless, and it is time to start again with the sublime ideal of the university in mind. Perhaps yet again, the Spirit of God who raised

---

22 Doidge, 2018, p. xxi

Christ from the dead and western civilization from dissolution after the fall of Rome, is even now beginning to form a creative agenda in which Christians around the world could join to produce something even better, with that model in mind.

Bibliography

• Anderson, R. T. (2018). *When Harry became Sally: Responding to the Transgender Moment*. Encounter Books.

• Baker, J. (2014). Academic Freedom as a Constraint on Freedom of Religion. In J. Turk (Ed.), *Academic Freedom in Conflict: The Struggle over Free Speech Rights in the University* (pp. 127-144). James Lorimer & Company Ltd.

• Barnes, M., & Florencio, P. S. (2002). Financial Conflicts of Interest in Human Subjects Research: The Problem of Institutional Conflicts. *The Journal of Law, Medicine & Ethics*, 30(3), 390-402. https://doi.org/10.1111/j.1748-720X.2002.tb00408.x

• Brooks, D. (2018, Jan. 26,). The Jordan Peterson Moment. *The New York Times*. https://www.nytimes.com/2018/01/25/opinion/jordan-peterson-moment.html

• Byrne, J. P. (1989). Academic Freedom: A "Special Concern of the First Amendment". *The Yale Law Journal*, 99(2), 251-340.

• Culler, J. D. (1988). *Framing the Sign: Criticism and its Institutions* (1st ed.). University of Oklahoma Press.

• Dales, R. C. (1980). *The Intellectual Life of Western Europe in the Middle Ages*. University Press of America.

• Doidge, N. (2018). Foreword. In *12 Rules for Life: An Antidote to Chaos*. Random House.

• Dworkin, R. (1996). We Need a New Interpretation of Academic Freedom. In L. Menand (Ed.), *The Future of Academic Freedom* (pp. 183-191). University of Chicago Press.

• Finkin, M. W., & Post, R. (2009). *For the Common Good: Principles of American Academic Freedom*. Yale University Press.

- Gallin, A. (1986). *Midwives to Nazism: University Professors in Weimar Germany*, 1925-1933. Mercer.

- Gerbrandt, G. (2014). Academic Freedom from a Christian University Perspective: A Personal Reflection. In J. Turk (Ed.), *Academic Freedom in Conflict: The Struggle over Free Speech Rights in the University.* (pp. 172-182). James Lorimer & Company Ltd.

- Haskins, C. H. (1965). *The Rise of Universities.* Cornell University Press.

- Hopper, T. (2017, Nov 21,). Here's the full recording of Wilfrid Laurier reprimanding Lindsay Shepherd for showing a Jordan Peterson video. *National Post.* https://nationalpost.com/news/ canada/heres-the-full-recording-of-wilfrid-laurier-reprimanding-lindsay-shepherd-for-showing-a-jordan-peterson-video

- Koterski, J. W. (2009). Taking a Catholic View on Academic Freedom. In P. J. Reilly & T. W. Mead (Eds.), *The Enduring Nature of the Catholic University* (pp. 43-50). The Cardinal Newman Society.

- Krimsky, S. (2014). Academic Freedom and the Growth of University-Industry Collaborations. In J. Turk (Ed.), *Academic Freedom in Conflict: The Struggle over Free Speech Rights in the University* (pp. 231-249). James Lorimer & Company Ltd. .

- Little, C. (2017, Sept. 13,). Replace Shakespeare? Diversity in literature should be about 'and' not 'or'. *The Globe and Mail.* https://www.theglobeandmail.com/ opinion/dont-replace-shake-speare-diversity-in-literature-needs-to-be-about-and-not-or/ article36248964/

- Mayer, L. S., & McHugh, P. R. (2016). Sexuality and Gender. *The New Atlantis,* 50, 4-143.

- McHugh, P. R. (2004). Surgical Sex. Why We stopped doing Sex Change Operations. *First Things.* https://www.firstthings.com/ article/2004/11/surgical-sex

- Money, J. (1955). Hermaphroditism, Gender and Precocity in Hyperadrenocorticism: Psychologic Findings. *Bulletin of the John Hopkins Hospital,* 95(6), 253–264.

- Muñoz Iturrieta, P. (2019). *Atrapado en el cuerpo equivocado: La ideología de género frente a la ciencia y la filosofía.* Editorial Katejón.

- Muñoz Iturrieta, P. (2020). Hanna Arendt's Notion of Political Freedom. In C. Rosental & R. H. Scott (Eds.), *Freedom and Society: Essays on Autonomy, Identity, and Political Freedom*. Mercer University Press.

- Newman, J. H. (1959). *The Idea of a University*. Image Books.

- Paglia, C. (2017). *Free Women, Free Men: Sex, Gender, Feminism.* Vintage Books.

- Schauer, F. (2006). Is there a Right to Academic Freedom? *University of Colorado Law Review*, 77(4), 907.

- Solzhenitsyn, A. I. (1973). *The Gulag Archipelago, 1918-1956: An Experiment in Literary Investigation I-II* (1st ed.). Harper & Row.

- Turk, J. (2014). *Academic Freedom in Conflict: The Struggle over Free Speech Rights in the University*. James Lorimer & Company Ltd.

- Veysey, L. R. (1965). *The Emergence of the American University*. University of Chicago Press. An Act to amend the Canadian Human Rights Act and the Criminal Code, (2016). https://openparliament.ca/bills/42-1/C-16/

Chapter 19

Kids in Contemporary Cultural Chaos

David McDonald[1]

My people are destroyed for lack of knowledge; because you have rejected knowledge, I reject you from being a priest to me.

And since you have forgotten the law of your God, I also will forget your children.
Hosea 4:6

There is nothing new under the sun.
Ecclesiastes 1:9

"Atheism Doubles Among Generation Z," reads the headline. The author explains:

> "The influence of Christianity in the United States is waning. Rates of church attendance, religious affiliation, belief in God, prayer and Bible-reading have been dropping for decades. Americans' beliefs are becoming more post-Christian and, concurrently, religious identity is changing. Enter Generation Z: Born between 1999 and 2015, they are the first truly "post-Christian" generation."

For the present cohort of youth, the reporter notes: "'atheist' is no longer a dirty word:" Indeed, the percentage of teens who are atheists is double that of other Americans.

These statistics are staggering but not surprising. The church seems numb to the hemorrhaging of our youth: numb - not due to indifference but, like a frog in water, unaware of how quickly the temperature of the environment is changing.

1 David McDonald received his doctorate from the University of Washington in 1998. As a Director for Health Teams International, Dr. McDonald has led medical mission teams to help the poor across the globe. He regularly lectures on Biblical Worldview, parenting and World Religions both domestically and internationally. He also serves as the Director of Business Operations for the Education Revolution.

Moreover, our culture embraces a patently anti-Biblical worldview at an ever-escalating pace. Politicians celebrate America's post-Christian state as a strength. Christians are being inundated at every side, and even within the church, by the shameless mocking of Biblical principles. The worldview of modern secular culture is reflected in the song *Hymn* by Grammy-award-winning pop star Kesha, which proudly proclaims:

> "This is a hymn for the hymnless, kids with no religion, Yeah we keep on sinning, yeah we keep on singing, don't need no forgiveness, 'cause if there is a heaven, don't care if we get in."

Taylor Swift mocks traditional marriage advocates in her video, "*You Need To Calm Down*", portraying Christians as uneducated, hate- filled lunatics. Netflix seems to glorify pedophilia in a film, "*Cuties*" that purports to warn against pedophilia. The movie is described as "Maïmouna Doucouré's sweet-spirited French coming-of-age drama" while showing close ups of pre-adolescent children dancing in a purposely titillating manner. Those who decried such sexual exploitation of young children were described as "the pedophile-obsessed American right" by NBC's contributing writer Sam Theilman.

The attack on children's innocence has expanded to academics. TEDx speaker Mirjam Heine explained that "pedophilia is an unchangeable sexual orientation," so we should "overcome our negative feelings about pedophiles."

The keynote of our era is emotive reasoning, with facts secondary to feelings. Discussion is crushed as entire ethnic groups are called "racists" due to the color of their skin and accused of a vaguely defined and unfalsifiable "systemic racism." Cities are burnt and businesses looted in what the Media describes as "peaceful protests." In one particularly flagrant example the self-delusion of our media masters borders on the surreal. In Kenosha, Wisconsin, CNN national correspondent, Omar Jimenez, broadcasts with a gas mask on his neck and goggles on his forehead, standing in front of cars that have been torched as flames soar high into the air. The caption displayed on the screen reads, "*Fiery But Mostly Peaceful Protest.*" Such Orwellian "spin" on patently obvious facts disturbingly typifies the "mainstream narrative."

Legislation increasingly reflects the same hostility to a Christian worldview with the laser focus on children. What was once called "abuse" is now called "loving" and what was once "loving" is now called "abuse." Parents with children struggling with gender dysphoria who send those children to loving pastors or professional counsellors are now called abusive, and laws banning this type of counsel have been passed in 20 states.

Legislators in Canada have been particularly vocal in this realm, and passed broad sweeping laws that serve as beacons to the direction in which the movement is headed. The intent of Bill 89 Ontario, Canada, *Supporting Children, Youth and Families* Act, 2017, was described by Michael Coteau, the Minister of Child and Family Services, who introduced it:

> "I would consider that a form of abuse, when a child identifies one way and a caregiver is saying no, you need to do this differently. If it's abuse, and if it's within the definition, a child can be removed from that environment and placed into protection where the abuse stops."

This bill was passed by an overwhelming margin of 63-23, and applies to foster children. It was mirrored in a similar law in Illinois, which states:

> "In no instance should LGBTQ Children/youth be placed with a non-affirming caregiver who is opposed to sexual orientations that differ from the caregiver's own."

Both of these laws apply to the foster care system and have not jumped over to break up biological families until recently. In Hamilton County, Ohio, parents lost custody of their minor child for wanting to delay hormonal treatment until the child was 18 years old. In a state where a child cannot receive a dental filling without parental consent, now the state becomes the parent for what is often irreversible treatment. Municipalities threaten pastors for what they teach from the pulpit as they flex political muscles to threaten those who oppose their agenda. They often understand the influence of the Church better than Christians do. The city of Houston, TX issued subpoenas demanding that pastors turn over sermons dealing with homosexuality or gender identity. Pastors who failed to comply were told that they would be held in contempt of court. Thankfully in this case the churchmen refused to comply.

Many Christians ask how things have changed so quickly. Many believers retreat into depression, anger, isolation and fear. If such horrors are recognized as symptoms of a diseased culture, understanding the causes of the spiritual diseases we suffer from may lead to proper treatment.

Instead of merely blaming our ideological opponents, let us consider where we as Christians have failed. We must remember that our faith is based upon the foundation of the Bible. We must embrace our responsibility to disciple our children. We must remember that our enemy is "seeking to devour." When we understand the problems, we can soberly seek solutions to the seemingly overwhelming threats of our day.

Rebuilding Our Foundations

"My people are destroyed for lack of knowledge" (Hosea 4:6).

Poor Biblical literacy is the heart of the problem. Multiple print copies of the Bible sit in our homes and scores of digital versions are at our fingertips. Yet biblical illiteracy grows. Atheist TV personality Bill Maher, who was raised as a Catholic, succinctly sums up the situation with this stinging rebuke.

> "To most Christians, the Bible is like a software license. Nobody actually reads it. They just scroll to the bottom and click 'I agree.'"

You may recognize the words, "My people are destroyed for lack of knowledge", but be less familiar with two sentences later in the same verse: "Because you have rejected knowledge ... and since you have forgotten the law of your God, I also will forget your children. The more they increased, the more they sinned against me." Our lack of Biblical literacy is an active rejection, not a lack of access to knowledge. This active rejection is reflected in our comfort with sin and in apathy towards the future that our children face.

Failure to Pass on Our Spiritual Legacy

The failure to shepherd and disciple the next generation is not a novel error. "There is nothing new under the sun" (Ecclesiastes 1:9). We read in the Book of Judges how the Children of Israel, who had witnessed the work of God with their own eyes, served Him during the time of Joshua and for a time after. But then:

> "There arose another generation after them who did not know the Lord or the work that he had done for Israel. And the people of Israel did what was evil in the sight of the Lord and served the Baals. And they abandoned the Lord, the God of their fathers" (Judges 2:7, 10-12).

Judges tells how Israel habitually slid into apostasy, provoking divine chastening. The nation urgently appealed to God in times of crisis, moving the Lord to raise up leaders (judges) to deliver the people from foreign oppressors and restore the land to peace. But as a summary of the book explains:

> "Israel quickly forgot the acts of God that had given them birth and had established them in the land. Consequently they lost sight of their unique identity as God's people, chosen and called to be his army and the loyal citizens of his emerging kingdom. They settled down and attached themselves to Canaan's peoples together with Canaanite morals, gods, and religious beliefs and practices as readily as to Canaan's agriculture and social life. …. They stopped fighting the Lord's battles, turned to the gods of Canaan to secure the blessings of family, flocks and fields, and abandoned God's laws for daily living."

One sees, then, that apostasy and back-sliding consist less often of denying God's existence (atheism), than of forgetting or ignoring Him. At the same time we also forget the Enemy of our Souls and the wiles by which he deceives nations.

The Roaring Lion

"Be sober-minded; be watchful. Your adversary the devil prowls around like a roaring lion, seeking someone to devour." (1 Peter 5:8)

"… in order that Satan might not outwit us. For we are not unaware of his schemes" (2 Corinthians 2:11).

A mother puffin letting her chicks fly for the first time, must beware of arctic foxes. A mother wildebeest crossing a river must watch out for crocodiles. Should not we be even more keenly aware of the fact that the Enemy is after our children? He calls that negligence "enlightenment" and "progress"; his slogans fill classrooms and brainwash the next generation.

We have seen the work of many anti-Christs in modern times, sub-contractors to the builder of altars upon which the souls of youth have been sacrificed. Carefully observe those "subs." We see Satan's plan reflected in Nazism and Communism and in the educational philosophies described in the previous three chapters. The wolves have made their ravenous plans clear, but we have ignored the warnings in the Bible and even our own ears. Names like "Hitler," "Marx" and "Stalin" are invoked so often that we barely hear them anymore. But hear what they themselves have said, and carefully ruminate on the implications of the plans they openly confessed.

Adolf Hitler called children "the most valuable possession a people can have", explaining his program boldly in *Mein Kampf*:

> "The State must assert itself as the trustee of a millennial future, in face of which the egotistic desires of the individual count for nothing and will have to give way before the ruling of the State."

The purpose of education, then, was to indoctrinate youth. On May Day, 1933, Hitler taunted parents:

> "When an opponent declares, "I will not come over to your side," I calmly say, "Your child belongs to us already... What are you? You will pass on. Your descendants, however, now stand in the new camp. In a short time they will know nothing else but this new community."

Hitler also gloated that "our success in the universities" made him more confident than anything of "the victory of our ideas." If you visit Auschwitz you will see a plaque of Hilter's boast:

> "I freed Germany from the stupid and degrading fallacies of conscience and morality …. We will train young people before whom the world will tremble. I want young people capable of violence – imperious, relentless and cruel."

The psychologist Viktor Frankl, MD, survived that concentration camp. He warned of the link between the intelligentsia and the horrors of the camps:

> "I am absolutely convinced that the gas chambers of Auschwitz, Treblinka, and Maidanek were ultimately prepared not in some ministry or other in Berlin, but rather at the desks and in lecture halls of nihilistic scientists and philosophers."

The other great totalitarian movement of our times, Marxism-Leninism, if anything, placed even greater emphasis on education. In *The Communist Manifesto*, a lion with a long mane, Karl Marx, already in the mid-19th Century recognized the central importance of schools:

> "The education of all children, from the moment that they can get

along without a mother's care, shall be in state institutions at state expense."

Joseph Stalin had the chance to fulfill this prophecy as absolute ruler of the Soviet Union. He spoke of schools in militaristic terms:
> "Education is a weapon whose effects depend on who holds it in his hands and at whom it is aimed."

Why are the foxes, crocodiles, and lions so focused on their prey – our children – while we make them cross the river unprotected and unaided?

Our children are the most valuable possession that God has entrusted to us. We need to become at least as militant, and as bold, in shepherding them in a godly way, as our Enemy is in trying to destroy them. Satan obviously did not throw in the towel with the defeat of 20th Century totalitarianism. Rather, he evolved a new breed of Marxism, marrying Narcissism and Hedonism to increase the potency on university campuses.

Satan's Use of The Western Education System

The public-school system is systematically abolishing God from the school, as other writers have already noted. This is by design. Horace Mann, a father of the public educational system, was clear about his goals:
> "What the Church has been for medieval man, the public school must become for democratic and rational man. God would be replaced by the concept of the public good."

John Dewey, considered a father of modern progressive education and a signer of the *Humanist Manifesto* I, agreed:
> "There is no God and there is no soul. Hence, there are no needs for the props of traditional religion. With dogma and creed excluded, immutable truth is also dead and buried. There is no room for fixed, natural laws or moral absolutes."

In 1973, *Humanist Manifesto II* updated the ideals of the original. In his contribution to this second document John Dunphy emphasized the role that education should take in spreading Humanist ideals:
> "The battle for humankind's future must be waged and won in the public school classroom by teachers who correctly perceive their role as the proselytizers of a new faith: a religion of humanity that

recognizes and respects the spark of what theologians call divinity in every human being."

Dunphy wrote of "...utilizing a classroom instead of a pulpit to convey humanist values" in every subject, "regardless of the educational level — preschool day care or large state university."

The National Education Association (NEA) is the largest labor union in the United States. The power and influence of the NEA cannot be understated. The website nea.org states that it "is more than 3 million people" who use "the power of public education to transform lives."

Leaders within the NEA recognize that their values are often at odds with those of parents. Echoing Hitler's May Day harangue, National Education Association Specialist Paul Haubner explained the need to change the student's parent-centered value system:

> "The schools cannot allow parents to influence the kind of values education their children receive in school; that is what is wrong with those who say there is a universal system of values. Our goals are incompatible with theirs. We must change their values."

Baptist theologian Albert Mohler described the agenda of this new wave of humanist educators:

> "Aided and abetted by strategic court decisions, the schools became transformative instruments for the secularization of the American worldview. Dewey's atheism was not a minor factor in this development, as he and like-minded theorists saw the public schools as a means of liberating children from the religious convictions of their parents. Parental authority was undermined by the fact that the schools took on functions that had previously been left to parents only. Gradually, school officials began to speak of parents as 'partners' in the educational process. Many schools now treat parents as extensions of the school's own mission and purpose—a great reversal from the time when schools saw themselves as extensions of the parents' authority.'

Most people understand that the philosophy of the school room in one generation becomes the philosophy of government in the next. This is why the Homeschool Movement, private Christian education and school choice initiatives are all under pressure from secular education leaders and legislatures.

In their May-June 2020 issue, Harvard Magazine unleashed an attack on homeschooling in an article titled *"The Risks of Homeschooling."* The article, written by Erin O'Donnel, profiled the ideas of Harvard Law Professor Elizabeth Bartholet, faculty director for the Law School's Child Advocacy Program. To be sure, some of Bartholet's concerns were legitimate: the danger of child abuse (which also occurs at a disheartening rate in public schools) and the need to make sure that children obtain a quality education. But Bartholet also zeroed in on what appeared to be ideological concerns:

> "Surveys of homeschoolers show that a majority of such families (by some estimates, up to 90 percent) are driven by conservative Christian beliefs, and seek to remove their children from mainstream culture . . . it's also important that children grow up exposed to community values, social values, democratic values, ideas about non-discrimination and tolerance of other people's viewpoints."

Bartholet noted that some European countries ban homeschooling. After all, outside of those "six or seven hours a day" (more like eight or nine, plus homework), can't parents influence their children enough after they come home from school?

> "The issue is, do we think that parents should have 24/7, essentially authoritarian control over their children from ages zero to 18? I think that's dangerous . . . I think it's always dangerous to put powerful people in charge of the powerless, and to give the powerful ones total authority."

Concentration of power is, indeed, dangerous. But studies show that biological parents are vastly less likely to abuse their own children physically or sexually than are unrelated adults. And it is not hard to discern, behind Bartholet's hand-waving, a religious agenda which, from a Christian point of view, might be described as a wolf's agenda.

Private schools are also under stress - both economically and legally. Education Secretary Betsy DeVos has called for federal funding to help the more than 160 private schools that have closed due to the coronavirus pandemic. Secretary DeVos' attempt to get additional aid to private schools was blocked by U.S. District Judge Friedrich in response to lawsuits filed by pro-public-school advocates and the NAACP.

The scheme of Satan is clear. He means to keep the next generation from knowing the truth. To do so, from an early as possible age, hand children into the care of teachers who deny revelation, for as much of the day as possible, thereby ensuring future generations know even less about God and His loving plan for His creation.

What Can We Do?

The Bible repeatedly commands the righteous to boldly speak up against evil:

> Walk as children of light (for the fruit of light is found in all that is good and right and true) and try to discern what is pleasing to the Lord. Take no part in the unfruitful works of darkness, but instead expose them. (Ep 5:8-11)

> Who will stand up for me against evildoers? Who will take his stand for me against those who do wickedness? (Ps 94:16)

> We demolish arguments and every pretension that sets itself up against the knowledge of God. (2 Co 10:5)

> I have made you a watchman for the house of Israel. Whenever you hear a word from My mouth, give them a warning from Me. If I say to the wicked man, 'You will surely die,' but you do not warn him or speak out to warn him from his wicked way to save his life, that wicked man will die in his iniquity, and I will hold you responsible for his blood. (Ek 3:17-18, Ek 33:8)

Education must be based on some worldview, which teaches particular notions of Origin, Meaning, Morality and Destiny. Nazis, Communists and Secular Humanists tell their stories divorced from the Author of Life, with warped senses of meaning and dead-end destinations. This is why Christian theology must form the heart of education, as Douglas Wilson eloquently explains:

> "Theology is the queen of sciences, and sound theology is the study of the triune God revealed in Scripture. It must be strongly emphasized that classical and Christian schools are evangelical Christian schools. We reject both the mind-numbing errors of theological liberalism and the superficial inanities of a reactionary fundamentalism. It is very important that Christians realize that they do not have to choose between genuine learning and a love

for Christ. The greatest commandment includes the requirement that we love the Lord our God with all our brains."

Pastor Voddie Baucham, Jr., put the matter more succinctly:
> "We cannot continue to send our children to Caesar for their education and be surprised when they come home as Romans."

Count the number of hours we lend our children to be discipled by persons with an anti-Biblical worldview! No wonder we find ourselves in such a mess.

In 1865 William Ross Wallace published a poem entitled "What rules the World?", Which celebrated the "divine mission" of mothers. From this poem came the common proverb "The Hand That Rocks the Cradle, Is the Hand That Rules the World." But the role of mothers (and fathers, who, research has shown, deeply influence how children turn out) has been diminished. Commonly a "blessing" is now thought to involve money. Let us quickly recover the biblical understanding of children as our ultimate earthly blessing. In three gospels, Jesus warned us that children would be under attack:
> "It is inevitable that stumbling blocks will come, but woe to the one through whom they come! It would be better for him to have a millstone hung around his neck and to be thrown into the sea than to cause one of these little ones to stumble." (Luke 17:1-2)

Stumbling blocks come, but how many parents are complicit as "the one through whom they come"?

Look at what Satan is accomplishing, and we may grow depressed or angry. There is time for anger! We need to be vigilant, combating evil influences in the Education system intelligently and with determination. But at the same time, our eyes must be ultimately fixed on Christ. And we must pray that those eyes be opened, as famously happened to Elisha's servant during a siege:
> "Oh no, my lord! What shall we do?"
> "Don't be afraid . . . Those who are with us are more than those who are with them."
> "Open his eyes, Lord, so that he may see" (2 Kings 6:15-17).

Discipleship through education can increase those who are with us, generation by generation.

The biblical vision is for planning from one generation to the next, like a seed planted and nurtured to grow into a tree. From one can come many. Would you rather be paid 1 million dollars for a month of work or would you rather be paid one penny for the first day of work but every day thereafter your wage would double until the end of the month? If you took the cool million, you would lose eight million dollars in a 31-day month. Paul planned for the Gospel to likewise grow from one generation to the next:

> "What you have heard from me in the presence of many witnesses, entrust to faithful men, who will be able to teach others also." (2 Timothy 2:2)

In this verse one finds three generations of disciples: Paul, Timothy ("you" and "many witnesses") and "faithful men, who will be able to teach others." This is the principle of exponential growth. Sociologist Rodney Stark argues that exponential growth, from generation to generation, was responsible for turning Rome Christian in three centuries. A seed, planted in the ground, grew into a tree.

God's people have often been faced with such circumstances, with the same devourer masquerading as light. The plan enunciated by Jesus and then Paul, can work again. The heart of the *"Third Education Revolution"* is reflected in 1 Peter 2:9 and Revelation 5:10. These verses refer to a "royal priesthood" and calls God's followers "kings and priests." What flows from the heart of this revolution is the goal of discipling the next generation of kings and priests for God's Kingdom through an educational system grounded in a biblical worldview.

Chapter 20

Reclaiming the Heritage of Western Civilization

Gayne John Anacker[1]

We Have a Problem

It is now clear that Christianity in the United States is in deep trouble. Due to various trends discussed in this book, Christianity is no longer the dominating force that guides the development of western culture. It is losing the ability to speak openly about some of the most important elements of life and faith.

The steep decline of Christian leadership in the United States is a fairly recent development. Noted scholar of law and jurisprudence Mary Ann Glendon, the Learned Hand Professor of Law at Harvard University and President of the Pontifical Academy of Social Sciences, stated that the decline began in a marked way in 1947, when a United States Supreme Court decision invoked what we now know how to be a fateful metaphor, the "wall of separation between church and state".[2] Although the ruling in this particular case[3] did not directly challenge the position of religion in the United States, the court's sweeping language, detailing its understanding of a "wall of separation" between Church and State, nevertheless became the tool in subsequent years by which subsequent court decisions were used to push religion aside.

---

1 Prof. Dr. Gayne Anacker is a Trustee of the C.S. Lewis Foundation, which he also served as Vice President for Academic Affairs for over 20 years. In 2020, he retired from his position as Professor of Philosophy and Director of the University Honors Program at California Baptist University. He also served this institution as Dean of the College of Arts and Sciences for 15 years.

2 Glendon, 2015, p. 4

3 Everson v. Board of Education

In the last 70 years, we have seen a dramatic roll-back of the ability to exercise religious faith in public forums. Prayer in public schools is now unthinkable, though it had once been common. In many jurisdictions, among many other restrictions, students are not allowed to hold Bible club meetings in public schools during lunch or after class; churches may not rent public school space on weekends; and teachers may not use the word "Christmas" to describe a class party, or refer to "winter" vacation.

Beginning under the Obama Administration, the secular challenge has fallen heavily on religious understandings of marriage and sexuality or sexual identity. Businesses have been subjected to grave legal challenges for refusing to support same-sex "wedding" celebrations. In 2012, Jack Phillips, owner of Masterpiece Cake Shop in Lakewood, Colorado, declined on religious grounds to create a wedding cake celebrating a same-sex "marriage". In 2013, Barronelle Stutzman, owner of Arlene's Flowers in Richland, WA, similarly declined to create floral arrangements to celebrate one of her customers' same-sex wedding. In 2015, Memories Pizza in Walkerton, Indiana declined for the same reasons to serve pizza for a reception celebrating a same-sex wedding. Memories Pizza closed its doors rather than fight the extended legal battles. Phillips and Stutzman are still in expensive litigation that stretches, in both cases, all the way to the United States Supreme Court. This quick survey does not even address the issue of gays in the military, use of restrooms by transgender persons, the censoring or de-platforming of speech deemed to be hateful or inaccurate, or many more. All of this has the effect (as intended) of forcing biblically-minded Christians and other conservative religious people to refrain from public discussion of their views about marriage or sexual identity, on pain of being hounded in the press, social media and the courtroom. This is the goal of secularism.

Two especially significant rulings should be noted. First, in 2015, by a 5-4 ruling, the U.S. Supreme Court required all 50 states to perform and recognize same-sex "marriages", overturning democratically enacted laws in fifteen states.[4] Justice Clarence Thomas, writing in a dissenting opinion on a recent case in which the ruling flowed from *Obergefell*, stated that, until *Obergefell* is "fixed", it would continue to have "ruinous consequences for religious liberty".[5] Finally, in a June, 2020 ruling, the Supreme Court pro-

---

4 Obergefell v. Hodges, 2015

5 Olson, 2020

hibited workplace discrimination on the basis of sexual preference and identity.[6] The implications of these curtailments of public expression of religious beliefs are staggering.

The hostility displayed by the courts to religion marks a fundamental change in American beliefs, especially among the educated and powerful. Without the support of numerous often powerful citizens, such legal rulings would not have been possible. These rulings are a public record of what has been happening in the hearts and minds of American citizens.

There is a word for this growing hostility — *secularism*. In this chapter "secular" refers to the idea that religion no longer has a substantive role to play in public intellectual discourse about society, culture, education or government. Religion may be acceptable as a private practice, giving meaning to one's personal life, but has little relevance for public matters.

Of course, Christians throughout the world and throughout time, have endured persecution much greater than this. The profound, open hostility to Christian faith we are witnessing is new only in the U.S. Throughout most of the West, secularism has been a functional reality for well over a century.[7]

How Should We Respond?

In responding to the challenge of secularism, we must remember that first of all, we are called to *be not afraid*, but to get on with the business which God has set before us. The Apostle Paul told Timothy:

> For this reason I remind you to fan into flame the gift of God, which is in you through the laying on of my hands, *for God gave us a spirit not of fear but of power and love and self-control.*[8]

Hundreds of scriptures call upon us to look to God, trust in him, and do the work to which He has called us. (1Cor.12:1, 7, 11, 27-31)

And what work is that? The title of Anthony Esolen's Touch- stone article sets out the essence of our response on the level of culture: "No Option:

6 Bostock v. Clayton County, 2020

7 Mat.24:9-12; Luk.18:8(b); Jas.5:7

8 2 Timothy 1:6-7, ESV, emphasis added

Clear Out the Rubble and Rebuild". In order to clear out and rebuild, many things need to be done by people with varied callings and training.

In order to ensure that God's will is done in the West, we need to reclaim biblical foundations of western civilization. The Church created, adapted and transmitted so much of the world's art, knowledge, and wisdom. It is time we take back our heritage. We need to fill our minds, and churches, with the art, economics, engineering, history, language, literature, languages, math, morality, philosophy, theology, science and technology that "those who have gone before us" have achieved. Whether through institutions like C. S. Lewis College which David Bastedo and I described in Chapter 10, through Collegepedia and the work of academic pastors, or other means, Christians must become literate in our own civilization.

In order to reclaim the West, we need to understand how a civilization, once saturated with Christian faith, has "lost its flavor", as Jesus put it - at least in public institutions.

The Roots of Secularity in the West

Secularism has grown since about 1600. In the United States it gained real power roughly when the Baby Boomers generation went to college in the 1960s and 70s. By that time most faculty members largely agreed that religion had little worth in how society should be managed.

What are the origins of this move towards secularity? The basic problem is spiritual in nature: rebellion against God. We learn from biblical history that humanity has a pronounced tendency to *ignore* God's claim upon our lives, act as if we dwell in his absence and, eventually, many *believe* that He does not exist. Why? Biblical religion unpleasantly informs us that we are sinners, that we need God's forgiveness, and that peace with God means complete reliance on him. As the prophets predicted, many people in the West became tired of God as wealth and success grew during the late-Middle Ages and the Renaissance. It became annoying to take God and his claims seriously, to organize one's life and thought around him and his demands upon us and our lives.

The biggest general impetus to secularism, however, came as the result of astounding developments in mathematics and the natural sciences during the Modern era. This is ironic, given that so many of the leading mathematicians and scientists of that time were devout Christians (Copernicus, Galileo, Kepler, Descartes, Pascal, Boyle, Leibniz, Newton, Euler, and many more). The "narrative", however, was that not the Bible, but mathematics and its application to the natural sciences, provided (so-called) "precise" understanding of the world. The Bible seemed to be a collection of myths, old-fashioned and irrelevant, compared with the astonishing discoveries flowing from the natural sciences. By the 19th Century it became common for people to assume that science and religion were in great opposition to each other. Science was the realm of reason, religion the realm of blind faith.

The biggest single development that gave license to thinking people to leave theism behind was Darwin's publication of *On the Origin of Species* in 1859. Darwin's theory of evolution provided the last piece of the puzzle needed for many to dispense with God. It was widely thought that his theory provided a solid explanation of how life could begin as a simple organism and evolve naturally into highly complex animal species without requiring the intervention of a designing and creating God. Intellectuals now thought they were free of God. God was not needed to explain life and the world. (Of course, many questions and challenges can be raised, but the account in this section focuses on the development of ideas, not their merits.) There were still many thinkers of faith, but they found it increasingly difficult to make the case for a biblically informed worldview within an Academy that had largely left religion behind.

Rejecting God and His revelation resurrects fundamental questions that had been settled by Christian confessions. These include: Who are we? Why do we matter? What is goodness? How shall we live? Extreme postmodernists know that evolutionary worldview cannot offer acceptable answers to such questions. So they say that human reason, being a product of blind chance, is incapable of validating answers to such questions. They doubt if human reason can even verify worldviews constructed to answer such questions. A key thinker in the movement, the French philosopher Jean-François Lyotard, wrote, "Simplifying to the extreme, I define postmodern as incredulity toward metanarratives".[9] "Metanarrative" is Lyotard's word for worldview, and he is saying that rational people must realize that worldviews are not rationally believable. This view has become widespread within academia and the ruling elite that thinks that human beings are nothing more than a species of animals.

---

9 [1979] 1984, p. xxiv, emphasis in the original

The preceding points about the roots of secularism describe what was happening in the culture around the church, but not necessarily *within* the church. Has the church been blameless in this process of cultural reversal?

Several prominent evangelical thinkers have, in recent decades, decried the ability of biblically oriented Christians to understand and effectively critique the deepest and most troubling patterns in Western civilization. The first of these was the Anglican theologian and writer Harry Blamires who studied under C.S. Lewis at Oxford University. In the opening sentence of his book *The Christian Mind*, written in 1961, Blamires wrote: "There is no longer a Christian mind" (p. 3). This might seem rather extreme, especially given that, at the time of that writing, both Lewis and J.R.R. Tolkien were still living, along with many other strong Christian thinkers. Blamires, however, was offering a generalization on the number and stature of Christian thinkers within the learned discourse of his day, and his conclusion was that "to-day there is no public pool of discourse fed by Christianly committed thought on the world we live in".[10] Quite a warning.

In 1994 Mark Noll repeated Blamires' charge in his *The Scandal of the Evangelical Mind*, saying in his very first sentence: "*The scandal of the Evangelical Mind* is that there is not much of an evangelical mind".[11] Noll was not denying that Christians have often succeeded in the modern academy, but that that is the full measure of a Christian mind:

> The much more important matter is what it means to think like a Christian about the nature and workings of the physical world, the character of human social structures like government and the economy, the meaning of the past, the nature of artistic creation, and the circumstances attending our perception of the world outside ourselves. Failure to exercise the mind for Christ in these areas has become acute in the twentieth century. That failure is *The Scandal of the Evangelical Mind*.[12]

To summarize: we know that Christianity had come *in some sense* to saturate the West by about 800 AD but that, within the last few centuries or so Christianity, and indeed all religions, have been pushed to the margins of society, divorcing Christianity from the civilization it helped to create.

---

10 Noll, 13

11 Noll, 3

12 272 Noll, 1994, 7

So, recognizing that Christianity is in real trouble, and as others have argued in this volume, world civilization with it, what shall we do?

Taking Back Western Civilization

What does it mean to reclaim the heritage of our civilization? Of course, we need well-educated Christians in all walks of life: doctors, lawyers, scientists, literary historians and so on. In addition, as we argued in an earlier chapter, we need to become literate in our civilization. Some level of civilizing literacy can be achieved by anyone, with study. But we do not just need a few rare individuals here or there. We need thousands of Christians who understand the fabric of ideas, events and artistic developments of our civilization, to engage the secular leadership of society with authority, for at least four reasons:

> 1) In addition to being called to share the Good News of Christ, we are also called to be agents of preservation (salt) and illumination (light) in a world that is decaying and descending into darkness (Mt 5:13-16). We have to understand civilization if we are going to preserve what is good in it.

> 2) Christians need to know the intellectual dimensions of the culture well enough to refute the world's reasons for dismissing our faith. Our knowledge of culture and faith must be sufficient to answer particular critiques. We must also show its intellectual credibility and power to explain morality and human nature, and why alternative views, such as atheism, fail to do so.

> 3) Since many influential secularists possess an extensive knowledge of our culture, Christians who contend with them intellectually must enjoy a similar breadth. Unless we know what we are talking about, we will not get a hearing. Powerful narratives that interpret human history are created by people who have great knowledge of the civilization they wish to influence. Most people have no clue about the role that Christianity played in creating modern science and western civilization. The Church needs a critical mass of believers who know history and can authoritatively tell the world what really happened and why.

4) In addition, when we do our homework by studying and carefully pondering the full legacy of faith, or its absence, we *honor* God. Mark Noll praised the life and work of Jonathan Edwards for displaying his commitment to using his mind to search out God's truth across an array of fields, knowing that all of these areas impinge on life as God's creatures.

Noll said it well:

> It is not simply advantageous to love the Lord with the mind; it is also good, sweet, holy, beautiful and honoring to God. The last reward to be had from the exercise of a Christian mind is to know God better, and that reward requires no other justification.[13]

Attaining civilizational literacy is no simple challenge. But in recent years, both Christians and non-Christians have created works which give one a running start. For instance: in the preface to his remarkable 2019 book *Dominion: How the Christian Revolution Remade the World*, historian Tom Holland states:

> "The civilization into which I had been born was Christendom . . . So profound has been the impact of Christianity on the development of Western civilization that it has come to be hidden from view" (p. 17).

Vishal Mangalwadi, co-editor of this volume, has described that impact in detail and in several works over the past two decades. Rodney Stark, the eminent sociologist and historian, has further described the core contributions of Christianity to civilization in a series of ground-breaking works.[14] In an interview Dr. Stark told our other co-editor, David Marshall:

> "I wrote my way back" to Christian faith by studying the impact of the gospel on human civilization.

To highlight the need for understanding the history of western ideas and the role Christianity plays in them, let me offer a little pop quiz, with just five questions to try your knowledge.

....

13 Noll, 1994, pp. 79-80

14 1996, 2003, 2005, 2015

A Western Civ Quiz for Readers

Question #1: Around 700 BC an explosion of organized learning and artistic expression in Greek culture began, unrivaled anywhere else in the ancient world (and which later continued in universities). The roots of most academic disciplines can be traced to this era. *Why did this happen in Greece? Were Socrates and his friends just smarter than everyone else?*

Answer: Some unknown Greek thinker invented a tool that made it possible for learning to be shared among a vast pool of literate persons — the Greek alphabet. It was the first short, phonetically complete alphabet in the world (including vowels as well as consonants, unlike Phoenician, from which it derived), encouraging wide-spread literacy. Because it was short, it could be learned by three-year-olds. Because it was phonetically complete, it fully replicated the spoken language. Anyone who could speak Greek could easily learn to read it.

Alexander's military conquests of much of the world made it possible for ancient Greek civilization to have many more readers than any other ancient culture. This led to greater intellectual foment and greater intellectual and artistic output. According to classicist David Mulroy, this theory about the origin of the ancient Greek explosion of learning is a well-known secret in classics departments.[15]

Question #2: *Why did Christianity gain ascendancy in the West in fewer than 300 years?*

Answer: Many reasons can be credibly cited, one of which is the philosophical adequacy of Christian theology. Plato and Aristotle, in the 4th century BC, had offered sophisticated, rigorous arguments about ultimate reality. The boisterous and seemingly juvenile pagan polytheism of Greco-Roman religion lacked the depth and richness to satisfy the hunger for a transcendent religious explanation of *all* reality. The great Catholic historian Christopher Dawson put it this way:

> From the time of Plato the Hellenic *paideia* [education] was a humanism in search for a theology, and the religious traditions of Greek culture were neither deep nor wide enough to provide the answer. The religious needs of the ancient world were satisfied not by philosophy but by the new religion which had emerged

15 Mulroy, 1999, p. 43

so suddenly and unpredictably from beneath the surface of the dominant culture.[16]

The clear superiority of Christian theism to its competitors gives us some reason to think this revelation was inspired by God.

Question #3: *Why did the West lead in the abolition of slavery?*

Answer: The Judeo-Christian tradition affirms that all men are created in the image of God, are sinners in need of God's grace and who stand before God as equals, receiving grace and forgiveness as we respond. If we are equal in so many ways, there can ultimately be no moral justification for one man owning another. The Bible began to be written when God sent Moses to liberate the Hebrews from their slavery in Egypt. The Bible saw slavery as a result of sin, and freedom as God's gift to those who repent and seek Him as the Savior. This made the Bible the matrix of western struggles for liberty for all.

One could ask similar questions about the abolition of polygamy and the consequent strength of the family in the West: the Rule of Law, Free Enterprise, Separation of Church and State and other core values that have formed world civilization. I leave these questions as a take-home exam. Feel free to "cheat" by reading the writers mentioned above!

But let me conclude this section with two "trick" questions.

Question #4: *What set of arguments, what thinker, or thinkers, decisively demonstrated that religion is best left out of the public domain?*

Answer: None. Secularism is grounded on an intellectual fashion that has developed and become firmly lodged in high places, but no one ever proved its essential premises. Mind you: this is a bold claim which I do not make glibly: one must do one's homework first.
The first major thinker to openly deny the relevance of religion was the Swiss German philosopher Friedrich Nietzsche, writing roughly from 1870-1890. And he did not give what could normally be called arguments to support his claim. He denied believing in objective reason, so he could not provide such arguments. He strongly implied, however, that modern science had made belief in God irrelevant. His enigmatic but powerful lit-

16 Dawson, [1961] 2010, p. 7

tle parable, often called "The Madman and the Death of God", is a classic statement of his views.[17] Nietzsche is one of the thinkers most responsible for the development of secularism and postmodernism. Christians who wish to influence the culture must know his work.

Question #5: *What set of arguments, thinker, or group of thinkers, clearly established that a biblically-based morality is irrational?*

Answer: Again: none. In fact, it is the secular understanding of morality that has been routed from the field of philosophical battle.
Over the past half-century, while Christian morality was shoved off the public square as irrelevant, a less-observed development occurred in the world of ideas.

As Christian influence waned, secularists considered how to replace its influence. Five or six competing theories of morality were suggested, and two emerged as leading contenders. The first was Utilitarianism, initially introduced by Jeremey Bentham in 1780, and later given its early definitive statement by John Stuart Mill in 1863.

Consider a morally significant act, say, "Shall I steal the loaf of bread, or not?"

Bentham and Mill argued that right and wrong could be calculated by determining which answer maximized happiness — often interpreted as pleasure — for the greatest number of people: "The greatest happiness for the greatest number." By contrast a moral theory based on duty, called Deontology, was proposed by Immanuel Kant around 1785.

These theories are mutually exclusive and cannot both be true but, for nearly 200 years, most philosophers have assumed that one or other would emerge victorious as the most sound basis for secular morality.

But within the past four decades, it has become clear to philosophers that both theories are fatally defective. They simply do not work any more than a bad computer program. They have design flaws which result in failure, even deadly failure. There is now a growing consensus that neither can be repaired. So among thinkers, we now have no moral theory that provides a widely accepted basis for belief in good and bad, right and wrong.

17 Nietzsche [1887] 1974, Sec. 125, pp. 181-182

Thus secularists who denounce Christian morality are standing on empty air. The Church needs to recognize that its competitors have gone bankrupt and must now boldly affirm that goodness comes from God; that He has placed knowledge of it in our hearts and has revealed the code to this knowledge in the Bible.

Final Quiz for the Author

Now that you have answered my questions, perhaps you have some for me.

1) Are you saying that everyone needs to become an expert in Western Civilization? Some of this study would do all well-educated Christians good. It is essential, however, that many of our most capable students be well-prepared in understanding the roots of Western thought and progress.

2) So is this mostly about history, literature and philosophy? No. The task ultimately encompasses all organized learning, including maths and the natural and social sciences. But who can master all of this? In their fully-developed modern forms, no one can. But those who are called to specialize in civilizational literacy can, over time, acquire basic understanding of all the foundational fields of study and move on toward mastery of some key fields of interest to them.

3) Are you saying that "The West is the best? No. That would be too simplistic. All nations are made up of sinners who need God's grace, but who were nevertheless made in the image of God. So every culture is a mix of good and evil. The West has, however, become the dominant civilization over the last six centuries (again, for good ánd ill). It has developed ideas that inspire, or repulse, people around the world. We do not promote cultural superiority or jingoism. Our point is that the most praiseworthy developments in the West are due to God's grace - most often manifest through His followers as they obey His will. The people of the West are sinners needing the grace of God, just like everyone else. The grace of God, flowing through the life of the Church over two millennia, is not something for which humans can take credit. To God alone be the glory. As the influence of Christian faith wanes, the Church will lose power to do good, especially if we fail to grasp the origins, assumptions, challenges and important turning points of our civilization.

4) Do you mean to imply that other cultures need not be studied by people in the West? Absolutely not. Many of those who gain a basic understanding of Western civilization will naturally seek to study other civilizations as well. Still, one best understands other cultures by first getting to know one's own. The most effective missionaries, like Matteo Ricci and James Legge, were often those who understood Western civilization the most deeply, before seeking a similar understanding of foreign cultures.

5) Do you mean to say, though, that people of other cultures should study the Western civilization? I leave this question for my fellow contributors from around the world to consider in the context of their own church's needs and history. It lies beyond my scope in this chapter.

6) Are you saying that, because of the grace of God, everything the West has achieved is good, true, and beautiful? Of course not! You need to read this chapter over again! Every civilization is a mixture of error and truth, goodness and evil, beauty and ugliness. It is through understanding the dialogue of theories over time that we learn to think carefully about truth and falsehood. For example: it took thinkers in the West well over 1400 years to recognize that Ptolemy's astronomy was profoundly wrong, and to adopt Copernican theory in its place. Western science had to develop a great deal in order to reach the truth of the matter. In the same way many of us consider Marx's theory of economics and politics to be profoundly false and destructive. Still, the challenge of Marxism helps us to more deeply appreciate the value of economic and other freedoms in its light. One of the glories of the West, now seemingly fading, lies in treating the "Great Conversation" as a principled heuristic - a fallible search for ever-growing insight into truth.

Bibliography:

- Blamires, Harry. [1963] 1978. *The Christian Mind: How Should a Christian Think?* Servant Publications, Ann Arbor, MI (1978).

- Bostock v. Clayton County, 590 U.S. (2020).

- Esolen, Anthony. 2020. "No Option: Clear Out the Rubble and Rebuild," *Touchstone*, July/August 2020, https://www.touchstonemag.com/archives/article.php?id=33-04-028-f (accessed Sept. 5, 2020).

- Everson v. Board of Education, 330 U.S. 1 (1947).

- Glendon, Mary Ann. 2015. "Religious Freedom: Yesterday, Today and Tomorrow," The 2015 Cardinal Egan Lecture, https://www.magnificat.net/foundation/pdf/M_A Glendon_ 2015.pdf (accessed October 16, 2020).

- Holland, Tom. 2019. *Dominion: How the Christian Revolution Remade the World.* Basic Books.

- Jefferson, Thomas. 1802. "Letter to the Danbury Baptist Association," https://www.digitalhistory.uh.edu/disp_textbook. cfm?smtID=3&psid=1276 (accessed October 16, 2020).

- Lyotard, Jean-Francois. [1979] 1984. "Introduction," The Post modern Condition: A Report on Knowledge, trans. Geoff Bennington and Brian Massumi, Foreword by Fredric Jameson, in *Theory and History of Literature*, Vol. 10, University of Minnesota (published by Manchester University Press).

- Mangalwadi, Vishal. 2011. *The Book that Made Your World: How the Bible Created the Soul of Western Civilization.* Thomas Nelson.

- Mangalwadi, Vishal. 2019. *This Book Changed Everything: Volume 1: The Bible's Amazing Impact on our World*, with contributions from Ashish Alexander and Jenny Taylor. Thomas Nelson.

- Mulroy, David. 1999. *"Alphabetic Literacy and the Revitalization of the Liberal Arts."* Academic Questions, Vol. 12, No. 2 (Spring 1999): 43-47.

- Nietzsche, Friedrich. [1887] 1974. *The Gay Science, with a Prelude in Rhymes and an Appendix of Songs, Translated*, with commentary, by Walter Kaufmann. Random House.

- Noll, Mark A. 1994. *The Scandal of the Evangelical Mind.* William B. Eerdmans Publishing Company.

- Obergefell v. Hodges, 576 U.S. 644 (2015).

- Olson, Tyler. 2020. "Justices Thomas, Alito slam Obergefell same- sex marriage decision as Supreme Court denies Kim Davis case," Fox News, https://www.fox-news.com/politics/thomas-alito-kim- davis-obergefell-decision-same-sex-marriage

- Stark, Rodney. - 1996. *The Rise of Christianity: How the Obscure, Marginal Jesus Movement became the Dominant Religious Force in the Western World in a Few Centuries -* Princeton University Press.
- 2003. *For the Glory of God: How Monotheism Led to Reformations, Science, Witch-Hunts, and the End of Slavery.* Princeton University Press.
- 2005. *The Victory of Reason: How Christianity Led to Freedom, Capitalism, and Western Success.*
- 2015. *How the West won: The Neglected Story of the Triumph of Modernity.* Intercollegiate Studies Institute.

III

The Great Commission to Educate Nations

Chapter 21

The Great Commission And the Healing of the Nations

Bruce Friesen[1]

The ideology taught in schools in one generation
will shape the next generation's government and other spheres of influence.

Not Discipling Nations Is Costly: Nigeria

During the past ten years about 70,000 Christians have been killed in Nigeria, approximately 2000 churches have been destroyed and nearly five million Christians have been displaced. Those are just some of the fruits of a gospel that saves souls from hell but refuses to disciple nations.

As a geo-political-legal entity, modern Nigeria is largely a creation of British Christianity — evangelical and liberal. It has approximately 90 million Christians and 90 million Muslims. And yet,

- In 1999 Nigeria's Constitution became Sharia compliant.
- In 1999 many Nigerian Northern states declared Sharia as their judiciary system. Meanwhile, Christian Association of Nigeria (CAN) prayed and protested against such unconstitutional actions.
- In 2014 Politicians formed a political party with Muslim majority leadership and won the 2015 general election.
- In 2016 all top military and security positions were occupied by Muslims, while CAN raised its voice against it and protested.
- In 2019 most significant places of authority and influence - President, Heads of Legislature, Chief Justice, Court of Appeal, Federal High Court, top military and government positions were secured by Muslims.

---

1 Bruce Friesen is the founder of Children Arise Ministry, which disciples nations by discipling the next generation through the sphere of education. He is also the founder of Lifetree Churches and the Global Transformation Collective, which focuses on the transformation of all spheres of influence, by discipling people in the truths and principles of God's Word.

How did this happen?

It happened because, after World War II, Western Christianity became so individualistic and escapist that its missions lost interest in discipling nations.

Protestantism that globalized the biblical idea of "nations" decided that God cares for souls, not nations. The Antichrist's will - not God's - should be done on the earth.

In his book *"The Grand Design: God's ultimate purpose for Africa"*, Professor Vincent Anigbogu explains why Nigeria is descending into a new dark age.

In 1976 The Christian Association of Nigeria (CAN) was inspired by the military-political leadership of the nation, which wanted to establish a national Christian body to represent the Christian interest in government. CAN had no visión to see God's kingdom in Nigeria. It had little interest in seeing God's will done in every sphere of public and national life. It's "vision" was to ensure that:
- Nothing disturbs the peace of the secluded Christian communities;
- The Church prays regularly for the nation, especially for those in authority;
- The welfare of the Christian church is protected; and
- The internal unity of the 5 major church denominational streams are maintained.

Thirteen years later, in 1989, the Organization of Islamic Cooperation (OIC) was formed as a member of the international OIC founded in 1969. OIC had clear goals for Nigeria:
- To win Africa for Islam;
- To install Muslim ideals through the education system;
- To establish economic alliances with Islamic States worldwide;
- To ensure that only Muslims are elected to all political posts;
- To eradicate all forms and ramifications of non-Muslim religions;
- To replace all Western forms of legal and judicial systems with sharia in all nations; and
- To ensure that only Muslims are appointed in strategic and international posts.

OIC wanted Allah's will done in Africa. CAN, in contrast, remained an organization that observed, prayed and protested. While Christians united in prayer and protest, Muslim's organized and advanced their agenda.

Prayer and protests are praiseworthy. However, contemporary Muslim Nigeria, Communist China and Hindu India have demonstrated that darkness will overtake a nation if its Christian leaders do not wake up to sow the seeds of God's kingdom of peace, justice and righteousness into the soul of the next generation.

Nigeria is paying a terrible price for the catastrophic failure of Christian leadership and theology that does not understand the gospel of the Kingdom and the Great Commission to disciple nations.

Professor Anigbogu believes that sound, value-based education can reform the African mindset. There is no reason why Africa cannot have leaders with national and continental vision, integrity and high quality management skills.

An education is needed that produces leaders who transform their organizations, communities and nations. For this reason Prof. Anigbogu leads the Institute for National Transformation (INT) out of Lagos, Nigeria, to train leaders who proffer performance instead of pronouncements; expertise and competence instead of title and position; who pioneer bold and progressive initiatives instead of dictatorship and control. Such leaders will leave lasting legacies in a continent that is currently led by strongmen who make excuses for their failures.

The Divine Mandate to Disciple Nations Through Education

From Genesis to Revelation, discipling the next generation is a basic biblical mandate. The Lord Jesus made our duty clear in the Great Commission:
> *"Go and make disciples of all nations, baptizing them in the name of the Father and of the Son and of the Holy Spirit, and teaching them to obey everything I have commanded you.* (Matt 28:18-20 NIV)

What children learn in the schoolroom often becomes the next generation's philosophy of government. As Gottfried Sommer and Steven McDowell showed in earlier chapters, The Protestant Reformation built great nations by disciplining youth in Christian schools and universities.

Nineteenth century missions followed the Reformers' example. They spread out around the world and planted Churches along with schools, colleges and universities. The education that those institutions furnished, trained leaders who transformed nations. But then, on continent after continent, the Church handed over education to secularism, even within institutions managed by Churches. That education, everywhere, has produced corrupt leaders who put self-interest above their neighbour's needs. It is time for the Church to commit itself again to discipling nations, starting from childhood.

An Epiphany on Discipleship

In May of 2008 I was preaching at evangelistic meetings in Uganda. For two days we saw few results. I gathered our team and we prayed. On the third day two boys, ages five and eight, were brought to us. They had been born blind, deaf and dumb, but God healed them instantly. Their eyes turned from a murky grey to white sclera with brown pupils, before my eyes. That's when I heard the Lord say: *"This is nothing in comparison to what I'm about to do."*

I pondered what that meant. I heard the Lord again: *"Uganda will be a prototype of a transformed nation. It will become a light of hope to the countries of Africa and send ripples of hope around the world."*

I found myself asking: "Lord how are you going to do this?" The Lord said, *"Disciple the nation by discipling the next generation through education."*

Later the Lord reminded me of how He confronted Saul and sent him on a mission to open peoples' eyes. *It will be your mission to open their eyes so that they may turn from darkness to light and from the kingdom of Satan to the kingdom of God.* (Acts 26:18 TPT).

The Lord said to me, *"The two boys healed in Uganda represent the opening of the spiritual eyes and ears of the next generation in Uganda."*

This inner spiritual encounter with the living God began to open my eyes. I began to see the Lord's strategy in discipling nations by discipling the next generation. This revelatory encounter was vivid and life-changing. Yet I felt compelled to research and establish a solid biblical foundation for discipling nations. I needed to know if Scripture supported the idea of discipling nations by investing in the discipling of the next generation. Is there implicit or explicit scriptural support for discipling the next generation through education? If this revelation is scriptural, is it supported in history; specifically in the reformation and mission history? I became curious to know: to what degree can we expect the kingdom of heaven to transform entire nations by discipling the next generation?

In 1999 I had read *"The Legacy of William Carey: A Model for the Transformation of a Culture"* by Vishal and Ruth Mangalwadi. In 2007 I read *"The Book That Transforms Nations"* by Loren Cunningham. Father God began to build my faith: heaven's Kingdom can transform nations if they are re-built on God's Word.

Does the gospel of the Kingdom have the power to transform nations? If it does, then the truths and principles for building godly nations had to be there in the Bible. In 2012 I met Landa Cope in Cape Town, SA. Her book *"The Old Testament Template: Rediscovering God's Principles for Discipling All Nations"* provided the biblical foundation I was searching for. I realized that Jesus' commission to disciple nations was built upon the foundation that had been laid through Abraham and Moses. God's Word gave them the wisdom needed to build good nations.

Jesus saves our souls. That means that the Holy Spirit gives us a new birth. He writes God's law in our hearts and renews our minds by teaching us truth. People who are transformed inwardly transform nations. They challenge false beliefs and inspire people to seek what is true and noble. God's kingdom is an inside-out process. Like leaven it begins in individual hearts but goes on to change social circles and spheres of influence. Principles, precepts, truths and systems, even under the Mosaic covenant, are not sustainable apart from God's Spirit living within us.

Abraham Our Father Laid the Foundation

Christ's command to make disciples of nations was not something new. It began two thousand years before Christ, when Abraham was commanded to disciple his people so that they may bless all nations. Four hundred years after him God revealed to Moses the non-material, spiritual resources necessary to build Israel into a great nation.

Israel often disobeyed and then suffered oppression, poverty, corruption, injustice and slavery. It was revived when it repented and chose to obey God's word. Revival of godliness resulted in national flourishing. Israel's long history of being blessed and cursed made it a template, prototype or strategic pattern for discipling nations. Nations flourish when they are built according to the patterns revealed from heaven. Nations perish when they refuse to walk in the light of the knowledge of the Lord. Just as plants require light to be healthy, nations require the light of God's Word to blossom.

God Himself commanded Abraham to disciple the next generation by teaching (i.e. educating) them to keep God's ways, doing what is good and righteous, showing mercy and justice to all others. This was a generational pattern.

> *After all, Abraham will become the father of a great and powerful nation, and all the other nations of the earth will find their blessing in him. I have chosen him for a reason, namely that he will carefully teach and instruct his children and his household after him to keep themselves strong in relationship to Me and to walk in My ways by doing what is good and right in the world and by showing mercy and justice to all others. I know he will uphold his end of the covenant, so that he can ensure My promises to him will be fulfilled and upheld as well.* (Genesis 18:18-19 AMP)

God upholds His end of the covenant promises if Abraham and his children uphold their end. God's covenant promises were conditional upon their obedience. Possessing the land, becoming a great nation that blesses all nations depended upon Israel teaching the next generation what God had taught them. Generational succession of God's blessings depend upon discipling the next generation to disciple the following generation. Blessings are inherited by walking in God's ways, doing good, being righteous, showing justice and mercy to all.

God's multiple promises to Abraham took over 730 years to be partially realized. Through Abraham God laid the foundation for Israel to be a great nation. Moses discipled Israel with principles and precepts revealed from heaven. The full realization of the promises could occur only after Christ's atonement, resurrection and the outpouring of the Holy Spirit. Jesus explained his crucifixion: it was like a grain of wheat that dies in order to reproduce. Jesus died so that He might reproduce Himself in His disciples. Christ's disciples must internalize all that Christ's atonement has redeemed so that His kingdom is established in us and on the earth. Jesus defeated Satan judicially by His death, resurrection and ascension. He gave executive power and authority to His disciples to enforce the judicial victory won at Calvary. Christ's kingdom comes on earth only as His disciples exercise their executive power to teach the nations to obey all God's commands from Genesis to Revelation.

Through Moses God Built His Nation Upon the Foundations Laid through Abraham

At the end of his life Moses reminded Israel:

See, I have taught you decrees and laws as the Lord my God commanded me, so that you may follow them in the land you are entering to take possession of it. Observe them carefully, for this will show your wisdom and understanding to the nations, who will hear about all these decrees and say, "Surely this great nation is a wise and understanding people." What other nation is so great as to have their gods near them the way the Lord our God is near us whenever we pray to him? And what other nation is so great as to have such righteous decrees and laws as this body of laws I am setting before you today? (Deut 4:5-8)

Moses went on to teach ancient Israel the secret of becoming a great nation:

"So commit yourselves wholeheartedly to these words of mine. Tie them to your hands and wear them on your forehead as reminders. Teach them to your children. Talk about them when you are at home and when you are on the road, when you are going to bed and when you are getting up. Write them on the doorposts of your house and on your gates, so that as long as the sky remains above the earth, you and your children may flourish in the land the Lord swore to give your ancestors." (Deut 11:18-21)

Israel had grown from 70 descendants of Abraham to over 3 million people who lived as slaves in Egypt for over 300 years. God chose Moses to deliver and disciple Israel. Following their deliverance from slavery of Egypt, God spent 40 years discipling Israel in the desert. Through Moses God instructed Israel to establish a religious system which taught them how to relate to God, to each other and to the earth. Divine instructions benefitted their relationships in marriage, family and parenting. God instructed them in government, education, economics, agriculture, science, medicine, communication, the arts, diet and hygiene. He taught them a wide range of systems and subsystems. Every instruction was designed for Israel to become great, to prosper and be successful, personally and nationally.

Israel became a numerous, displaced people-group who had to migrate through a desert. They were called to conquer sinful nations in Canaan that sacrificed their children to false gods instead of nurturing them. God punished their sins by asking Israel to possess the land, develop it and become a great nation so that all the nations may learn that God does not want their children's blood. He wants them to love and build up their children. Later, when the Israelites began to sacrifice their own children to false gods, the living God brought Assyrians and Babylonians to destroy and enslave Israel until they learn repentance.

Hundreds of years of slavery in Egypt had impoverished Israelites materially and intellectually. They were oppressed, uneducated and illiterate. They had no knowledge or understanding of the systems required to build a great nation that could flourish in sustainable ways. The challenge of developing as a free nation that governs itself well, needed to begin with finding their true identity. As a people no longer enslaved, they had to become a people dependent on God. The exodus from slavery meant that they no longer had a king or master. Therefore they needed to internalize God's law in their hearts to govern themselves. Egypt governed them with the fear of man. Freedom could work only if they learned to fear God.

It took 40 years in the wilderness for God to teach Israel how to be a nation. God made Moses their Academic Pastor - not just their liberator. Moses had to listen to God in order to teach truths that could transform a bunch of slaves into a wise nation. Exodus 33: 7-10 tells us that,

> *Moses used to take a tent and pitch it outside the camp some distance away, calling it the "tent of meeting." Anyone inquiring of the Lord would go to the tent of meeting outside the camp. And whenever Moses went out to the tent, all the people rose and stood at the entrances to their tents, watching Moses until he entered the tent. As Moses went into the tent, the pillar of cloud would come down and stay at the entrance, while the Lord spoke with Moses. The Lord would speak to Moses face to face, as one speaks to a friend.*

On occasions Moses disappeared for days to be alone with God on a mountain peak. Exodus 34: 29-30 tells us,

> *When Moses came down from Mount Sinai with the two tablets of the covenant law in his hands, he was not aware that his face was radiant because he had spoken with the Lord. When Aaron and all the Israelites saw Moses, his face was radiant, and they were afraid to come near him.*

After Moses, for centuries God continued teaching Israel the way to life through judges. Then God gave them David and Solomon to make Israel the healthiest, wealthiest, happiest and greatest nation on the earth. All through this long period God kept inspiring individuals to record Israel's failures, repentance and successes. These scriptures, including what was written by David and Solomon, enabled Israel to fulfill their prophetic destiny of being a blessing to other nations. God's word taught the world the wisdom of God's ways, His justice and righteousness. History records:

> *"And kings from every nation sent their ambassadors to listen to the wisdom of Solomon."* (1 Kings 4:34)

The Queen of Sheba exclaimed to the king:

> *"Everything I heard in my country about your achievements and wisdom is true! I didn't believe what was said until I arrived here and saw it with my own eyes. In fact, I had not heard the half of it! Your wisdom and prosperity are far beyond what I was told. How happy your people must be! What a privilege for your officials to stand here day after day, listening to your wisdom! Praise the Lord your God, who delights in you and has placed you on the throne of Israel. Because of the Lord's eternal love for Israel, he has made you king so you can govern with justice and righteousness."* (1 Kings 10:6-9)

Solomon asked God for an understanding heart (discernment), so that he could govern Israel in justice and righteousness. God was pleased with Solomon's request and therefore also gave him wisdom, riches and honor. (1 Kings 3:9,14)

Israel began to experience the blessings promised to Abraham and through Moses. It became a model, a prototype of a transformed nation as they obeyed God's Word:

> *"The Lord will set you high above all other nations.*
> *You will lend to other nations but not need to borrow.*
> *The Lord will make you the head, not the tail.*
> *You will always be at the top, never at the bottom."* (Deut 28:1-14)

The Hub of Education

The most important question for the 21st century is: What will serve as the hub of education — human ideology or divine revelation?

Beginning with *"Let there be light"* in Genesis 1:3, the entire Bible is inspired by God for humanity's education. We can know truth because God has revealed it. For this reason: to educate our children in God's ways means to make theology the hub of all education. All wisdom and knowledge within each sphere needs to be a spoke firmly connected to the hub — the knowledge of God. Humanist education makes human folly the hub of God-less education. The 20th century has already experienced the horrors of that choice.

Nazi Ideology

Hitler understood the significance of moulding students' minds. Therefore Public Enlightenment and Propaganda influenced every aspect of Nazi Germany. Education of the youth became Nazism's first agenda. When Hitler wrote *Mein Kampf* or *My Struggle* he was serving out a prison sentence at Landsberg. He opined "whoever has the youth has the future". He insisted that "Youth belongs to us and we will yield them to no one."

> *'I begin with the young. We older ones are used up. We are rotten to the marrow. But my magnificent youngsters! Are there any finer ones in the world? Look at these young men and boys! What material. With them I can make a new world. My teaching will be hard. Weakness will be knocked out of them. A violently active, dominating, brutal youth – that is what I am after. Youth must be indifferent to pain. There must be no weakness and tenderness in it. I want to see once more in its eyes the gleam of pride and independence of the beast of prey. I will have no intellectual training. Knowledge is ruin to my young men. I would have them learn only what takes their fancy. But one thing they must learn – self-command. They shall learn to overcome their fear of death under the severest tests. This is the heroic stage of youth. Out of it will come the creative man, the god-man." (Adolf Hitler Letter and Notes?)*

The Nazis implemented Hitler's strategy as soon as they had won power. They began infiltrating schools and education. Jews and others who didn't agree with the National Socialist agenda for education, were marginalized. Curricula were revised to indoctrinate the next generation with Nazi ideology and values.

Louis Snyder, the author of *Roots of German Nationalism*, says:
> "The ultimate purpose of education was to fashion citizen's conscience of the glory of the country and filled with fanatical devotion to the national cause. National Socialism would furnish the necessary elite for the nation."

If the young were going to belong to the Nazi Party, then the very youngest were targeted for an education based on Hitler's educational philosophy. Hitler required schools to push national pride and race issues within the lessons taught, regardless of the age of the pupils. Every spoke of the wheel of knowledge had to connect to Nazi ideology. So, *History* became historicism – the study of history for political purposes. It taught Nazi values and assumptions, reinforcing the myth of Aryan supremacy. History books were filled with tales of Germanic heroes and warriors, political leaders and military conquests.

Biology was used as a vehicle to push race ideas, 'enlightening' children about Aryan supremacy and the despicable traits of untermensch (sub-human people and races).

Nazi education used Physical Education to develop a child's physical well-being, at the service of the ideology.

In July 1926, a young party member named Kurt Gruber established the Hitler Youth. Nazi youth policy also revolved around several party-run youth groups such as the Hitler Youth for boys aged 14-18. These groups began haphazardly but were eventually organized on a national level by the National Socialist German Workers' Party (NSDAP).

Nazi youth groups combined paramilitary style training and skills with National Socialist teachings and indoctrination, such as worship of Hitler and the significance of racial purity.

There were also several NSDAP-run girls' groups, such as the Bund Deutscher Madel or BDM. These groups also circulated Nazi ideology and reinforced traditional conceptions about the roles of women.

Communism Embraces the Bible's Emphasis on Education

The People's Republic of China makes no distinction between education and Propaganda or indoctrination. It makes indoctrinating the next generation through education a primary communist strategy.

Vladimir Lenin, who won Russia for Communism, is famous for saying: "Give me just one generation of youth, and I'll transform the whole world." Lenin was following Karl Marx who prescribed the strategy of making a nation Communist: "The education of all children, from the moment they can get along without a mothers care, shall be in the state institutions at the state expense."

New Age Ideology

Alice Bailey (1880-1949) and her husband Foster were leaders in the Theosophical Society. They founded the *Lucifer Trust* and edited Messenger magazine. Alice Bailey, one of the first writers to use the phrase "New Age", wrote out a ten-point plan in "Discipleship in the New Age Volume 2" to destroy Christianity. Here is a summary of her proposals:

1) Take God and prayer out of the education system;
2) Reduce parental authority over the children;
3) Destroy the Judeo-Christian family structure or the traditional Christian family structure;
4) If sex is free, then make abortion legal and make it easy;
5) Make divorce easy and legal, free people from the concept of marriage for life;
6) Make homosexuality an alternative lifestyle;
7) Debase art, make it run mad;
8) Use media to promote and change mindsets;
9) Create an interfaith movement; and
10) Get governments to set all these into law, and get the churches to endorse these changes.

Expanded versions of Alice Bailey's ten-point plan are available on the internet. One hundred years ago these ideas were ridiculed, but now every point is being realized in Western culture. Governments, education systems, media, arts and entertainment spheres have embraced this ideology.

As the first chapter in this volume points out, Martin Luther began re-forming Europe by discipling the next generation through education. He realized that God's will cannot be done on earth unless everyone knows God's Word and serves Him as priest and king. The goal of getting every-one to serve God as His child required the church to take responsibility for education. It also made theology the mother or the hub of all other sciences.

Every Protestant reformer who followed Luther — Zwingly, Katharina and Bullinger in Zurich, Melanchthon in Whittenberg, Calvin and Beza in Geneva, Knox and Melville in Scotland, John Amos Comenius in London, Sweden and Amsterdam, saw education as the means of discipling nations.

Originally America's great universities such as Harvard, Yale and Princeton were based on the Geneva Academy and Immanuel College in Cambridge. Western civilization is disintegrating because it has made "man the mea-sure of all things." Yet the Church can reform the West by redeeming education and making it a pursuit of truth and righteousness.

Needed: a New Reformation

Revival involves turning the hearts of the fathers to the children. God cares for children. Therefore He promised through the prophet Malachi:
> *"See, I will send you the prophet Elijah before that great and dreadful day of the Lord comes. He will turn the hearts of the fathers to their children, and the hearts of the children to their fathers; or else I will come and strike the land with a curse."* (Malachi 4:5-6)

This prophecy was initially fulfilled in John the Baptist. However, the spir-itual principle it stated is ongoing. When the prophets, priests and kings of a nation forget God, their nation is cursed. When they, as fathers, turn the hearts of the children towards the heavenly Father, their nations are blessed.

Hezekiah was ill, Isaiah came and told him he was about to die. Hezekiah cried out to the Lord and received a fifteen year extension. Isaiah then told Hezekiah that all the generational inheritance stored up by his forefathers would be taken to Babylon, your sons will be made eunuchs and made to serve in the palace of Babylon's king. Hezekiah said to Isaiah, the word of the Lord is good, but in his heart, all this evil is meant for the future, at least I will have peace and security in my lifetime. (2 Kings 20). We need spiritual fathers and leaders who care more for their children and future generations than they do for their own peace and security.

We need a revival. That means we need the Spirit of Elijah to awaken the fathers in our nations to turn their hearts towards the children. If they do, the hearts of the children will be turned towards the fathers and towards Father God. Then they will experience His favour and blessing in every sphere of influence.

Deuteronomy is the second giving of the law. It was written about 40 days before Israel crossed the Jordan to possess the promised land. God's concern for Israel was two-fold. Obedience and teaching the next generation to obey, so they would experience all God's promised covenant blessings.

But after Joshua and the elders died, the next generation didn't obey. The older generation had not taught the younger generation to know the Lord neither all that God had done for them.

> *After that whole generation had been gathered to their fathers, another generation grew up, who knew neither the Lord nor what he had done for Israel. Then the Israelites did evil in the eyes of the Lord and served the Baals. They forsook the Lord, the God of their fathers, who had brought them out of Egypt. They followed and worshiped various gods of the peoples around them.* (Judges 2:10 -12)

Jesus authorized His disciples to make disciples of nations, to immerse nations into the essence of the nature and authority of the Father, Son and Holy Spirit. Discipling and immersing nations would be achieved by teaching nations all Jesus commanded, from Genesis to Revelation.

Jesus only authorized His disciples to make disciples of nations and immerse nations. The only authorized curricula are the truths of God's Word. Therefore all others are unauthorized and all curricula not founded on the truths of God's Word is illegal. When Jesus disciples abdicate their authority and vacate their role of responsibility, unauthorized people use illegal ideologies to disciple the nations.

To effectively disciple the nations requires the church to disciple the nations through the sphere of education, with kingdom ideology.

This tragic cycle was often repeated in Israel's history. Then repeated in church history. Now it is being repeated in our nations that were built on God's Word. The Kingdom education revolution offers a strategy to the church to reclaim the sphere of education from the spirit of the antichrist and make God's enemies His footstool.

Chapter 22

Indonesia: How Education Revolution Began

Takim Andriono[1]

"Education is the most powerful weapon, which you can use to change the world."
- Nelson Mandela

Indonesia is now the world's fourth most populous nation, with 267 million people, consisting of more than three hundred ethnic groups scattered across thousands of islands. As World Bank Indonesia notes, currently our country has the world's 10th largest economy in terms of Purchasing Power Parity (PPP), and is a member of the G-20.

Yet Indonesia struggles with great inequality. Recently President Jokowi formulated a policy to accelerate the development of sixty-two "left behind" regions, mostly with a Christian majority, such as Papua, East Nusa Tenggara and Maluku. The Human Development Index in these regions is far below the national average. In fact before Indonesia declared independence in 1945, East Nusa Tenggara and Maluku were known for their quality Christian schools, founded by local churches. In the past, Indonesian Christian schools contributed a lot to the country. Many national leaders, including non-Christians, graduated from these institutes. Unfortunately many are now struggling to survive.

Although Indonesia still has a number of quality schools, even with international reputations, and some of them are Christian, the OECD's Program for International Student Assessment (PISA) reveals serious problems. This assessment gives Indonesia among the lowest scores in Reading (Literacy), Mathematics, and Science. Morality is also a critical issue. As reported by Transparency International, the Corruption Perception Index

---

1 Dr. Takim Andriono is Chairman of TRAMPIL Indonesia Foundation and Visi & Misi Education Foundation, Advisory Board Member of University of the Nations, Board Member of Petra Christian Schools, Advisor of the Council of Christian Education in Indonesia (East Java Chapter).

of Indonesia in 2019 was a mere 40 out of 100, putting Indonesia 85th among 179 surveyed countries.

It has long been noted that education in Indonesia needs a major reform, if not a revolution. This is especially true for Christian education. One can say that, without dramatic changes, the continued existence and contribution of these schools lies in doubt.

The technological revolution, and more recently the COVID-19 pandemic, have caused major disruptions to schools around the world. Changes have far outpaced the capacity of current governing systems to respond. As recognized by many researchers, a top-down approach to designing and implementing education reform is no longer ideal.

The Indonesian Ministry of Education and Culture thus recently formulated new policies to encourage educators and communities to be involved in this innovation. The initiative that I will describe in this chapter comes in response to such felt needs. It is also a response to a Christian vision to revolutionize education and place it back in the hands of a newly-awakened Church.

The Incubation Period: From Vision to Experimentation (2009 - 2010)

"The only thing worse than being blind is having sight and no vision."
- Helen Keller

An important vision was introduced during the 2009 Asia-Pacific Transformation Conference (APTC) in Jakarta. And the visionary is the Co-editor of this book, an Indian philosopher, Vishal Mangalwadi. His advice prompted an education revolution that has been rumbling across Indonesia for the past decade.

The focus of this conference was on the need to transform nations in seven spheres, including Education. During a group session, conference participants were clustered into groups according to their spheres of interest. A number of Christian educators and observers gathered in one room to discuss crucial problems of education in Indonesia. (I was not present, but became involved soon afterwards, when Dr. Iman Santoso shared Vishal's vision with me.)

Among other topics, participants discussed how many Christian schools in rural districts had experienced serious setbacks since the 1970s. Many had been closed due to a lack of resources and the founding of new public schools which charged little for tuition.

Indonesia is an archipelago with some 17,000 islands (six thousand inhabited). In recent decades, disparity in education quality has increased between schools in major cities and in the countryside, also in Java or on other islands, especially in regions where Christians are the majority (we refer to these regions as "Pearls of the Archipelago").

Along with Catholic schools, there are more than 5,000 Protestant schools throughout Indonesia, belonging to some 500 foundations, registered members of the Council of Christian Education in Indonesia. About ten percent are located in major cities. Most of these schools serve pupils from the middle class or above, although they also provide scholarships for the needy. In addition, the Association of Christian Universities and Colleges in Indonesia includes 49 members, aside from seminaries and Bible colleges.

Churches founded almost all these institutions. Unfortunately many are no longer well nurtured by their founding churches. Some have become essentially secular, with only Christian names to mark their origin.

After listening to an outpour of concerns, with no great break- through solutions offered, Vishal shared his vision on how to revitalize Christian education. Since Indonesia is an archipelago, church-based e-learning would be the best solution, he suggested. Children can learn at churches. An "academic pastor" (AP) can mentor them while high-quality materials arrive digitally from distant teachers.

Dr. Iman Santoso, one of the initiators of the 2009-APTC and the coordinator of the Transformation-Connection Indonesia (TCI), shared Vishal's vision with many Christian educators, including myself. Upon receiving this vision, which I believe came from the Lord, I became deeply enthusiastic, especially since I had just started a pilot project for training Christian principals on-line, still a new concept at the time.

Several meetings were then held in Jakarta to further clarify this vision. Our team in Surabaya, East Java, together with Romi Budiarjo, my co-worker at that time, started to implement the vision. We began to try our wings. The Information-Communication Technology Learning Centre was set up on the grounds of the Indonesia Christian Church in Jombang, East Java, about 80 kilometers from Surabaya. To provide a good internet service, a Base Transceiver Station (BTS) was prepared with a 50 meter antenna. Some teachers who served at schools run by the church, gathered in this center once a week so as to be equipped by Christian Education experts from Surabaya and other cities. Vishal and Iman had visited at different times prior to the 2010 Asia-Pacific Transformation Conference in Jakarta. This experiment showed that the technology and general concept were viable.

Start-Up Period: From Experimentation to Realization (2010 - 2013)

"Success is the progressive realization of a worthy goal or ideal"
- Earl Nightingale

In early 2011 Mangalwadi was invited to speak as a guest lecturer at the Graduate School of Community Development, University of Nations, at Youth With a Mission in Kona, Hawaii. The students of this school were located in several countries across many time zones. Again, a blended learning mode was used. Material was made available in a Learning Management System: face-to-face lectures were conducted at the Kona campus while being broadcast via teleconference to distant students. Since Vishal thought the Indonesian team should get a "feel" of this style, he invited me to attend his sessions in Kona for two weeks in order to learn and experience the blended process.

During this visit, I met Loren Cunningham and other YWAM leaders and received moral support in the form of a commitment by the University of Nations to help the movement in Indonesia, especially by training ICT Learning Centre facilitators.

A government regulation was enacted requiring all presently serving teachers to obtain at least a Bachelor's Degree in Education within five-years (2012-2020) as a minimum qualification. Thousands of teachers in Christian schools lacked that qualification. We decided to set this need as our top priority. With such a scattered population, access to tertiary education was almost impossible unless teachers moved to major cities which had colleges of education, to pursue their degrees. Furthermore, these teachers would need scholarships in that case, since most did not earn enough to afford the fees. Church-based e-learning looked like the ideal solution.

And so a formal task force, called Transformation through Education using E-Learning (TRAMPIL from the Indonesian words) was established under the Council of Christian Education in Indonesia. This team aimed at first to work with Christian teacher colleges and local churches to meet this need. However, not even education colleges were allowed to offer degree programs while using distance learning without a special permit. The Ministry of Education and Culture suggested that we collaborate with the Open University, a tertiary state institution assigned to conduct distanced learning across the country.

In order to form this public-private partnership, a legal entity was founded in February 2013 called TRAMPIL Indonesia Foundation. It was agreed that the Open University would provide a Bachelor's Degree in Education, using a blended learning mode. Participants would learn independently and meet face-to-face during weekends. Half the classes would be taught by Open University instructors, the other half by TRAMPIL, which would equip participants in such central matters as Biblical Foundation of Teaching, Christ-like character development, and some contemporary issues in education. Face-to- face sessions were carried out with TRAMPIL via web-conferences.

Under this legal structure, TRAMPIL set up ICT Learning Centers in various locations, using rooms in churches or Christian schools. At each center two local people were selected to serve part-time as learning and technical facilitators. These facilitators were trained spiritually and technically. Leaders from the University of the Nations leaders, such as Mark Brokenshire and Christine Colby, led teams to Indonesia to assist in these trainings. TRAMPIL invited local pastors to serve as learning facilitators. However, only a few committed to this ministry. Most facilitators were therefore selected from among principals, senior teachers and IT technicians. Having set up centers and facilitators, TRAMPIL began to recruit and select participants, teachers serving Christian kindergarten and primary schools.

A Period of Challenge (2013 - 2019)

"God's work done in God's way will never lack God's supply"
- Hudson Taylor

TRAMPIL sent teams to the target regions to carry out tests and interviews. Each candidate was required to submit two letters of recommendation - from their school principal or board chairperson - and from their pastor. With this relatively strict selection process, we hoped that all participants would be able to maintain themselves as eligible recipients of scholarships from TRAMPIL until they completed their studies and obtained the required degree.

The project did not always run smoothly. Teachers encountered numerous roadblocks. Some husbands insisted that their wives should resign after one or two semesters from joining the program, in order to attend to family matters. Other students gave up for other reasons. Out of 1200 participants, only around a third (410 participants) were successfully approaching the finishing line. To date 330 participants have graduated and another eighty are due to graduate soon. It is no easy matter to juggle parenting and teaching obligations with part- time studies. We found that serious commitment is vital to success.

Most participants were teachers with low salaries serving Christian schools in rural areas, so scholarships were needed to pay tuition fees to Open University and for biblical training. TRAMPIL is grateful for the financial support provided by a mega-church and several others. Unfortunately the biggest portion of this initial support was terminated after two semesters, leaving TRAMPIL in financial difficulty. The staff of TRAMPIL then learned to depend more deeply upon God's providence. It seems fitting to offer a tribute to the late Mr. Suwadji Widaja, a member of our Board of Trustees. He encouraged his family members and church to take part in this ministry by giving scholarships to two hundred participants. Eventually all debts, which exceeded $1 million, were paid off by the end of 2019.

During this challenging period, TRAMPIL also faced and overcame technical problems, such as poor internet connections in some areas, ICT equipment which expired earlier than advertised, and lack of commitment among some facilitators. We see all these problems as lessons learned on the path to growth.

The Development Period: Learning to Bear More Fruit
(2019 and Beyond)

"I am the vine; you are the branches. Whoever abides in me and I in him, he it is that bears much fruit, for apart from me you can do nothing"
- John 15:5 (ESV)

COVID-19 has disrupted schools and universities around the globe and forced people to relocate academics from campus to home. Suddenly, students everywhere are relying on digital technology. Web-conferences are used daily by teachers and students - from preschool and onwards. So far no one knows exactly when this situation will end. It has been a period of struggle for many but, in retrospect, this crisis may prove to be a blessing in disguise.

At the end of 2019 the Ministry of Education and Culture (MOEC) of Indonesia launched a new policy called "Freedom of Learning" to improve education on a broader and more equitable basis. One strategy is to prepare 10,000 K-12 model schools. TRAMPIL was selected by MOEC, due to its successful track record, to serve as one of the NGOs to train teachers and principals of these models. The idea is that the staff of these high-quality schools would then train colleagues serving in the surrounding schools. For the first time, MOEC has embraced a combination of bottom-up and top-down educational models, rather than the conventional hierarchical model. Selected training centers, including TRAMPIL, have been given freedom to propose best practices for training teachers and principals in order to create those model schools.

TRAMPIL sees this new policy as another rumbling of the volcano awakening the Church to join the Education Revolution by developing church-based model schools, especially in rural "Pearls of the Archipelago" regions. Many more churches are expected to open their doors for use as ICT Learning Centers, allowing young people to learn and be equipped to help develop their villages. The shepherds of those churches may also serve as mentors or academic pastors. Meanwhile, Christian university professors and experts, from within Indonesia and overseas, are invited to provide quality learning materials to these Church-based ICT learning centers.

So to date, TRAMPIL has implemented or partnered in implementing three nation-wide programs, and stands at various stages of planning or preparing three more:

1) Learn & Teach We have helped working teachers who need to obtain minimum academic qualifications. Cooperating with the Open University, TRAMPIL has graduated 330 participants, with eighty more due to graduate soon. In addition, TRAMPIL and Open University also run a three-semester program for more than 170 working teachers in Christian kindergarten and primary schools who have a Bachelor's degree in other fields, but still need qualification in Early Childhood or Primary Education. Altogether, then, this aspect of our program has served 580 teachers, not including those forced to drop out.

2) Learn & Educate: We are also working to equip other practicing teachers with more advanced biblical-based training to become more reliable and self-initiating Christian teachers, ready to disciple other teachers. So far some two hundred students have joined this part of our program.

3)Learn & Lead: We partner to train school leaders and other candidates with biblical-based leadership and managerial skills so that they may help their schools become more innovative.

4) Learn & Serve: Another of our goals is to equip students of Christian institutions of higher education with useful biblical-based knowledge and skills so they can serve in rural areas.
5) Learn & Grow: In addition we plan to prepare biblical-based high-quality learning contents for students in needy Christian schools so that they can grow up as well-informed students with Christ-like character.

6) Learn & Develop: Finally, we have the long-term goal of helping young people in rural areas (especially in Pearls of the Indonesian Archipelago) to learn and develop their villages.

So far, TRAMPIL has implemented the first two programs. The Visi & Misi Education Foundation, one of the founding institutions of TRAMPIL, has conducted the third program, i.e. Learn & Lead, since 2009, and has graduated more than two hundred school leaders. Putting these three programs altogether, TRAMPIL and our partners have equipped, or are presently training, more than a thousand teachers and principals.

Jesus said, "I am the vine, you are the branches." To bear fruit, all board members and executives of TRAMPIL must be, like other believers, attached to the vine, daily seeking fresh encounters with the Spirit of God. But as vines spread out, so, by God's grace, we are also growing. The time may be drawing near when this Education Revolution will yield the fruit of a godly and effective education for brothers and sisters across the many islands of Indonesia.

Conclusion:

As can be seen from our experiments in Indonesia, there is no easy path to realizing the full vision of *The Third Education Revolution*. Challenges come to all who seek to implement great visions. For us, the experimental stage was vital in that it gave us time to learn by trial and error and prepare to "vamp up" our programs on a larger scale. We must be prepared to meet those challenges with faith in God, Who will lead the way.

Our first phase is nearing completion and the executive team must now be prepared to take on larger assignments. Momentum is building just as the Ministry of Education and Culture introduces new policies. We invite churches and Christian schools around the world to join this exciting and vital movement with us.

Chapter 23

Education for Transforming Uganda

Bishop Joshua Lwere[1]

Like the rest of Africa, Uganda faces major challenges. We must forthrightly admit that, foremost among those challenges, is corruption, which poisons politics and results in devastating poverty. Before explaining how a revolution in education can transform my country, let me begin with a brief overview of the history of education here.

The Missionary Foundation

Uganda got off on a good footing when formal education was introduced by British and Italian missionaries under the patronage of a local king, Kabaka Mutesa 1, even before the colonial state was born. In June 1877 the Church Missionary Society from England arrived in Uganda. One of the team leaders, Alexander Mackay, was a Scottish Presbyterian engineer. Their approach to Christianity and civilization was rather holistic. The same approach was adopted by the Catholic missionaries.

When Mackay arrived at the East African coast, he decided to construct a road from the coast inland about 230 miles. This was his first major project, though it was cut short when his colleagues started dying of tropical diseases. The second major project was writing the alphabet in the local dialect in order to translate the Bible into the local vernacular. Africans were excited to learn to read and write and in the process many converted from African traditionalism to Christianity. These converts were referred to as "Abasomi", meaning "readers" or "the learned". The only textbook they had by which to practice reading and writing was the Bible. In other words, education was first understood in the context of God, and vice-versa.

----

1 Bishop Joshua Lwere is the General Overseer of about 30,000 National Fellowship of Born Again Pentecostal Churches in Uganda.

The missionaries also taught life skills that were associated with both God and education, including artisan skills like carpentry and hygiene. The African people were so excited to learn these new ideas that the Anglican and Roman Catholic missionaries had brought, that they became a great, committed following. Their devotion was so unwavering that some of them were martyred, willingly enduring death by fire while singing songs of praise to God.

Missionary education targeted the whole person, in tandem with the Hebrew approach to the whole person: heart, head, hands and house (community responsibility). I will elaborate more on this later.

It became fashionable to be a Christian: to be baptized and receive a Christian name, to be officially wed in church and to become a pillar in the Church. Soon it was no longer a response of the heart but the prestige that counted. In addition, traditional beliefs and ancestral worship, deeply ingrained in the people, mixed with Christianity in a syncretistic blend.

After a series of military confrontations between factions in Uganda had broken out, this good foundation was disrupted by bitter rivalry between religious groups. This rivalry greatly affected our understanding of Christianity. Schools were started and religiously segregated. Christian leaders sought to develop all aspects of life, but many cared more about "our religion" than about following biblical principles.

The powerful, sweeping East African Revival of the 1930s infused a new spiritual lease on life but failed to imbue solid biblical discipleship. It produced key social reforms in some areas but not corresponding intellectual results, as had the Welsh Revival and the Great Awakenings in the United States. And so schools became more secular as time went by. The missionary spirit sought to bless Uganda, but some of the curricula were also developed by colonial masters. Sometimes their aim was limited to producing clerks who would serve imperial administrations.

Although Ugandans received independence just under 60 years ago, the education system has not changed much since then. It does not produce people with the knowledge, skills and character to disciple the nation in the 21st century. Throughout the last century, mission schools were progressively converted into government schools (meaning government-aided). The Church relaxed its grip on these institutions which, in the process, became more and more secular, losing spiritual and moral features.

Current Education

We applaud all efforts by the government to improve education. Government has invested heavily in the education sector. According to available statistics, 92% of all parishes in Uganda now have a government-aided primary school, while 71% of all sub-counties have a government-aided secondary school. All major regions of the country now also host a public university. In addition the government has promoted participation of the private sector in education. Due to the Universal Primary and Secondary Education Program initiated by the government in 1997, enrollment increased not only among small children but also in tertiary institutions and universities.

The aggregate impact of all this is an increase in literacy rate to 74%, and to an average of 6.1 years of schooling (Uganda National Development Plan III). However, the education that African nations inherited from their colonial masters remains essentially the same. This undermines anti-colonial rhetoric that paints all white missionaries and rulers as evil. The fact is that African leaders have retained many of the defects from the colonial era.

The most notable of the defects is that the focus lies not on teaching students to learn and imagine a better future, but to pass exams. This leads to a culture of cramming not thinking critically. The average educated person is the one who has crammed and jumped through examination hoops: primary, secondary, tertiary and university. We cram every fact we can find: American agriculture, European history, Asian monarchs - you name it.

Unfortunately most of the accumulated facts cannot be applied to real life. We have countless university-trained scientists and yet we are not inventing anything significant to transform our societies. That is why so many educated people are roaming streets looking for jobs instead of creating them. Every year 40,000 students graduate from universities, yet only 8,000 can be absorbed into the labor market. This is a cause of deep concern and raises many questions about our present education system.

Information Without Formation

Secondly, the African education system focuses on educating the mind (head) and skills (hands) but does not adequately address issues of character (heart) and community consciousness and responsibility (house). We have leaders who are informed but not transformed, and those who are transformed are not informed. For example: our accountants and auditors are so skilled that, when they embezzle funds, they can cover all their audit trails without a trace. They are talented at dipping their hands into the public coffers and looting with impunity what is meant to improve the lives in poor communities.

I think that the secularization of much of the education sector partly explains the high levels of corruption in our country since the moral code has drained from the national consciousness. In the Transparency International 2019 Report, Uganda scored 28 out of 100 and was ranked 137 out of 183 countries among the most corrupt countries in the world. This corruption is not only rampant in the public service but in every sphere. Head is filled, hands are busy, but heart becomes cold, and the house is shoved off its foundation of compassion and community responsibility.

Government has put in place a strong legal framework intended to stamp out corruption but instead, it grows more complex every day. Uganda has among the best anti-corruption and accountability policies and legal frameworks in Africa, yet this has not stopped the vice from spreading like a cancer throughout the body politic. Crooks are well networked and adroit at beating the system. I heard of a case in which the government had spent 80 million shillings in order to investigate the theft of 50 million shillings. The thief pays a few million of his ill-gotten wealth to bribe the investigators, and the nation ended up losing 130 million in total.

Commercializing Education

Education has been commercialized. Schools are considered among the most lucrative businesses and therefore many who invest are motivated first and foremost by monetary gains. Stiff competition for pupils is the order of the day, while passing exams is far more important than the effectiveness of training. Every year the names of the schools that perform best are published in newspapers. The schools with the largest number of students who distinguish themselves can expect the biggest enrollment for the next year. So they hike tuition, knowing that parents must pay. After all, more than 70% of candidates from such schools will be admitted into publicly-sponsored universities.

Students study day and night - not so much to learn to think, improve knowledge and become their Father's image - creative and holy, but mainly to cram answers and pass exams. This practice starts early in kindergarten. As a result, children end up hating the very idea of schooling because of the pressure at school and compulsory home-work, which follows them into the holidays. Any free time has to be used to pump as much learning material into children as possible. Parents pay extra money to teachers to privately coach their children, otherwise they will lag behind.
In a bid to curb this trend, the government banned holiday coaching with serious penalties for those who fail to obey. However, parents and teachers creatively find ways around the rules. With such mindless competition, it seems that more tests are taken than learning achieved. Most children pass exams but know little, and graduate half-baked. And so more semi-skilled youths join the labor market. There is a critical mismatch between education and the demands of the market. Consequently, progressive organizations employ foreigners in managerial positions while Ugandans, irrespective of paper credentials, take unskilled employment.

Uganda has the lowest literacy and numeracy levels in East Africa. The low quality of education, and a high school dropout rate of 38.5 %, means that drop-outs need to be retrained to meet the labor demand, or we will waste the "demographic dividend", the boost in economic productivity that a young population with lowering fertility rates should bring.

The Evangelical Church

Evangelizing Africa has been the global Church's commendable obedience. But the indigenous church it produced has become anti-intellectual and escapist. So many souls are saved but Africa is not progressing apace - socially, economically or politically. The modern Church emphasizes evacuation over occupation (Luke 19:13). It focuses exclusively on heaven and portrays a Jesus who comes back to take individual souls to their mansions in heaven, but lacks the interest or power to improve the slums and transform nations.

That Gospel rightly promotes moral and ethical values for personal piety, but neglects our mandate to transform government, markets, schools, literacy dens and science labs. The Great Commission is reduced to saving souls, without discipling the soul of the nations where those souls dwell. Therefore, the modern evangelical Gospel fails to equip the church to guide the nation. It is an individualistic, introverted and narcissistic Gospel mostly about blessing me but with no power to reform, heal or bless the community, and therefore recognized as almost irrelevant to public life.

This is the challenge we are trying to address in Uganda before we embark on the education revolution. The Church has to first recognize her role in society.

Does Uganda need an Education Revolution?

With that in mind: does Uganda need an Education Revolution? The answer is an emphatic yes! Uganda needs schooling that will marry truth and virtue, character with information and skills. But even more: we need Christian education with a holistic take on the Great Commission.

One could say that we have focused on national hardware but have neglected the software. Our focus has been on how to maximize natural resources, minerals, agriculture, tourism, industries, infrastructure and increased revenue collection, but we neglected to develop our people by re-forming them into the image of God..

Our greatest treasure is not natural- but human resources. A country that does not invest in its human capital, mortgages its future to foreigners. Well-educated, enlightened and healthy humans are essential to sustainable development. This has been proven by nations like Singapore, which was poorer than many nations in Africa at the time of our independence in the early 1960s. But now, with hardly any natural resource, Singapore has prospered by building human capital. Currently at 88%, Singapore's Human Development Index (HDI) is the highest in the world. (World Bank: Human Development Index, 2020). In the same report Uganda was classified in the lowest HDI category. Uganda's Human Capital Index (HCI) is 38%, implying that, with the current state of education and health, a child born in Uganda today is expected to achieve only 38% of his or her productive potential by age 18. This is a serious problem!

The Uganda Vision 2040 identifies human capital development as the key to allowing our young workforce to fully develop the country.

A 2016 report by UNICEF showed that about 2.4 million Ugandan children (6% of our population) were stunted - an effect which cannot be reversed. 68.9% of our population is still dependent on subsistence farming, and 76% live in rural areas (World Bank, 2019). This is in spite of massive investments over almost six decades. Alarmingly, many of these investments have come through foreign aid and high interest long-term loans which our children and grandchildren will continue to pay long after we are gone.

If our education and health systems only help our people achieve 38% of their potential, then clearly that education needs dramatic change. This responsibility should not be left to the government alone, but should be shared by the Church.

Even worse than physical stuntedness: we face the moral and ethical retardation of our population. Our schools neglect character development. Rather, we focus on:

Level	Emphasis
Primary	Literacy and numeracy skills
Secondary	Problem solving
Tertiary	Competence and skills
University	Research and innovation

When a Ugandese student graduates from university, the education he or she has received has centered around knowledge (head) and skills (hands), but has neglected character formation and social responsibility. The Education revolution we envisage will develop the whole person.

The vocation of teaching is to educate the nation in the divine truth which permeates all aspects of life. Satan seeks to deceive the world (John 8:44; Revelation 12:9) and has founded his worldly strongholds upon lies of every kind. God counters those lies with His truth which permeates every sphere of society (Matthew 28; 1 Timothy 2:4; Habakkuk 2:14). As Jesus has said: "The reason I was born and came into the world is to testify to the truth. Everyone on the side of truth listens to me." (John 18:37).

In order to fulfil the Cultural or Dominion Mandate (Gen 1:26-28) and the Great Commission (Mat 28:18-20) we must view education holistically as the means to communicate truth in every sphere of society. I agree with the comprehensive approach which Dr. Stephen McDowell takes to the Great Commission: seeing education as God's main tool to transmit His truth to the nations.

God Wishes All Men to Know the Truth

All Christian activities, including education, are ultimately mandated by the Great Commission. The Great Commission is recorded in all four gospels, each emphasizing a different aspect. Mark focuses on individuals, while Matthew focuses on nations.

> "And Jesus came to them and spoke to them, saying, All authority has been given to me in heaven and on earth. Go ye therefore, and make <u>disciples</u> of all the <u>nations</u>, … <u>teaching</u>… <u>whatsoever I commanded</u> you …" (Mat 28:18-19).

So for the past fifteen years we have asked ourselves what we need to do in order to disciple Uganda as a model nation. Since the fall of Idi Amin there has been an evangelistic revival across the country, but with little discipleship. But Jesus told his disciples to "teach all nations whatever I commanded you" - which implies the central role of education.

We are called to influence all society with truth, so that the knowledge of the Lord may fill the whole earth as the waters cover the sea (Habakkuk 2:14; Isaiah 11·9). God desires all men (a) "to be saved" and (b) "to come to the knowledge of the truth." (I Tim. 2: 4-5).

This means that we are called to prepare students to touch every sphere of life with the Grace of God, including these ten:

1) Church: Seek and receive truth through revelation.
We will produce reformers in coming generations. Every major move of God is preceded by a special revelation and a release of God's special grace upon that generation.

2) Family: Model truth through love.

God anchored education in the family, starting with every father (Deut. 6:7). Education is primarily the role of the family, whereby parents model truth to their children in a loving environment. The Pilgrims saw education as one of the four major pillars of society and defined the essence of education as the wisdom of maturity meeting obedience from the youth. The New Testament reveals love as the aim (or goal) of all forms of education (1Timothy 1:5).

3) Science: Discover truth.

God's truth is revealed through three books: His words, His reason in us, and His works (Romans 1:20) which can be explored through science. Truths about the universe, nature and culture can be discovered by observation. Jesus reprimanded the Pharisees that they fail to know the scriptures (the book of His Words) or the power of God (the book of His Works). The Lord expects us to discover truth through observation of His works. When we study biology, for example, the anatomy of man and the twelve systems that make the human body, we echo the Psalmist, who marveled about how man is fearfully and wonderfully made (Psalms 139:5). In the same way when we study astronomy and observe with the Psalmist the moon and the stars which God has ordained (Psalms 8), we discover truth and end in worship (Psalms 111:2). We are to teach students to observe and discover truth through science, which leads to worship of the Creator.

4) Technology: Apply Truth.

The truth discovered through science can be applied to improve life. As Sue Victor (1120AD) said, we need technology to supplement our physical weakness which came as a result of the fall and subjected us to the punishment of toil. But more than that: by exercising dominion over nature, we confirm the dignity of having been created in the image of God.

5) Humanities: Interpret Truth

Humanities is the study of society, culture and how people process and document their experience of the world through philosophy, history, language, literature, art, music, etc. If our students interpret human experience in the light of God's work, they will see history as "His Story." This will produce Christians whose worldview is comprehensive like that of St. Augustine, who was the first Christian to offer a comprehensive philosophy of history. Augustine described the two cities of Babylon and

Jerusalem, whose conflict runs down through history, lending the story of man its ultimate significance.

6) **Business:** Truth in the Market

We have been called to stewardship till Jesus returns (Luke 19:13). The New KJV says, "Do business till I come." These words were spoken in the parable of talents, in which Christ emphasizes that the portion allotted to each of us can be multiplied.In business we illustrate truth through creativity,faithful stewardship, entrepreneurship and management capability. God wants us to create wealth and to use it to bless those around us. Believers who understood this call have greatly blessed their communities and nations. Businessmen (like Cyrus McCormick, the founder of International Harvester, who donated $10,000 to help Dwight Moody found the YMCA among other causes) understood their calling and greatly blessed their own and subsequent generations.

7) **Reform:** Contend for the Truth

The enemy seeks to drown out the truth in lies, leading to oppression of the weak and the voiceless. By preaching the truth we set captives free. But often we contend with forces that hold whole communities in bondage. Students need to understand that we cannot sit back when truth is trodden underfoot. It is not Christian to keep silent when people are oppressed. Edmund Burke famously said: "All that evil needs to flourish is when good people do nothing." Godly men must rise up and lead movements to liberate the oppressed. So William Wilberforce in England and Charles Finney in America sought to liberate slaves; Alexander Mackay in Uganda insisted on teaching the people practical skills; William Carey helped end the burning of widows in India; and Martin Luther King Jr.protested against racial segregation during the Civil Rights Movement in the American South.

8) **Education, Media & Arts:** Communicate Truth

The truth of God should be imparted by the most effective means possible under the power and anointing of the Holy Spirit.The three best ways to communicate truth are through education, media and arts. Teachers, whether in class, behind a microphone or with brush in hand, should not merely describe facts, but impart life to those to whom they speak. Art is an effective means of communicating truth because it appeals to the senses without being offensive. Whatever falsehoods children are taught in European cities, they need only gaze at the cathedrals that have beautified those cities for centuries, and much of the art inside them, to be reminded of the glory of God. Art speaks to the heart and the subconscious and inspires action. We need to recapture these spheres from the Devil for the glory of God.

9) Government and Law: Conserve truth and Justice
Government influences all spheres of life. That is why the devil is so happy when the church abdicates its divine mandate to lead and dismisses political involvement as too dirty to get involved in.

10) Religion: Worship in Truth.
The Church is called to worship the Lord in Spirit and in Truth (John 4:4). We are therefore expected to raise leaders who will take worship to another level and scale this mountain. In the past Christians have created some of the most glorious music in the world, in many styles and forms, to praise God and to call to Him.

Students should study all three of God's books:
1) Bible: The Book of God's Words - Proverbs 25:2 (Revelation);
2) Conscience: The Book of God's Reason within us -
Romans 2:15 (Conscience)
3) Nature and History: The Book of God's works - Science & Culture - Matthew 22:29 (Observation).

God Targets Whole Nations

Besides desiring all people to be saved, God wants all people to come to the knowledge of the truth. That means education for all. This was the gospel that He preached to Abraham in Genesis 12:1-3 and has remained His ultimate goal (Galatians 3:8).

God carried out His pilot "mass education" project in Israel. When the Jews escaped from Egypt, He gave them the Law and commanded them to study it (Deut. 6). This model was to be replicated elsewhere in order to bless all nations. We are convinced that this is God's will for Uganda. To make education affordable, achievable, accessible and effective, education should meet people at their own level.

The language of the Bible itself is evidence that mass education is God's plan. The Hebrew alphabet had only 22 characters compared to other far more complex written languages of the day. For example, Hittite writing had 375 cuneiform; Akkadian in Mesopotamia had 1,500; Egyptian had 3,000 hieroglyphics. To read Chinese, you should learn about 4-5000 often complex characters. It was a relative cakewalk for the Hebrews to learn to spell out their language. Making it easy to learn, democratizes knowledge and facilitates mass education. But one also requires vision, which the biblical revelation amply supplies:

> For the earth will be filled with the knowledge of the glory of the Lord, as the waters cover the sea. Habakkuk 2:14

A student can graduate with honors with cognitive knowledge of systematic theology yet still be a debased character. The revolution we envisage seeks to inform and transform.

World-Wide Scope

Our goal is to furnish the masses with a biblically-centered education covering every aspect of life: the universal priesthood of believers. We want a renewed education that will <u>permeate</u> all <u>society</u> with <u>truth</u> without necessarily quoting a book and a verse: thinking Bible but speaking Babylonian. Based in every church, it aims to transform every individual, family and community.

This agrees with the Hebrew model that has made the Jewish communities succeed wherever they were. Presently at least twenty percent of Nobel Prize winners are Jewish, and a similar percentage are Ivy League professors.) One of the secrets of the Jewish community is the education model they have maintained throughout the ages. After the Babylonian Captivity, this program evolved into a three-tier education structure (Deus 6:1-9):

Level	Location	Leader
Primary	Home	Every Father (Both parents)
Secondary	Synagogue	Synagogue Leader
University	Temple	Lawyers & Scribes

Every Jewish child had an opportunity to study. One of Israel's major secrets for advancement is that they value holistic education. This is why you find Jewish scholars among the best in every field.

The Church's Obligation

The role of the Church is twofold: theological and practical. Theology informs our philosophy of life which, in turn, molds politics and economics, resulting in appropriate policies and laws.

The reformation in Europe started with a change in theology. Martin Luther discovered by God's revelation that "the just shall live by faith," (Romans 1:17); then the universal priesthood of all believers (1Peter 2:9). He and the other reformers emphasized the "Five Solas."

- Sola scriptura ("by Scripture alone")
- Sola fide ("by faith alone")
- Sola gratia ("by grace alone")
- Solus Christus ("Christ alone")
- Soli Deo gloria ("glory to God alone")

Theological change birthed social change. Fresh revelations emerged from the Word of God to spark revivals and reforms, beginning with godly kings in the Old Testament.

But a theological change in the last 150 years also made the global Church lose her grip on the dominion mandate and she withdrew from culture. The Church lost her universities, think tanks, leadership in science and technology and more. Liberals and atheists first infiltrated the education system with their ideologies before taking over whole institutions, and then society at large.

The Church's neglect or disdain of her theological and intellectual heritage cost her her leadership role, and it cost society deeply, too. The Church allowed an intellectual vacuum to develop which Charles Darwin, Alice Bailey, Karl Marx and others filled, leading to many of the great tragedies of modern times.

The Church needs a fresh revelation of God to regain her leadership position, starting with education. This revelation must be articulated under the anointing of God's Word, preached, taught, explained and defended in the marketplace of ideas in every sphere of influence so that we can influence policy and shape public opinion. That will move the Church from the current victim mentality to the true *"ekklesia"* - a company of people called out to labor here on earth, and rightly influence society on behalf of the Kingdom of God.

I believe that, for the Church in Uganda to bring about the educational revolution we seek, our theology and philosophy will have to change. To recapture education, the Church must regain the original Protestant vision of the Great Commission. A mis-reading of scripture dichotomized the believer's life and reduced the Great Commission to individual benefits. Such a believer is spiritual only in church, but ineffective in transforming the marketplace.

This is where we are placing our emphasis. At a national level we are mobilizing pastors and marketplace leaders to set aside their denominational biases and collaborate for the Kingdom. Our grand vision of discipling the whole nation calls for us to synergize, network and strategize to impact every sphere, including education.

We envision an approach to education that will equip every pastor, local church and student with a biblical worldview that targets the whole person, church, community, city and nation, in every sphere of life.

For a free government to be sustained, people need more than knowledge or facts - they need moral and principled education: Head, Heart, Hands and House.

An ignorant people will quickly become enslaved. Only a well-instructed citizenry can be permanently free (John 8:32). To preserve liberty in a nation, the whole population must understand the principles upon which a free government is based. When they do, they will prevent their leaders from eroding their God-given rights.

Our Goals in Uganda

The Inter-Religious Council brings together the seven leaders of the seven major faiths in Uganda. This council is respected by the government and so we decided to use our clout to weigh in on the current national campaign against corruption. So in a recent three-day retreat, in collaboration with the Uganda Joint Christian Council (UJCC), we discussed our role in education and the campaign against corruption. We invited government agencies mandated to fight vice to participate.

Our unanimous conclusion was that we should take the lead in this fight. After all, government agencies fight corruption mainly in public service, but corrupt people emerge from our churches, families and communities, where these agencies do not exercise direct control.

We also concluded that we must begin the fight against corruption in the classroom. We have to go back and recapture our grip on church institutions of learning, and instil ethical values starting with the little children, right through university.

Most schools in Uganda were started by the Church. Along the way, Christians partly abdicated their responsibility to disciple the youth and surrendered it to the state. But all is not lost yet: most of the population still identifies with either Christianity or Islam. (Christians constitute 84% of the population, and Muslims 13%.) Although the majority does not practice what they profess, most Ugandans respect the things of God.

Some argue that the rule of Idi Amin and the subsequent years of civil war and unrest undermined cultural norms and the family. But leaders are still respected in our country and therefore any effective revolution in our country needs to have them on board. It is still national policy to teach religious education, and our leaders profess to believe in God. We agreed to exploit this window of opportunity. The Uganda Joint Christian Council (UJCC) will meet to decide on a joint strategy. We also agreed to return to the holistic education model based in the teachings of Jesus and biblical truths.

Training the Whole Person

Jesus invoked the whole man when he commanded:
> "Love the Lord your God with all your (Heart) and with all your soul and with all your mind (Head) and with all your strength (Hands). The second is this: Love your neighbor (House) as yourself. There is no commandment greater than these. All the Law and the Prophets hang on these two commandments." (Mark 12:29; Mathew 22:37; Luke 10:29)

We educate the *head, heart, hands* and *house.* The house has to do with community consciousness and social responsibility. That fourfold transformation is how Jesus taught, and how Uganda must be transformed. Again and again we see these four invoked:

> "And David shepherded them with integrity of heart and with skillfulness of *hands* he led them." (Psalms 78:72)
>
> "He who has a clean hands and a pure *heart*, who doesn't lift up his soul [head] to falsehood nor sworn deceitfully." (Psalms 24:3,4)

The Gospel speaks truth to individuals, but recognizes the effect of that truth on relationships. The best way to gauge how effective the gospel is working in our lives is to take note of how we apply what we have learnt in day to day life and how we treat others around us.

Community consciousness, including patriotism, is critical. We have many wealthy people who refuse to help a neighbor struggling for a day's meal. The "filthy-rich" embezzle billions of shillings meant for eradicating poverty among the needy.

Pastors Take the Challenge

In January 2019 the General Assembly of the National Fellowship of Born Again Pentecostal Churches of Uganda was held at Ndejje University in central Uganda. This is an umbrella body of more than 30,000 churches across the nation. I currently serve as the General Overseer, with fourteen bishops under me, but with structured and elected leadership down to the sub counties. We decided to spend most of the time discussing our role in national transformation, especially in education.

I invited Dr. Vishal Mangalwadi to be with us throughout this retreat. He spent the biggest part of this retreat teaching and explaining to the pastors the mandate we have, and the opportunity to use the local church as a platform to educate and disciple the nation. After days of deliberation, we unanimously voted to take up the challenge. A team of professionals under our Education Minister/Department and a few Elders were tasked to operationalize this undertaking. This retreat achieved the following, among other things:

> 1) We agreed that this is our corporate responsibility as the body of Christ.
>
> 2) It is a united, multi-denominational effort.
> We should stay united by this one grand vision, not by narrow denominational interests.
>
> 3) We have the task to educate the whole nation holistically.

4) We may not live to see all the fruit, nor its full effect. So we need to birth a movement that will outlive us.

5) We must return to the biblical core of what education is meant to be.

6) The Education Revolution must transcend mere academic papers or adding courses in universities.

7) We must think beyond short-term financial benefits.

8) Education must be available to all, not only to a privileged few.

9) It will take a reformed Church to educate the Nation.

10) We have to revise our theology and emphases if we are to bring healing and renewal to Uganda.

11) We agreed to strengthen our grip on schools founded by churches.

12) Uganda needs an education revolution in which the Church, through a web-based curriculum, provides high quality, yet affordable education to the masses.

The Challenge

The Inter-Religious Council of Uganda (IRCU) and Uganda Joint Christian Council (UJCC) agree that education must be one means of salvaging the soul of the nation. There are many details still to be hammered out and, no doubt, much discussion about strategies. But we agree, provisionally that these reforms are the path to solving our chief national challenges, especially corruption, and have put a task force in place to blaze the path forward.

The National Fellowship of Born Again Pentecostal Churches of Uganda, the Association which I lead, working with four leading Christian universities, agreed to develop a joint curriculum. Consequently a team, chaired by Dr. Gillian Kasirye, our minister in charge of education, was formed. Under the guidance and continued inspiration of Vishal, they have made good progress. Soon this curriculum will be ready to be presented to the National Council of Higher Education for approval. Besides that a complete business plan is being developed by our experts to roll out this revolution over the next twenty years. We are also reaching out to the various Christian organizations to join us. We now have the full blessing of the Association of Pentecostals and Evangelicals of Uganda (APEU). This association brings together other Christian denominations like Baptists and Presbyterians.

The current government is supporting our efforts. Many people in the Ministry of Education, and elsewhere in the government, are excited about this approach. Our Minister of Education, and also First Lady Janet Museveni, who has served in the Cabinet as Minister of Education and Sports, as well as the deputy ministers under her, are all passionate about restoring moral values to education.

Covid-19: Challenge or Opportunity?

The Covid pandemic, which was intended for evil by the devil, now benefits our cause because it is now easy to explain the need for a web-based program to be rolled out nation-wide. The state is already working on it through the Ministry of Education. While pupils have been unable to go back to school, the government still cannot provide internet-based classes, opting instead to provide a free radio for every household, and two TV sets for every village so that pupils can study again as soon as possible.

Admittedly there are challenges to this approach. In some rural areas men will take these radios away from their families. In addition to a host of other challenges, some families find it hard to buy batteries while some villages lack electricity.

All these challenges help us towards explaining the need to invest in a nation-wide web-based education system as soon as possible. If the Church can provide web-based education, we will be able to lead the nation in its time of need, as we ought to.

A Vision for Uganda

We aim to position Uganda as a model nation for the 21st century Education Revolution. We seek to be a Church that is fully discipled and passionately reaching and discipling nations. We are praying and trusting God that we will not miss any opportunity that He may provide. We especially believe that the problems surrounding the Covid pandemic be turned into opportunities for the Church to disciple the nation. Our God is not limited by anything, much less a virus. We must grasp God's will for the nations. There is no better opportunity than now for the Kingdom of God to flourish. Amen.

Chapter 24

Discipling South America: Getting it Right This Time!

Ricardo Rodriguez[1]

Why have Protestant churches failed to transform the nations of South America? In this chapter, I aim to describe some of the key cultural and historical causes of that failure. I will then present what must be done, pointing to encouraging developments and highlighting the role the Church can play through the reform of education.

The Encounter of Two Worlds

When Spanish conquerors arrived in America in 1492, their vessels were occupied by unaccompanied men. Hundreds of lonely conquistadors had sexual relations with indigenous women from the villages they subdued.[2]

As the Spanish advanced, they encountered agricultural societies with little social development, with men and women who wore simple clothing that barely covered their bodies. Christopher Columbus and his people felt they were meeting creatures inferior to themselves.[3] Europeans would only confront a well-organized empire with high social development in the year 1519, when they entered Aztec lands. That was twenty-seven years after their arrival on San Salvador Island.[4]

---

1 Dr. Ricardo Alberto Rodríguez is Professor of the University of the Nations, Director of the School of Biblical Worldview, Director of the School of Educators in Chile, 2020 and International conference speaker on worldview perspectives in education, politics, economics and the church. He is an Argentinian, living in Chile for the last 41 years.

2 Fábrega C.. (1963). El Mestizaje en América. 08 18, 2015, de Universidad del Bio Bio Sitio web: http://revistas.ubiobio.cl/index.php/TYE/article/view/1986/1862

3 Colon C.. (1880). Cartas que escribió sobre el descubrimiento de América y testamento que hizo a su muerte. 2006, de Biblioteca virtual Miguel de Cervantes

4 Francisco López De Gómara, (1552), *Historia general de las Indias*, edición 2013, editorial Hardpress Publishing .

With this sense of superiority numerous abuses were committed, including slavery. In 1511 the Dominican friar Antonio de Montesino asked:
> "With what right and what justice do you have in such a cruel and horrible servitude these Indians?"[5]

To answer that question Fernando de Aragón summoned a meeting in Spain the next year, called "Junta de Burgos" in which theologians and jurists studied complaints about the treatment of indigenous peoples.[6] The result of this meeting was the approval of the Laws of Burgos - rules that began to regulate the treatment of American-Indians, though they were often ignored.[7]

This "Burgos Gathering" was followed by the so-called "Controversy of Natives" or "Junta de Valladolid" a theological debate between 1550 and 1551. Arguing for the colonists was Gines de Sepulveda, a Catholic priest, philosopher and jurist who claimed that the Spaniards had a right to subdue the Indians in order to culturize and evangelize them:
> "With the perfect right the Spaniards dominate over these Barbarians of the New World and the islands, which in prudence and humanity are as inferior to the Spanish as children are to adults... It is convenient and healthy to be submitted to the empire... They, who barely deserved the title of human beings".[8]

Taking the opposing stance was Friar Bartolome de las Casas. De las Casas argued that Indians should be cared for, because they were God's creatures. The Spanish should respect them and preach the Gospel. Some writers claim that Bartolome de las Casas proposed that the Spanish return the conquered lands and return to Spain.[9]

---

5 José María Iraburu, 2003, *Hechos de los apóstoles de América*, Pamplona, España, Editorial Fundación Gratis Date.

6 Sánchez R.. (Septiembre 01, 2012). Las Leyes de Burgos de 1512. *Revista Jurídica de Castilla y León*, 28, pp 1-55.

7 de las Casas, B.. (2006). *Brevísima relación de la Destrucción de las Indias*. Alicante, Biblioteca virtual Miguel de Cervantes: Universidad de Antioquía.

8 Morán, L.. (2002). Visión del Indio en la obra de Juan Ginés de Sepúlveda. *Revista de Filosofía*, 42, pp, 1-16.

9 Faundes, J. (2012). Fray Bartolomé de las Casas: Testimonio y legado de un hombre luchador. 2012, de Universidad Católica de Temuco Sitio web: http://repositoriodigital.uct.cl/

Sepulveda saw Indians as "little men" and even "homunculi"[10], not fully formed human beings, and his ideas and the ideas of like- minded priests influenced the conquerors. When the Spaniards joined with Indian women, the act was construed as inherently perverse. The conquerors also often had a family in Spain, and was committing adultery. We should not be surprised that he therefore felt doubly ashamed of such a union.

So often, the resulting "mestizo" child was rejected by its European father, accepted by the Indian mother and despised by his indigenous peers. On account of those half-hearted relations many historians trace a certain chill in relations between Latin American men and their children to this day.[11]

In this mix the Spaniard was always male, and the conquered indigenous person was female. I suspect that it is to this that we can trace the root of Latin American Machismo (male dominance). The mestizo is essentially a son without a father, feeling deep rejection.[12] He will seek affirmation in affection and appreciation at home, subjugating his wife, but also look for other women outside the home.

It is not a surprise that a deep inferiority complex developed as a result of European power. Sadly, this rejection and abandonment, coupled with a search for validation due to the lack of a father, continues to affect millions of men and women in South America to this day.

----

10 Sepúlveda J.G. (1987). Democrates Alter de Justis Belli Causis Apud Indios. Edición bilingüe latin-español: Tratado sobre las Justas Causas de la Guerra contra los Indios. México: Fondo de Cultura Económica. pp 101.
A homunculus is a very small human being. The term, which has its etymological root in the Latin word homuncŭlus, is usually used in a derogatory sense, according to what is indicated by the Royal Spanish Academy, Dictionary of the Spanish Language, 23rd ed., Madrid: Espasa, 2014.

11 Catelli, L. (2010). Los Hijos de la Conquista: otras perspectivas sobre el "Mestizo" y la traducción a partir de El Nueva Corónica y el Buen Gobierno de Felipe Guaman Poma de Ayala. *Revista de Historia de la Traducción*, 4, p.2.
-Guerrero Vinueza, G. (2008) El "otro oro" en la conquista de américa: las Mujeres indias, el surgimiento del mestizaje, *Revista de la Universidad de Nariño*, Colombia, https://revistas. udenar.edu.co/index.php/rceilat/article/download/1343/1637/
-Rodríguez García, Huascar (2011). *Cuadernos Inter.c.a.mbio* Año 8, n. 9, Barcelona, España, Fundación Dialnet, Universidad de la Rioja, España.

12 Mörner, Magnus (1967). *Race mixture in the History of Latin América*. Boston, USA: Little, Brown and Co.

Allah, Muhammad and The Koran

We must also consider the influence Islam had on our continent.

The Arabs began conquering Spain in 711 AD and remained there until 1492, when the city of Granada - the last Muslim stronghold - fell.[13] These centuries of dominance influenced not only our local customs and our emerging language, but also the concept of holy war which the Muslims had introduced.[14] Islamic fatalism may also be counted as an import: "*Que sera, sera*, Whatever will be, will be"[15] - which affected our sense of innovation and encouraged passivity.

When the Spaniards arrived in America, their concept of evangelism was the one they had practiced against the Muslims.[16] Evangelizing was not about sharing the Good News of salvation but about defeating the enemy by arms, taking their possessions and imposing religion by force.[17]

This concept was consolidated with the establishment of the Inquisition in Spain, which peaked in 1480. The Spanish Inquisition was led by Tomas de Torquemada, known to history and literature as "The Grand Inquisitor". Torquemada was a Dominican friar and one of three confessors of Queen Isabella of Castile and King Ferdinand of Aragon who sponsored Columbus' voyages.[18] Hernán Cortés arrived in Mexico in 1519 with this distorted concept of evangelism, prepared to "spread the Gospel" throughout Latin America. Ginés de Sepulveda justified this warfare from

---

13 Suárez, L.. (1989). *Los Reyes Católicos: el tiempo de la Guerra de Granada.* Madrid: Rialp, S.A.

14 Christie, N.. (2016). *The Book of the Jihad of ʿAli ibn Tahir al-Sulami* (d.1106). New York, USA. Rouledge.

15 Salgado, FM.. (1995). Doctrina Islámica: Principios y Prácticas. 1995, de Universidad de Salamanca Sitio web: www.dialnet.unirioja.es

16 de León Azcárate, JL. (2015). La Biblia y la evangelización del Nuevo Mundo durante el siglo XVI. *Veritas*, 32, pp. 195-227.

17 Raskolnikov's, V.. (Octubre 2, 2008). *La Metodología en la Evangelización de América Latina.* Octubre 2, 2008, de Centro de tesis y publicaciones Monografías.com Sitio web: www. monografias.com/usuario/perfiles/vladirmir_raskalnikovs

18 Dedieu, JP.. (1992). Denunciar-denunciarse. La delación inquisitorial en Castilla la Nueva en los siglos XVI-XVII. *Revista de la Inquisición*, 2, pp.96-10

Aristotle and the Bible.[19] Evangelization, as the Conquistadors understood it, was an important goal. Everything they did was in the name of Jesus. They destroyed the idols, gave cities Christian names, and taught Catholic doctrine. They read a document to the Indians, requiring them to declare submission to God. Many priests participated in the conquest, in concert with the conquerors.

If it wasn't for the decisive actions of brother Bartolomé de las Casas and other theologians (such as the Jesuit Francisco Suárez and the Dominican Francisco de Vitoria), the enslaving and killing of indigenous people would have been worse.[20]

Riches, Prestige and Power

The conquerors of the new world asked the King of Spain for three things: gold, titles, and lands.[21]

Gold proved to be insufficient for individuals as well as for the Spanish Kingdom. Most conquerors died poor and Spain, the first empire to have dominions on five continents,[22] fell into bankruptcy three times during the reign of Felipe II, due to constant wars with France, England and the Netherlands, causing national havoc.[23]

Spanish Kings did not want to grant titles in America either, because they had enough problems with the nobility in Spain and did not want a new social class creating the same problems thousands of miles away.

19 Ginés, J.. (1941). *Tratado Sobre Las Justas Causas De La Guerra Contra Los Indios.* México D.F.: Fondo de Cultura Económica.

20 de Las Casas, B. (1550). *Brevísima Relación de la Destrucción de las Indias,* España. Editorial Fontamara 2010.

21 Fernández, J.. (1999). La Figura del Conquistador. 2018, de Hispanoamérica - Historiae Instituciones Sitio web: http://www.hispanoteca.eu/Hispanoamérica/La%20figura%20del%20 conquistador.htm

22 Uriarte, J.. (Abril 23, 2020). Imperio Español; Resumen y Características. Abril 23, 2020, de Características.co Sitio web: https://www.caracteristicas.co/imperio-espanol/

Ruiza, M., Fernández, T., y Tamaro, E.. (2004). Felipe II. Septiembre 17, 2020, de Biografías y Vidas. La enciclopedia biográfica en línea Sitio web: https://www.biografiasyvidas. com/biografia/f/felipe_ii.htm

What they did grant were vast expanses of land in America.[24]

But land was useless without people to work it. So an institution called "La Encomienda" (The Entrustment) was created, whereby Indians were given to Spanish lords to work their lands for free in exchange for protection and teaching the Catholic religion.[25]

This is how the "latifundios" were born in Latin America. Such landowners were the first families in our continent to become rich, doing so at the expense of the natives. Thus a sense of injustice and oppression in obtaining wealth was born in our continent, as was a social system with Europeans at the apex and Indians at the bottom of this new society.

In the first decade of the 19th century Latin American elite, noting that King Ferdinand VII of Spain had been kidnapped by Napoleon, sought autonomy, then independence.[26] Colonialism began to give way to locally-ruled republics, which inaugurated a new time of hope and social well-being.

But who benefited? An economic, political and religious ruling class formed by American-born Spaniards called "criollos". What about the natives? Indians and Mestizos made up the bulk of the population, but they saw little improvement, and some indigenous communities continue to be treated with contempt and degradation to this day.[27]

Protestant America, Catholic America

Colonization of the United States and Latin America reveal great differences worth careful attention. The Pilgrims, who were mostly Puritan

---

24 de Paredes, I. (1681). Recopilación de leyes de los reinos de las Indias : mandadas imprimir y publicar por la Majestad Católica del rey Don Carlos II, nuestro señor. Madrid, España: Biblioteca Nacional de Chile.

25 Bacigalupo, A. (2007). La encomienda y la evangelización. 2020, de blogspot: aprendiendo Sitio web: http://arianna-aprendiendo.blogspot.com/2007/06/la-encomienda-y-la-evangelizacin.html

26 Zaragoza, G. (2004). *América Latina: La Independencia.* España: Anaya.

27 Agüero,O.. (dic. 2002). Sociedades indígenas, racismo y discriminación. 2020, de Horizontes Antropológicos Sitio web: https://www.scielo.br/scielo.php?script=sci_arttext&pid=S0104-71832002000200011&lng=es&tlng=es

Christians, arrived on the east coast of North America in 1620 aboard the Mayflower.[28] Their main reason for leaving Europe was not to conquer territory or steal gold, but to find a place far from the persecution they had suffered in England, so as to practice their religion freely.[29] These Pilgrims arrived as families, unlike the crews on the first two voyages of Columbus.[30]

After their arrival the Pilgrims worked the land with seeds they had brought with, and in the spring of the following year harvested crops. Since their families had come with them, they pestered the local women much less than did the Spanish conquerors.

In 1621 these Puritans invited local natives, from whom they had received help during the harsh winter, to join them to celebrate and thank God for their first harvest, a fraternal meeting where both groups brought food that was joyfully shared.[31] This would have been unthinkable during the Spanish colonization, since the Spanish never saw the Indians as equals.

It was after the Civil War, in the second half of the 19th Century, that American citizens confronted native peoples most violently, mostly in "the Wild West" as single men occupied lands, built railroads, and hunted bison almost to extinction.[32] Wealth in North America originated mostly from individual effort. The Pilgrims held to what was later called the Protestant Work Ethic, since work should honor God.[33]

---

28 Uribe, D. (2017, marzo 27). Los peregrinos del Mayflower y la formación de los Estados Unidos. El Espectador.

29 IDEM

30 Redi, C.. (June 2017). Conquista y Colonización en América: un estudio comparado entre España e Inglaterra, Siglos XVI y XVII. European Scientific Journal, Special edition, pp.94-117. June 2017, De www.core.ac.uk Base de datos.

31 Whitney, F.. (1949-50). Los Albores de Norteamérica. En *Reseña de la Historia de los Estados Unidos*(5). Estados Unidos: Oficina de Información Internacional del Departamento de Estado.

32 Berkin, Carol, et. al. (2006): *Making America*, p. 373.

33 Ferguson, Niall (8 de junio de 2003). The World; Why America Outpaces Europe (Clue: The God Factor). The New York Times (Nueva York, Estados Unidos). Consultado el 17 de Septiembre de 2020.

In my classes on Biblical Worldview I normally do an experiment, the results of which always surprise my students. I first ask them a question and challenge them to be honest in their answers:

> "What does the concept of wealth produce to you? What do you think about rich people?"

The answers given by most Latins are strongly negative. Students from Europe and North America, by contrast, consider wealth something positive, the fruit of personal effort. Then I explain to both groups the difference in how great wealth in our respective regions has usually been created.

It is not surprising, given our history, that in Latin America wealth is associated with something morally suspicious, something that borders on the illegal, implying a certain guilt. Much of our wealth was, indeed, generated by exploitation, corruption and drug trafficking, or at least by nabbing a government position, or living at the expense of the state through bonds and subsidies.

Culture of Control

The desire for control is also deeply rooted in our Latin culture. For example: economic freedom cannot be found in our traditions. Spain exercised a strong monopoly over the colonies throughout the continent through the "Casa de Contratación" (House of Hiring), which prevented the cities of the continent from trading with other European powers.

The British colonies in North America experienced something different since, from the beginning, they governed themselves with little pressure from London.[34] A famous uprising resulted when England tried to tax them without their consent.

Hierarchical control is a feature of our culture, expressed in families, churches, schools, the market and government.

The monopoly which the Roman Catholic Church exercised in Latin America and its political dominance strengthened this attitude. The Catholic Church favored hierarchical and pyramidal rule, unlike the congregations influenced by The Reformation, which proclaimed individual freedom to read and study the Bible and organized Congregationalist

---

34 Lucena, M.. (2008). *Historia de Iberoamérica*. España: Cátedra.

churches with a horizontal power structure.[35] In the latter, church members were involved in decision-making.

The North American colonies extended the example of their churches to govern themselves.[36] Latin America likewise followed the example of the hegemonic Church. (Other churches were admitted only in the 19th century, and under many restrictions).[37]James Thompson, a Scottish Baptist pastor, was welcomed by liberal rulers like Bernardino Rivadavia in Argentina, and Bernardo O'Higgins in Chile. These two were tired of the dominance of the Catholic Church over their education systems. Thompson introduced the Bible as a textbook in the Lancaster system of education that he spread to various parts of South America[38], enabling greater literacy in many countries.[39]

Education is an important step in achieving God's call for discipling our continent. Good biblical education can help us break free of a sense of inferiority, controlling leadership and mistrust of wealth honestly acquired. Education based on the Word of God and guided by the Holy Spirit will help heal us and show us how to bring transformation to our countries.

Freedom and the Growth of the Gospel

At the end of the 19th century there arose a continent-wide debate over whether the Church or State should handle education (and other institutions). A movement called "laicism"[40] took control out of the hands of the

35 Max Savelle, *Seeds of Liberty: The Genesis of the American Mind* (2005)

36 Jefferson, E.. (2013). *Congregationalism*. Estados Unidos.

37 Gómez, R. (2009). El Poder Político Y La Religión En El Puritanismo: La Colonia Norteamericana De La Bahía De Massachusetts. *Revista Española De Derecho Constitucional*, (86), 145-182. Retrieved September 18, 2020, from http://www.jstor.org/stable/24885983

38 Romero, F. (Diciembre 5, 2012). Diego Thompson. Consultado el 18 Septiembre, 2020, de Sendas Sitio web: http://www.sendas.cl/biografias/diego-thompson/#sdfootnote1sym

39 IDEM

40 Sang Ben, Mu-Kien Adriana. (2015). Liberalismo versus conservadurismo en América Latina y el Caribe del siglo XIX: Reflexión desde una perspectiva crítica. *Memorias: Revista Digital de Historia y Arqueología desde el Caribe*, (27), 1-34. https://dx.doi.org/10.14482/ memor.27.8009

Church and secularized it. By the first half of the 20th century all Latin American countries had adopted these ideas, implementing laws more in line with the liberal position[41] which positively affected the freedom of the individual in society.

At this point evangelical churches had not yet established much of a presence in Latin America. That began to change in the 1960s. The Second Vatican Council declared that Protestants were no longer heretics, but "separated brethren".[42] So now evangelicals were not going to hell anymore for holding non-Catholic beliefs.

Then missionaries arrived from Europe, and even more from the United States. This coincided with the "Cold War", a hostile worldwide confrontation between communist states (especially the Warsaw Pact) and NATO and its largely democratic allies.[43]

With the Cuban Revolution in 1959, and the missile crisis in 1962, Latin America became politically polarized. The Cold War had a big impact in this part of the world, especially from the 1970`s, when right-wing military regimes and left-wing guerrilla movements emerged in many countries.[44]

41 Osés, J.. (2013, abril-junio). Laicismo: Del Concepto a los Modelos. Revista de Estudios Políticos, Núm.160, p.143. Madrid.
Arredondo, A.. (2017). Educación Laica en América Latina y el Caribe. En Historia Caribe, Vol.12 Núm.30(p.19). Barranquilla: Universidad del Atlántico.

42 IDEM

43 Dussel, E.. (1983). *Historia general de la iglesia en América Latina*. Tomo I : introducción general a la historia de la iglesia en América Latina. Salamanca: Ediciones Sígueme CEHILA

44 Revolución Cubana y Crisis de los Misiles: Kruijt, D.. (2019, Junio 1). Cuba y sus lazos con América Latina y el Caribe, 1959 - presente. Revista Uruguaya de Ciencia Política, Vol.28 Núm.1, Uruguay.
-Guerra Fría y Regímenes Militares de Derecha: Victoriano, F.. (2010, diciembre). Estado, golpes de Estado y militarización en América Latina: una reflexión histórico política. Argumentos (México, D.F.), Vol.23 No.64 y pp.179-187, 185. México.
- Movimientos de izquierda: Victoriano, F.. (2010, diciembre). Estado, golpes de Estado y militarización en América Latina: una reflexión histórico política. Argumentos (México, D.F.), Vol.23 No.64, p.182. México.
-Goicovic, I.. (2017, Julio-Diciembre). La Revolución Bolchevique y el Movimiento de Izquierda Revolucionaria (MIR) chileno (1965-1973). Adhesiones y distancias. Avances del Cesor, Vol.14 Núm. 17, pp. 98-103. Chile.

The growing suspicion in the political climate of the United States also affected mission work. Senator Joseph McCarthy accused hundreds of people of communist connections, including those in government and other fields.

Most of the missionaries who brought the Gospel from the United States to Latin America, failed to fully understand the times that our Latin American nations were living in, and preferred to distance themselves from social and political matters. They preached a gospel based on personal salvation and changed individual behavior but failed to teach responsibility for transforming unfair structures in society.

For the first 40 years of my life I never heard a message about biblical justice although that is the second-most mentioned sin in the Old Testament after idolatry, and a deep problem in Latin America. How could the Gospel ignore the problems of poverty, discrimination, corruption and concentration of wealth, which are endemic to Latin societies? Our concept of the separation of Church and State was defective, resulting in a church which did not seek to transform all of society for the Glory of God.

Our sense of passiveness, even pride at being "non-political", gained us followers. For decades the impending return of Christ was preached with a pessimistic eschatology. Christ is coming, so why study? What is to be gained by changing the world around us? The Bible says everything will go from bad to worse.

This Cold War pessimism caused the Evangelical Church to stay aloof from meeting social needs. A large percentage of believers in our continent are now Pentecostal.[45] This Church encourages free expression and incorporates elements of the peasant society that new members brought to the city.

However, until recently pastors of these churches lacked theological preparation. They focused on leading godly personal and family lives and left society alone.

---

45 Semán, P.. (Mayo 15, 2019). Pentecostalismo, política y secularización en América Latina. 17 de Septiembre del 2020, de Open Democracy
- Ruíz, N.. (Marzo 1, 2013). Los pentecostales representan el 70% de los protestantes en el mundo 17 de Septiembre del 2020, de NC Noticia Cristiana.com

In the light of these great needs, and in the absence of a theology that would confront social problems, the so-called "Theology of Liberation" emerged, based on a Marxist praxis, far removed from the gospel of Christ.[46] Few evangelicals followed it, but it caused a great stir among the Catholics. Some priests and laymen went so far as to take up arms and proclaim a revolution.[47]

One Bible, Two Realities

Over many years a Church was formed that was not of this world, but neither was salt and light in the world. A complex evangelical culture developed, divorced from reality around us. Believers lived dualistically, between religious and secular lives. The Bible became a book of religion, of intimate life with God, touching the family, but not the streets.

Every good work within the Church, however small, was warmly welcomed: preaching, teaching, singing in the choir, working with children and youth, evangelism in the parks. Each such effort was indeed precious but failed to introduce salt and light into a dark and tasteless world. Love of God was shut within four walls. Believers were not challenged to bring the Truth to bear to mend a broken society.

Intimations of Change

Over the last several years interesting changes have occurred. We now have the greatest number of evangelical believers in Latin America ever.[48] Some faithful businessmen, sports- and social leaders have come to occupy political positions.[49]

---

46 Garrigues, A.. (Mayo 8, 1979). La teología de la liberación. 17 de Septiembre del 2020, de *El País* Sitio web: https://elpais.com/diario/1979/05/09/opinion/295048811_850215.html

47 Tahar, M.. (2007, Julio-Septiembre). La teología de la liberación en América Latina: una relectura sociológica. *Revista Mexicana de Sociología* , Vol. 69 Núm. 3, pp.429-448. México.

48 Semán, P.. (Mayo 15, 2019). Pentecostalismo, política y secularización en América Latina. 17 de Septiembre del 2020, de Open Democracy Sitio web: https://www.open- democracy.net/es/democraciaabierta-es/pentecostalismo-pol%C3%ADtica-y-secular- izaci%C3%B3n-en-am%C3%A9rica-latina/

49 Cargo Político: Vera, D.. (Abril 28, 2020). Bolsonaro nombra a pastor >>Cont

Many believing youth have gained technical or professional education.[50]

We also see an incipient awakening in training in areas like Apologetics and Biblical Worldview. L'Abri and Transforma conduct training in Brazil, while Youth With A Mission holds worldview schools in countries like Chile, Argentina, Mexico and Brazil, among other courses offered by various Christian organizations.

This movement is still in its early stages, but I see it as charged with promise for the future.

The "Indi-Structural" Gospel

The Church of the 21st century needs to be "Indistructural", by which I mean that it must aim to change not only the individual, but also the structures that shape society.

Jesus often attended to individual needs. We can see Jesus' personal touch with the Samaritan woman (John 4: 1-30) and with Nicodemus (John 3:1-21). He also fed the hungry (Matthew 14:13-21, John 6:1-14), healed the sick (Jesus healed: a blind man in John 9:17; a mute in Matthew 9: 32-33; a paralytic in Mark 2: 1-12), raised the dead (John 11:1-44) and showed compassion for those who suffered (Matthew 9:35-38). The early Christians shared a common purpose of helping the poor (John 13:29).
At the same time that Jesus ministered to individuals, he challenged the social thinking of his time to the core.

<< Cont.. evangélico como ministro de Justicia tras renuncia del exjuez Sergio Moro. 17 de Septiembre del 2020, de biobiochile.cl Sitio web: https://www.biobiochile.cl/noticias/internacional/america-latina/2020/04/28/bolsonaro-nom-   bra-a-pastor-evangelico-como-ministro-de-justicia-tras-renuncia-del-exjuez-sergio-moro.shtml Jara, A.. (Noviembre 20, 2017). Los candidatos evangélicos que triunfaron en las elecciones parlamentarias. 17 de Septiembre del 2020, de La Tercera Sitio web: https://www.latercera. com/noticia/los-candidatos-evangelicos-triunfaron-las-elecciones-parlamentarias/

50 Pérez, F.. (Diciembre 23, 2019). El estallido evangélico en universidades laicas y su soterrada influencia política. 17 de Septiembre del 2020, de El Mostrador Sitio web: https:// www.elmostrador.cl/destacado/2019/12/23/el-estallido-evangeli-co-en-universidades-la- icas-y-su-soterrada-influencia-politica/

What could be more revolutionary than to tell people to love, and not to hate, their enemies? (Matthew 5:44).

The Law of Moses said "an eye for an eye and a tooth for a tooth" (Exodus 21:24). That was the legal limitation, and it was up to the judges to set the exact penalty. In other words, they could not kill someone who had broken someone's tooth. To hate one's enemy was a mindset as rooted in Jewish tradition as it is in human nature, which Jesus challenged in Matthew 5:43-45.

The Law commanded rest on the Sabbath (Exodus 20: 8-11). But this commandment did not prohibit one from loving one's neighbor, and the Lord of the Sabbath often chose that day to work miracles, angering the religious Powers-That-Be (Matthew 12: 2).

Pharisees would not eat with publicans and sinners, but Jesus dined with Zacchaeus, Matthew and other publicans (Matthew 9: 10-13; Luke 19: 5-10), challenging the norm in doing so.The Christians later likewise challenged many Roman institutions and laws.

While the Twelve Tables of the Roman law mandated the death of children born weak or deformed,[51] the *Didache*, likely written before 100 AD, ordered believers not to commit infanticide.[52]

The laws of the cruel Caesar and Christ, who "came to give life", clashed at many points. The legal dilemma was partly resolved in 374 A.D., when the Justinian Code made it a crime to kill children.[53] Such examples abound in Christian history, when the followers of Jesus not only changed laws, but created new institutions.

Among them was the modern hospital. In 369 AD in the East[54] Basil and

---

51 Antequera, J.M. (1874). *Historia de la legislación romana desde los tiempos más remotos hasta nuestros días.* España: P. Infante. pp., 273-283

52 Ropero, A. (2018). *Obras escogidas de los padres apostólicos.* España: Clie. p. 95.

53 «*Codex Theodosianus*» 9, 14, 1

54 Villanueva L.A. (2005, julio agosto). Las transformaciones históricas y sociales del sistema hospitalario. *Revista de la Facultad de Medicina UNAM*, 48, 158.

the godly Roman matron St. Fabiola in Rome itself,[55] founded hospices to welcome visitors and heal the sick - a concern pagan Romans had not felt.[56]

Meanwhile Christians suppressed ungodly institutions like the coliseum, where, for seven centuries, gladiators had killed one other to delight the cruel tastes of the Romans.[57]

In order for the Good News of Christ to be relevant in society, we must move from a Gospel that concentrates only on individual change, to applying a Gospel that confronts unjust and cruel structures and mindsets. We are called to proclaim the "life more abundant" of which Jesus spoke. For that purpose society must be reformed, beginning with schools.

Important Steps in Education

If we wish to transform our continent our first challenge is to multiply schools with a biblical worldview throughout Latin America.

For some time I have challenged church leaders to adopt a vision for education in their congregations. When they build a church facility, for instance, consider erecting a school and using it to house the church. The school's auditorium can be used for worship, and classrooms for Sunday school classes. This way they can use the facility every day of the week and bring great blessing - not just on the weekend.

Such schools should become tools of evangelism. Non-Christian families whose children attend this educational center will come to the Lord and naturally attend this church.

Thus the school-church will develop an organic relationship with the community even while it redeems education. Admittedly this is not an easy

---

55 T. E. C. Jr. (1987, abril 1). Fabiola, a fourth century roman lady, and the origin of the first public hospital. Pediatrics, official journal of the american academy of pediatrics, 79, (4) 528.

56 Chuaqui, B. (2000). El concepto de dignidad en la antigua Roma y después. Estudio de Viktor Poschel. *Revista ARS MEDICA* revista de ciencias médicas, Vol.29 Núm.1, p.3. de la Pontificia Universidad Católica de Chile.

57 Mañas, A. (2011). *Munera Gladiatoria: Origen del deporte espectáculo de masas* (tesis doctoral). Universidad de Granada.

task: for one thing, each country sets its own code for school construction. But having met those specifications, the building should also easily meet requirements for a church as well.

A good building is just a first step. Running a Christian school that lacks a biblical worldview is like swimming in a pool with no water.

The Foundations of Education

The biblical view of education should be based on 2 Peter 1:5: "Add to faith, virtue and to virtue, knowledge."All education has to begin with faith, and this faith comes by hearing the voice of God (Romans 10:17).

Can a five-year-old child hear the voice of God? Of course he can! Experts tell us that the first five years of life is when children learn the most. So we can teach students how to hear God's voice from the earliest grades. But one of the principles of Christian education is to do first, then teach. If the educator has never heard the voice of God, he cannot teach his students how to do it.

Secondly, this verse speaks about virtue, which essentially con- sists of the willingness of the soul to act according to the moral law. Imagine parents and teachers teaching children to forgive at the age of six. If we keep this principle as a constant practice in the classroom and at home, our children will grow up emotionally healthy.

Adults need to take a whole Star Wars series of courses to straighten out our souls after all they have gone through: Inner Healing I, Inner Healing II, Inner Healing Strikes back, the Return of Inner Healing. But if we teach virtue as a lifestyle from a young age, what a chance to raise a generation of children who know how to forgive, who understand the value of commitment and the benefits that responsibility brings! The world has never seen such a band of spiritually-healthy youth.

Training in virtue will also help children deal with bullying, especially if we raise a "Culture of Blessing" in opposition.

The first time I gave a talk about the Culture of Blessing was at a school in northern Chile. I had originally been invited to speak to the teachers, but my class ended up being for kids in the last two years of high school.

I was warned that these eighty students had no interest in religion, and that the previous day they threw a cake at a teacher's face. That did not encourage me much.

I started talking about how we can bless fellow students through expressing gratitude. I said we should recognize one another's abilities, and be intentional about highlighting the positive character traits of those around us. We should also share the benefits of asking for forgiveness.

Then I invited students to express words of blessing to each other publicly. Suddenly a student stood up and said he wanted to apologize to the teacher for throwing the cake in his face. Then a girl got up and then another youth, all expressing the same thing. They approached and hugged the teacher. The atmosphere had changed radically. A young girl expressed many words of blessing to a classmate, then another, and another, and so forth. As time was running out, I asked them to leave their seats to bless as many as they could. Groups of six, eight and ten students were formed, all hugging each other in tears. But one person was crying the most: the school principal. The Lord had brought a solution to a problem that was affecting them greatly.

After this experience, I have conducted such lectures in schools in many Latin American countries, all with similar results. Most of these schools where I have been invited are not Christian, but God's principles apply to everyone, because "the law of the Lord is perfect, converting the soul" (Psalm 19: 7).

The third element mentioned in this verse is Knowledge. In a humanistic worldview, knowledge is fragmented, which means that we study subjects discreetly, out of the context of their origin, as Principal David Marshall mentioned in Chapter Two. We study mountains, the respiratory system and many other objects, without explaining why they came to exist. This knowledge is like one grain of sugar taken out of a bowl. So I define this type of education as granulated.

Truth, by contrast, is fibrous, from a biblical perspective. Unlike a grain of sugar, a root is a fiber that only has life and fulfills its func- tion if it is connected to the tree. Every phenomenon in creation is connected with the Creator. We do not start talking about the cycle of water from the moment the sun heats the water and it evaporates to create the clouds, we must start by saying: "In the beginning God created the heavens and the earth". And then God separated the waters from the waters, and then the sun heated the waters, and so on (Genesis 1:1-7). We do not start in step 3, but from the beginning.

In other words: all knowledge is connected to God, as the root is connected to the tree. Therefore everything we teach becomes an act of worship. Let everything that has breath praise the Lord (Psalm 150: 6).

Involving God in all the content of studies must be a top priority for the educational reform that we are promoting.

Final Points

As Latin Americans we must change our thinking about the church.

First we must end dualism between secular and religious life. Secondly we must also break down the division between laymen and ministers, which accentuates this dualism. A missionary calling is not something that is directed to a select group of people, but to everyone. As Paul said,

> "Whether you eat or drink, or whatever you do, do it all for the glory of God" (1 Corinthians: 10 : 31).

Let me integrate these final three points into one. Every Christian has a calling from God (the *Vocatio Dei*). We should not ask the Lord whether or not we have such a calling. Yes, we do! What we must ask is: how, where, and when should we exercise that calling?

Maybe our calling is to serve in India, or in our hometown; it may be to work as a cross-cultural missionary to a tribe in Africa, or a professor at a prestigious university. Our calling may begin right now or we may need to prepare. But we all have a missionary calling because we all have a mission to fulfill in life.

Years ago, in our YWAM School of Biblical Christian Worldview in Santiago de Chile, we received a professor of molecular biology, who taught at a university in Lima, Peru. She thought that the only way to serve Christ was to stop teaching at the university and become a pastor. She saw a huge dichotomy between secular work and service to the Lord. By the end of our course she returned home with a new perspective on where God had called her to serve. She turned her university professorship into a mission field. She realized that pastors have great difficulty reaching universities, but she was already there as a missionary. Her work of evangelism is formidable and she does it all by teaching how a cell is formed. Recently she was recognized by the university as one of the most successful and creative of their teachers.

Imagine if, throughout Latin America, every committed Christian were to become a missionary in his or her area of work. Imagine them not only leading souls to Christ, but also transforming the fields in which they labor!

That is my hope for Latin America and the world. A Gospel that declares to us our true identity, salt and light, called to challenge every error and lie in each area of society. A people who are trained and empowered by the Word of God, knowing that we have a God who will again heal the broken hearted, who continues to call us to repentance and to live holy lives. Faith in a God who has given us the tools to work in each of our nations and especially in this beloved Latin America, which has waited so long for the manifestation of the children of God in every area of society.

Chapter 25

Brazil - A Beauty In Search of Her Soul

Heliel Gomes de Carvalho[1] &

Paulo Borges Júnior[2]

Brazil should be one of the world's strongest economies. It is the world's sixth largest nation in population and the fifth largest in area. In terms of natural resources it is richer than the nations that are bigger.

Brazil has not been able to harness her resources because her students rank among the ten worst nations according to PISA - the inter-governmental 'Program for International Students Assessment. In the year 2000, 13.6% Brazilians, 15-years or older, were illiterate. In 2018, many teenagers enrolled in schools, but 43% failed to obtain a minimum level in reading, mathematics and science. These cold statistics remind us that the Portuguese who colonized Brazil were very different from the Puritans who colonized North America.

Brazil's oldest university, The Federal University of Amazonas, was founded only in 1909. That is, over four hundred years after Pedro Alvares Cabral "discovered" Brazil on April 22, 1500. In contrast, the "Pilgrims" landed in New England on November 11, 1620. Within two decades, in 1636, they had established what became the Harvard University. The difference? Pilgrims sought God; the Portuguese gold.

Pilgrims and Puritans came to North America as FAMILIES that valued children. For the Bible taught Protestant reformers that the Family was the

1 Heliel Gomes de Carvalho is Specialist in University Teaching, holds a Master's degree in Environmental Sciences from the University Center of Anápolis, UniEvangélica and is currently a Professor at UniEvangélica and Coordinator of the Institutional Chaplaincy of Associação Educativa Evangélica.

2 Paulo Borges Júnior is Co-founder and one of the coordinators of the Ministry of Salt of the Earth. He has received University training in theology and civil engineering. He is president of Instituto Total.

"School of Character." God required parents to educate children with the help of the Church and the state. In contrast, early Portuguese who sailed to Brazil, left their wives behind in Europe. They took native women and fathered children, often to abandon them to be raised by single, illiterate mothers without church-support.

During the Council of Trent (1545-48) that began the Roman Catholic counter-reformation, the Jesuits accepted the Protestant belief that education was the Church's mandate. A church that does not take the responsibility to educate God's children disobeys God's word. That reform within Catholicism could have changed Brazil had slavery not begun in 1568. The first groups of African slaves were brought in that year starting a terrible phase of Brazil's history.

The unjust oppression of more than 5 million people lasted for about 320 years. It produced a nation of miscegenated people, born of native Indians, Europeans and Africans. Brazil's success in football shows that her biological DNA was enriched by the fusion of their ancestors' diversity. However, human culture is created by the "soul" - which transcends biology.

A nation's "soul" is not an immortal, metaphysical entity. It shapes a people's behavior as it is forged by their shared beliefs. The individual soul is responsible for sin, but biblical prophets called for national repentance because God judges nations when they fail to teach what is right and glorify and institutionalize sin. Temples are turned into centers of prostitution, a mother's womb into a slaughter house of the innocent, the sacred profession of teaching into another trade-union.

We are commanded to disciple "nations" because a nation's soul is shaped by its education, literature, and social institutions that shape individuals' character.

A revolution that reforms the church, family, and education will produce the character that glorifies God and brings forth the best of Brazil.

Why Jesuit Education Failed

The Jesuit 'Society of Jesus' was active in the Portuguese colony of Brazil from 1549-1759. It educated the leading layer in the metropolis. Native Indians and the black people of African origin were educated mainly to serve as catechesis. Although this was seen as a formal, limited and uncritical education for men-only, it could have laid good moral foundations for Brazil. Unfortunately the "Liberal Enlightenment" reforms of Marquês de Pombal expelled Jesuits' educational mission. The "Liberals" wanted public education run by lay people, not clergy. They accused Jesuits for wanting an "ideological domination over the Indians, converting them to the Catholic faith".[3] However, most historians agree that driving Jesuits out, harmed Brazil's educational situation. Brazil lost whatever teaching of godliness that it did have. The teaching profession lost cultural respect since a teacher was no longer a "Father", a priest, obeying his divine calling to teach.

Early Protestant Educational Initiatives

In the 1550s three hundred French people arrived at Guanabara Bay in Rio de Janeiro. Among them were fourteen Protestants and two pastors sent by John Calvin. In the next century the Dutch arrived in the northeast of Brazil. Two Potiguara Indians chose to live in Holland from 1625-1630. There they studied and embraced the Protestant faith. They returned to exercise administrative, educational, military and spiritual functions in Brazil. Due to their intense efforts, within seven years, Brazil had Indian school teachers, pastors and the first Protestant church. At least four Indians had become schoolmasters. "Maybe these could have been the first Brazilian teachers: Álvaro Jacó, Bento da Costa, Melchior Francisco and João Gonçalves".[4] Calvinism reinforced the Roman Catholic idea that teaching was a divine calling.

It was a sacred profession; a gift of the Holy Spirit.
Hundreds of indigenous people started the "Igreja Reformada Potiguara". This alarmed the Portuguese who sent a priest, Antônio VieiraIn, in 1660, to investigate the situation. He published the "list of the Serra de Ibiapaba mission", and called Serra de Ibiapaba a "Geneva of the entire frontier." He wrote that so many Indians had become "so Calvinist and Lutherans that they seemed to be born in England or Germany".[5] As a result the French and the Dutch Protestants were expelled from Brazil and some were martyred.

---

3 MELO, 2012, pp. 11, 12

4 VIRAÇÃO, 2013, p. 68

5 VIRAÇÃO, 2013

This robbed Brazil of the best educational opportunity. In 1808 the first signs of some religious tolerance and investment in education came with Dom João VI, the king of Portugal. He fled to Brazil from Napoleon Bonaparte's invasion of Portugal and introduced vocational training, including for administrators for his court. The first institution to train doctors began soon after that.

On September 7, 1822, the country became independent and the "colony" was made the seat of the empire. That brought European migrants, including some Protestants. They limited themselves to caring for their regions, spiritually and educationally. In the Brazilian Constitution of 1824 an article introduced the idea of a "free and primary education for all citizens". But there was very little zeal for educating Brazil. For example: in 1844 Brazil had around 250,000 children, but the network for basic education served just over 2,400 students.

The mission to educate Brazil received fresh impulse with the arrival of Protestant Missionaries. A significant milestone was the work of Scottish Dr. Robert Raid Kalley (1809-1888). He first worked in the Island of Madeira in 1838. The island's poverty, illiteracy, alcoholism and human needs motivated him to start a hospital with 12 beds and one pharmacy.

Along with friends he created an educational system based in homes. A student who knew more taught others who knew less. Children studied during the day and adults at night. These "schools" emerged in various parts of the island. "Thus, a century before the celebrated Laubach Method, Dr. Kalley was already instituting the pro-literacy movement, known by the motto – "each one teaches another".[6] In six years, more than two thousand people learned to read. They were instructed in the Scriptures. Bibles and other literature were distributed and hymns were composed.

As Madeira's people began developing, persecution started. Kalley and many Christians were arrested. Some were expelled from the island and the doctor's house and hospital were burnt down. About 2000 Madeirans fled to the islands of Trinidad and Tobago. Later, some of them went to Illinois in the United States and Kalley brokered the reception of these refugees.[7]

....

6 TESTA, 1963, p. 31

7 TESTA, 1963

Kalley fled the Island and a few years later he visited the Madeiran refugees in the United States with his wife Sarah. There he learned about Brazil's needs and arrived in Rio de Janeiro on May 10, 1855.

In August Kalley and Sarah started a Sunday School. The following year, encouraged by the school's growth, they started to teach German, English and Portuguese to children over 8 years old. Three decades before the abolition of slavery, Kalley already had a class to teach the blacks. In 1865 he wrote articles combating slavery. Kalley returned to Scotland where he died in 1888. Perhaps due to the difficulties he had encountered in Madeira, Kalley made efforts in his relationship with civil authorities. He became a friend of Emperor D. Pedro II. Together they worked on principles of religious and educational freedom in Brazil.

After Robert Kalley Protestant missionaries from Europe and North America started coming to Brazil. For them education was an integral part of evangelization. It trained the nation's leadership. The early missionaries knew that between 1780 and 1860 nine educational institutions had grown to two hundred in North America, thanks to the Presbyterians, Congregationalists, Episcopelians, Baptists, Methodists and others.[8] "Missionaries, in addition to evangelists, played the role of teachers, and the missionary companies included women education specialists as part of this missionary enterprise ... some of these have gained recognition in Brazilian education, such as Carlota Kemper, Márcia Brown and Martha Watts".[9]

Scholars such as Hilsdorf (1977) have defended the thesis that missionary work in education took place through small and large schools. Among these are Mackenzie Presbyterian University (1870), the Southern Presbyterian Seminary in Campinas (1873) and Methodist University of Piracicaba (1881). This education sought to make individual Brazilian followers of Christ and also to transform Brazil's general culture. Initially the second aspect was supported by republicans and liberals but, before it could shape the nation's soul, secularism took over education. Corruption followed.

---

8 MENDONÇA, 1986, p.60

9 MENDONÇA, 1986, p. 93

Secularization of Education

In 1889 Brazil became a Federative Republic. The worldview of the governing elite was most influenced by August Comte's French positivism. It promoted what it considered "scientific" and atheistic education. For example: the Federal Constitution of 1891 was promulgated in the name of the Family, the Fatherland and Humanity. The idea of being a nation "under the protection of God" was discarded. Positivism insisted that morality should be based on science, not spirituality. That proved impossible because science describes what is, not what ought to be. A scientist can observe that students steal, fight and cheat. How is he to know that students ought to study, share, love, and serve - not plagiarize. Understandably the Catholic brotherhoods reacted to this corruption of education in the name of science. It founded schools throughout Brazil.

Secular education created another profound cultural problem: It robbed the teaching profession of its sacredness - its dignified status as a divine service rendered by "Fathers," "Mothers," priests and missionaries. Secularized teaching could no longer be seen as a calling, a sacred gift. Teaching became just another "job" like washing dishes in a restaurant to earn a living. When a teacher ceased being an Academic Pastor, the culture lost appreciation of teachers. Sociologists have noted that secularization of education led to the "natural removal of intelligent people from a poorly paid function and that it finds in the public opinion the consideration to which it is entitled".[10] In the year 1900, 65% of Brazilians were illiterate, compared to 3% British. Teaching profession can be made attractive by increasing teachers' wages. That, however, is insufficient in itself to increase the quality of a teacher's devotion to his pupils or profession. Improving pay-scale, perks and benefits is helpful, but the real challenge is to restore respect for the profession. That is one of the objectives of making an Academic Pastor the heart of the education revolution, the point person relating to students, families, church, university and the education bank.

Secularization of education gained momentum in the 1920s when World War I ended and the impetus of the Industrial Revolutions brought new immigrants in large numbers. That strengthened the Escola Nova movement which aimed at an "inclusive" education. Education could have imparted whatever good the culture had. Instead it avoided discussing the questions of truth, ethics and meaning of life. It focused on imparting

---

10 ALMEIDA, 2000, p. 65

practical studies, preparing students for jobs, not life. Once public education was taken over by John Dewey's Pragmatism (see Chapter 1 by Vishal Mangalwadi), it became incapable of giving any purpose to the pursuit of knowledge and wisdom. Earning one's livelihood by means fair or foul became the only purpose of studies.

The 1934 Constitution recognized the harm education was doing by preparing students for a meaningless life. It was robbing the very soul of the nation. Therefore the constitution devoted 17 articles to education. Article 149 said: "Education is the right of all and must be given, by the family and by the Public Powers, [...] so that it enables efficient factors of the nation's moral and economic life, and develops in a Brazilian spirit the awareness of human solidarity".[11] This opened the nation to religious education which was prohibited previously. Now it was made available as an optional course. However, it had to be taught according to the student's creed.

Secularists attacked the new policy. Campos wrote, for example: "this re-introduction of religious education in schools did not only have a political dimension, in the sense of obtaining the support of the Catholic Church for the Vargas Government". The policy was about "using Catholic doctrine as an instrument to fight internationalist ideologies, to legitimize authoritarianism and to affirm the national. Religious education could also better fulfill its function of "recovering lost values", that is, those linked to religion".[12]

Industrial education was launched in early 1940. It targeted the poorest strata of the population. Military Dictatorship (1964-1984) also leveraged higher education for its own purposes. The first Leide Diretrizes e Bases da Educação (LDB) aimed to think about the education system as a whole, emphasizing greater participation of women. The LDB was improved until 1996 when elementary and high schooling were recognized as basic education. None of this, however, has given Brazil a set of commonly shared ideas and ideals - a national *soul* which enables our nation to know God's will, let alone to do it. We remain a nation confused by man's "wisdom" (Rom.1:22) and folly, "goodness" (Luk.18:19) and sinfulness. Might, not right, tends to rule over us. Five centuries of educational struggles

---

11 BRASIL, 1934

12 CAMPOS, 1941, p. 155

have left us as one of the most corrupt countries in the world. Immorality that dominates the souls of our educated elite makes sure that too many poor continue to live with complete or functional illiteracy.

Why did state-controlled secular education fail Brazil? It failed for the same reason as atheistic education failed in communist Russia and its satellites. Its goal was to produce good workers, not good human beings. Artificial Intelligence can feed tons of excellent information, mathematical and linguistic skills into a robot. That will make extremely useful tools for agriculture, industry, services or the information age. The challenge, however, is how to change the human heart. How to nurture free citizens who choose what is good, not merely "profitable" for one's private or company's interests. It may be easy to program a robot to blow itself up in a war, but how do you cultivate virtues that inspire individuals to deny themselves, take up their cross and sacrifice their self-interest for others - their families, neighbors and nations?

A Lighthouse Amidst the Encircling Gloom

The foregoing survey appreciates the wonderful steps that dedicated visionaries took to educate Brazil. Each confronted darkness. Some failed but none were useless. They showed that Brazil needs to learn from them to do better. An ongoing exception has been in the state of Goiás in the center of the nation. "There was no school in Goiás until 1787".[13] The light of salvation and education came in 1860 with Protestant evangelists.

The Bible taught the missionary movement that Jesus had sent out His disciples to heal and to teach. Therefore, they focussed on health care and education, especially in the beginning of the 20th century. In the 1920s they obeyed Christ by building up a lighthouse in the city of Anápolis, in Brazilian Midwest. A lighthouse may be a small structure, but its life-saving influence must not be underestimated.

The missionary families that came together to shine light were supported by the Evangelical Union of South America (1911) - specifically by Archibald Tipple (1888-1972), an English peddler who arrived in Brazil in 1912, and physician James Fanstone (1890-1987) who came to Anápolis in 1924 with his wife Dayse. The young doctor had graduated from the University of London with a master's and doctorate in medicine in tropi-

---

13 MORAES, 2012, p. 33

cal diseases and a degree in hygiene. He studied the Bible at the Glasgow Bible Training Institute in Scotland.[14]

Fanstone's choice to settle on the border of Central Brazil proved strategic. The railroad reached the city in 1935. That made it possible to transfer the Federal Capital away from the coast to the center of the country. Educational mission turned out to be more important than geography or railways. Even before Anápolis became a city, the Spirit-led missionaries had created a chapel as "a class of first letters for the male." Twenty years later the first class for women began.[15]

Within a year of Fanstone's arrival in 1925, a group of visionaries joined hands together to found the first high school in the city - the Instituto de Ciências e Letras. It also offered teacher training. That inspired the government to found its own School Group in February 1926. The following year, in 1927, the missionary doctor Fanstone inaugurated Hospital Evangélico Goiano (HEG). This was the second hospital in the Brazilian central west, at that time inhabited by around half a million people.[16]

In 1932 began the activities of Colégio Couto Magalhães under the leadership of the prosecutor Carlos Pereira, James Fanstone and other protestants. This was to become the state's first confessional college. In addition to education this pioneering group also worked to improve health, justice, spirituality and social action on behalf of the poor. Back then, in the 1930s, formal nursing education was non-existent in Brazil. The demand for nursing professionals was overshadowed by cultural prejudice. Dr. James Fanstone responded by starting the Florence Nightingale Nursing School (1933). This was the first nursing school in Goiás and the third in Brazil. In about three decades the school trained 220 nurses. Currently it has more than 450 students.[17]

Critics say that missionaries come to colonize the soul. In 1941 Dayse Fanstone invested her personal inheritance to build the city's first building suitable for a school. Their evangelism was accompanied with running at least 4 clinics for the poor and lepers along with Christian education for all.

----

14 FANSTONE, 2017; CARVALHO, 2015

15 Borges, 1974

16 FANSTONE, 2017; CARVALHO, 2015

17 CARVALHO, 2015

Dr. James Fanstone's example inspired another missionary physician, Dr. Donald Gordon and his nurse wife Helen Gary Gordon, to start the second hospital and nursing school in Goiás state (1937). Other hospitals and schools followed in different cities in Goiás. Today, one of them has at least 8 higher education courses serving students from dozens of cities.[18]

World War II made it difficult for Ginásio Couto Magalhães to sustain itself. The challenge was accepted by a North American missionary, Arthur Wesley Archibald (1906-1986). He had started a theological seminary in Anápolis (SETECEB). He bought the Colégio Couto Magalhães and founded Associação Educativa Evangélica (AEE) on March 31, 1947. These nine founders represented five Protestant confessions from three countries.

The Association incorporated Colégio Couto Magalhães, a theological seminary, and started Colégio Álvaro de Melo in Ceres. In the 1950s it started three more schools that incorporated agriculture into education. As a result the state of Goiás, that used to be a poor frontier, produced about 27.18 million tons of grains in 2019 and 2020. Crops included soy, corn, sugar cane, accounting for 10% of Brazil's production. Much of it was exported.[19] Goiás remains an innovator in agri-business in Brazil. AEE schools train many of these professionals through their courses in Agronomy, Biological Sciences and Business Administration.

Higher level teacher training began in 1960 when AEE started the first higher education institution in the interior of the state. It taught courses in Education, Portuguese, Mathematics, History and Geography. Then came the Law Schools of Anápolis (1969), the Faculty of Dentistry (1971) and so on. In 1993, these colleges were united, constituting the Integrated Faculties of the AEE. This education is based explicitly on Christian ethics and democratic values. That draws students from different parts of the Midwest of Brazil. In 2004 these colleges were accredited as Centro Universitário de Anápolis. This became the first Centro Universitário of Goiás, now known as UniEVANGÉLICA.

AEE has taken its mission to educate beyond Anápolis to seven other cities in the state of Goiás. In 2019 AEE had about 16,000 students. Six of

---

18 CARVALHO, 2017

19 Agro in Data, SEAPA, 2020

its institutions offer 49 undergraduate courses to thousands of students served by more than 700 teachers. Besides basic education the Institution offers masters in pharmaceutical sciences, dentistry and a master's and doctorate in human movements and environmental sciences.

The extension programs serve more than 500 children from the suburbs. In the project Criar e Tocar, students also receive food, music training for orchestra and scholarships in schools and colleges. These education and health projects operate in poor communities to realize the pioneers' dream of a Christian university in the Brazilian midwest.

Reflection on History Should Shape Our Future

Brazil was Portugal's colony as Israel had been Egypt's slave for four centuries. External, political slavery can be ended in one night but the inner spirit of slavery can last a long time. If the "yeast" (worldview or the spirit) of slavery remains in people's minds it prevents them from becoming a free nation: wise and great. That is why to 'disciple a nation' means to educate that nation. Freedom is a matter of the spirit. The Bible says: "Now the Lord is the Spirit, and where the Spirit of the Lord is, there is freedom" (2 Corinthians 3:17). In the same letter to the Corinthians - a Roman colony - the apostle Paul teaches that our struggle is not against human structures or social circumstances but against forms of thought that have the appearance of truth but are sophistry. They have a certain logic but, in the end, they enslave people in deception. These deceptive worldviews become fortresses that imprison the mind. Truth has to be taught to destroy deceptive ideologies (2 Corinthians 10: 3-5).

Brazil is no longer a colony but it is wandering in the wilderness as did Israel after its miraculous exodus from Egypt. Those liberated slaves were marching to the Promised Land but they did not stop thinking like slaves. Their slave mentality made them wander in the desert for 40 years. Even there they were sustained miraculously. The Father's care was evident but their unbelieving thoughts and disobedient hearts prevented them from becoming a genuine community - a family under one Father.

God used those decades in the desert to drive the enslaving worldview out of their souls. The rebellious generation that did not believe that God was able to make them a great nation had to die out. The new generation had to be circumcised. It had to renew the covenant to serve God and take responsibility for each other. No child was circumcised during the years they were in the desert. Circumcising each other was a deliberate decision in collective obedience. To choose to be circumcised together was to become God's nation. It was a choice to be one community under God, caring for each other - materially and spiritually.

Their spirit of slavery manifested itself in the wilderness in difficult times. Their instinctive response was to transfer the responsibility onto someone else. Immediately they wanted to return to slavery in Egypt. They found it harder to go forward into a responsible freedom under God.

The Israelites were delivered from the "reproach of Egypt" only after they circumcised each other (Joshua 5: 2-9). That step of collective obedience was a renewal of their national covenant. It was a commitment to walk in God's ways as one people - one community. It made Abraham's biological descendants his children in faith, in a living relationship with God and each other. This was a milestone in forging the soul of a new and free nation. Of course, the process had begun much earlier. Pooling their resources to build God's Tabernacle among them was one step. They called it the "Tent of Meeting" with God. Their new, unique identity as God's people had begun to emerge when they put God's law, the Ark of the Covenant, in the very center of their camp. It was an affirmation that God and His word, not Egypt, were to have the ultimate authority over their lives, individually and as a nation.

Brazil is yet to find its identity as a nation under God and His law. Some Europeans came here seeking wealth; others were exiled from Portugal as "criminals"; still others were brought here from Africa, against their will, as slaves. What makes us one people, a nation?

Franciscan Friar Vicente do Salvador was the first to use the term "Brazilian" in a pejorative way to identify someone in terms of the accident of his birth and the poor moral quality of his activities. Following that we continue to define ourselves as an extractive, exploitative, gold-digging, opportunistic people who find it challenging to get along with each other. Our origin as a nation is no more exemplary than the Hebrew origin as Egyptian slaves. Will we remain slaves, uncomfortable with each other, or become one as children of one Father, doing His will on earth?

So, who are we as Brazilians?

Our messy beginning makes it hard to define Brazilian identity or soul in a positive way. What will define us? Three and a half centuries of slavery? Or 130 years of wanderings without direction and light? Who will teach us that practice of equity is more important than the entitlement of "rights?" Must Brazilian democracy mean the right of the majority or the good of the whole? Does winning an election mean obtaining power over others, or is it the responsibility to care for everyone? Where shall we find the light of life in a culture where education is the pursuit of power and status rather than wisdom and humility?

What does secularization of education do to a college?

Secularization has turned a college into a shopping mall; the teacher has become an anonymous vendor. His job is to lure students to buy his department's wares. The customer can choose an expensive brand or have fun with cheap consumer goods. This sham, called 'Higher Education', cannot make Brazil a great nation. It has become incapable of attracting gifted teachers. Who wants to join a violent, dangerous, precarious, unworthy, impoverished, poorly paid and commercially exploitative profession? Education is ripe for a revolution described in this book.

Bibliography:

- CARVALHO, Heliel Gomes de. *James Fanstone:* Protestantismo, medicina como vocação e legado social na Fronteira Goiás na Primeira Metade do Século XX. Centro Universitário de Anápolis- UniEvangelica: 2015. Dissertação de Mestrado em Ciências Ambientais.

- FANSTONE, James. *Aventura Missionária no Brasil. A Incrível História do Hospital de Anápolis tirada das "memórias" de seu fundador.* São Paulo: Fonte Editorial. 2017.

- FERREIRA, Haydée Jayme. *Anápolis: sua vida, seu povo.* Brasília: Senado Federal, 1981.

- McGRATH, Alister. *A Revolução Protestante.* Brasília: Palavra, 2012.

- DUARTE, Crissiana de Almeida. *Enfermagem em Anápolis* (1933-1963). Universidade Católica de Goiás, Goiânia, 2007.

- HILSDORF, M.L.S. – *Escolas Americanas de Confissão Protestantes na província de São Paulo: um estudo de suas origens.* São Paulo 1977. Dissertação de Mestrado em Educação – Faculdade de Educação da Universidade de São Paulo.

- MELO, Josimeire Medeiros Silveira de. *História da Educação no Brasil;* Coordenação Cassandra Ribeiro Joye. - 2 ed. Fortaleza: UAB/IFCE, 2012.

- MENDONÇA, A. G. O. *Celeste Porvir – A inserção do protestantismo no Brasil.* Paulinas, São Paulo, 1986.

- PNUD, ed. (14 de setembro de 2018). "Human Development Indices and Indicators - 2018 Statistical Update" (PDF). Sept 11 2020.

- VERCELLI, Ligia de Carvalho Abões. O pensamento Educacional de Martinho Lutero. Universidade Nove de Julho. *Revista de Educação: Educere et Educere*, Vol. 7 n° 14 jul./dez. 2012, p. 46-53.

- VIRAÇÃO, Francisca Jaquelini de Souza. *A primeira igreja Protestante do Brasil.* São Paulo: Mackenzie, 2013.

Chapter 26

Revolution Across Cultures

Mark Harris[1]

As the kingdom of God spread, over centuries it developed a variety of forms. Missiologists have long discussed how the Gospel can be preached in varying ways from place to place, so as to speak to different cultures. But it seems less common to contextualize education to these varied patterns. Teachers may think that classroom instruction is simply a matter of finding one-size-fits-all "best practices" when, in fact, teaching methods that work in one culture may flop in another.

As servants of God we appreciate His multicultural world in its variety, by allowing God's truth to take root in ways that fit each setting. In addition, while we must allow God's truth to correct the sins of cultures, we also celebrate those aspects of each culture that display the glory of the Creator in unique ways. By magnifying these strengths in how we teach, we encourage students to participate joyfully and to succeed in beautiful ways.

A Lesson for the Instructor

In the late 1990's I was teaching economics to an international group of undergraduates in a Russian-American business university where most of the students were Russian. However, this class included one American and two students from India. I decided to give them a group assignment for which each group would write up and act out a few skits which illustrated one or more of the principles I was teaching.

The Russian students formed several groups, while the lone American joined the Indian students. The Russian groups followed a common protocol. They identified the most talented thinker in their group and supported

1 Dr. Mark Harris is a businessman, accountant, and missiologist who has served in multiple roles both in the USA and overseas. He earned his DIS while living in Russia for 9 years in the 1990's. He started an accounting company and two nonprofits after returning to the USA in 2002. He now lives with his wife in Lynchburg, VA.

that student, who presented a cogent argument for the economic principle they had chosen. Although I had instructed every student to fully participate, most Russian presentations were done by one student whose mastery of the subject, or lack thereof, determined the group's degree of success.

The Indian-American group, by contrast, sat down and started to plan democratically how to work together to imagine and present their skits. They all took part in their presentation, using creativity and humor, and effectively illustrated the economic principles. Their presentation was much more basic and "folksy" in approach. They had more accurately followed my intended form, but their depth of understanding of the principles was no greater than that of the Russian teams.

I was initially disappointed with the Russian groups because they had not done their presentations as directed. I didn't notice that I was using an educational method that I myself had enjoyed as an undergrad and seminarian, assuming it would be universally understood and enjoyed. The American and the Indians had experienced similar methods in school and immediately knew what to do. For the Russians, however, it was very unusual: they lacked classroom experience in organizing themselves, choosing a topic together, and working as a team to present effectively. But they did know how to find the most capable student and support him or her. Surprisingly, the two methods produced comparable results.

I am sure the students learned from this project, but maybe I learned more. As their instructor I gained an introduction to the wonders and challenges of cross-cultural education. I subsequently did missiological research that helped me to better understand cultural issues, and Russian culture in particular.

Cultural Change

We who desire to impact our students, rightly focus on the content of our lectures, lessons and materials, but we should also adopt cultural forms that best help learners gain understanding, change attitudes and acquire skills. Those who teach or write for audiences in other cultures, employing forms and methods from home, may find that their lessons misinform, seem irrelevant, embarrass learners or fail to bring about the desired change.

Lessons succeed to the extent that they meet the learning needs of people within their culture.

As we plan a revolution in education it is important to avoid exporting fully-formed educational systems from the West, or from the North, East or South for that matter. There is no "one size fits all" program that can be packaged and uniformly taught around the world. Rather: we must seek to discover which locally acceptable forms and methods will work within a given culture, in order to change those that local educators, parents and students find tailored to their needs and values. These forms and methods must not feel "foreign."

In this chapter I explain several cultural variables that affect intercultural learning. These variables interact in a variety of ways in each cultural setting. Although it takes difficult, time-consuming work to gain a clear understanding of another culture, those efforts tend to pay off in the long run. Understanding and applying these principles will foster sustainable, replicable systems that outlast our involvement, bringing fruit which can multiply on native soils, to the glory of God.

Layers of Culture

For our purposes culture can be defined as "a system of behaviors, beliefs, values, and products that are characteristic of a society." Members of a society acquire these elements mostly informally, through years of inter-action within families, friendships and social structures.

Culture is like an onion: it consists of layers that move from the visible outer to the invisible inner. The outer layer is observable behavior which includes how adults educate their young. Below that is the more basic layer of social authority, patterns of group behavior that may be enforced by laws, customs and mores. The next layer consists of collective and per-sonal experience or history that define a society's worldview and expecta-tions. The deepest layer, or cultural core, consists of fundamental beliefs: assumptions that seem self-evident and which few people question.

People in a given culture can explain its social rules, how authority works, and how one is expected to behave, well enough to outsiders. But they cannot always put their finger on basic assumptions which underlie that behavior. Core values are taken for granted. "That's just the way things are." They may even feel surprise or irritation when others question those assumptions, even if they are unsure where their culture's most basic intuitions came from in the first place.

There is an old Chinese proverb: "If you want to know what water is, don't ask the fish." Those who swim in the ocean of their own culture are not fully aware of that ocean.

Educational forms ultimately derive from invisible, core beliefs and values on which behavior rests, and lending it stability. Those core assumptions are now "common sense" to educators, parents, and teachers. The changes outsiders introduce may fail to take root, because they fail to take those assumptions into account.

It is true that some aspects of every culture are antagonistic to the ways of God and beg reform. But most are morally neutral. Every culture has strengths and weaknesses. For example: Russian culture tends to produce strong leaders and deep thinkers who love the mysteries of God, as evidenced in the great Russian literary tradition. American culture tends to produce good collaborators and amiable conversationalists who work together as teams, as practiced in the great American business tradition. Both traditions have something important to offer each other, as I learned in many ways during my years in Russia.

Sound education requires wise mentors guiding motivated students toward mutually-agreed goals. So the genius of any system requires utilizing elements of culture so that wisdom is effectively understood, internalized and shared.

Plants indigenous to local soil and climate need no "hot house" to artificially sustain them. It would be foolish to plant palm trees in Alaska, or apple orchards in Arizona. One studies the soil and climate before introducing new vegetation.

Dimensions of Culture

In *Cultures and Organizations*, Geert Hofstede identified four dimensions across which educational systems differ from culture to culture, which have to do with attitudes towards power, how people work together, uncertainty and gender.

1) Power Distance (PD) – How does one see authority and dependence? In societies with a large PD, citizens accept that power is distributed unequally. Students in such cultures depend on instructors for learning. Students deeply respect their teachers, and do not question, let alone challenge them regarding their knowledge or approach.

Low PD cultures expect power to be distributed more equally and thus students will tend to see teachers as equals, freely challenging them, addressing them on familiar terms, and perhaps becoming friends outside of class.

Those in low PD cultures tend to assume that students in high PD cultures must feel oppressed and constrained, but this is usually not the case. Students find comfort in learning quietly from a respected expert, and may feel nervous in the presence of a low PD teacher who expects students to become familiar, forcing them to think for themselves.

My Russian students were more comfortable and effective with higher PD structures, while the Americans thrived in a lower PD environment. This difference was displayed in their contrasting approaches to my economics assignment. In addition, when I taught accounting my Russian students expected to memorize large amounts of information. Even though they had the disadvantage of being taught in a second language, they usually surpassed my American students who expected more lenience and accommodation rather than rigid demands from the respected authority.

2) Individualism and Collectivism (IC) – How strongly are people integrated into groups to which they are expected to remain loyal and adapt their behavior? In collectivist societies, the interests of the group prevail over the interests of the individual. A student thinks more about pleasing his family than finding his way in the world.

Individualist societies, which are in the minority, empower students to study what they like, while parents tend to allow children to study whatever topics will fulfill them as individuals.

3) Uncertainty Avoidance (AV) – How threatened do people in a given culture feel in the face of uncertain situations? Those with high AV tend to treat as dangerous new ideas or behavior. Those with low AV tend to be more curious and accepting novelties. A student in a high AV society will favor structured learning situations with clear objectives and in which there is only one correct answer to be discovered. Students in low AV societies much more enjoy open-ended learning situations where originality is rewarded.

The extent to which students tolerate uncertainty is important because they will often feel great stress when facing a system or teacher at variance with their expectations. Young people have learned what is expected and generally feel comfortable with the style they have been taught. They are often thrown into anxiety by an unfamiliar style.

4) Masculinity and Femininity (MF) – How far do gender roles overlap or remain distinct, and to what extent do traditional masculine values dominate? In more masculine-oriented societies aggressiveness and competition tend to be stronger than cooperation and security, which affects how both genders operate. Women in masculine-oriented societies seem more "masculine" than women in feminine-oriented societies.

Masculine-oriented students strive to be the best, and are comfortable with competition for grades. In addition there are clearer distinctions between masculine and feminine subjects. In feminine-oriented societies it is preferable to be a cooperative average student than to stand out.

The "mental programming" reflected in these four dimensions of power, individuality, uncertainty and gender, affect every aspect of society, so at school, too, people think and act consistent with general patterns. Parents, teachers and students tend to feel comfortable with the educational forms adopted within their cultures and to resist alien systems. A student or teacher may more easily adapt while being a guest in another culture, but will expect his "home" to maintain the status quo.

Cultural Learning Styles

"Learning style" has been defined as "How you take in information; how you perceive, remember, think; how you apprehend, store, transform, and use information."

The learning styles prevalent in a given culture are influenced by the dimensions of culture described above, among other factors. Although individual temperaments differ, students are in their most receptive stage of life, and the general pattern by which they learn derives from these social patterns.

Three culturally-rooted learning styles are common:

Synthetic vs Analytic – Do students isolate and examine the individual elements of a subject, or do they tend to see it as a whole? Synthetic (or "big picture") learners are most comfortable if they can see how a specific subject touches everything else. They especially value practical application. Analytic learners are comfortable with learning individual elements of a subject in isolation, being less concerned about fitting them into a global picture or applying them to their lives.

Formal educational systems reward students who are adept at analyzing and reproducing information from isolated topics. Those who are naturally strong in this ability tend to rise to the top of their classes, but every student in such a culture becomes more adept in cramming information and regurgitating it for an exam.

Informal systems tend more to pass down practical wisdom that can be applied to life. Consider a child growing up on a farm. What he learns tends to relate to the overall system that must be cooperatively managed by a capable leader. Bookish analysis of topics that do not enhance those abilities would be a waste of time. Similarly, traditional education for women often focused on developing her ability to run a household.

Cooperative vs. Competitive – Do students expect to learn a subject in a group, or to master it alone? And will a student be graded as part of a group, or for personal achievement?

Competitive systems are often less concerned with how the educational process fits students into society, and more oriented toward scholastic achievement. There are practical reasons for this, but the result may be that graduates fail to smoothly integrate into worksites after years of mastering isolated bits of information. (A problem several contributors describe in various countries.)

Concepts vs Skills – Do students want to learn first with hands or minds? Would they rather do first, then perceive what they have done, or understand first, then do it? The answer may depend on how long a given society has been literate. Some newly-literate cultures continue to transmit lessons orally and in groups, and feel uncomfortable mastering information from texts.

Students from highly literate cultures may look down on such young people. But youths in such cultures may handily memorize and retain large quantities of material orally. They are unused to relying on books, developing powerful memories instead. Students in such cultures may be reluctant to waste time learning "trivial" facts that do not directly contribute to social intercourse or to a trade.

Learning styles are developed in culture and solidify as adolescents become adults. All styles can assist young people in gaining skills and spiritual maturity. Programs that rely on culturally dominant styles will, at their best, prepare young people to thrive within the cultures that developed those methods. Of course, cultures change over time and what works in one era may fail later on.

Teaching Approaches

Teachers who are honored as masters of their craft in one culture do not necessarily begin as masters in another culture. Those of us with cross-cultural teaching experience have felt the confusion that arises when there is a clash of expectations between students and teachers. The issues outlined above should help the reader appreciate why transitions can be difficult. In this final section, in the light of these diverse cultural patterns, let us examine three common teaching approaches and see why they meet with varying results across cultures.

I draw here on the approach of Herbert M. Kliebard as developed recently by James Plueddemann to describe three approaches to teaching which can be described in terms of production, growth, and travel.

Production – The student is seen as raw material that will be shaped by the technician into a finished product. As in a factory, efficiency and predictability are key to keeping the product rolling off the conveyor belt. This is a business model, in which one calculates cost per student, and hires skilled workers so that return on investment will be maximized.

This approach has become common worldwide. What it gains in efficiency and standardization, it loses in serving the individual needs of students and to mentor students, which transfers culture as well as ideas.

Growth – In this approach the student is seen as a unique plant that needs to be tended by a master gardener in order to flower and bear rich fruit. The tending may not seem efficient and cannot be standardized. Teachers require the insight to know students as well as they know subjects. While the production model might produce good soldiers, the growth model resembles the training of athletes to harness their inborn physical and mental potentiality. Paul, indeed, compared spiritual growth to the training through which a boxer or runner goes. The disciple-maker needs to understand the spiritual gifting of each disciple in order to adapt training to his or her needs.

Travel – This approach pictures student and teacher as fellow travelers. The teacher is a wise guide, having gone ahead and gained familiarity with the territory, but he sees himself as traveling the same road and can still learn even from a less-experienced traveler. The fellow traveler model works only within a culture with comparatively low power distance. But the one who has gone ahead is still recognized as a respected guide, so teacher and student are not simply "traveling buddies."

Curriculum Design and Outcomes

To be effective, curricula must, from the beginning, be designed with the target culture in mind. Universal truths must be made understandable and applicable to the lives of the students within their own worldview.

This should be obvious, but curriculum designers are often enamored with efficient "time-saving" systems that are scalable and transferable. Young Russians whom I interviewed had little patience with the discipleship booklets that Americans had packaged and translated. They wanted deep discussion and distrusted simplified and formulaic lessons.

However, all this may prove secondary to students who only seek a diploma. It is frustrating for an educator with high ambitions to encounter students who only care about acquiring credentials. If they value superficial outcome over genuine accomplishment, they will find ways to "work the system". often gaining the cooperation of local administrators.

Conclusion

All education should have the ultimate purpose of bringing glory to God. Christian education must draw on the Scriptures for spiritual formation. But training must also be adapted to the needs and values of the local culture. Just as God created incredible variety in the natural world, human variety is also part of His plan and brings Him glory. We should keep this in mind as we prepare to teach cross-culturally.

An international revolution in education must, therefore, reflect human diversity and involve cooperation on the deepest levels. Indeed, the cooperative character of this book should not be seen as an accident, but as a theological statement. Experts from diverse cultures must be full partners in designing approaches that will best reach students wherever they are. They may tell you, as I once heard a Russian trainer say to an American audience, "Bring us the general principles, but allow us to apply them to our own situation."

Cultures vary, and learning and teaching styles need to follow suit. They will vary again, whether we apply them in the classroom, to field study, to rooms with fifty students or one-on-one mentor relationships. But in each case cultural differences need to be treated with respect, for that is part of respecting the students we are called to mentor.

Chapter 28

Mastering the Media

Vishal Mangalwadi[1]

Human beings create culture because we use words. Language and Literature collect and communicate information and insights, truth and falsehood, wisdom and folly, traditions and innovations. Language creates culture because it unites our souls in a common bond. Our species uses words because the Triune God made us in the image of the divine Word (logos) who envisioned, created and sustains the cosmos.

Four revolutions in communication have shaped human history:

Writing came first. While script was invented in Sumer and alphabets perfected by the Phoenicians, it was the Jews who transformed the world through the written medium. Numerically they were never a big nation. Unlike Assyrians, Persians, Greeks or Romans, the Jews never became an empire to conquer and rule a large portion of the world. They were a People of the Book. Their global influence came from the written word.

In my native India, Brahmins also had sacred "scriptures", the Vedas, even though they never developed a *script* to write down their *scriptures*. Sanskrit, their sacred language, had well developed grammar but, without a script, it remained inaccessible. The Brahmins chose not to write down their magical mantras. Exclusive commitment to orality allowed learned priests to keep their knowledge to themselves. Orality makes a student dependent upon his teacher or guru. Without written texts he has no way to check his teacher's facts.

This tight control over oral knowledge and memorization was intended to sustain tradition. It made the priest the authority; truth was subservient to the teacher. That precluded the possibility of reforming religion and society. Consequently India's reform had to wait until after missionaries

---

1 Prof. Vishal Mangalwadi, M.A. LLD is the visionary behind *The Third Education Revolution*.

had arrived in the 18th-19th centuries. They began to translate the Bible as well as Hindu Scriptures into vernaculars, making it possible for the people to study truth.

Missionaries wrote because God Himself had commanded Moses, the prophets and apostles to write down the revelations that they had seen, heard, experienced and understood. The biblical tradition made the priest a teacher. One of his duties was to teach his disciples to read God's Word, reflect upon it, copy it and then *pass on that knowledge to his students in turn.*

This religious tradition of a preacher-teacher/pastor-master arose from the fact that God promised to make Israel a wise nation, a light to all the nations that walk in darkness (Deuteronomy 4:5-8; Isaiah 2: 3-5 etc.). Most pagans saw religion as a matter of rightly-performed rituals, even if those rituals sounded like magical mumbo-jumbo. By contrast the priest, as an educator, made God's Word intelligible. He made understanding and wisdom the social matrix of Shalom: peace, with justice and prosperity.

Printing was the second revolution in communication that shaped history. What you hand-write is read by one person at a time. What you print can be read by many at the same time. Printing thus turns writing into 'mass communication'. Widely-disseminated literature, in turn, consolidates and advances a culture.

The Buddhists and Confucian literati printed their sacred texts in China and Korea hundreds of years before Johannes Gutenberg invented the printing press in Europe around 1450. However, printing technology did not reform China, Korea or pre-Reformation Germany. Printed texts, including the Gutenberg Bible, looked beautiful.

They were works of art. Printing did not reform because the Buddhist scriptures taught that words cannot communicate truth. It had to be "realized" in a mystical experience, achieved via meditation that empties or silences one's mind of words and thoughts. For Confucian scholars, mastery of the Classics was a door to political power, ideally used to pa-tronize the good of the people, but certainly to bring honor and riches to one's own family.

The Gutenberg Bible was printed in Latin that very few people read. A single copy of that Bible cost the same amount of money as a German townhouse. Only kings and bishops could afford the Gutenberg Bible. It was a revered work of religious art for display, not for study.

Printing technology contributed to the opening of the European mind only after the Protestant Reformation made God's Word affordable for the common man in his mother-tongue. Studying God's Word demystified religion. As people sought truth, they were able to question human authority, enslaving superstitions and myths.

Audio-visual communication, epitomized by Hollywood, was the third revolution in communication. Christianity lost the West partly because it allowed secular nihilism to monopolize this media. For much of the 20th century Christian leaders advised their followers to stay away from sinful films and entertainment. Fundamentalists thought that, by banning idol-making, God had banned visual arts. God did command us not to make *His* images. They would necessarily be false because God is Spirit, without a physical form. However, to assume that God was against making visual images was a costly misunderstanding of the first two of the Ten Commandments. For the Bible was clear that God had made His own image — man: male and female. Sin damaged that image, that is why the Son of God came to help us see what the image of God in us should look like. Jesus is the visible image of the invisible God. The fact that God makes His own image in Christ and in us should have encouraged Christians to artistic, linguistic, and scientific creativity. The Creator gave His Word *because* the gift of language and writing are creative arts: not just poetry, but all writing, including biography and history is a creative art.

Now the electronic media has evolved into *digital* media. The usefulness and affordability of this new medium is making it virtually omnipresent. This is the fourth and the latest revolution in communication. It has already grown bigger and more influential than all the previous communication revolutions combined.

Social Media: A Worldwide Beast?

Silicon Valley inventor and business magnate, Steve Jobs (1955-2011), named his digital brand "Apple" for a variety of reasons. He was on a fruitarian diet, visiting a commune with an apple orchard when the name of "Apple" occurred to him. The brand name made sense because "Apple" would appear before its rival Atari in a phone book.

At some stage its cultural significance became apparent: the invention played a role similar to the proverbial fruit of "the tree of the knowledge of good and evil" that Eve and Adam ate in Eden:

> "When the woman saw that the fruit of the tree was good for food and pleasing to the eye, and also desirable for gaining wisdom, she took some and ate it. She also gave some to her husband, who was with her, and he ate it. Then the eyes of both of them were opened, and they realized they were naked; so they sewed fig leaves together and made coverings for themselves." (Genesis 3: 6-7)

Digital media is the most seductive fruit on the planet. Its charm and million-and-one benefits are well-known. Contemporary life is inconceivable without it. It drives everything from conversation to conferences to cars and capital exchange. Yet eating this fruit also opens eyes. Even Silicon Valley can now see human nakedness.

Anyone whose eyes are still closed ought to watch the 2020 Netflix docudrama, *The Social Dilemma.* This 94-minute film, directed by Jeff Orlowski, is intended to horrify you. The film is created by industry insiders who know that they have created a real-life Frankenstein.

Social media, the film says, makes a few people super wealthy by dehumanizing two billion "users." Only two kinds of businessmen describe their customers as "users": drug pushers and social media tycoons. The industry insiders lamented that this invention is destroying not just the social fabric of civilization such as family and church, but also democracy and truth. One of these creators-turned-critics is candid in admitting that social media's "short term" contribution to America will be a "civil war."

Why? Wasn't "social media" created for social networking? What turned it into a deadly force that is dividing society?

The film explains that social media is free only because advertisers pay for it. What do advertisers get in return? They get to target you, the user, even if you never become an addict. Social media's success is proportional to making you too weak to resist the advertisers' subtle hold over you.

Once addicted you cease being the "user." Social media uses you. You are turned into the product that social media sells to advertisers.

Don't get me wrong. Social media doesn't violate your privacy. They are smart enough to know that they can't give away their only capital — you, their esteemed "user."

The media knows more about you than you think. Google, Facebook, Twitter, Instagram and other social media giants use super-computers and artificial intelligence to keep track of every second you spend on phone or online. Your every search, "like," dislike or contact is customized at a lightening speed and linked to targeted marketing.

This divides your loved ones. It ensures that a "pro-life" voter sees mainly those ads and ideas that interest him or her. The "pro-death" voter sees what reinforces his or her bias. Opponents' prejudices are continuously reinforced to the point that they become enemy combatants.
A dear woman lamented that, in order to pressure her to vote for their political preference, her children have "unfriended" her on Facebook and "blocked" her. She can no longer see her grandchildren's photos, let alone cuddle them and feed them! Grandchildren can't comprehend why their parents have become so mean as to punish their beloved grandparents.

Is Media the Problem?

No! The film *The Social Dilemma* makes it clear that the digital media is not the root problem. Nor do its creators and capitalists want to destroy anyone's family or democracy.

Yet, the film has a prophetic edge. It diagnoses one of our new and contemporary problems: a monster has been unleashed upon the post-truth world with awesome memory and artificial intelligence, but without a conscience. This has happened at a time when our nihilistic intellectual culture has lost agreed-upon standards to distinguish true from false and good from evil.

Consider that grandmother's pain for a moment: is it a moral absolute that children should honor their mother even if they disagree with her political preference?

Who commanded, "Children honor your father and your mother?"

Does God even exist? Is He capable of speaking?

Who gave Him the authority to issue such a command?

Is language a gift from heaven? Or did it evolve in the jungles of Africa when our ancestors were fighting over mates and food?

Do parents teach children to honor them out of mere self-interest? Is morality anything more than a tool by which the powerful protect their personal interests?

Social media users empower media moguls, but the moguls are not "drug mafia dons" who control drug cartels. Some of them are innovators, successful businessmen and philanthropists. Facebook didn't make anyone an addict in order to use them. *The social dilemma* is that our age had already crucified the spirit that could tame the beastly machine before the monster was created.

Truth, morality, wisdom and self-control are matters of the spirit. The power to deny yourself, to let spirit rule over flesh, comes from spiritual disciplines such as fasting and prayer. *The Third Education Revolution* must resurrect the spirit of truth before the amoral monster of artificial intelligence devours the culture that created it.

Resurrection of the spirit can make digital media, the world's largest educational platform and eco-system, a force for good. The 21st Century will thus belong to a spirit-filled worldview that has the power to tame this worldwide beast.

The film, *The Social Dilemma*, presents a simple truth: The creators and owners of social media have the world's most creative teams, financial resources and prestige. What they lack are the spiritual and intellectual resources to harness the beast that they have created. Such resources can transform digital media into a power for good.

For digital media makes global reformation possible. It is so far-reaching and so affordable that even a tiny, dedicated minority can win the intellectual war of worldviews. Many dedicated minorities have already used the media to mislead the masses and even their leaders. *The Third Education Revolution* will win because our numerical, social and moral strength will come from millions of partnering churches. They seek God's Spirit of truth, holiness, liberty and love.

Harnessing technology and artificial intelligence will help the Church create a new intellectual environment that promotes Veritas and Virtue. Digital media is a mountain that can be summitted.

A revolution, like a fire, requires certain elements to be present before it blazes forth: social weather that favors change, the fuel of a group of people prepared to act, then the spark of timely ideas. This book transmits the key ideas of *The Third Education Revolution*. You, the follower of Christ, are part of the forest which we pray will blaze forth to transform our increasingly chilly and dark modern world.

Your role in reading this book will not, we pray, be merely passive. We need you to fall on your knees and seek the role God may have prepared for you in transforming the modern world. The world needs those who will "speak the truth in love": truths that have been neglected, even abandoned and scorned, for too long.

Practical Proposals

Chapters by Dr. Ashish Alexander, Giftson Selladurai, and Hans Joachim Hahn describe some of the initial steps being planned to harness digital media. Let me introduce two of the media projects in which you can participate proactively.

Restoring Civilization's Ruined Foundations

The film *The Social Dilemma* is our culture's heart-wrenching cry for help. That cry to fill a materialistic machine with soul and humanity must be heeded. Some of the creators of the social media are pleading with us to restore the soul of modern education: re-make it so as to be a pursuit of truth, virtue and relationships. Therefore, our mission intends to create a compelling documentary series that can revive the roots of our ailing civilizational tree.

The reality style documentary series we are planning will not be confined to Western civilization. It will also examine the Bible's impact on modern Africa, Indonesia, India, Korea, Japan, China and South America. As various chapters in this volume suggest, networks of scholars are already studying and publishing how the Bible changed these cultures. Our creative team will pool this research to create authentic books and documentaries on how the Bible is the DNA in the soul of the modern world. Atheists, Critical Theorists, Environmentalists, Marxists, Rationalists, Secular Humanists, and Skeptical Scientists who condemn and marginalize the Bible are, themselves, products of a civilization birthed by the Bible. They do not know that their rebellion is burning down the house in which they were born and continue to live.

This multi-part series will be distributed through network, cable and video streaming services. The research will be turned into books. Extensive footage gathered from around the world will be used to create online courses on the Bible and civilization for college, seminary, and senior high school students.

The series will explore the thesis presented in my books that the modern world which pursued truth and goodness was built upon the Bible. Modern civilization is crumbling because nihilists have destroyed its foundations.

The main series, as currently conceptualized, will present five international scholars as hosts. They are studying five different fields of study but come together because they are reading my books and want to test the thesis that the Bible is the soul of the modern world. They will take an intellectual journey to find the soul amputated by the postmodern world. The series will explore how their initial opinions and convictions change with increased understanding.

The five investigators will visit locations where history was made. They will interact with experts with conflicting convictions. Live encounters with historians, philosophers, educators, artists, scientists and statesmen will challenge the host-scholars to critically examine prominent interpretations of the modern world. At the end of each segment and at the end of the series the researchers will debate the thesis of the series. They will discuss the strengths and weaknesses of various viewpoints and share how their experience has or has not changed their initial opinion.

Experts will identify the core historical elements to be included in the series. Entertainment tone, format and other aspects that affect marketability will be shaped by experienced professionals. Practitioners of online pedagogy will be involved in developing the project from the beginning. After filming they will use the extensive footage to create educational curricula.

Several books have been published already to support the proposed do-cuseries. "Treatments" for four episodes have also been written. These will allow a creative team to hit the ground running as soon as funding becomes available. A vast quantity of additional research exists and more research is being done. A business plan is being prepared for this aspect of *The Third Education Revolution.* Meanwhile, we are seeking God's guidance to build our team and momentum with the following more short-term project.

Human Sexuality, Gender Confusion and Worldviews

The Western family is falling apart. Jewish scholar Mona Charen, in *Sex Matters: How Modern Feminism Lost Touch with Science, Love, and Common Sense* (2018), concludes that lack of monogamous sexual discipline is destroying America's inner cities. And yet, media moguls, including Wikipedia, have become so intolerant that they will not accept a person as an editor who believes that marriage means a permanent and exclusive union of one man and one woman.

This bigotry is amazing, given that almost a century ago, English ethnologist and social anthropologist Joseph Daniel Unwin (1895–1936) studied sexual mores in 80 primitive tribes and 6 developed civilizations over the preceding 5,000 years. In his magisterial study, <u>Sex and Culture</u> (1934), he concluded that sexual discipline in monogamy was the key to empowerment of women and societal development.

If what these scholars have found is true, how did western universities, judges, public intellectuals and politicians come to a point that they no longer understand what is male and female, love and sex, marriage and family? Such a moment of the cultural elite is ripe for a new dawn. The wood is dry, and the wind is hot. With your help we can ignite a wild-fire that will burn dead leaves and trees.

In order to build a creative team with grassroots support, we propose to invite established professors to guide a team to study these questions and write books for the general and educational market. This research will be turned into a 90-minute documentary and online curriculum for Behavioral Sciences 101. Professors in our team will partner with accredited universities to offer these courses for college credit through local churches. Participating churches will invite high school and college students to come to host churches two or three times a week and take these online courses for college credits.

Our Times Call For Action

A popular movement of readers like you is needed to unite in prayer. We have to act when we "see the fields, white for the harvest." If you are able, and agree with our goals, we invite you in addition to prayer, to help crowd-fund this pilot project for 2021. Success on this front will make it easier to build a creative community to put more of the army of Christian soldiers into the field for *The Third Education Revolution*.

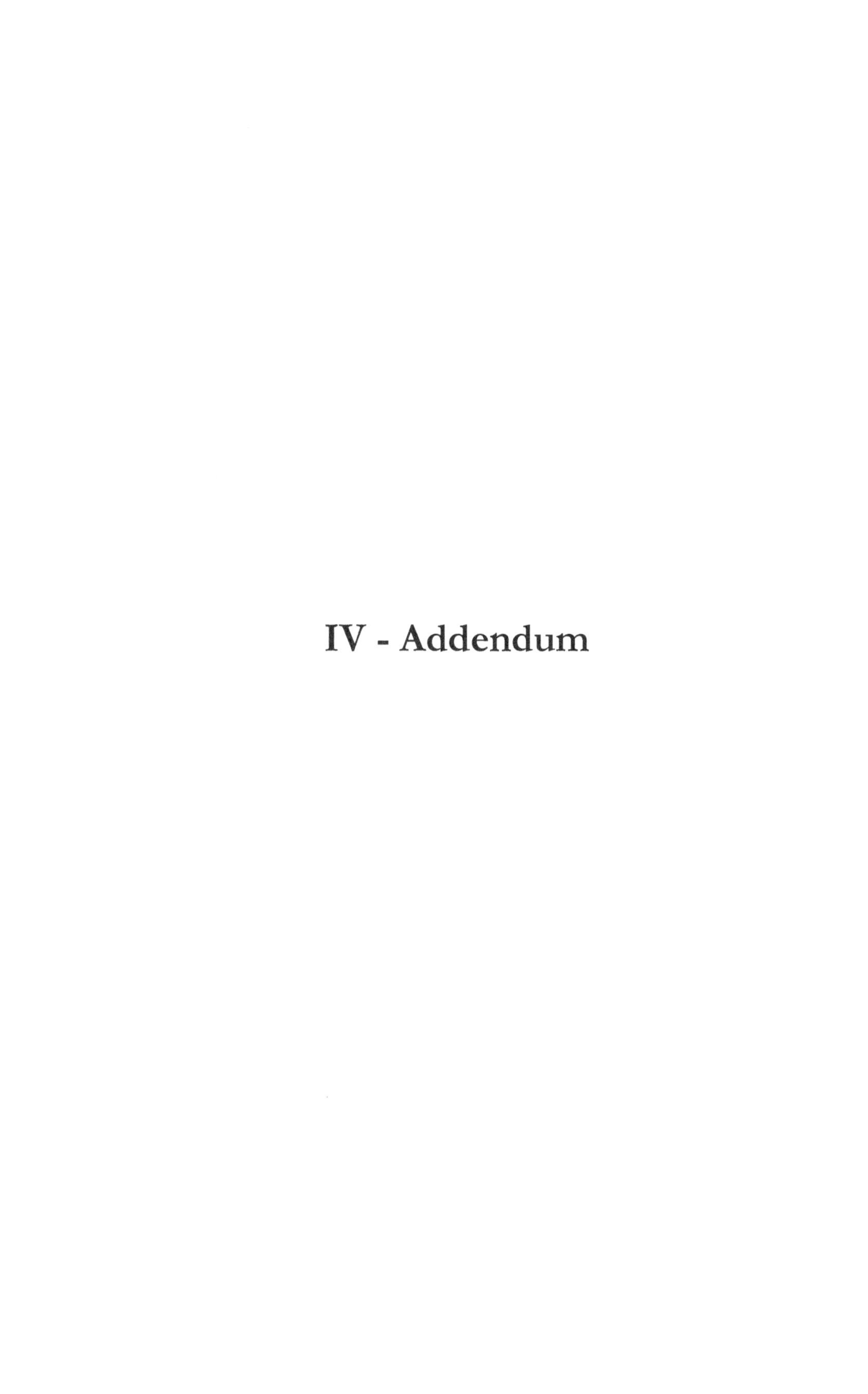

IV - Addendum

EDUCATION:

WHY AND HOW TO CHANGE IT?

We are not the first ones to say that secular education needs a revolution. Many have pleaded for change, especially since the two world wars.

The Jews were not the only ones persecuted in countries such as Russia or Germany. Totalitarian Internationalism was robbing private citizens and entire nations of their sovereignty, rights to life, liberty and property. This prompted Luis Finkelstein, a rabbi and Talmud scholar to initiate a conference on "Science, Philosophy and Religion and Their Relation to the Democratic Way of Life" from September 9-11, 1940. New York's Jewish Theological Seminary (JTS) hosted it out of a sense of solidarity with the tortured. High profile public figures felt obliged to participate in the conversation: Why was the West at war against its own soul?

Prof. Mortimer Adler (1902-2001), a non-observant Jew, shocked the learned participants by asserting that the greatest threat to America's democratic civilization came not from Adolf Hitler but from average university professor.

Adler was an esteemed pioneer of the Great Books curriculum in the University of Chicago. The school's president, Robert Maynard Hutchins, had invited Adler to Chicago to help reform America's decaying educa-tion. One of America's prominent philosophers of education, Hutchins believed the thesis that Adler articulated: the university had become the greatest threat to Western freedom.

After the War, Hutchins became Chicago University's Chancellor. He partnered with Adler in editing the 54-volume Great Books of the West-ern World (1952). Adler went on to plan and direct the creation of the University's two-volume index of great ideas, *A Syntopicon: An Index to The Great Ideas* (1952; second edition, 1990). Adler became a Christian only in 1984, when he was 82-years old. By then he had realized that his heroic efforts to reform education had failed.

Philosopher John Dewey (1859-1952) and his life-long disciple, Sidney Hook, early on recognized the threat that Adler posed to their own work. Dewey had taught at the University of Chicago from 1894- 1904 and founded The University of Chicago Laboratory Schools. Dewey and Hook hit back at Adler's assertion because they realized that Adler was attacking Pragmatism. Thanks to Dewey, Pragmatism had replaced Christianity as America's reigning philosophy of education.

Positivism, which came from England, and Pragmatism, born in America, had replaced the West's biblical morality with relativism. These philosophies were human speculations and had little relationship to truth. They could not help professors conjure up out of their magical hats any credible standard of justice that would allow them to say to a Stalin or a Hitler: "Thou shalt not take away a citizen's or a nation's property, liberty or life."

An enemy could destroy a Pearl Harbour but moral relativism, taught by university professors, was destroying the very foundations of the American way of life. The West's freedoms had been built upon the rock-solid truths revealed in the Bible that "all men are created equal . . . and are endowed by their Creator with inalienable rights to life, liberty and pursuit of happiness."

So, at the start of World War II, the great challenge confronting the free world was: how can 'Science, Philosophy, and Religion' come together to restore the foundations of Western civilization? Or, must the USA also go the way of the birthplace of Protestant Reformation — Germany? Could America degenerate to murdering millions of innocent?

Christian seminaries had made themselves incapable of speaking on public issues; therefore the Jewish Theological Seminary had to raise the question: What is God's will on this existential matter of the state trampling upon citizens' inalienable rights?

Scholars could not get together without disagreeing with each other. But the West had set itself on a path to self-destruction. Therefore, personal pride and prejudices had to be set aside; the Enlightenment's crisis had to be understood; solutions had to be found. The thinkers disagreed, but continued their deliberations through most of World War II.

As a 14-year old Jew, Adler had discovered St. Thomas Aquinas when he dropped out of school and began working as a copy boy for the New York Sun. His interest in Aristotle and Aquinas continued to grow even after he became a philosopher in his own right. He thought that universities could restore the foundations of Western Civilization by teaching great books and great ideas of the West.

Dewey, however, dismissed Adler as utterly naïve: Yes, Aristotle and Aquinas had been important in Europe's Renaissance... but only because, back then, Europe had one 'Papa' in Rome with a well established reserve bank of Europe's intellectual capital — the Roman Catholic Church. It was the Church that had canonized Aquinas as a saint and allowed its universities to teach Aristotle. The sixteenth century Reformation had undermined Roman Catholicism. That made Protestant nations such as the USA intellectual orphans. Orphans were free to believe whatever they wanted to and do what seemed right. The nanny State still accredited universities but lacked the means to decide who was or was not a saint: "A" (Aquinas) or "B" (the Buddha).

The secular state had no authority to tell university professors whether they should teach pre-marital abstinence or permissiveness. The Prince had been accrediting Post-Reformation Universities, but no one had authorized pagan governments to say whether the Creator had given an inalienable right to life to every person or if parents had the right to kill their babies to suite their convenience. A state (as a state) is not baptized with the Spirit of Truth. Therefore it cannot decide if God is Trinity or if worshiping idols is sin.

The Contemporary West's moral-intellectual cacophony is a fruit of the fact that, subject to student-mobs, every professor is free to play off his own music sheet. Every teacher has his own truth (or rather, her own "story"). No one can insist that history and mere story are two totally different beasts.

Even before coming to power, Hitler agreed with Adler that the public education system had paved the way for his cruel acts:

> "Nothing makes me more certain of the victory of our ideas than our success in the universities."

Following the war, one Auschwitz concentration camp survivor, Dr. Victor Frankl, echoed this sobering analysis: "I am absolutely convinced that the gas chambers of Auschwitz, were ultimately prepared not in some ministry or other in Berlin, but rather at the desks and in lecture halls of nihilistic scientists and philosophers."

And yet, . . . Dewey's criticism of Adler also turned out to be correct.

Alan Bloom, another Professor from Chicago University, summarized the failure of Adler and Hutchins in his 1987 block-buster, *The Closing of the American Mind: How Higher Education Has Failed Democracy and Impoverished the Souls of Today's Students.*

Bloom condemned liberal "openness" to relativism in academia and society as the paradoxical cause of the great "closing" of the American mind. Four decades of teaching in Chicago convinced him that Academic "openness" undermines critical thinking. It compels everyone to make up his/her own truth and morality. Openness to everyone's truth means eliminating objective standards, the "point of view" that could define and critique opinions and cultures.

Unlike Dewey and Hook, Alan Bloom did not blame Adler or the Great Books curricula. He had figured out that Adler's dream of reforming the university did not materialize because public high schools made students incapable of understanding the West's great books, art, music, architecture, literature, laws and institutions. How could one possibly understand Bunyan or Bach, Milton or Michelangelo, Locke and Law, Luther and Liberty, Newton and Natural Science without knowing the Bible. The Bible was the source of all that was great in the West and yet, western education, including the Great Books curriculum, had turned its back on the sacred text that made the West a thinking civilization.

Bloom was not a Christian. He was a Jew and a practicing homosexual who died of HIV/AIDS. His insight was correct: Great Books program, an improvement on crass Pragmatism, failed because biblically illiterate students, parents and universities had no interest or ability to study the great source of Western civilization. Biblical illiteracy made university professors and students incapable of understanding their culture's taproot.

So . . . what is the greatest threat to Western civilization?

Now, a generation later, a professor or a pundit is likely to answer: Western civilization deserves to be canceled. There was never anything great about the Pilgrims and Puritans, Washingtons and Jeffersons, Edwards and Finny, the Declaration or the Bill of Rights.

The souls of sixty million babies will most likely agree with these well-paid professors. How can they respect their murderers — their biological fathers and mothers, doctors and politicians, the press and the presidents who authorized their massacre in their own mothers' wombs? A university that turns a mother into a murderer is indeed more brutal than Hitlerism.

Great Books alone cannot rebuild a humane West. Anyone who builds his house on the shifting sands of human stories is a fool. The flood-waters will surely rise and bring down the fool's house. A wise man, taught the Master-Builder, builds his house upon the rock of God's word (Matthew 7: 24-27). The "Cornerstone" (Acts 4:11-12; Ephesians 2: 19-21) that built up the West's imperfect but humane civilization can rebuild the ancient ruins again.

The Third Education Revolution is a global movement. You are invited to participate whether you are a child, a parent, a pastor, or a professor. Please visit www:ThirdEducationRevolution.com and contact one of our offices.

CONTRIBUTORS

Alexander, Ashish (India)

Dr. Ashish Alexander is Dean of the School of Film and Mass Communication and Head of the English department in Sam Higginbottom University of Agriculture, Technology and Sciences at Prayagraj (formerly Allahabad), UP, India. He has a Ph.D. in English from Panjab University, Chandigarh, India. He worked as a development editor at Pearson Education India and later served as the editor of FORWARD Press magazine. Dr Alexander also worked briefly as a freelance journalist and has contributed to various national publications. The intellectual formation of modern India is one of his chief areas of interest. He is married to a journalist and has two children.

Anacker, Gayne (USA)

Dr. Gayne Anacker is a Trustee of the C.S. Lewis Foundation, which he also served as Vice President for Academic Affairs for over 20 years. In 2020, he retired from his position as Professor of Philosophy and Director of the University Honors Program at California Baptist University. He also served that institution as Dean of the College of Arts and Sciences for 15 years. Earlier, Dr. Anacker served as Founding President of Community Christian College, based in Redlands, CA. He began his teaching career at Orange Coast College, Costa Mesa, CA, where he was Professor of Philosophy and Religious Studies for 14 years.

Dr. Anacker speaks and writes on C.S. Lewis, virtue ethics, theory of truth, and Christian worldview. He holds a B.A. in philosophy from Westmont College, an M.A. from Washington State University, and a Ph.D. from the University of California, Irvine. He also earned the Master of Theological Studies from Gordon-Conwell Theological Seminary.

Andriono, Takim (Indonesia)

Dr. Takim Andriono is Chairman of TRAMPIL Indonesia Foundation and Visi & Misi Education Foundation, Advisory Board Member of University of the Nations, Board Member of Petra Christian Schools, and Advisor to the Council of Christian Education in Indonesia (East Java Chapter). He Formerly served as the Vice Rector for Academic Affairs of Petra Christian University.

Bastedo, David (USA)

David Bastedo is the founding President of CS Lewis College an arm of the CS Lewis Foundation. He is a member of the board of trustees of the college. He is a life-long educator who began his teaching career at the high school level and has spent over 45 years as an instructor. He has taught English composition and literature, mathematics, chemistry, and various subjects in biology at the high school level. While teaching in high school level he was also a staff member of Youth for Christ. He is currently Professor of Anatomy at San Bernardino Valley College in Southern California. He has served as the Chair of the Biology Department and Faculty Chair of the College Technology committee. He readily incorporates current educational technologies into his teaching and has been awarded Innovator of the Year at SBVC.

Benedict, Jason (USA)

Dr. Jason Benedit is an entrepreneur, business strategist, author, missionary, theologian and international trainer. In the early years of their ministry in Africa Jason and his wife Kim directed an interdenominational Bible school that served a number of local African denominations. In the early 2000s, Jason facilitated the funding and establishment of a Christian primary school in Niger. He and Kimberly also developed a field-based missionary internship that is still being used by their missionary agency today.

In 2008, Jason became a strategist with the Regent University Center for Entrepreneurship (a university think tank) where he co-founded the center's training-based business incubator model (the BDC model). They have founded eight BDCs in seven nations. In addition to his international missions work, Jason runs his own enterprise development-consulting firm. From 2009 – 2015 Jason worked in finance and investment banking and continues to consult the industry periodically.

Borges Júnior, Paulo (Brazil)

Paulo Borges Junior is married to Lana, and a father of five children. He is co-founder and one of the coordinators of the Ministry of Salt of the Earth. He served a mission in Edinburgh, Scotland. Paulo has a strong ministry in the area of teaching, as well as in the training leaders, church planters and people who work in the most varied areas of society. He has training in theology and civil engineering. He is president of Instituto Total.

de Carvalho, Heliel Gomes (Brazil)

Heliel Gomes and his wife Fernanda live in Anápolis with their children Isaías, Joyce and Anthony. He has a Master of Theology degree from the Andrew Jumper Presbyterian Graduate Center, Mackenzie University and a Master in Environmental Sciences from the University Center of Anápolis, UniEvangélica. He is presently both a PhD student in History at the Federal University of Goiás, and a professor at UniEvangelica and Coordinator of the Institutional Chaplaincy of Associação Educativa Evangélica. He also serves as pastor of the Presbyterian Church of Brazil in Anápolis.

Esolen, Anthony (USA)

Anthony M. Esolen is a writer, social commentator, translator of classical poetry, and Writer-in-Residence at Magdalen College of the Liberal Arts. He taught at Furman University and Providence College before transferring to the Thomas More College of Liberal Arts in 2017 and Magdalen in 2019.

Esolen has translated into English Dante's *Divine Comedy*, Lucretius' *On the Nature of Things*, and Torquato Tasso's *Jerusalem Delivered*. In addition to multiple books, he is the author of numerous articles in such publications as The Modern Age, The Catholic World Report, Chronicles, The Claremont Review of Books, The Public Discourse, First Things, Crisis Magazine, The Catholic Thing, and Touchstone, for which he serves as a senior editor. He is a regular contributor to Magnificat, and has written frequently for a host of other online journals.

Forbes, Amanda (USA)

Dr. Amanda Forbes is the co-founder and executive director of Trinity Education (www.TrinityEducationGlobal.org), an international nonprofit focused on equipping least-served students around the world with Christian worldview and vocational skills. She has extensive experience working with education partners in Haiti and various parts of Africa and Asia. Amanda also serves on the boards of City Vision University and Union University of California, along with having experience as an adjunct faculty member at City Vision University. She holds degrees from Pepperdine University (B.A.), Vanderbilt University (M.Ed.), and the University of Minnesota (Ph.D.). She resides with her husband in Nevada.

Friesen, Bruce (Canada)

Bruce Friesen is the founder of Children Arise Ministry, which disciples nations by discipling the next generation through education. He is the founder of Lifetree Churches and the Global Transformation Collective, which focuses on the transformation of all spheres of influence, by discipling people in the truths and principles of God's Word. Bruce lives in Victoria BC with his wife Lorraine. They have three married children and ten grandchildren.

Glesne, David (USA)

Dr. David Glesne is a native Minnesotan who received a B.A. from Concordia College, Moorhead, Minnesota, a M. Div. from Luther Seminary, St. Paul, Minnesota, and a D. Min. degree from Fuller Theological Seminary, Pasadena, California.He has been a pastor of churches in Illinois, California, and Minnesota. He most recently served the Redeemer Lutheran Church in Fridley and Coon Rapids.

Hahn, Hans-Joachim (Germany)

Hans-Joachim Hahn initiated the German Professorenforum, a network of Christian professors who promote a Biblical worldview in education and stand for a culture of freedom of thought and search for truth. (www.professorenforum.de) The Forum is committed to help raise a new generation of Christian academics with a Biblical worldview. Though trained as a teacher in English and Physical Education (highschool), Hans-Joachim followed God's call to work with Campus for Christ Germany, where he served as student-counsellor, National Director and in other functions.

He teaches Ethics in Economics at various universities. Bringing Vishal Mangalwadi to the stage and acting as his interpreter at more than 160 events since 2015 he has helped make Mangalwadi and his message known in German-speaking Europe, which laid the groundwork for Truth and Transformation. Hans-Joachim is married to Dorothee; they have two adult children.

Harris, Mark (USA)

Dr. Mark Harris was raised in a nominal Christian home in Idaho, and became a Christian in 1978, a year after graduating from college and becoming a CPA. He decided to turn his attention to ministry and graduated in 1984 with a Masters in New Testament from Western Seminary. After graduation he continued as an accountant, and then in 1993 moved to Russia where he was involved in evangelism and pastor training.

He also completed his doctorate in Intercultural Studies, studying the effects of Western evangelism among Russian youth. Upon returning to the USA in 2002 he continued traveling and teaching overseas, and also built up his accounting business that served mostly Christian nonprofits. He is currently President or CFO for five Christian nonprofits, and Instructor in Global Studies for Liberty University. He and his wife live in Lynchburg, VA.

Iturrieta, Pablo Munoz (Canada)
Dr. Pablo Munoz Iturrieta holds a doctorate in political philosophy from Carleton University (Canada), and is the author of four books on philosophy of knowledge, religious freedom, a critique of gender ideology, and the problem of education today. In the last few months he has been invited to give conferences to thousands of people at different universities and associations, legislative assemblies and Senates in 10 countries.

Lwere, Joshua (Uganda)
Bishop Joshua Lwere is the General Overseer of the National Fellowship of Born-Again Pentecostal Churches of Uganda, one of the major denominations of the country with more than 30.000 member churches.

Mangalwadi, Vishal (USA)
Prof. Dr. Vishal Mangalwadi studied philosophy in Indian universities, Hindu Ashrams and L'abri Fellowship in Switzerland. Along with his wife, Ruth, he founded a community to serve the rural poor in central India and organized lower castes as a political force. Vishal's 21 books have been translated into a total of 16 languages. Six of them have been taught at university level. William Carey International University honored him as a Legum Doctor. From 2014-16, he served as an Honorary Professor of Applied Theology at the Sam Higginbottom University of Agriculture, Technology and Sciences in Allahabad (UP) India. Vishal and Ruth have two daughters and six grandchildren.

Marshall, David (USA)
Dr. David Marshall has taught at the college and high school levels in America, China, and Japan. Author of a dozen books on "How Jesus Fulfills the Chinese Culture," "the New Atheism," the historicity of the gospels, world literature, and other subjects, Marshall has lectured in many countries, and writes frequently at The Stream. After riots broke out in the spring of 2020, he wrote an ebook entitled "Letter to a 'Racist' Nation, an experience which focused his attention on the corrupting influence

of modern education. It was then that Vishal Mangalwadi invited him to co-edit this book. Dr. Marshall is presently writing books entitled "The Case for Aslan: Evidence for Jesus in the Land of Narnia" and "How Jesus Liberates Women," while looking for the right teaching position, after Covid cut him off from his research students in China.

Mcdonald, David (USA)

Dr. David Mcdonald received his doctorate from the University of Washington in 1998. He is a father of 5 children and two grandchildren. As a Director for Health Teams International, Dr. McDonald has led medical mission teams to help the poor across the globe. He regularly lectures on Biblical Worldview, parenting and world religions, both domestically and internationally.

McDowell, Stephen (USA)

Stephen McDowell, co-founder and President of the Providence Foundation, has trained people from one hundred countries to apply biblical truth in all spheres of life. He has consulted with government officials, assisted in writing political documents, advised political parties, and aided in starting Christian schools and Biblical Worldview training centers. He has authored and co-authored over forty books, videos, and training courses including Liberating the Nations, America's Providential History, and Ruling Over the Earth, A Biblical View of Civil Government. Stephen's books and writings have been translated into eighteen languages and distributed to more than one million people. McDowell holds a master's degree in geophysics, served for several years as a pastor, and has been an adjunct professor at Regent University.

Osburn, Robert (USA)

Robert Osburn is a Senior Fellow with Wilberforce International Institute and trains international students to be redemptive change agents in their home societies. He has a BA from the University of Michigan, a ThM from Dallas Theological Seminary, and a PhD in international education from the University of Minnesota. He is the author of *Taming the Beast: Can We Bridle the Culture of Corruption?* (2016) and speaks and writes frequently on corruption, wealth development, comparative worldviews, and discipleship for redemptive change. He has been married to Susan for 45 years. They have four sons and 11 grandchildren, and reside in the Twin Cities of Minnesota.

Perry, Karla (USA)

Karla Perry, worldview revitalizer and author of Back to the Future: Rebuilding America's Stability and her new release The Reformation of America, is an avid writer with a penetrating and thought-provoking style. Karla helps people develop healthy worldviews through biblical Kingdom-based thinking. She earned her bachelor's degree from Old Dominion University where she majored in English and minored in American History. Karla is a co-founder of The Serve Initiative - an organization designed to equip and empower believers for the work of reformation. Karla lives with her husband, Joseph, in Virginia Beach, VA, where they pastored for eleven years. You can find more of Karla's work at www.karlaperry.com.

Rodriguez, Ricardo (Chile)

Ricardo Rodriguez is a lawyer from the University of Buenos Aires (1988), Member of the Global Leadership Team in YWAM from 1999 to 2017. He co-founded YWAM Chile in 1979 and has served as the leader of YWAM Chile from 1980 until now. Rodriguez has served as a Professor of the University of the Nations, Director of the School of Biblical Worldview since 2010, Leader of YWAM South Cone in South America 1984 until 2017, Director of the School of Educators in Chile 2020, an international spokesman about worldview perspectives in education, politics, economics and the church. Ricardo is an Argentinian, and a missionary in Chile from 1979 until now. He is married to Luisa Manzano, and a father of 2 children.

Rudmik, Tom (USA)

Tom Rudmik, educator and entrepreneur, is the founder of Master's Academy and College and Imaginal Education and Imaginal Transformation Inc. Tom is passionate about implementing REAL change and is committed to researching and developing breakthroughs in learning and sharing them with the world. Today, Imaginal Education is working with schools and government leaders in eight countries. Tom is also an international speaker who is instructing and guiding organizations that confront issues of obsolescence and the need for transformation. He has created an innovative and organizational transformation model for becoming an Imaginal Organization and leader, he developed the Imaginal Transformation Workshop and the Imaginal Thinking process of seeing and creating the future. Tom is the author of the book *Becoming Imaginal: Seeing and Creating the Future of Education*. Tom received an Honorary Doctorate in May 2017 from Canada Christian College.

Selladurai, Giftson (Australia)

Giftson Selladurai is a results-oriented leader with over 12 years of experience in Information Technology. An alumnus of LaTrobe University, Melbourne, Giftson also holds an international patent for his innovative approach towards Social Media engagement. Giftson's heart and passion is to make the utmost use of technology as a tool to transform nations, be it through online education or through disruptive applications, that deliver women/child safety, bridge the unreached and deliver justice through hack proof security. He is Currently the CEO of Ruah Tech, an IT solutions company based in Australia that works across emerging technologies like AR/VR, Blockchain, AI and the like.

Selladurai, Samson (India)

Samson Selladurai is a serial entrepreneur who has pioneered many ventures, in both business and missions. An alumnus of University of South Australia, he participated in the prestigious Lachlan Macquarie Internship in Canberra, Australia, that trains leaders in politics and public policy. His passion is to see kingdom leaders across business, church and government work together in unity to transform cities and nations. Samson and his twin brother Giftson, currently lead Ruah Tech Solutions, an innovative technology firm based in Australia, that helps develop world changing ideas to reality.

Senyonyi, John (Uganda)

Dr. John Senyonyi holds a PhD in Mathematical Statistics, a Bachelor of Science Degree, and a Master of Arts degree in Evangelism/ Theology. He is an academic, evangelist and public speaker. He was deeply influenced by the East African Revival and came to faith in Jesus Christ as an undergraduate in 1976. In August 2020, he retired from heading Uganda Christian University (UCU). He serves on two international boards among other things. He is married to Dr. Ruth Nantege Senyonyi, a counselling psychologist and they have four adult children and four grandchildren.

Sommer, Gottfried (Germany)

Dr. Gottfried Sommer, living in Trossingen, Germany, was born in Bad Reichenhall (Bavaria), Germany; he has German, Austrian and Hungarian roots. He is married to Juliánna, they have three children. He has an M.div. (FTH Gießen), Lic, Theol. (ETF Leuven), and a Ph.D. in church history (ETF Leuven). He currently is self-employed as an Information-technology instructor (MCT). He has worked for some ten years as a part-time pastor of Pentecostal Churches (CoG) in Singen and Rottweil (Germany).

His Vision: Finding the key to the re-Christianization of Germany, educating the people of God, strengthening the family and nation.

Suozzo, Joe (USA)

Joe and his wife Dianne have been serving in missions and pastoral ministry for 30 years. God has graciously given Joe and Dianne two beautiful girls. While serving in Asia, they had the privilege of planting a network of house churches among the untouchable people. That network has grown to over 40 churches and is completely in the hands of national leadership today. Since 2000 Joe began serving in pastoral ministry. He earned his BA from Moody Bible Institute, holds an MA in International Studies from Columbia International University and a Graduate degree in Indian Philosophy and Religion from Banares University, India.

Wieland, Andreas (Germany)

Andreas Wieland is a German theologian and business psychologist. He holds a M.Div. equiv. from Freie Theologische Akademie in Germany, a M.Th. in Missiology from University of South Africa, Pretoria and a M.A. in Business Psychology, Leadership and Management from SRH University, Germany. He is Founder and President of the European organization Truth and Transformation e.V. (www. truthandtransformation.org). He is part of the global leadership team of The Third Education Revolution, which this book describes. He also is a church planter in Stuttgart, Germany, where he lives with his wife Cinzia and their daughter (www. stuttgartprojekt.de).

HISTORY

&

ACKNOWLEDGEMENTS

"Light is the true cure of darkness" wrote Charles Grant, India's first prophet of education in 1792. As a civil servant who became a Christian in India, Grant saw not only the darkness of his heart but also of the Indian culture and of the colonial rule. His study of the Bible and of Europe's reforms convinced him that God's word can also reform India.

With help from William Wilberforce and the Evangelical "Clapham Sect," Grant became a Member of Parliament and the director of the British East India Company. He inspired and supported other great men and women who educated South Asia to create modern Bangladesh, India and Pakistan.

Vishal and Ruth Mangalwadi explored the Bible's impact on India as they authored three books that became the "seeds" of this education reformation:
- *The Legacy of William Carey: A Model for The Transformation of a Culture* (1992, '93, '99),
- *Missionary Conspiracy: Letters to A Postmodern Hindu* (1996), and
- *India: The Grand Experiment* (1997).

The builders of modern South Asia had their flaws, but no one ever accused Gandhi, Jinnah, Nehru, Ambedkar or Shastri of financial corruption. The founders of modern India were educated to be men of character; serving the public with integrity. Politicians and civil servants of the 1970s were very different. Secularization of education had corrupted a university degree into a license to loot helpless citizens as well as public treasury.

Vishal first presented the vision of blessing nations by reforming education in Garden Valley, Texas in 1996. The event was convened by Christine Colby of the University of the Nations. The participants included Darrow Miller, Bob Moffitt, Bob Osburn, and Scott Allen. Out of that consultation emerged Disciple Nation Alliance (DNA) and later BOMI/ Revelation Movement.

In the year 2000, Vishal and Ruth Mangalwadi were in Cambridge UK, researching for what became a lecture series "Must The Sun Set on The West." These lectures were delivered for the MacLaurin Institute at the University of Minnesota and published in, *"The Book That Made Your World: How the Bible Created The Soul of Western Civilization"* (2011).

The seed began to sprout: in 2009 YWAM, Seattle, WA published *"Truth And Transformation: A Manifesto For Ailing Nations."* Within days of its release at the "Transform World" conference, an Indonesian group began translating that book. They invited Vishal to launch the Indonesian version at the "Transform Indonesia" conference in October 2009. The educational vision presented in Appendix 3 inspired Dr. Takim Andriono and others to take up the challenge of transforming Indonesia by reforming education. A base was set up in Surabaya (Eastern Sumatra) in 2010. The development of this ministry is recorded in Dr. Andriono's chapter in this book.

The vision spread from these roots: South Americans who read these books began inviting Vishal and Bob Moffitt to travel and explain how nations could be transformed through church- based education. This led to the first international consultation in Florida in 2012. That birthed CaCHE, now www.trinityeducationglobal.org led by Dr. Amanda Forbes who contributed the chapter on blended, student-centered education.

The buds appeared as *"The Book That Made Your World"* became a game-changer. In the summer of 2014, while he was serving as a Professor of Applied Theology in India, a Lutheran church in the Twin Cities, Minnesota, invited Vishal to spend ten weeks exploring the theme of the "Church and the Healing of the Nations" in the Bible. Some of these Church leaders were concerned about the fact that in the 1980s their synod was confirming around 120,000 young people every year. By 2010s, the number had dropped to around 60,000 a year. Secular college education was luring students away from the church. That left the American Church with two options: Stop sending students to college OR take education back from destructive anti-Christian ideologies. Those ten weeks climaxed in the formation of www.VirtuesCampus. com. This ministry is led by Dr. David Glesne who wrote the chapter on Academic Pastors. He resigned from his position as Senior Pastor at a two-campus church to develop the dream into reality.

Around the same time a European publisher, Fontis, started publishing Vishal's books in German. *"The Book That Made Your World"* became an instant best-seller. Its success demonstrated that German Rationalism had reached a dead-end. People were willing to take a fresh look at alternatives offered by the New Age and Buddhism and also reconsider God's revelation in the Bible. Hans-Joachim Hahn, the founder of the Professors' Forum (Europe), felt called by the Holy Spirit to organize Vishal's lecture-tours throughout Germany, Austria, and Switzerland.

The roots grew deep: the Holy Spirit used this groundswell of popular interest in the Bible's cultural impact to nudge at the heart of a Church Planter, theologian, and a University lecturer of business psychology, Andreas Wieland. He volunteered his skills to organize prayer and consultation events across Germany to channel enthusiasm into an organization now called Truth and Transformation.

Simultaneously, a Swiss group of talented young people decided to summarize Vishal's teachings in ten short videos www.TruthMatters.tv. The German version of these DVDs were presented to every member of the German Parliament with the aid of the German Evangelical Alliance.

Flowers develop in anticipation of a harvest. In the Autumn of 2018, Canadian pastor/missionary, Bruce Friesen, invited Vishal and Ruth to Uganda to minister to national leaders in the government, judiciary, business, churches, and education. Those meetings led to an invitation from Bishop Joshua Lwere, the General Overseer of the Association of Born Again Pentecostal Churches in Uganda. In January 2019, for five days Vishal interacted with 200+ leaders of this dynamic "denomination." That became a critical milestone. Unanimously the bishops/overseers and senior pastors voted to upgrade every one of their 30,000 churches into centers of hybrid education. That is the background of Bishop Lwere's chapter in this book. Within months, Rev. Canon Dr. John Senyonyi, the then Vice Chancellor of Uganda Christian University invited Vishal to give the convocation address in his university. Those interactions stimulated several Christian universities in Uganda to explore how they may use their institutions to bless the whole nation. Prof Senyonyi's chapter explores possible future partnership between the university and the church.

The breakthrough in Uganda called for a Strategy Consultation in Phoenix, AZ (2019) hosted, by Bob Moffitt/DNA. Dr. Young David Lee, the then Vice-Chancellor of Kumi University in Uganda, was one of the participants. He invited the "Consultation" leaders to a second round in South Korea along with the leaders of a network of twenty Christian universities established by South Korean missionaries.

Dr. James Hwang, the Chairman of Erom Company, the Founder of the Kingdom Dream School and the Chancellor of the Kumi University in Uganda hosted the South Korean Consultation in February 2020. Out of this consultation was born the Kingdom Education Fellowship.
Fields ripened for the harvest: Covid-19 hit the world while we were meeting in Korea. The lockdowns forced the cancellation of our 2020 calendars and compelled the world to experiment with online education, That is when Bruce Friesen connected us with Ian Green, an English visionary, who inspired us to "write the vision" and to be "bold" in asking for the resources to fertilize this global education movement.

We were modest, calling our education initiative a "Fellowship." Prof. Gillian Kasirye, who has taught education for decades in Uganda's oldest and largest university, challenged us to be honest and admit that our "Fellowship" was, in fact calling for a "revolution." Such exhortations gave us the courage to write this book.

We are grateful to Prof Anthony Esolen for giving us the permission to use his essay, "No Option! Clear Out The Rubble and Rebuild" as a guest postscript. Copy editing was done by Chuck Harmon and Gideon Aggenbag. G.Santhosh Kumar, Andrew Jerome and S.Vijay of Ruah Tech Solutions designed the book and the book cover. Thanks to each of you.